FREE WILL AND REACTIVE ATTITUDES

The philosophical debate about free will and responsibility has been of great importance throughout the history of philosophy. In modern times this debate has received an enormous resurgence of interest and the contribution in 1962 by P.F. Strawson with the publication of his essay "Freedom and Resentment" has generated a wide range of discussion and criticism in the philosophical community and beyond.

The debate is of central importance to recent developments in the free will literature and has shaped the way contemporary philosophers now approach the problem. This volume brings together a focused selection of the major contributions and reactions to the free will and responsibility debate inspired by Strawson's contribution. McKenna and Russell also provide a comprehensive overview of the debate. This book will be of great value to scholars of Strawson and those interested in the free will debate more generally.

Free Will and Reactive Attitudes
Perspectives on P.F. Strawson's "Freedom and Resentment"

Edited by

MICHAEL McKENNA
Florida State University, USA

PAUL RUSSELL
University of British Columbia, Canada

ASHGATE

© Michael McKenna and Paul Russell 2008

All rights reserved. No part of this publication may be reproduced, stored in a retrieval system or transmitted in any form or by any means, electronic, mechanical, photocopying, recording or otherwise without the prior permission of the publisher.

Michael McKenna and Paul Russell have asserted their right under the Copyright, Designs and Patents Act, 1988, to be identified as the editors of this work.

Published by
Ashgate Publishing Limited
Wey Court East
Union Road
Farnham
Surrey GU9 7PT
England

Ashgate Publishing Company
Suite 420
101 Cherry Street
Burlington, VT 05401-4405
USA

Ashgate website: http://www.ashgate.com

British Library Cataloguing in Publication Data
Free will and reactive attitudes : perspectives on P.F. Strawson's
  Freedom and resentment
  1. Strawson, P.F. Freedom and resentment 2. Free will and
  determinism
  I. McKenna, Michael, 1963– II. Russell, Paul, 1955–
  123.5'092

Library of Congress Cataloging-in-Publication Data
Free will and reactive attitudes : perspectives on P.F. Strawson's Freedom and resentment / edited by Michael S. McKenna and Paul Russell.
   p. cm.
   Includes index.
   ISBN 978-0-7546-4059-2 (hardcover : alk. paper) 1. Strawson, P.F. Freedom and resentment. 2. Free will and determinism. I. McKenna, Michael, 1963– II. Russell, Paul, 1955–

B1667.S383F7433 2007
123'.5--dc22
                                                                            2007002612

ISBN: 978 0 7546 4059 2

Printed and bound in Great Britain by
MPG Books Ltd, Bodmin, Cornwall.

Contents

List of Contributors		*vii*
Acknowledgements		*xi*

Introduction: Perspectives on P.F. Strawson's "Freedom and Resentment" *Michael McKenna and Paul Russell*		1
1	Freedom and Resentment *Peter Strawson*	19
2	Free Will and Rationality *A.J. Ayer*	37
3	Accountability (II) *Jonathan Bennett*	47
4	The Importance of Free Will *Susan Wolf*	69
5	On "Freedom and Resentment" *Galen Strawson*	85
6	Responsibility and the Limits of Evil: Variations on a Strawsonian Theme *Gary Watson*	115
7	Strawson's Way of Naturalizing Responsibility *Paul Russell*	143
8	Emotions, Expectations and Responsibility *R. Jay Wallace*	157
9	Blaming, Understanding and Justification: A Defence of Strawson's Naturalism about Moral Responsibility *Kevin Magill*	187
10	The Limits of Evil and the Role of Moral Address: A Defense of Strawsonian Compatibilism *Michael McKenna*	201
11	Revising the Reactive Attitudes *Derk Pereboom*	219
12	Free Will: From Nature to Illusion *Saul Smilansky*	235

13	Thinking with your Hypothalamus: Reflections on a Cognitive Role for the Reactive Emotions *David Zimmerman*	255
14	Doing without Desert *Erin Kelly*	273
15	Responsibility and the Aims of Theory: Strawson and Revisionism *Manuel Vargas*	297

Suggested Further Readings   *319*
Index   *323*

List of Contributors

P.F. Strawson (1919–2006) spent most of his academic career at Oxford University, where he was Waynflete Professor of Metaphysics from 1968 to 1987. His wide-ranging and influential writings include *Introduction to Logical Theory* (1952), *Individuals* (1959), and *The Bounds of Sense* (1966). P.F. Strawson was also the author of a number of highly influential papers on topics covering logic, language, mind, as well as several other areas of philosophy. Among his many honours, he was elected a Fellow of the British Academy (1960) and knighted (1977). His contribution, "Freedom and Resentment," which is the centerpiece of this volume, originally appeared in the *Proceedings of the British Academy*, 48 (1962), 187–211.

A.J. Ayer (1910–1989) was Wykeham Professor of Logic at Oxford University from 1959 to 1978. He was the author of many well-known philosophical works, including *Language, Truth and Logic* (1936) and *Problem of Knowledge* (1956). He was knighted in 1970. His contribution, "Free-will and Rationality," originally appeared in Zak van Straaten (ed.), *Philosophical Subjects* (Oxford University Press, 1980), pp. 1–13.

Jonathan Bennett has taught at Cambridge University, the University of British Columbia, and Syracuse University. Since 1997 he has lived in retirement on an island near Vancouver, BC, preparing student-friendly versions of the classics of early modern philosophy and placing them at www.earlymoderntexts.com. The most recent of his books are *Learning from Six Philosophers* (Oxford University Press, 2001) and *A Philosophical Guide to Conditionals* (Oxford University Press, 2003). His contribution, "Accountability II," is an original piece that has not previously appeared in print. It is, however, based upon his highly influential paper, "Accountability," which appeared in Zak van Straaten (ed.), *Philosophical Subjects* (Oxford University Press, 1980), pp. 14–47.

Erin Kelly is Associate Professor of Philosophy at Tufts University. Her research interests are in moral and political philosophy and the philosophy of law, with a focus on questions about justice, the nature of moral reasons, moral responsibility and desert, and theories of punishment. Her publications include, "The Burdens of Collective Liability," in D. Chatterjee and D. Scheid (eds), *Ethics and Foreign Intervention* (Cambridge University Press, 2003) and "Personal Concern," published in the *Canadian Journal of Philosophy*. Her contribution, "Doing without Desert," originally appeared in *Pacific Philosophical Quarterly*, 83 (2002), 180–205. Reprinted with kind permission of Blackwell Press.

Michael McKenna is Professor of Philosophy at Florida State University. Until recently, he was an Associate Professor in the Department of Philosophy and Religion at Ithaca College and also held a position as a visiting Assistant Professor at Bryn Mawr College. He has published several articles, mostly on the topics of free will and moral responsibility. He has also co-edited *Moral Responsibility and Alternative Possibilities* (Ashgate Publishing, 2003). His contribution, "The Limits of Evil and the Role of Moral Address: A Defense of Strawsonian Compatibilism," originally appeared in *Journal of Ethics*, 2 (1998), 123–42. Reprinted with kind permission of Kluwer Academic Publishers.

Kevin Magill is Associate Dean and a member of the Department of Philosophy, School of Humanities, Languages and Social Sciences at the University of Wolverhampton. He is the author of *Freedom and Experience: Self-Determination Without Illusions* (MacMillan, 1997) and "The Idea of a Justification for Punishment," *Critical Review Of International Social And Political Philosophy*, 1 (1998). His contribution, "Blaming, Understanding, and Justification: A Defense of Strawson's Naturalism about Moral Responsibility," is excerpted from *Freedom and Experience: Self-Determination Without Illusions*. Reprinted with kind permission of Palgrave MacMillan. It also appeared as a freestanding piece in T. van den Beld (ed.), *Moral Responsibility and Ontology* (Kluwer Academic Publishers, 2000), pp. 183–97. Reprinted with kind permission of Springer Science and Business Media.

Derk Pereboom is Professor of Philosophy at Cornell University. On free will and moral responsibility he has published a number of articles, including "Determinism al Dente" (*Noûs*, 1995), a book, *Living Without Free Will* (Cambridge University Press, 2001) and, more recently, he is one of the contributors to *Four Views on Free Will: A Debate* with John Martin Fischer, Robert Kane, and Manuel Vargas (Blackwell, 2007). He has also published articles in philosophy of mind, philosophy of religion, and on the philosophy of Immanuel Kant. His contribution, "Revising the Reactive Attitudes" is excerpted from his book *Living Without Free Will*, pp. 90–100, and 199–207. Reprinted with kind permission of the publisher and the author.

Paul Russell is Professor in Philosophy at the University of British Columbia, where he has been teaching since 1987. He has held visiting positions at Virginia (1988), Stanford (1989–90) and Pittsburgh (1996–97). In 2005 he was a Visiting Professor (Kenan Distinguished Visitor) at the University of North Carolina at Chapel Hill. His principal research interests include problems of free will and moral responsibility and the history of early modern philosophy. He is the author of *Freedom and Moral Sentiment: Hume's Way of Naturalizing Responsibility* (Oxford University Press, 1995) and *The Riddle of Hume's Treatise: Skepticism, Naturalism, and Irreligion* (Oxford University Press, 2008). He is currently working on a book *The Limits of Free Will: A Critical Introduction to the Contemporary Debate* (Blackwell). His contribution, "Strawson's Way of Naturalizing Responsibility," originally appeared in *Ethics*, 102 (1992), 287–302. Reprinted with kind permission of The University of Chicago Press. All Rights Reserved.

List of Contributors

Saul Smilansky is Professor of Philosophy at the University of Haifa. He is the author of *Free Will and Illusion* (Oxford University Press, 2000), *Ten Moral Paradoxes* (Blackwell, 2007), and numerous articles on moral philosophy. His contribution, "Free Will: From Nature to Illusion," originally appeared in *Proceedings of the Aristotelian Society*, 101 (2001), 71–95. Reprinted with kind permission of Blackwell Press.

Galen Strawson is Professor of Philosophy at the University of Reading and Distinguished Professor of Philosophy at City University of New York Graduate Center. He is an editorial consultant at the Times Literary Supplement. In 1993 he was a Visiting Fellow at the Research School of Social Sciences, Australian National University. In 1997 he was a Visiting Professor at New York University, and in 2000 a Visiting Professor at Rutgers University. He is the author of books on free will, causation, and the philosophy of mind: *Freedom and Belief* (Oxford University Press, 1986; reprinted 1991), *The Secret Connexion: Realism, Causation, and David Hume* (Oxford University Press, 1989; revised edition 1992), and *Mental Reality* (MIT Press, 1994). His contribution, "On 'Freedom and Resentment'," is excerpted from his book *Freedom and Belief*, pp. 84–120. Reprinted with kind permission of Oxford University Press.

Manuel Vargas is Assistant Professor of Philosophy at the University of San Francisco. He has been a Visiting Assistant Professor at the University of California, Berkeley and at the California Institute of Technology, as well as an Acting Assistant Professor at Stanford University. He has published articles on practical rationality, free will, moral responsibility, and various topics in Latin American philosophy. He is one of the authors of *Four Views on Free Will: A Debate* with John Martin Fischer, Robert Kane, and Derk Pereboom (Blackwell, 2007). He received a Joint Ph.D. in Philosophy and Humanities from Stanford University in 2001. His contribution, "Responsibility and the Aims of Theory: Strawson and Revisionism" originally appeared in *Pacific Philosophical Quarterly*, 85 (2004), 218–41. Reprinted with kind permission of Blackwell Publishers.

R. Jay Wallace is Professor and Chair in the Department of Philosophy at the University of California, Berkeley. He is the author of *Responsibility and the Moral Sentiments* (Harvard University Press, 1994) and *Normativity and the Will. Selected Essays on Moral Psychology and Practical Reason* (Oxford University Press, 2006). His contribution, "Emotions, Expectations, and Responsibility," is excerpted from his book *Responsibility and the Moral Sentiments*, pp. 18–40, 51–2, and 62–83. Reprinted with kind permission of the publisher and the author.

Gary Watson is Professor of Philosophy at the University of California, Riverside. He has published numerous essays on human action, free agency, and moral philosophy. He is the author of *Agency and Answerability* (Oxford University Press, 2004). His contribution, "Responsibility and the Limits of Evil: Variations on a Strawsonian Theme," originally appeared in F. Schoeman (ed.), *Responsibility, Character, and the Emotions* (1987), pp. 256–86. Reprinted with kind permission of the author and Cambridge University Press.

Susan Wolf is the Edna J. Koury Professor of Philosophy at the University of North Carolina at Chapel Hill. She is the author of *Freedom Within Reason*, (Oxford University Press, 1990) and numerous articles on ethics and the philosophy of mind. Her current research focuses on the relations among happiness, morality, and meaningfulness in life. Her contribution, "The Importance of Free Will," originally appeared in *Mind*, 90 (1981), 386–405. Reprinted with kind permission of Oxford University Press.

David Zimmerman is Professor of Philosophy at Simon Fraser University. He works mainly in ethics and the philosophy of mind. His articles in those areas include "Coercive Wage Offers" (*Philosophy & Public Affairs*, 10, 1981) and "That Was Then, This is Now: Personal History vs. Psychological Structure in Compatibilist Theories of Autonomous Agency" *Nous*, 37 (2003), 638–71. He is co-editor (with David Copp) of *Morality, Reason and Truth: New Essays on the Foundations of Ethics* (Rowman & Allanheld, 1985). His contribution, "Thinking with your Hypothalamus: Reflections on a Cognitive Role for the Reactive Emotions," originally appeared in *Philosophy and Phenomenological Research*, 63 (2001), 521–41. Reprinted with kind permission of the journal.

Acknowledgements

The origins of this project can be traced back to a time in the late 1980s when the editors of this volume, one as a visiting professor, another as a graduate student, were both based in the Department of Philosophy at the University of Virginia. As a way of showing our appreciation for this unusually congenial place to study and teach philosophy, we would like to dedicate this volume to our friends and colleagues at UVA.

We wish to thank James Kelleher, for his careful and diligent editorial assistance. Also, we are indebted to the Social Science and Humanities Research Council of Canada, the Office of the Provost at Ithaca College, and the Department of Philosophy at Florida State University for their generous financial assistance with aspects of this project. Finally, we would like to thank Paul Coulam at Ashgate Publishing for his support for our project.

Introduction

Perspectives on P.F. Strawson's "Freedom and Resentment"

Michael McKenna and Paul Russell

> We are naturally social beings; and given with our natural commitment to social existence is a natural commitment to that whole web or structure of human personal and moral attitudes and feelings, and judgments of which I spoke. Our natural disposition to such attitudes and judgments is naturally secured against arguments suggesting they are in principle unwarranted or unjustified ...
>
> – P.F. Strawson, Skepticism and Naturalism

During the past half century the free will problem has received a considerable amount of philosophical attention. This activity has resulted in a significant advance in the level of sophistication and subtlety in the various theories on offer. P.F. Strawson's "Freedom and Resentment", which was first published in 1962, is among the most important and influential of the contributions produced during this period.[1] In order to appreciate the significance of Strawson's contribution fully his paper must be viewed from two directions. On one side, it must be viewed from the perspective of the "classical" free will debate as it was generally understood around the middle of the twentieth century. On the other side, we need to consider "Freedom and Resentment" in terms of the critical responses and debates that it has generated. The aim of this introduction is to provide the reader with a general framework for understanding the significance of Strawson's contribution from both these perspectives.

I. The Classical Debate and the Dilemma of Determinism

As Strawson presents the issue, the problems that primarily concern the classical free will debate can be described in terms of the dilemma of determinism. The thesis of determinism, as generally understood within this debate, is the claim that everything that happens in the world—including all human thought and action—is subject to causal laws and that this involves the necessitation of effects by antecedent causal conditions.[2]

---

1 Page references for "Freedom and Resentment" are to pages 19–36 of this volume, followed by (after the slash) the corresponding pages of Gary Watson (ed.), *Free Will* (1982). (Thus, 'FR, 19/59' refers to this volume, p. 19/and *Free Will*, p. 59.)

2 On the standard empiricist account associated with classical compatibilism these laws are themselves analysed in terms of regularities or constant conjunctions of resembling events. However, this account of causal relations and causal laws is not essential to classical compatibilism.

The initial difficulty we are presented with is that free will and moral responsibility seem to be impossible if our actions are causally necessitated. At the same time, free will and moral responsibility also seem to be impossible if our actions are not causally necessitated. If both these claims are correct then free will and moral responsibility are impossible *whatever* view we take concerning the truth of determinism.

Why should the causal necessitation of action be viewed as incompatible with freedom and responsibility? One argument that classical incompatibilists have put forward is that moral responsibility requires free will and this requires that the agent could have acted otherwise or had alternative possibilities. However, if our actions are causally necessitated then the agent could not have done otherwise or had no open alternative possibilities. In these circumstances, the argument concludes, the agent is neither free nor responsible. On the other hand, when we move over to the side of indeterminism, we encounter a different set of problems. Classical compatibilists have argued that there is a difference between an action being free and an action being simply uncaused. If an action lacks any cause, they maintain, then it is merely a chance event that cannot be attributed to any agent. (For example, the random "swerves" of an Epicurean atom do not constitute freedom of the kind that is required for moral responsibility.) Clearly, then, denying the thesis of determinism serves only to present us with a different set of problems—those that are associated with the horn of chance.

The two main parties in the classical free will debate both attempt to avoid the skeptical conclusion reached by this argument. Classical compatibilism argues that it is a mistake to suppose that causal necessity is incompatible with freedom and responsibility. One core argument of this compatibilist position is that it is mere confusion to suppose that freedom implies the absence of causal necessitation. What freedom requires is only the absence of compulsion and coercion. Conduct is compelled or coerced when it is caused *in a certain way*: namely when it is produced without or against the agent's will and desires. However, when an action is caused by the agent's desires and willings then it is attributable to the agent and the agent can be said to act freely in the sense required for moral responsibility (Ayer, 1954; Schlick, 1930; Hobart, 1934; Nowell-Smith, 1948; Smart, 1963).[3] Responsible agents, compatibilists have argued, are those who can be appropriately influenced by the incentives of praise and blame and rewards and punishments. In circumstances where action is caused by the agent's own desires and willings we can influence the agent's future conduct by means of these incentives. The only sort of freedom required for moral responsibility, therefore, is the freedom to act according to the determination of our own will. From these arguments we can conclude, according to classical compatibilists, that the thesis of determinism poses no threat to moral responsibility.[4]

---

3   More recently, of course, compatibilists have introduced a number of fine-grained distinctions and more precise definitions concerning freedom, free will, acting freely on so on. However, for the purpose of describing classical compatibilist commitments these distinctions are not needed.

4   Many classical compatibilists also made it a central fixture of their positions to argue directly against the incompatibilist thesis that if determinism if true, no one can do otherwise. They argue that "could have done otherwise" claims should be analysed *conditionally* in terms of what the agent would have done *if* he had chosen or willed differently. (See, among others, Moore, 1912; Nowell-Smith, 1948; Ayer; 1954; and Smart, 1963). It is a curious fact about

Classical incompatibilists have objected to this strategy on several different grounds. One point of particular importance is that they reject the forward-looking, utilitarian understanding of moral responsibility provided by the compatibilist. We know that responsibility is not just a matter of our conduct being capable of being changed or influenced by rewards and punishments because it is evident that both children and animals can be influenced in these ways and they are, nevertheless, paradigmatically not responsible agents (Campbell, 1951). Clearly, then, something is missing from this classical compatibilist account of freedom and moral responsibility. What, then, is missing? According to incompatibilists what is missing is a sufficiently *deep* account of moral responsibility. More specifically, we must be able to account for the importance of moral *desert* and this requires that the agent is, in some relevant way, the *ultimate originator* of her conduct. For this to be possible, the incompatibilst continues, the agent must be able to choose between genuinely open alternatives and this requires the falsity of determinism. Some incompatibilists, known as *libertarians*, have argued that these conditions can be met (Campbell, 1951; Chisholm, 1964, 1967; and Taylor, 1954, 1974). Others, known as *hard determinists*, claim that this demand cannot be satisfied (Edwards, 1958; and Hospers, 1957).

The difficulty that libertarians have faced is to provide some account of free will that extends beyond the simple negative claim that our actions are not causally necessitated. The problem here is to give coherent content to some notion of free will that does not collapse into mere chance or capriciousness. According to classical compatibilists, when libertarians set about to meet this challenge their metaphysical commitments tend to take the form of speculative, anti-naturalistic accounts that are both obscure in themselves and difficult to integrate with the natural order of events in the world (Schlick, 1930; Hobart, 1934). It may be suggested, for example, that free will requires agents who are entirely distinct from their (given) character and desires and who are capable of a form of causality that is different in kind from (efficient) causation in nature.[5] From the classical compatibilist perspective, libertarian theories of this kind are hopelessly obscure and unintelligible.

The dynamics of the classical free will debate, as formulated along the lines of the dilemma of determinism, move us sharply in the direction of the conclusion that moral responsibility is *impossible*—since no plausible interpretation of free will can be provided by either of the two non-skeptical parties in this debate. The problem with this radical skeptical conclusion is that it seems both intellectually incredible and humanly impossible for us to accept or live with.

"Freedom and Resentment" that Strawson seemed not to concern himself with this central classical compatibilist topic. (For a reading of "Freedom and Resentment" that suggests otherwise, see McKenna, 2005; Scanlon, 1998, also suggests that Strawson did indeed have in his sights some treatment of "could have done otherwise", though Scanlon does not develop that point.)

5   One view of this kind is that agents are substances of a distinct kind or non-empirical rational selves who somehow directly bring about those events that are their actions. (See, among others, Campbell, 1951, Taylor, 1958; and Chisholm, 1964.)

II. Strawson's "Reconciling Project" and the Naturalistic Turn

Strawson presents his basic objective in "Freedom and Resentment" as an attempt to "reconcile" the two main parties in the free will dispute. For the purpose of his discussion he adopts his own labels for the various parties he is concerned with. This is both a strength and a weakness of his presentation. Strawson refers to compatibilists as "optimists", those who maintain that our attitudes and practices associated with moral responsibility would in no way be discredited by the thesis of determinism.[6] He refers to incompatibilists as "pessimists", those who believe that the truth of the thesis of determinism would discredit and undermine our commitment to these attitudes and practices. "Pessimists" may, on this account, be either libertarians or moral skeptics. The libertarian, as we have noted, holds that free will requires the falsity of determinism, that free will exists, and that free will serves to support a deep conception of moral responsibility. The moral skeptic is not only a "pessimist" on the assumption that determinism is true but also on the assumption that determinism is false. In other words, the moral skeptic is a *systematic pessimist* who concludes that the dilemma of determinism is intractable.[7] Although there is a sense in which Strawson's labels are confusing, they are nevertheless valuable in so far as they highlight the fact that the free will debate is not merely a matter of abstract, theoretical controversy. On the contrary, this is an issue that is taken to have a relevance to our attitude to life and the human condition, depending on where we stand on this matter.[8] More specifically, the pessimist/incompatibilist takes the view that there is something depressing or dispiriting about the (possible) truth of the thesis of determinism. In contrast with this, the optimist/compatibilist wants to show that there is no basis for worries and anxieties of this kind. Strawson's use of the labels "optimist" and "pessimist" are consistent with his wider objective in "Freedom and Resentment" to explain why the free will debate has the emotional significance for us that it has. It is Strawson's view that the main parties in this dispute have failed to identify what really matters to us in this sphere. His idiosyncratic terminology helps to illuminate and highlight this point.[9]

---

6   Strawson claims to be of "the party of those who do not know what the thesis of determinism is" (FR, 19/59). However, this does not prevent him from going on to characterize the dispute in terms of the general disagreement about the theoretical and practical implications of the truth of determinism.

7   Cp. Galen Strawson (1994).

8   Other great metaphysical questions, such as the existence of God and the immortality of the soul, may also be understood to have deeper significance for our attitude to life and the human condition (i.e. depending on what view we take on these issues). Certainly these are problems that are not merely of abstract, theoretical interest for us.

9   On Strawson's account the free will dispute is produced primarily by the confusions of philosophers. Ordinary life carries on unaffected and unconcerned by these (artificial) problems and difficulties. So considered, the free will dispute is presented as something of a "pseudo-problem", requiring diagnosis and philosophical therapy. Note, however, that this view sits uncomfortably with the view that the free will issue is one that affects our fundamental attitude to life and the human predicament (see the comments in note 8 above).

Strawson's attempt to "reconcile" the optimist and pessimist accepts that the pessimist is correct in holding that the optimist's account of moral responsibility leaves out "something vital". On the other hand, Strawson rejects the suggestion that what is needed is the falsity of determinism and some form of "contra-causal freedom" (FR, 35/79).[10] Although something is indeed missing from the optimist's story this gap is not to be filled using the "obscure and panicky metaphysics of libertarianism" (FR, 36/80). To find what is missing from the optimist and pessimist accounts we require a more radical shift in our philosophical approach to this problem. This involves what may be described as Strawson's "naturalistic turn".

Strawson's strategy in "Freedom and Resentment" involves turning away from conceptual issues about the analysis of "freedom" and "responsibility" and taking a closer look at what actually goes on when we *hold* a person responsible. That is to say, his methodology depends less on conceptual analysis and more on a descriptive account of actual human moral psychology. The place where our investigations ought to begin, Strawson suggests, is with "the very great importance that we attach to the attitudes and intentions towards us of other human beings, and the great extent to which our *personal feelings and reactions* depend upon, or involve, our beliefs about these attitudes and intentions" (FR, 22/62—our emphasis). Where we must begin, therefore, is with "that complicated web of attitudes and feelings which form moral life as we know it" (FR, 34/78). In this way, Strawson's "naturalistic turn" involves, not just a methodological turn away from conceptual analysis to moral psychology, but also an emphasis on the importance of emotion in moral life.[11] What is essential, on this view of things, is that we must not "over-intellectualize" the free will debate—a mistake that is common to both optimist and pessimist strategies (FR, 34–5/78–9).

How does an understanding of our "reactive attitudes and feelings" help us to resolve the free will problem? Strawson's approach is to describe carefully those circumstances in which we consider ourselves required to withdraw or suspend our reactive attitudes towards other individuals. He begins with an examination of the personal reactive attitude of resentment—where we believe that a person has injured or harmed us in some way or failed to show appropriate good will towards us (FR, 23/64).[12] In situations of this kind we are disposed "to modify or mollify" our feeling of resentment when certain relevant excusing considerations are brought to our attention. Strawson distinguishes between two important groups of excuses. The first aims to show that in the particular circumstances the agent's conduct lacked any degree of ill-will or disregard. Although some injury may have occurred, it was accidental, inadvertent or unintentional in some respect or other. Another kind of

---

10 See Campbell (1951). Campbell's paper is a reply to Nowell-Smith (1948), which Strawson cites as representative of the "optimist" viewpoint. Campbell's views are particularly representative of the (libertarian) "pessimist" outlook that Strawson is concerned with.

11 Strawson's turn away from conceptual analysis is probably one reason why he does not directly concern himself with the debate between his compatibilist and incompatibilist contemporaries over the proper analysis of "could have done otherwise". (See note 4.)

12 Strawson's interest in the case of resentment and its relation to our reactive attitudes is anticipated by Adam Smith in his *Theory of Moral Sentiments* (1759). See also Joseph Butler, "On Resentment" (1726).

excusing consideration goes much further than this and suggests that resentment is not called for on the ground that the agent is somehow an "inappropriate" target of any attitude of resentment because she is "abnormal or immature" and thus not a normal adult who we can reasonably expect to show due care and concern for others.

This analysis of the rationale of excuses as they concern our reactive attitudes suggests that there are two different stances that we can take up in our "human relationships". The first is a "participant" attitude where we believe the person we are dealing with is generally a normal adult who is an appropriate target of our reactive attitudes. The other is the "objective" stance, where we believe that the person we are dealing with is in some way incapacitated for normal adult human relationships and so reactive attitudes are inappropriate when directed at individuals of this kind. In cases of this kind we see the person as "an object of social policy; as a subject for what, in a wide range of sense, might be called treatment ... to be managed or handled or cured or trained" (FR, 25/66). In general, however, there is no question of us choosing or needing to justify the fact that we are liable to reactive attitudes and feelings in the normal case. This is simply a "given" of our human nature and without it we would hardly recognize an individual or community as being fully *human*.

Strawson maintains that these observations about human psychology and society are fundamental for understanding what has gone wrong with the classical free will debate. What influence, he asks, would the truth of determinism have upon our personal reactive attitudes such as resentment? More specifically, would the acceptance of this thesis "lead to the repudiation of all such attitudes"? (FR, 25/67). Strawson answers this question at several different levels. In the first place he argues that the truth of determinism in no way serves (theoretically) to discredit our reactive attitudes in any systematic way. For this to be so, he claims, determinism would have to imply that one or other of the two basic forms of excusing considerations hold universally. We have, however, no reason to suppose that this follows. Certainly determinism does not imply that any injury caused by someone is always done accidentally or inadvertently. That is to say, determinism does not imply that no one's conduct ever manifests ill will or lacks proper regard for others. Nor does determinism imply that every agent is somehow abnormal or immature, or in some way incapacitated for adult relationships. We may conclude, therefore, that the truth of the thesis of determinism in no way discredits or theoretically undermines our commitment to reactive attitudes of this kind.

Strawson argues for two further points beyond this. Even if we had some theoretical reason to abandon or suspend these reactive attitudes it would be psychologically impossible for us to do this. To do this would involve "adopting a thoroughgoing objectivity of attitude to others" which is something we are *incapable* of (FR, 27–8/69–70). While it is possible for us to choose to take up the objective stance on occasion—even sometimes when we are dealing with normal, mature adults—the fact is that we cannot do this with regard to all people all of the time *whatever* theoretical view we may hold. Furthermore, even if we were to be given a ("god-like") choice on this matter and could decide for ourselves whether or not to retain "our natural human commitment to ordinary inter-personal attitudes", this choice must be decided in terms of "the gains and losses to human life, its enrichment or impoverishment" (FR, 28, 31–2/70, 74). Obviously we have little or no reason to choose a life that is emotionally impoverished and de-humanized, so the truth of determinism is itself irrelevant to any choice of this kind.

According to Strawson the very same arguments and considerations apply to our moral reactive attitudes, which are simply "generalized or vicarious analogues of the personal reactive attitudes" (FR, 29/71). These various forms of reactive attitude, Strawson maintains, are all "humanly connected" and subject to the same rational and psychological constraints. Clearly, then, the truth of the thesis of determinism provides us with no theoretical reason to entirely suspend or abandon our commitment to our (moral) reactive attitudes and we have, furthermore, no pragmatic reason to *want* to take an exclusively objective stance toward all other people. More importantly, whatever our theoretical or pragmatic views may be, any effort of this kind is "practically inconceivable", since our commitment to moral reactive attitudes is no less fundamental to human nature than it is in the case of other forms of reactive attitudes (FR, 31–2/74–5).[13]

Strawson draws several important conclusions from these arguments. In the first place, he identifies the respective failings of both the optimist and pessimist positions. The optimist generally attempts to show that the truth of determinism does not prevent rewards and punishments from "regulating behaviour in socially desirable ways".

> The picture painted by the optimist is painted in a style appropriate to a situation envisaged as wholly dominated by objectivity of attitude. The only operative notions involved in this picture are such as those of policy, treatment, control. But a thoroughgoing objectivity of attitude, excluding as it does the moral reactive attitudes, excludes at the same time essential elements in the concepts of *moral* condemnation and *moral* responsibility. (FR, 33/76—Strawson's emphasis)

Strawson argues that the pessimist is right to "recoil" at this picture of things but makes the mistake of concluding that the reactive attitudes cannot be all that we require to "fill the gap in the optimist's account" (FR, 35/79). This leads the pessimist to conclude that "the gap can be filled only if some general metaphysical proposition is repeatedly verified, verified in all cases where it is appropriate to attribute moral responsibility" (FR, 35/79). This proposition, Strawson claims, "is as difficult to state coherently and with intelligible relevance as its determinist contradictory" (FR, 35/79).

Behind their disagreement both the optimist and pessimist are guilty of a shared misunderstanding.

> Both seek, in different ways, to over-intellectualize the facts. Inside the general structure or web of human attitudes and feelings of which I have been speaking, there is endless room for modification, redirection, criticism, and justification. But questions of justification

---

13 Along with the personal and moral reactive attitudes Strawson also distinguishes a third group, the self-reactive attitudes. These are "associated with demands on oneself for others" (FR, 29/71).

are internal to the structure or relate to modifications internal to it. The existence of the general framework of attitudes itself is something we are given with the fact of human society. As a whole, it neither calls for, nor permits, an external 'rational' justification. Pessimist and optimist alike show themselves, in different ways, unable to accept this. (FR, 35/78–9)

With this point in place Strawson goes on to conclude that "if we sufficiently, that is radically, modify the view of the optimist, his view is the right one" (FR, 36/80). What needs to be done is to fill the "lacuna" in the optimist's account—the neglect of our human attitudes and feelings—without falling into the "obscure and panicky metaphysics of libertarianism" (FR, 36/80). We must ask the pessimist to "surrender his metaphysics" and the optimist to concede that there is "something vital" missing in his account. If both parties can agree to these terms then "reconciliation" will be achieved.

Strawson's naturalistic turn in "Freedom and Resentment" has two important features and each draws on (related) historical sources. The first is the role of *emotion* in Strawson's account of the nature and conditions of moral responsibility. Strawson makes clear that his interest in reactive attitudes constitutes a return to the moral sense tradition in ethical theory.[14] Although Strawson does not cite any specific influences, several key claims and insights in his paper can be found (in a more fully worked out form) in the writings of predecessors such as David Hume (Hume, 1739–40) and Adam Smith (Smith, 1759). The most fundamental of these claims is that our moral reactions to other human beings is a given of our human nature and involve feelings and attitudes produced by our beliefs about conduct and character. It is, nevertheless, a significant fact that the moral sense tradition is itself divided on the free will issue.[15]

Another important dimension of Strawson's "naturalistic turn" is his way of discrediting the skeptical challenge by reference to the inescapable, psychological mechanisms that guide human thought and action. This is a theme that Strawson directly addresses in his more recent work *Skepticism and Naturalism* (hereafter abbreviated as SN), where he explicitly acknowledges both his historical sources and the wider application of this form of naturalism to philosophical skepticism. In this context, Strawson observes that Thomas Reid drew "an explicit parallel between our natural commitments to belief in external things and our natural proneness to moral or quasi-moral response" (SN, 33). In this respect, says Strawson: "we see Reid aligning himself with Hume the naturalist against Hume the skeptic" (SN, 33). He elaborates on this theme further below:

---

14 "It is a pity that talk of the moral sentiments has fallen out of favour ..." (FR, 35/79).

15 Hume, for example, is clearly an optimist/compatibilist. In contrast with this, Butler defends a pessimist/libertarian position [*Analogy of Religion*, Pt. I, Ch. 4.]. Smith is simply silent on the problem of free will. On the striking resemblance between Hume's and Strawson's strategy as it concerns moral responsibility and the free will problem see, Russell (1995), esp. Ch. 5. For a more general discussion of Strawson's views as they relate to the compatibilist tradition see McKenna (2004).

[Reid's point ...] is that argument, reasonings, either for or against the skeptical position, are, in practice, equally inefficacious and idle ... Where Nature thus determines us, we have an original non-rational commitment which sets the bounds within which, or the stage upon which, reason can effectively operate, and within which the question of rationality or irrationality, justification or lack of justification, of this or that particular judgment or belief can come up. I then played roughly the same game, as one might put it, with the moral life. We are naturally social beings; and given with our natural commitment to social existence is a natural commitment to that whole web or structure of human personal and moral reactive attitudes, feelings, and judgments of which I spoke. Our natural disposition to such attitudes and judgments is naturally secured against arguments suggesting that they are in principle unwarranted or unjustified just as our natural disposition to belief in the existence of body is naturally secured against arguments suggesting that it is in principle uncertain. (SN, 39)

Strawson's "naturalist way" with the moral skeptic not only parallels the naturalist way with the skeptic about the existence of the external world, it also parallels (Hume's) naturalist way of dealing with skepticism about induction.[16] Clearly, then, as Strawson indicates, his own naturalistic way of refuting pessimism and moral skepticism, as it arises out of the free will dispute, has parallels with the way that Hume, Reid and others have dealt with structurally similar skeptical challenges.[17]

III. Critical Themes Concerning "Freedom and Resentment"

At the time "Freedom and Resentment" first appeared Anglo-American philosophy was tightly in the grip of "ordinary language" or "conceptual" analysis. As we have noted, around the middle of the twentieth century it was widely held that the right way to solve the free will problem was to provide the correct analysis of the logical relations among the terms "freedom", "causation", "responsibility" and "could have done otherwise". Lying behind this approach is the assumption that there is some identifiable, determinate meaning to each of the relevant terms and that this procedure of "conceptual analysis" could put an end to the whole controversy. Related to this assumption is the view that language embodies all the logical distinctions that are needed for everyday moral conversation and practice. Confusion in this sphere, therefore, is a peculiar product philosophical reflection rather than a real difficulty that presents itself in ordinary moral life.

It is evident that Strawson's naturalistic approach to the free will problem involves a fundamental shift away from this kind of philosophical methodology. However, although Strawson's naturalistic turn recommends that we begin with the

---

16 SN, 18–19; and FR, 35n7/79n7. In the latter passage Strawson suggests that any attempt to justify the general framework of our reactive attitudes is misguided in much the same way that any attempt to justify induction is mistaken. For Strawson's views on induction see Strawson (1952), Ch. 9.

17 According to Strawson, Hume's naturalist way of dealing with skepticism finds a "powerful later-day exponent of a closely related position" in Wittgenstein (SN, 10,14f). This indicates that, in some respects, Strawson's own strategy in "Freedom and Resentment" takes a Wittgensteinian approach.

facts of human moral psychology, as opposed to a pure conceptual analysis, there are features of his methodology that follow the ordinary language approach in a number of ways. It may be argued, for example, that Strawson's naturalistic commitments in "Freedom and Resentment" manifest his own preference for "descriptive" over "revisionary" metaphysics. This distinction is introduced by Strawson in *Individuals*, which was published three years before "Freedom and Resentment".

> Descriptive metaphysics is content to describe the actual structure of our thought about the world, revisionary metaphysics is concerned to produce a better structure ... The idea of descriptive metaphysics is liable to be met with skepticism. How should it differ from what is called philosophical, or logical, or conceptual analysis? It does not differ in kind of intention, but only in scope or generality. Aiming to lay bare the most general features of our conceptual structure, it can take far less for granted than a more limited and partial conceptual inquiry. [Strawson (1959), p. 9]

Strawson goes on to say that while metaphysics may be an instrument of conceptual change, there is, nevertheless, "a massive central core of human thinking which has no history ... there are categories and concepts which, in their most fundamental character, change not at all" [Strawson (1959), p. 10]. Strawson also makes clear that his work in *Individuals* is intended as a contribution to descriptive as opposed to revisionary metaphysics. The same "descriptive" spirit is evident in "Freedom and Resentment". Strawson wants to account for the *natural* foundation of our "concepts and practices associated with moral responsibility" in the "web" of human reactive attitudes and feelings. Although he does not deny that there are "local and temporary" variations in the way our moral sentiments and reactive attitudes may be manifest and directed. (FR, 36/80) he insists, nevertheless, that "in the absence of *any* forms of these attitudes it is doubtful whether we should have anything that *we* could find intelligible as a system of human relationships, as a human society". (FR, 36/80, Strawson's emphasis). This aspect of his approach in "Freedom and Resentment" is entirely consistent with his more general descriptive commitments and orientation.

These features of Strawson's naturalism and descriptivist metaphysics may be challenged from two related points of view. In the first place, it may be argued that our human commitment to the framework of reactive attitudes or moral sentiments is not so essential to human nature as Strawson suggests.[18] The reactive attitudes are not permanent, inescapable features of human nature, like other more basic emotions such as fear or love. Rather they should be viewed as cultural artifacts produced in particular historical and social conditions. Reactive attitudes, the critic maintains, involve a set of socially acquired dispositions and expectations and we can well imagine more radical shifts and transformations in human relationships and attitudes than Strawson allows for. Related to this point, it may also be argued that Strawson's form of descriptivist metaphysics and naturalism commits him to a "static" and "conservative" account of our basic concepts and practices as they relate to moral responsibility. Although Strawson allows that there is "endless room for modification, redirection, criticism and justification", he pointedly blocks-off

---

18 See, for example, Watson (1987; reprinted in this volume, pp. 117–43); or Wallace (1994; excerpt reprinted in this volume, pp. 159–87).

any radical revisionist account of responsibility that would take us in the direction of a purely utilitarian or consequentialist theory (FR, 34–5/78–9). The critic may argue that our attitudes and practices in this sphere are more flexible and plastic than Strawson's picture suggests and that our theoretical reflections may push us in the direction of more fundamental changes of a "revisionist" kind.[19]

A central theme of "Freedom and Resentment" is that both optimists and pessimists seek to "over-intellectualize the facts" as they relate to justifying responsibility. More specifically, it is a mistake, Strawson argues, to aim to provide any "external 'rational' justification" for responsibility. Beyond this, however, Strawson is clear that reason has an important role to play "inside the general structure or web of human attitudes and feelings" that he is concerned with. Be this as it may, it remains a matter of some debate about the exact role that reason can play in justifying our reactive attitudes. Here too, we encounter two related difficulties. The first concerns Strawson's understanding of the cognitive aspects of emotion. Should moral sentiments or reactive attitudes be interpreted as mere feelings, without propositional content, or should they be regarded as necessarily involving beliefs of some relevant kind?[20] Similarly, what role does reason play in justifying the (moral) demands and standards associated with the reactive attitudes and feelings?[21] Are these demands and standards part of the "given framework" of human nature or do they vary with local conventions and customs? The deeper issue here concerns the open or noncommittal nature of Strawson's theoretical commitments as they relate to moral reasons and justification *within* the framework of reactive attitudes.[22]

Strawson's discussion in "Freedom and Resentment" turns on several sharp dichotomies that may also be questioned. Among these is the fundamental opposition between the "objective" and "participant" stances. A number of problems present themselves in relation to this dichotomy. It may be suggested, for example, that we may altogether avoid reactive attitudes toward an individual (e.g. on the ground that they are severely incapacitated) but still engage in other forms of personal, emotional response or engagement (e.g. parental love). Another general difficulty relating to this dichotomy is how it is possible to "dispel" or set-aside our reactive attitudes when we take up the objective stance in the "normal" case without thereby discrediting them? In other words, it may be argued that the constraints imposed by embracing the objective stance as an acceptable option for inter-personal relations

---

19 For a strong argument for this point see Pereboom (2001). For an interesting way to *support* Strawson along revisionist lines, see Vargas (2004; reprinted in this volume, pp. 301–20).

20 See, for example, Bennett (1980; see also "Accountability (II)" at pp. 47–69 of this volume); Wallace (1994; excerpt reprinted in this volume, pp. 159–87). The background worry here is that Strawson's account depends on a feeling theory of emotion that would make it impossible to assess (tokens of) emotions or reactive attitudes and feelings as themselves reasonable or unreasonable. This difficulty has deeper roots in the moral sense tradition dating back to Hume's views on this subject. On this issue see Russell (1995), Ch. 6.

21 On this point see Ayer (1980; reprinted in this volume, pp. 37–46) and Wolf (1981; reprinted in this volume, pp. 71–85).

22 For differing positions on this issue, see Magill (1997; and see the excerpt reprinted in this volume, pp. 189–202) and Kelly (2002; reprinted in this volume, 275–98).

are such that it is not possible to continue to endorse the reactive attitudes as in any way appropriate in these circumstances. If these observations are correct then the objective/participant dichotomy is more problematic for Strawson's project than he has acknowledged.[23]

Another dichotomy that that has attracted critical comment concerns the gap between holding and being responsible. Critics, such as John Martin Fischer and Mark Ravizza, have argued that Strawson is insufficiently sensitive to this gap and that this vitiates much of his strategy in "Freedom and Resentment".

> ... Strawson's theory may reasonably be said to give an account of what it is for agents to be held responsible, but there seems to be a difference between being *held* responsible and actually *being* responsible. Surely it is possible that one can be held responsible even though one in fact is not responsible, and conversely that one can be responsible even though one is actually not treated as a responsible agent. By understanding responsibility primarily in terms of our actual practices of adopting or not adopting certain attitudes towards agents Strawson's theory risks blurring the difference between these two issues. [Fischer and Ravizza (1993), p.18—their emphasis]

It is important to be careful about interpreting the exact nature of this criticism. It is clear that Strawson wants to allow that in *particular* cases our reactive attitudes may fail to properly track moral responsibility (e.g. we feel an inappropriate reactive attitude because we have incorrect beliefs about the agent's intentions or state of mind). Similarly, sometimes we may fail to feel any sentiment of approval or disapproval but would do so if we were fully and properly informed about the agent's conduct and character. These are not, however, the sort of difficulties that concern Fischer and Ravizza.

The problem that they are concerned with is the possibility that there could be a *systematic* lack of correlation between our reactive attitudes and their appropriate and legitimate objects. It could be, for example, that an entire community has its reactive attitudes switched on or off in the wrong way and at the wrong times. The very possibility of this suggests that there is more to being responsible than what is generally targeted by our reactive attitudes and feelings. A deeper difficulty, related to this, is that what does or does not make an individual an appropriate target of reactive attitudes must depend on some relevant interpretation of *moral capacity*— the capacities that establish a person as a "normal adult" who is capable of full participation in the moral community.[24] This is a crucial issue, since the pessimist/incompatibilist will argue that among the relevant capacities we must consider is the ability to act otherwise or (libertarian) free will. Unless Strawson can provide some

---

23 On these matters, see G. Strawson (1986; see also excerpt reprinted herein, pp. 87–115); Smilansky (2000; reprinted in this volume, pp. 237–56), (2001); and Zimmerman (2001; reprinted herein, pp. 257–74).

24 Several commentators have fixed upon this point. See, for example, Nagel (1986), Ch. 7; Watson (1987; reprinted in this volume, pp. 117–43); Russell (1992; reprinted, this volume, pp. 145–58), (1995); McKenna (1998; reprinted, this volume, pp. 203–20); and Scanlon (1998).

plausible account of moral capacity then it would appear there is a significant gap or "lacuna" in his own version of compatibilism.

Another problem for Strawson's theory, critics may argue, involves his ambiguous remarks about the relationship between resentment and retribution. Although Strawson maintains that "savage or civilized, we have some belief in the utility of [retributive] practices" (FR, 34/78) this leaves it open as to what role utilitarian considerations play in justifying punishment in general, as well as particular cases of punishment.[25] It is not clear, for example, whether the institution of punishment requires some "external 'rational' justification"—in contrast with the whole framework of reactive attitudes that serve to ground and structure retributive practices and the institutions associated with them.[26] Nor is it clear if our retributive practices, as distinct from our reactive attitudes which motivate them, are a "given" of human nature and something that it is practically inconceivable that we could altogether suspend or abandon.[27] Obviously it is one thing to claim that our emotional nature is fixed and incapable of fundamental alteration and quite another to say that the institutions and practices associated with them are also incapable of being eliminated or removed from human life. Certainly this is an issue that requires further interpretation and analysis. What is needed, therefore, is a more detailed account of the implications of Strawson's naturalistic account of responsibility for a theory of retributive justice.[28]

Perhaps the most fundamental problem with Strawson's theory in the eyes of his critics is that he has too little to say about the extent to which our reflections concerning the (historical) origins or sources of character and conduct can inhibit—if not altogether undermine—the (normal) operation of our reactive attitudes. The difficulty here can be brought to light by means of "implantation" cases. Suppose that our basic dispositions, which shape and direct our attitudes and intentions towards others, were somehow "implanted" by means of an artificial technique of some kind (e.g. neuro-surgery or genetic engineering). According to Strawson' theory, our reactive attitudes would still continue to operate in cases of this kind. That is to say, allowing that the agent is a "normal" (i.e. rational) adult who is capable of manifesting good or ill will towards others "theoretical" worries about implantation will not and cannot dislodge or discredit our reactive attitudes. Contrary to this view, however, critics will argue that implantation evidently eliminates the agent's moral responsibility and so there is something wrong with Strawson's theory.[29]

---

25 For a discussion of the general utilitarian justification for the reactive emotions see Magill (1997; excerpt reprinted in this volume, pp. 189–202) and Zimmerman (2001; reprinted, this volume, pp. 257–74).

26 On this see Russell (1995), Ch. 10.

27 See, for example, Mackie (1982). Mackie shows how naturalistic principles of a Strawsonian kind may be used to defend strong forms of retributivist punishment.

28 It is beyond the scope of this collection to take up the relevance of Strawson's views in "Freedom and Resentment" for the related topic of *distributive* justice. See, however, the valuable discussion in Scheffler (1992).

29 Similar difficulties arise in the theological context regarding worries about moral responsibility in circumstances where God is the ultimate source of the agent's character and conduct. (See Hume's influential discussion of this issue in his *Enquiry Concerning Human Understanding*, Sect. VIII.)

This line of criticism, based on worries about the history, origins or source of character and conduct, cannot be evaded by insisting that implantation is "abnormal" and that this is what excuses the agent. We may, for example, alter the factors at work in conditioning the agent's basic character and disposition and make them natural and/or ordinary social processes of various kinds.[30] In these circumstances the agent still has no control over the kind of moral character she has acquired and it is *this*—not implantation *per se*—that makes it impossible to sustain our commitment to reactive attitudes. Strawson's theory, the critic continues, simply presupposes that (historical) considerations of this kind are irrelevant to the legitimacy and functioning of our reactive attitudes. Most philosophers maintain that this view of things is neither psychologically credible nor philosophically defensible.[31] The fact that Strawson has so little to say about this general problem suggests, to some readers, that Strawson's naturalistic approach never adequately confronts the real problem lying at the heart of the free will dispute and thus fails to solve it.

The themes and criticisms described above are all raised in one form or another in the essays that follow. For the purpose of our introduction there is no need to summarize or paraphrase each individual essay. It is better for the contributors to speak for themselves in their own words.

IV. The Aim of This Volume

All the essays in this collection make a significant contribution to the interpretation and criticism of the strategy and arguments that are advanced in "Freedom and Resentment". Taken as a group, they constitute an important set of developments in the contemporary free will debate. The primary purpose of bringing this material together is to give our readers easy access to these contributions, which in some cases are not easily found. There are also several essays in this collection that present new material that has not appeared in print before or else substantially revise earlier work. This collection provides an opportunity to contrast and compare the various responses to "Freedom and Resentment" in a unified format that allows the reader to consider these responses and criticisms in a more systematic and coherent fashion. This process, we hope, will stimulate new avenues of criticism and encourage further development of the themes arising from Strawson's work. Finally, as with any project of this kind, due to limited space and publication costs we have not been able to include every relevant and worthwhile contribution that has already appeared in print. Several of these works are cited in the "suggestions for further reading" that appears at the end of this volume. The suggestions that we have made are not intended to cover all material relevant to "Freedom and Resentment" published over the past four decades. Our aim is simply to guide the reader to a few more notable contributions that are directly relevant to the particular discussions and arguments taken up in this volume.

---

30 This is one crucial point in Watson (1987; this volume, pp. 117–43).

31 For one noteworthy source of dissent, see Frankfurt (1975). In Strawson's defence, McKenna (1998) resists Watson's historical objections to Strawsonian compatibilism.

References

Ayer, A.J., "Freedom and Necessity", in *Philosophical Essays* (New York: St Martin's Press, 1954), pp. 3–20.
—— "Free Will and Rationality", in van Straaten (ed.), *Philosophical Subjects* (1980).
Bennett, Jonathan, "Accountability", in van Straaten (ed.), *Philosophical Subjects* (1980).
Berofsky, Bernard (ed.), *Free Will and Determinism* (New York: Harper & Row, 1966).
Butler, Joseph, "On Resentment" [Sermon 8], in *The Works of Joseph Butler*, Vol. 2.
—— *The Analogy of Religion*, in *The Works of Joseph Butler*, Vol. 1.
—— *The Works of Joseph Butler*, 2 vols, Samuel Halifax (ed.), (Oxford: Oxford University Press, 1849).
Campbell, C.A., "Is 'Freewill' a Pseudo-Problem?", *Mind*, 60 (1951), 446–65. Reprinted in Bernard Berofsky, (ed.), *Free Will and Determinism*.
Chisholm, Roderick, "Human Freedom and the Self", *The Lindley Lectures* (Department of Philosophy, University of Kansas, 1964).
—— "He Could Have Done Otherwise", *Journal of Philosophy*, 64 (1967), 409–18.
Edwards, Paul, "Hard and Soft Determinism", in Hook (ed.), *Determinism and Freedom* (1958).
Fischer, John M., "Responsibility and Control", *Journal of Philosophy*, 89 (1982), 24–40.
Fischer, John M. and Ravizza, Mark, (eds), *Perspectives on Moral Responsibility* (Ithaca: Cornell University Press, 1993).
Frankfurt, Harry, "Alternate Possibilities and Moral Responsibility", *Journal of Philosophy*, 68 (1969), 829–39.
—— "Freedom of the Will and the Concept of a Person", *Journal of Philosophy*, 68 (1971), 5–20.
—— "Three Concepts of Free Action", *Proceedings of the Aristotelian Society*, supp. vol. 2 (1975), 113–25.
Ginet, Carl, "Might We Have No Choice?" in Lehrer (ed.), *Freedom and Determinism* (1966).
—— *On Action* (Cambridge: Cambridge University Press, 1990).
Hobart, R.E., "Free Will as Involving Determination and Inconceivable Without It", *Mind*, 43 (1934), 1–27.
Hook, Sidney (ed.), *Determinism and Freedom in the Age of Modern Science* (New York: MacMillan, 1958).
Hume, David, *A Treatise of Human Nature* [1739–40], David Fate Norton and Mary J. Norton (eds), (Oxford: Oxford University Press, 2000).
—— *An Enquiry Concerning Human Understanding* [1748], Tom L. Beauchamp (ed.), (Oxford: Oxford University Press, 2000).
Kane, Robert, *The Significance of Free Will* (Oxford: Oxford University Press, 1996).

Kelly, Erin, "Doing Without Desert", *Pacific Philosophical Quarterly*, 83 (2002), 180–205.

Lehrer, Keith (ed.), *Freedom and Determinism* (New York: Random House, 1966).

Mackie, John, "Morality and the Retributive Emotions" [1988], reprinted in Mackie, *Persons and Values: Selected Papers Volume II* (Oxford: Oxford University Press, 1985), pp. 206–19.

Magill, Kevin, *Experience and Freedom: Self-Determination Without Illusions* (London: MacMillan, 1997).

McKenna, Michael, "The Limits of Evil and the Role of Moral Address: A Defense of Strawsonian Compatibilism", *Journal of Ethics*, 2 (1998), 123–42.

—— "Compatibilism", *The Stanford Encyclopedia of Philosophy* (Summer 2004 Edition), Edward N. Zalta (ed.), http://plato.stanford.edu/archives/sum2004/entries/compatibilism.

—— "Where Strawson and Frankfurt Meet", *Midwest Studies in Philosophy*, 29 (2005), 163–80.

Moore, G.E., *Ethics* (Oxford: Oxford University Press, 1912).

Nagel, Thomas, *The View From Nowhere* (Oxford: Oxford University Press, 1986).

Nowell-Smith, H.P., "Free Will and Moral Responsibility", *Mind*, 57 (1948), 45–61.

—— "Ifs and Cans", *Theoria*, 26 (1960), 85–101.

Pereboom, Derk, "Alternate Possibilities and Causal Histories", *Philosophical Perspectives*, 14 (2000), 119–38.

—— *Living Without Free Will* (Cambridge: Cambridge University Press, 2001).

Russell, Paul, "Strawson's Way of Naturalizing Responsibility", *Ethics*, 102 (1992), 287–302.

—— *Freedom and Moral Sentiment: Hume's Way of Naturalizing Responsibility* (Oxford: Oxford University Press, 1995).

Scanlon, T.M., "The Significance of Choice", in Sterling M. McMurrin (ed.), *The Tanner Lectures on Human Values* (Salt Lake City: University of Utah Press, 1998).

Scheffler, Samuel, "Responsibility, Reactive Attitudes, and Liberalism", *Philosophy and Public Affairs*, 21 (1992), 299–323.

Schlick, Moritz, "When Is a Man Responsible?" reprinted in Berofsky (ed.), *Free Will and Determinism* (1966).

Schoeman, Ferdinand (ed.), *Responsibility, Character, and the Emotions: New Essays in Moral Psychology* (Cambridge: Cambridge University Press, 1987).

Smart, J.J.C., "Free Will, Praise, and Blame", *Mind*, 70 (1963), 291–306.

Smilansky, Saul, *Free Will and Illusion* (Oxford: Oxford University Press, 2000).

—— "Free Will: From Nature to Illusion", *Proceedings of the Aristotelian Society*, 101 (2001), 71–95.

Smith, Adam, *The Theory Of Moral Sentiments* [1759], Knud Haakonssen (ed.), (Cambridge: Cambridge University Press, 2002).

Strawson, Galen, *Freedom and Belief* (Oxford: Oxford University Press, 1986).

Strawson, P.F., *Introduction to Logical Theory* (London: Methuen, 1952).

—— *Individuals: An Essay in Descriptive Metaphysics* (London: Methuen, 1959).

—— "Freedom and Resentment", *Proceedings of the British Academy*, 48 (1962), 187–211. Reprinted in Strawson (1974) and in Watson (1982).
—— *Freedom and Resentment and Other Essays* (London: Methuen, 1974).
—— *Skepticism and Naturalism* (New York: Columbia University Press, 1985).
Taylor, Richard, "Determinism and the Theory of Agency" in Hook (ed.), *Determinism and Freedom in the Age of Modern Science* (1958).
—— *Metaphysics* (Englewood Cliffs, NJ: Prentice Hall, 1974).
van Straaten, Zak (ed.), *Philosophical Subjects: Essays Presented to P. F. Strawson* (Oxford: Oxford University Press, 1980).
Vargas, Manuel, "Responsibility and the Aims of Theory: Strawson and Revisionism", *Pacific Philosophical Quarterly*, 85 (2004), 218–41.
Wallace, R. Jay, *Responsibility and the Moral Sentiments* (Cambridge MA: Harvard University Press, 1994).
Watson, Gary (ed.), *Free Will* (Oxford: Oxford University Press, 1982).
—— "Responsibility and the Limits of Evil: Variations on a Strawsonian Theme", in Schoeman (ed.), *Responsibility, Character, and the Emotions* (1987).
Wolf, Susan, "The Importance of Free Will", *Mind*, 90 (1981), 386–405.
Zimmerman, David, "Thinking With Your Hypothalamus: Reflections on a Cognitive Role for the Reactive Emotions", *Philosophy and Phenomenological Research*, 63 (2001), 521–41.

Chapter 1

Freedom and Resentment*

Peter Strawson

I.

Some philosophers say they do not know what the thesis of determinism is. Others say, or imply, that they do know what it is. Of these, some—the pessimists perhaps—hold that if the thesis is true, then the concepts of moral obligation and responsibility really have no application, and the practices of punishing and blaming, of expressing moral condemnation and approval, are really unjustified. Others—the optimists perhaps—hold that these concepts and practices in no way lose their raison d'etre if the thesis of determinism is true. Some hold even that the justification of these concepts and practices requires the truth of the thesis. There is another opinion which is less frequently voiced: the opinion, it might be said, of the genuine moral sceptic. This is that the notions of moral guilt, of blame, of moral responsibility are inherently confused and that we can see this to be so if we consider the consequences either of the truth of determinism or of its falsity. The holders of this opinion agree with the pessimists that these notions lack application if determinism is true, and add simply that they lack it if determinism is false. If I am asked which of these parties I belong to, I must say it is the first of all, the party of those who do not know what the thesis of determinism is. But this does not stop me from having some sympathy with the others, and a wish to reconcile them. Should not ignorance, rationally, inhibit such sympathies? Well, of course, though darkling, one has some inkling—some notion of what sort of thing is being talked about. This lecture is intended as a move towards reconciliation; so is likely to seem wrongheaded to everyone.

But can there be any possibility of reconciliation between such clearly [**60**]opposed opinions as those of pessimists and optimists about determinism? Well, there might be a formal withdrawal on one side in return for a substantial concession on the other. Thus, suppose the optimist's position were put like this: (1) the facts as we know them do not show determinism to be false; (2) the facts as we know them supply an adequate basis for the concepts and practices which the pessimist feels to be imperilled by the possibility of determinism's truth. Now it might be that the optimist is right in this, but is apt to give an inadequate account of the facts as we know them, and of how they constitute an adequate basis for the problematic

---

* This essay is reprinted in Gary Watson (ed.), *Free Will* (1st edn) (Oxford University Press, 1982), pp. 59–80. Watson's collection is the most commonly cited source of "Freedom and Resentment." Accordingly, we have inserted Watson's pagination in our own volume. For example, at p. 19 of this volume, '[**60**]' indicates the beginning of p. 60 of the Watson text.

concepts and practices; that the reasons he gives for the adequacy of the basis are themselves inadequate and leave out something vital. It might be that the pessimist is rightly anxious to get this vital thing back and, in the grip of his anxiety, feels he has to go beyond the facts as we know them; feels that the vital thing can be secure only if, beyond the facts as we know them, there is the further fact that determinism is false. Might *he* not be brought to make a formal withdrawal in return for a vital concession?

II.

Let me enlarge very briefly on this, by way of preliminary only. Some optimists about determinism point to the efficacy of the practices of punishment, and of moral condemnation and approval, in regulating behaviour in socially desirable ways.[1] In the fact of their efficacy, they suggest, is an adequate basis for these practices; and this fact certainly does not show determinism to be false. To this the pessimists reply, all in a rush, that *just* punishment and *moral* condemnation imply moral guilt and guilt implies moral responsibility and moral responsibility implies freedom and freedom implies the falsity of determinism. And to this the optimists are wont to reply in turn that it is true that these practices require freedom in a sense, and the existence of freedom in this sense is one of the facts as we know them. But what "freedom" means here is nothing but the absence of certain conditions the presence of which would make moral condemnation or punishment inappropriate. They have in mind conditions like compulsion by another, or innate incapacity, or insanity, or other less extreme forms of psychological disorder, or the existence of circumstances in which the making of any other choice would be morally inadmissible or would be too much to expect of any man. To this list they are constrained to add other factors which, without exactly being limitations of freedom, may also make moral condemnation or punishment inappropriate or mitigate their force: as some forms of ignorance, mistake, or accident. And the general reason [61] why moral condemnation or punishment is inappropriate when these factors or conditions are present is held to be that the practices in question will be generally efficacious means of regulating behaviour in desirable ways only in cases where these factors are *not* present. Now the pessimist admits that the facts as we know them include the existence of freedom, the occurrence of cases of free action, in the negative sense which the optimist concedes; and admits, or rather insists, that the existence of freedom in this sense is compatible with the truth of determinism. Then what does the pessimist find missing? When he tries to answer this question, his language is apt to alternate between the very familiar and the very unfamiliar.[2] Thus he may say, familiarly enough, that the man who is the subject of justified punishment, blame or moral condemnation must really *deserve* it; and then add, perhaps, that, in the case at least where he is blamed for a positive act rather than an omission, the condition of his really deserving blame is something that goes beyond the negative freedoms that the

---

1 Cf. P.H. Nowell-Smith, "Freewill and Moral Responsibility", *Mind* (1948).

2 As Nowell-Smith pointed out in a later article: "Determinism and Libertarians", *Mind* (1954).

optimist concedes. It is, say, a genuinely free identification of the will with the act. And this is the condition that is incompatible with the truth of determinism.

The conventional, but conciliatory, optimist need not give up yet. He may say: Well, people often decide to do things, really intend to do what they do, know just what they're doing in doing it: the reasons they think they have for doing what they do, often really are their reasons and not their rationalizations. These facts, too, are included in the facts as we know them. If this is what you mean by freedom—by the identification of the will with the act—then freedom may again be conceded. But again the concession is compatible with the truth of the determinist thesis. For it would not follow from that thesis that nobody decides to do anything; that nobody ever does anything intentionally; that it is false that people sometimes know perfectly well what they are doing. I tried to define freedom negatively. You want to give it a more positive look. But it comes to the same thing. Nobody denies freedom in this sense, or these senses, and nobody claims that the existence of freedom in these senses shows determinism to be false.

But it is here that the lacuna in the optimistic story can be made to show. For the pessimist may be supposed to ask: But *why* does freedom in this sense justify blame, etc.? You turn towards me first the negative, and then the positive, faces of a freedom which nobody challenges. But the only reason you have given for the practices of moral condemnation and punishment in cases where this freedom is present is the efficacy of these practices in regulating behaviour in socially desirable ways. But this is not **[62]** a sufficient basis, it is not even the right *sort* of basis, for these practices as we understand them.

Now my optimist, being the sort of man he is, is not likely to invoke an intuition of fittingness at this point. So he really has no more to say. And my pessimist, being the sort of man he is, has only one more thing to say; and that is that the admissibility of these practices, as we understand them, demands another kind of freedom, the kind that in turn demands the falsity of the thesis of determinism. But might we not induce the pessimist to give up saying this by giving the optimist something more to say?

III.

I have mentioned punishing and moral condemnation and approval; and it is in connection with these practices or attitudes that the issue between optimists and pessimists—or, if one is a pessimist, the issue between determinists and libertarians—is felt to be particularly important. But it is not of these practices and attitudes that I propose, at first, to speak. These practices or attitudes permit where they do not imply, a certain detachment from the actions or agents which are their objects. I want to speak, at least at first, of something else: of the non-detached attitudes and reactions of people directly involved in transactions with each other; of the attitudes and reactions of offended parties and beneficiaries; of such things as gratitude, resentment, forgiveness, love, and hurt feelings. Perhaps something like the issue between optimists and pessimists arises in this neighbouring field too; and since this field is less crowded with disputants, the issue might here be easier to settle; and if it is settled here, then it might become easier to settle it in the disputant-crowded field.

What I have to say consists largely of commonplaces. So my language, like that of commonplace generally, will be quite unscientific and imprecise. The central commonplace that I want to insist on is the very great importance that we attach to the attitudes and intentions towards us of other human beings, and the great extent to which our personal feelings and reactions depend upon, or involve, our beliefs about these attitudes and intentions. I can give no simple description of the field of phenomena at the centre of which stands this commonplace truth; for the field is too complex. Much imaginative literature is devoted to exploring its complexities; and we have a large vocabulary for the purpose. There are simplifying styles of handling it in a general way. Thus we may, like La Rochfoucauld, put self-love or self-esteem or vanity at the centre of the picture and point out how it may be caressed by the esteem, or wounded by the indifference or contempt, of others. We might speak, in another jargon, of the need for [63] love, and the loss of security which results from its withdrawal; or, in another, of human self-respect and its connection with the recognition of the individual's dignity. These simplifications are of use to me only if they help to emphasize how much we actually mind, how much it matters to us, whether the actions of other people—and particularly of *some* other people—reflect attitudes towards us of goodwill, affection, or esteem on the one hand or contempt, indifference, or malevolence on the other. If someone treads on my hand accidentally, while trying to help me, the pain may be no less acute than if he treads on it in contemptuous disregard of my existence or with a malevolent wish to injure me. But I shall generally feel in the second case a kind and degree of resentment that I shall not feel in the first. If someone's actions help me to some benefit I desire, then I am benefited in any case; but if he intended them so to benefit me because of his general goodwill towards me, I shall reasonably feel a gratitude which I should not feel at all if the benefit was an incidental consequence, unintended or even regretted by him, of some plan of action with a different aim.

These examples are of actions which confer benefits or inflict injuries over and above any conferred or inflicted by the mere manifestation of attitude and intention themselves. We should consider also in how much of our behaviour the benefit or injury resides mainly or entirely in the manifestation of attitude itself. So it is with good manners, and much of what we call kindness, on the one hand; with deliberate rudeness, studied indifference, or insult on the other.

Besides resentment and gratitude, I mentioned just now forgiveness. This is a rather unfashionable subject in moral philosophy at present; but to be forgiven is something we sometimes ask, and forgiving is something we sometimes say we do. To ask to be forgiven is in part to acknowledge that the attitude displayed in our actions was such as might properly be resented and in part to repudiate that attitude for the future (or at least for the immediate future); and to forgive is to accept the repudiation and to forswear the resentment.

We should think of the many different kinds of relationship which we can have with other people—as sharers of a common interest; as members of the same family; as colleagues; as friends; as lovers; as chance parties to an enormous range of transactions and encounters. Then we should think, in each of these connections in turn, and in others, of the kind of importance we attach to the attitudes and intentions towards us of those who stand in these relationships to us, and of the kinds of *reactive* attitudes and feelings to which we ourselves are prone. In general, we demand some degree of goodwill or regard on the part of those who stand in these relationships to us, though the forms we require it to take vary widely in different [64] connections. The range and intensity of our *reactive* attitudes towards goodwill, its absence or its opposite vary no less widely. I have mentioned, specifically, resentment and gratitude; and they are a usefully opposed pair. But, of course, there is a whole continuum of reactive attitude and feeling stretching on both sides of these and—the most comfortable area—in between them.

The object of these commonplaces is to try to keep before our minds something it is easy to forget when we are engaged in philosophy, especially in our cool, contemporary style, viz. what it is actually like to be involved in ordinary interpersonal relationships, ranging from the most intimate to the most casual.

IV.

It is one thing to ask about the general causes of these reactive attitudes I have alluded to; it is another to ask about the variations to which they are subject, the particular conditions in which they do or do not seem natural or reasonable or appropriate; and it is a third thing to ask what it would be like, what it *is* like, not to suffer them. I am not much concerned with the first question; but I am with the second; and perhaps even more with the third.

Let us consider, then, occasions for resentment: situations in which one person is offended or injured by the action of another and in which—in the absence of special considerations—the offended person might naturally or normally be expected to feel resentment. Then let us consider what sorts of special considerations might be expected to modify or mollify this feeling or remove it altogether. It needs no saying now how multifarious these considerations are. But, for my purpose, I think they can be roughly divided into two kinds. To the first group belong all those which might give occasion for the employment of such expressions as "He didn't mean to", "He hadn't realized", "He didn't know", and also all those which might give occasion for the use of the phrase "He couldn't help it", when this is supported by such phrases as "He was pushed", "He had to do it", "It was the only way", "They left him no alternative" etc. Obviously these various pleas, and the kinds of situations in which they would be appropriate, differ from each other in striking and important ways. But for my present purpose they have something still more important in common. None of them invites us to suspend towards the agent, either at the time of his action or in general, our ordinary reactive attitudes. They do not invite us to view the *agent* as one in respect of whom these attitudes are in any way inappropriate. They invite us to view the *injury* as one in respect of which a particular one of these [65] attitudes is inappropriate. They do not invite us to see the *agent* as other than a fully responsible agent. They invite us to see the *injury* as one for which he was not fully, or at all, responsible. They do not suggest that the agent is in any way an inappropriate object of that kind of demand for goodwill or regard which is reflected in our ordinary reactive attitudes. They suggest instead that the fact of injury was not in this case incompatible with that demand's being fulfilled, that the fact of injury was quite consistent with the agent's attitude and intentions being just what we demand they should be.[3] The agent was just ignorant of the injury he was causing, or had lost his balance through being pushed or had reluctantly to cause the injury for reasons which acceptably override his reluctance. The offering of such pleas by the agent and their acceptance by the sufferer is something in no way opposed to, or outside the context of, ordinary inter-personal relationships and the manifestation of ordinary reactive attitudes. Since things go wrong and situations are complicated, it is an essential and integral element in the transactions which are the life of these relationships.

The second group of considerations is very different. I shall take them in two sub-groups of which the first is far less important than the second. In connection with the first sub-group we may think of such statements as "He wasn't himself", "He has been under very great strain recently", "He was acting under post-hypnotic suggestion", in connection with the second, we may think of "He's only a child", "He's a hopeless schizophrenic", "His mind has been systematically perverted", "That's purely compulsive behaviour on his part." Such pleas as these do, as pleas of my first general group do not, invite us to suspend our ordinary reactive attitudes toward the agent, either at the time of his action or all the time. They do not invite us to see the agent's action in a way consistent with the full retention of ordinary interpersonal attitudes and merely inconsistent with one particular attitude. They invite us to view the agent himself in a different light from the light in which we should normally view one who has acted as he has acted. I shall not linger over the first subgroup of cases. Though they perhaps raise, in the short term, questions akin to those raised, in the long term, by the second subgroup, we may dismiss them without considering those questions by taking that admirably suggestive phrase, "He wasn't himself," with the seriousness that—for all its being logically comic—it deserves. We shall not feel resentment against the man he is for the action done by the man he is not; or at least we shall feel less. We normally have to deal with him under normal stresses; so we shall not feel towards him, when he acts as he does [66] under abnormal stresses, as we should have felt towards him had he acted as he did under normal stresses.

The second and more important subgroup of cases allows that the circumstances were normal, but presents the agent as psychologically abnormal—or as morally undeveloped. The agent was himself; but he is warped or deranged, neurotic or just a child. When we see someone in such a light as this, all our reactive attitudes tend to be profoundly modified. I must deal here in crude dichotomies and ignore the ever-interesting and ever-illuminating varieties of case. What I want to contrast is the attitude (or range of attitudes) of involvement or participation in a human relationship, on the one hand, and what might be called the objective attitude (or range of attitudes) to another human being, on the other. Even in the same situation, I must add, they are not altogether *exclusive* of each other; but they are, profoundly, *opposed* to each other. To adopt the objective attitude to another human being is to see

---

3   Perhaps not in every case *just* what we demand they should be, but in any case *not* just what we demand they should not be. For my present purpose these differences do not matter.

him, perhaps, as an object of social policy; as a subject for what, in a wide range of sense, might be called treatment; as something certainly to be taken account, perhaps precautionary account, of; to be managed or handled or cured or trained; perhaps simply to be avoided, though *this* gerundive is not peculiar to cases of objectivity of attitude. The objective attitude may be emotionally toned in many ways, but not in all ways: it may include repulsion or fear, it may include pity or even love, though not all kinds of love. But it cannot include the range of reactive feelings and attitudes which belong to involvement or participation with others in inter-personal human relationships; it cannot include resentment, gratitude, forgiveness, anger, or the sort of love which two adults can sometimes be said to feel reciprocally, for each other. If your attitude towards someone is wholly objective, then though you may fight him, you cannot quarrel with him, and though you may talk to him, even negotiate with him, you cannot reason with him. You can at most pretend to quarrel, or to reason, with him.

Seeing someone, then, as warped or deranged or compulsive in behaviour or peculiarly unfortunate in his formative circumstances—seeing someone so tends, at least to some extent, to set him apart from normal participant reactive attitudes on the part of one who sees him, tends to promote, at least in the civilized, objective attitudes. But there is something curious to add to this. The objective attitude is not only something we naturally tend to fall into in cases like these, where participant attitudes are partially or wholly inhibited by abnormalities or by immaturity. It is also something which is available as a resource in other cases too. We look with an objective eye on the compulsive behaviour of the neurotic or the tiresome behaviour of a very young child, thinking in terms of treatment or training. But we *can* [67] sometimes look with something like the same eye on the behaviour of the normal and the mature. We *have* this resource and can sometimes use it: as a refuge, say, from the strains of involvement; or as an aid to policy; or simply out of intellectual curiosity. Being human, we cannot, in the normal case, do this for long, or altogether. If the strains of involvement, say, continue to be too great, then we have to do something else—like severing a relationship. But what is above all interesting is the tension there is, in us, between the participant attitude and the objective attitude. One is tempted to say: between our humanity and our intelligence. But to say this would be to distort both notions.

What I have called the participant reactive attitudes are essentially natural human reactions to the good or ill will or indifference of others towards us, as displayed in *their* attitudes and actions. The question we have to ask is: What effect would, or should, the acceptance of the truth of a general thesis of determinism have upon these reactive attitudes? More specifically would, or should, the acceptance of the truth of the thesis lead to the decay or the repudiation of all such attitudes? Would, or should, it mean the end of gratitude, resentment, and forgiveness; of all reciprocated adult loves; of all the essentially *personal* antagonisms?

But how can I answer, or even pose, this question without knowing *exactly* what the thesis of determinism is? Well, there is one thing we do know: that if there is a coherent thesis of determinism, then there must be a sense of "determined" such that, if that thesis is true, then all behaviour whatever is determined in that sense. Remembering this, we can consider at least what possibilities lie formally open;

and then perhaps we shall see that the question can be answered *without* knowing exactly what the thesis of determinism is. We can consider what possibilities lie open because we have already before us an account of the ways in which particular reactive attitudes, or reactive attitudes in general, may be, and, sometimes, we judge, should be, inhibited. Thus I considered earlier a group of considerations which tend to inhibit, and, we judge, should inhibit, resentment, in particular cases of an agent causing an injury, without inhibiting reactive attitudes in general towards that agent. Obviously this group of considerations cannot strictly bear upon our question; for that question concerns reactive attitudes in general. But resentment has a particular interest; so it is worth adding that it has never been claimed as a consequence of the truth of determinism that one or another of *these* considerations was operative in every case of an injury being caused by an agent; that it would follow from the truth of determinism that anyone who caused an injury *either* was quite simply ignorant of causing it *or* had acceptably overriding reasons for acquiescing reluctantly in causing it *or* .... The prevalence of this happy **[68]** state of affairs would not be a consequence of the reign of universal determinism, but of the reign of universal goodwill. We cannot, then, find here the possibility of an affirmative answer to our question, even for the particular case of resentment.

Next, I remarked that the participant attitude, and the personal reactive attitudes in general, tend to give place, and, it is judged by the civilized, should give place, to objective attitudes, just in so far as the agent is seen as excluded from ordinary adult human relationships by deep-rooted abnormality—or simply by being a child. But it cannot be a consequence of any thesis which is not itself self-contradictory that abnormality is the universal condition.

Now this dismissal might seem altogether too facile; and so, in a sense, it is. But whatever is too quickly dismissed in this dismissal is allowed for in the only possible form of affirmative answer that remains. We can sometimes, and in part, I have remarked, look on the normal (those we rate as "normal") in the objective way in which we have learned to look on certain classified cases of abnormality. And our question reduces to this: could, or should the acceptance of the determinist thesis lead us always to look on everyone exclusively in this way? For this is the only condition worth considering under which the acceptance of determinism could lead to the decay or repudiation of participant reactive attitudes.

It does not seem to be self-contradictory to suppose that this might happen. So I suppose we must say that it is not absolutely inconceivable that it should happen. But I am strongly inclined to think that it is, for us as we are, practically inconceivable. The human commitment to participation in ordinary inter-personal relationships is, I think, too thoroughgoing and deeply rooted for us to take seriously the thought that a general theoretical conviction might so change our world that, in it, there were no longer any such things as inter-personal relationships as we normally understand them; and being involved in inter-personal relationships as we normally understand them precisely is being exposed to the range of reactive attitudes and feelings that is in question.

This, then, is a part of the reply to our question. A sustained objectivity of interpersonal attitude, and the human isolation which that would entail, does not seem to be something of which human beings would be capable, even if some general truth were a theoretical ground for it. But this is not all. There is a further point, implicit in the foregoing, which must be made explicit. Exceptionally, I have said, we can have direct dealings with human beings without any degree of personal involvement, treating them simply as creatures to be handled in our own interests, or our side's, or society's—or even theirs. In the extreme case of the mentally deranged, it is easy to see the [69] connection between the possibility of a wholly objective attitude and the impossibility of what we understand by ordinary inter-personal relationships. Given this latter impossibility, no other civilized attitude is available than that of viewing the deranged person simply as something to be understood and controlled in the most desirable fashion. To view him as outside the reach of personal relationships is already, for the civilized, to view him in this way. For reasons of policy or self-protection we may have occasion, perhaps temporary, to adopt a fundamentally similar attitude to a "normal" human being; to concentrate, that is, on understanding "how he works", with a view to determining our policy accordingly or to finding in that very understanding a relief from the strains of involvement. Now it is certainly true that in the case of the abnormal, though not in the case of the normal, our adoption or the objective attitude is a consequence of our viewing the agent as *incapacitated* in some or all respects for ordinary inter-personal relations. He is thus incapacitated, perhaps, by the fact that his picture of reality is pure fantasy, that he does not, in a sense, live in the real world at all; or by the fact that his behaviour is, in part, an unrealistic acting out of unconscious purposes; or by the fact that he is an idiot, or a moral idiot. But there is something else which, *because* this is true, is equally certainly *not* true. And that is that there is a sense of "determined" such that (1) if determinism is true, all behaviour is determined in this sense, and (2) determinism might be true, i.e., it is not inconsistent with the facts as we know them to suppose that all behaviour might be determined in this sense, and (3) our adoption of the objective attitude towards the abnormal is the result of prior embracing of the belief that the behaviour, or the relevant stretch of behaviour, of the human being in question *is* determined in this sense. Neither in the case of the normal, then, nor in the case of the abnormal is it true that, when we adopt an objective attitude, we do so *because* we hold such a belief. So my answer has two parts. The first is that we cannot, as we are, seriously envisage ourselves adopting a thoroughgoing objectivity of attitude to others as a result of theoretical conviction of the truth of determinism; and the second is that when we do in fact adopt such an attitude in a particular case, our doing so is not the consequence of a theoretical conviction which might be expressed as "Determinism in this case", but is a consequence of our abandoning, for different reasons in different cases, the ordinary inter-personal attitudes.

It might be said that all this leaves the real question unanswered, and that we cannot hope to answer it without knowing exactly what the thesis of determinism is. For the real question is not a question about what we actually do, or why we do it. It is not even a question about what we would *in fact* do if a certain theoretical conviction gained general acceptance. It is [70] a question about what it would be *rational* to do if determinism were true, a question about the rational justification of ordinary inter-personal attitudes in general. To this I shall reply, first, that such a question could seem real only to one who had utterly failed to grasp the purport of the preceding answer, the fact of our natural human commitment to ordinary interpersonal attitudes. This commitment is part of the general framework of human life, not something that can come up for review as particular cases can come up for review within this general framework. And I shall reply, second, that if we could imagine what we cannot have, viz. a choice in this matter, then we could choose rationally only in the light of an assessment of the gains and losses to human life, its enrichment or impoverishment; and the truth or falsity of a general thesis of determinism would not bear on the rationality of *this* choice.[4]

V.

The point of this discussion of the reactive attitudes in their relation—or lack of it—to the thesis of determinism was to bring us, if possible, nearer to a position of compromise in a more usual area of debate. We are not now to discuss reactive attitudes which are essentially those of offended parties or beneficiaries. We are to discuss reactive attitudes which are essentially not those, or only incidentally are those, of offended parties or beneficiaries, but are nevertheless, I shall claim, kindred attitudes to those I have discussed. I put resentment in the centre of the previous discussion. I shall put moral indignation—or, more weakly, moral disapprobation—in the centre of this one.

The reactive attitudes I have so far discussed are essentially reactions to the quality of others' wills towards us, as manifested in their behaviour: to their good or ill will or indifference or lack of concern. Thus resentment, or what I have called resentment, is a reaction to injury or indifference. The reactive attitudes I have now to discuss might be described as the sympathetic or vicarious or impersonal or disinterested or generalized analogues of the reactive attitudes I have already discussed. They are reactions to the qualities of others' wills, not towards ourselves, but towards others. Because of this impersonal or vicarious character, we give them [71] different names. Thus one who experiences the vicarious analogue of resentment is said to be indignant or disapproving, or morally indignant or disapproving. What we have here is, as it were, resentment on behalf of another, where one's own interest and dignity are not involved; and it is this impersonal or vicarious character of the attitude added to its others, which entitle it to the qualification "moral". Both my description of, and my name for, these attitudes are, in one important respect, a little misleading. It is not that these attitudes are essentially vicarious—one can feel indignation on one's own account—but that they are essentially capable of being vicarious. But I shall retain the name for the sake of is suggestiveness; and I hope that what is misleading about it will be corrected in what follows.

---

4   The question, then, of the connection between rationality and the adoption of the objective attitude to others is misposed when it is made to seem dependent on the issue of determinism. But there is another question which should be raised, if only to distinguish it from the misposed question. Quite apart from the issue of determinism might it not be said that we should be nearer to being purely rational creatures in proportion as our relation to others was in fact dominated by the objective attitude? I think this might be said; only it would have to be added, once more, that if such a choice were possible, it would not necessarily be rational to choose to be more purely rational than we are.

The personal reactive attitudes rest on, and reflect, an expectation of, and demand for, the manifestation of a certain degree of goodwill or regard on the part of other human beings towards ourselves; or at least on the expectation of, and demand for, an absence of the manifestation of active ill will or indifferent disregard. (What will, in particular cases, *count* as manifestations of good or ill will or disregard will vary in accordance with the particular relationship in which we stand to another human being.) The generalized or vicarious analogues of the personal reactive attitudes rest on, and reflect, exactly the same expectation or demand in a generalized form; they rest on, or reflect, that is, the demand for the manifestation of a reasonable degree of goodwill or regard, on the part of others, not simply towards oneself, but towards all those on whose behalf moral indignation may be felt, i.e. as we now think, towards all men. The generalized and non-generalized forms of demand and the vicarious and personal reactive attitudes which rest upon, and reflect, them are connected not merely logically. They are connected humanly; and not merely with each other. They are connected also with yet another set of attitudes which I must mention now in order to complete the picture. I have considered from two points of view the demands we make on others and our reactions to their possibly injurious actions. These were the points of view of one whose interest was directly involved (who suffers, say, the injury) and of others whose interest was not directly involved (who do not themselves suffer the injury). Thus I have spoken of personal reactive attitudes in the first connection and of their vicarious analogues in the second. But the picture is not complete unless we consider also the correlates of these attitudes on the part of those on whom the demands are made, on the part of the agents. Just as there are personal and vicarious reactive attitudes associated with demands on others for oneself and demands on others for others, so there are self-reactive attitudes associated with demands on oneself for others. And here we have to mention such phenomena as feeling bound or obliged (the **[72]** "sense of obligation"); feeling compunction; feeling guilty or remorseful or at least responsible; and the more complicated phenomenon of shame.

All these three types of attitude are humanly connected. One who manifested the personal reactive attitudes in a high degree but showed no inclination at all to their vicarious analogues would appear as an abnormal case of moral egocentricity, as a kind of moral solipsist. Let him be supposed fully to acknowledge the claims to regard that others had on him, to be susceptible of the whole range of self-reactive attitudes. He would then see himself as unique both as one (*the* one) who had a general claim on human regard and as one (*the* one) on whom human beings in general had such a claim. This would be a kind of moral solipsism. But it is barely more than a conceptual possibility; if it is that. In general, though within varying limits, we demand of others for others, as well as of ourselves for others, something of the regard which we demand of others for ourselves. Can we imagine, besides that of the moral solipsist, any other case of one or two of these three types of attitude being fully developed, but quite unaccompanied by any trace, however slight, of the remaining two or one? If we can, then we imagine something far below or far above the level of our common humanity—a moral idiot or a saint. For all these types of attitude alike have common roots in our human nature and our membership of human communities.

Now, as of the personal reactive attitudes, so of their vicarious analogues, we must ask in what ways, and by what considerations, they tend to be inhibited. Both types of attitude involve, or express, a certain sort of demand for inter-personal regard. The fact of injury constitutes a prima-facie appearance of this demand's being flouted or unfulfilled. We saw, in the case of resentment, how one class of considerations may show this appearance to be mere appearance, and hence inhibit resentment, *without* inhibiting, or displacing, the sort of demand of which resentment can be an expression, without in any way tending to make us suspend our ordinary inter-personal attitudes to the agent. Considerations of this class operate in just the same way, for just the same reasons, in connection with moral disapprobation or indignation; they inhibit indignation without in any way inhibiting the sort of demand on the agent of which indignation can be an expression, the range of attitudes towards him to which it belongs. But in this connection we may express the facts with a new emphasis. We may say, stressing the moral, the generalized aspect of the demand, considerations of this group have no tendency to make us see the agent as other than a morally responsible agent; they simply make us see the injury as one for which he was not morally responsible. The offering and acceptance of such exculpatory pleas as are here in question in no way detract in our eyes from the agent's [73] status as a term of moral relationships. On the contrary, since things go wrong and situations are complicated, it is an essential part of the life of such relationships.

But suppose we see the agent in a different light: as one whose picture of the world is an insane delusion; or as one whose behaviour, or a part of whose behaviour, is unintelligible to us, perhaps even to him, in terms of conscious purposes, and intelligible only in terms of unconscious purposes; or even, perhaps, as one wholly impervious to the self-reactive attitudes I spoke of, wholly lacking, as we say, in moral sense. Seeing an agent in such a light as this tends, I said, to inhibit resentment in a wholly different way. It tends to inhibit resentment because it tends to inhibit ordinary inter-personal attitudes in general, and the kind of demand and expectation which those attitudes involve; and tends to promote instead the purely objective view of the agent as one posing problems simply of intellectual understanding, management, treatment, and control. Again the parallel holds for those generalized or moral attitudes towards the agent which we are now concerned with. The same abnormal light which shows the agent to us as one in respect of whom the personal attitudes, the personal demand, are to be suspended, shows him to us also as one in respect of whom the impersonal attitudes, the generalized demand, are to be suspended. Only, abstracting now from direct personal interest, we may express the facts with a new emphasis. We may say: to the extent to which the agent is seen in this light, he is not seen as one on whom demands and expectations lie in that particular way in which we think of them as lying when we speak of moral obligation; he is not, to that extent, seen as a morally responsible agent, as a term of moral relationships, as a member of the moral community.

I remarked also that the suspension of ordinary inter-personal attitudes and the cultivation of a purely objective view is sometimes possible even when we have no such reasons for it as I have just mentioned. Is this possible also in the case of the moral reactive attitudes? I think so; and perhaps it is easier. But the motives for a total suspension of moral reactive attitudes are fewer, and perhaps weaker: fewer, because only where there is antecedent personal involvement can there be the motive of seeking refuge from the strains of such involvement; perhaps weaker, because the tension between objectivity of view and the moral reactive attitudes is perhaps less than the tension between objectivity of view and the personal reactive attitudes, so that we can in the case of the moral reactive attitudes more easily secure the speculative or political gains of objectivity of view by a kind of setting on one side, rather than a total suspension, of those attitudes.

These last remarks are uncertain; but also, for the present purpose, unimportant. What concerns us now is to inquire, as previously in [74] connection with the personal reactive attitudes, what relevance any general thesis of determinism might have to their vicarious analogues. The answers once more are parallel; though I shall take them in a slightly different order. First, we must note, as before, that when the suspension of such an attitude or such attitudes occurs in a particular case, it is *never* the consequence of the belief that the piece of behaviour in question was determined in a sense such that all behaviour *might be*, and, if determinism is true, all behaviour *is*, determined in that sense. For it is not a consequence of any general thesis of determinism which might be true that nobody knows what he's doing or that everybody's behaviour is unintelligible in terms of conscious purposes or that everybody lives in a world of delusion or that nobody has a moral sense, i.e. is susceptible of self-reactive attitudes, etc. In fact no such sense of "determined" as would be required for a general thesis of determinism is ever relevant to our actual suspensions of moral reactive attitudes. Second, suppose it granted, as I have already argued, that we cannot take seriously the thought that theoretical conviction of such a general thesis would lead to the total decay of the personal reactive attitudes. Can we then take seriously the thought that such a conviction—a conviction, after all, that many have held or said they held—would nevertheless lead to the total decay or repudiation of the vicarious analogues of these attitudes? I think that the change in our social world which would leave us exposed to the personal reactive attitudes but not to all their vicarious analogues, the generalization of abnormal egocentricity which this would entail, is perhaps even harder for us to envisage as a real possibility than the decay of both kinds of attitude together. Though there are some necessary and some contingent differences between the ways and cases in which these two kinds of attitudes operate or are inhibited in their operation, yet, as general human capacities or proneness, they stand or lapse together. Finally, to the further question whether it would not be *rational*, given a general theoretical conviction of the truth of determinism, so to change our world that in it all these attitudes were wholly suspended, I must answer, as before, that one who presses this question has wholly failed to grasp the import of the preceding answer, the nature of the human commitment that is here involved: it is *useless* to ask whether it would not be rational for us to do what it is not in our nature to (be able to) do. To this I must add, as before, that if there were, say, for a moment open to us the possibility of such a godlike choice, the rationality of making or refusing it would be determined by quite other considerations than the truth or falsity of the general theoretical doctrine in question. The latter would be simply irrelevant; and this becomes ironically clear when we remember that for those convinced that the truth of determinism nevertheless really would make the one choice [75] rational, there has always been the insuperable difficulty of explaining in intelligible terms how its falsity would make the opposite choice rational.

I am aware that in presenting the arguments as I have done, neglecting the ever-interesting varieties of case, I have presented nothing more than a schema, using sometimes a crude opposition of phrase where we have a great intricacy of phenomena. In particular the simple opposition of objective attitudes on the one hand and the various contrasted attitudes which I have opposed to them must seem as grossly crude as it is central. Let me pause to mitigate this crudity a little, and also to strengthen one of my central contentions, by mentioning some things which straddle these contrasted kinds of attitude. Thus parents and others concerned with the care and upbringing of young children cannot have to their charges either kind of attitude in a pure or unqualified form. They are dealing with creatures that are potentially and increasingly capable both of holding, and being objects of, the full range of human and moral attitudes, but are not yet truly capable of either. The treatment of such creatures must therefore represent a kind of compromise, constantly shifting in one direction, between objectivity of attitude and developed human attitudes. Rehearsals insensibly modulate towards true performances. The punishment of a child is both like and unlike the punishment of an adult. Suppose we try to relate this progressive emergence of the child as a responsible being, as an object of non-objective attitudes, to that sense of "determined" in which, if determinism is a possibly true thesis, all behaviour *may* be determined, and in which, if it is a true thesis, all behaviour *is* determined. What bearing *could* such a sense of "determined" have upon the progressive modification of attitudes towards the child? Would it not be grotesque to think of the development of the child as a progressive or patchy emergence from an area in which its behaviour is in this sense determined into an area in which it isn't? Whatever sense of "determined" is required for stating the thesis of determinism, it can scarcely be such as to allow of compromise, borderline style answers to the question, "Is this bit of behaviour determined or isn't it?" But in this matter of young children, it is essentially a borderline, penumbral area that we move in. Again, consider—a very different matter—the strain in the attitude of a psychoanalyst to his patient. *His* objectivity of attitude, *his* suspension of ordinary moral reactive attitudes, is profoundly modified by the fact that the aim of the enterprise is to make such suspension unnecessary or less necessary. Here we may and do naturally speak of restoring the agent's freedom. But here the restoring of freedom means bringing it about that the agent's behaviour shall be intelligible in terms of conscious purposes rather than in terms only of unconscious purposes. *This* is the object of the enterprise; and it is in so far as *this* object is attained that [76] the suspension, or half-suspension, of ordinary moral attitudes is deemed no longer necessary or appropriate. And in this we see once again the *irrelevance* of that concept of "being determined" which must be the central concept of determinism. For we cannot both agree that this object is attainable and that its attainment has this consequence and yet hold (1) that neurotic behaviour is determined in a sense in which, it may be, all behaviour is determined, and (2) that it is because neurotic behaviour is determined in this sense that objective attitudes are deemed appropriate to neurotic behaviour. Not, at least, without accusing ourselves of incoherence in our attitude to psychoanalytic treatment.

VI.

And now we can try to fill in the lacuna which the pessimist finds in the optimist's account of the concept of moral responsibility, and of the bases of moral condemnation and punishment; and to fill it in from the facts as we know them. For, as I have already remarked, when the pessimist himself seeks to fill it in, he rushes beyond the facts as we know them and proclaims that it cannot be filled in at all unless determinism is false.

Yet a partial sense of the facts as we know them is certainly present to the pessimist's mind. When his opponent, the optimist, undertakes to show that the truth of determinism would not shake the foundations of the concept of moral responsibility and of the practices of moral condemnation and punishment, he typically refers, in a more or less elaborated way, to the efficacy of these practices in regulating behaviour in socially desirable ways. These practices are represented solely as instruments of policy, as methods of individual treatment and social control. The pessimist recoils from this picture; and in his recoil there is, typically, an element of emotional shock. He is apt to say, among much else, that the humanity of the offender himself is offended by *this* picture of his condemnation and punishment.

The reasons for this recoil—the explanation of the sense of an emotional, as well as a conceptual, shock—we have already before us. The picture painted by the optimists is painted in a style appropriate to a situation envisaged as wholly dominated by objectivity of attitude. The only operative notions invoked in this picture are such as those of policy, treatment, control. But a thoroughgoing objectivity of attitude, excluding as it does the moral reactive attitudes, excludes at the same time essential elements in the concepts of *moral* condemnation and *moral* responsibility. This is the reason for the conceptual shock. The deeper emotional shock is a reaction, not simply to an inadequate conceptual analysis, but to the suggestion of a change in our world. I have remarked that it is possible to cultivate an [77] exclusive objectivity of attitude in some cases, and for some reasons, where the object of the attitude is not set aside from developed inter-personal and moral attitudes by immaturity or abnormality. And the suggestion which seems to be contained in the optimist's account is that such an attitude should be universally adopted to all offenders. This is shocking enough in the pessimist's eyes. But, sharpened by shock, his eyes see further. It would be hard to make *this* division in our natures. If to all offenders, then to all mankind. Moreover, to whom could this recommendation be, in any real sense, addressed? Only to the powerful, the authorities. So abysses seem to open.[5]

But we will confine our attention to the case of the offenders. The concepts we are concerned with are those of responsibility and guilt, qualified as "moral", on the one hand—together with that of membership of a moral community; of demand, indignation, disapprobation and condemnation, qualified as "moral", on the other hand—together with that of punishment. Indignation, disapprobation, like resentment, tend to inhibit or at least to limit our goodwill towards the object of these attitudes, tend to promote an at least partial and temporary withdrawal of

---

5 See J.D. Mabbott's "Freewill and Punishment", in *Contemporary British Philosophy*, 3rd ser. (London: Allen & Unwin, 1956).

goodwill; they do so in proportion as they are strong; and their strength is in general proportioned to what is felt to be the magnitude of the injury and to the degree to which the agent's will is identified with, or indifferent to, it. (These, of course, are not contingent connections.) But these attitudes of disapprobation and indignation are precisely the correlates of the moral demand in the case where the demand is felt to be disregarded. The making of the demand *is* the proneness to such attitudes. The holding of them does not, as the holding of objective attitudes does, involve as a part of itself viewing their object other than as a member of the moral community. The partial withdrawal of goodwill which *these* attitudes entail, the modification *they* entail of the general demand that another should, if possible, be spared suffering, is, rather, the consequence of *continuing* to view him as a member of the moral community; only as one who has offended against its demands. So the preparedness to acquiesce in that infliction of suffering on the offender which is an essential part of punishment is all of a piece with this whole range of attitudes of which I have been speaking. It is not only moral reactive attitudes towards the offender which are in question here. We must mention also the self-reactive attitudes of offenders themselves. Just as the other-reactive attitudes are associated with a readiness to acquiesce in the infliction of suffering on an offender, within the "institution" of punishment, so the self-reactive attitudes are associated with a readiness on the part of [78] the offender to acquiesce in such infliction *without* developing the reactions (e.g. of resentment) which he would normally develop to the infliction of injury upon him; i.e. with a readiness, as we say, to accept punishment[6] as "his due" or as "just".

I am not in the least suggesting that these readinesses to acquiesce, either on the part of the offender himself or on the part of others, are always or commonly accompanied or preceded by indignant boiling or remorseful pangs; only that we have here a continuum of attitudes and feelings to which these readinesses to acquiesce themselves belong. Nor am I in the least suggesting that it belongs to this continuum of attitudes that we should be ready to acquiesce in the infliction of injury on offenders in a fashion which we saw to be quite indiscriminate or in accordance with procedures which we knew to be wholly useless. On the contrary, savage or civilized, we have some belief in the utility of practices of condemnation and punishment. But the social utility of these practices, on which the optimist lays such exclusive stress, is not what is now in question. What is in question is the pessimist's justified sense that to speak in terms of social utility alone is to leave out something vital in our conception of these practices. The vital thing can be restored by attending to that complicated web of attitudes and feelings which form an essential part of the moral life as we know it, and which are quite opposed to objectivity of attitude. Only by attending to this range of attitudes can we recover from the facts as we know them a sense of what we mean, i.e. of *all* we mean, when, speaking the language of morals, we speak of desert, responsibility, guilt, condemnation, and justice. But we *do* recover it from the facts as we know them. We do not have to go beyond them. Because the optimist neglects or misconstrues these attitudes, the pessimist rightly

---

6 Of course not *any* punishment for *anything* deemed an offence.

claims to find a lacuna in his account. We can fill the lacuna for him. But in return we must demand of the pessimist a surrender of his metaphysics.

Optimist and pessimist misconstrue the facts in very different styles. But in a profound sense there is something in common to their misunderstandings. Both seek, in different ways, to over-intellectualize the facts. Inside the general structure or web of human attitudes and feelings of which I have been speaking, there is endless room for modification, redirection, criticism, and justification. But questions of justification are internal to the structure or relate to modifications internal to it. The existence of the general framework of attitudes itself is something we are given with the fact of human society. As a whole, it neither calls for, nor permits, an external "rational" justification. Pessimist and optimist alike show themselves, in [79] different ways, unable to accept this.[7] The optimist's style of over-intellectualizing the facts is that of a characteristically incomplete empiricism, a one-eyed utilitarianism. He seeks to find an adequate basis for certain social practices in calculated consequences, and loses sight (perhaps wishes to lose sight) of the human attitudes of which these practices are, in part, the expression. The pessimist does not lose sight of these attitudes, but is unable to accept the fact that it is just these attitudes themselves which fill the gap in the optimist's account. Because of this, he thinks the gap can be filled only if some general metaphysical proposition is repeatedly verified, verified in all cases where it is appropriate to attribute moral responsibility. This proposition he finds it as difficult to state coherently and with intelligible relevance as its determinist contradictory. Even when a formula has been found ("contra causal freedom" or something of the kind) there still seems to remain a gap between its applicability in particular cases and its supposed moral consequences. Sometimes he plugs this gap with an intuition of fittingness—a pitiful intellectualist trinket for a philosopher to wear as a charm against the recognition of his own humanity.

Even the moral sceptic is not immune from his own form of the wish to over-intellectualize such notions as those of moral responsibility, guilt, and blame. He sees that the optimist's account is inadequate and the pessimist's libertarian alternative inane; and finds no resource except to declare that the notions in question are inherently confused, that "blame is metaphysical". But the metaphysics was in the eye of the metaphysician. It is a pity that talk of the moral sentiments has fallen out of favour. The phrase would be quite a good name for that network of human attitudes in acknowledging the character and place of which we find, I suggest, the only possibility of reconciling these disputants to each other and the facts.

There are, at present, factors which add, in a slightly paradoxical way, to the difficulty of making this acknowledgment. These human attitudes themselves, in their development and in the variety of their manifestations, have to an increasing extent become objects of study in the social and psychological sciences; and this growth of human self-consciousness, which we might expect to reduce the difficulty

---

7 Compare the question of the justification of induction. The human commitment to inductive belief-formation is original, natural, non-rational (not *ir*rational), in no way something we choose or could give up. Yet rational criticism and reflection can refine standards and their application, supply "rules for judging of cause and effect". Ever since these facts were made clear by Hume, people have been resisting acceptance of them.

of acceptance, in fact increases it in several ways. One factor of comparatively minor importance is an increased historical and anthropological awareness of the great variety of forms which these human attitudes may take at different times and in different cultures. [80] This makes one rightly chary of claiming as essential features of the concept of morality in general, forms of these attitudes which may have a local and temporary prominence. No doubt to some extent my own descriptions of human attitudes have reflected local and temporary features of our own culture. But an awareness of variety of forms should not prevent us from acknowledging also that in the absence of *any* forms of these attitudes it is doubtful whether *we* should have anything that we could find intelligible as a system of human relationships, as human society. A quite different factor of greater importance is that psychological studies have made us rightly mistrustful of many particular manifestations of the attitudes I have spoken of. They are a prime realm of self-deception, of the ambiguous and the shady, of guilt-transference, unconscious sadism and the rest. But it is an exaggerated horror, itself suspect, which would make us unable to acknowledge the facts because of the seamy side of the facts. Finally, perhaps the most important factor of all is the prestige of these theoretical studies themselves. That prestige is great, and is apt to make us forget that in philosophy, though it also is a theoretical study, we have to take account of the facts in *all* their bearings; we are not to suppose that we are required, or permitted, as philosophers, to regard ourselves, as human beings, as detached from the attitudes which, as scientists, we study with detachment. This is in no way to deny the possibility and desirability of redirection and modification of our human attitudes in the light of these studies. But we may reasonably think it unlikely that our progressively greater understanding of certain aspects of ourselves will lead to the total disappearance of those aspects. Perhaps it is not inconceivable that it should; and perhaps, then, the dreams of some philosophers will be realized.

If we sufficiently, that is *radically*, modify the view of the optimist, his view is the right one. It is far from wrong to emphasize the efficacy of all those practices which express or manifest our moral attitudes, in regulating behaviour in ways considered desirable; or to add that when certain of our beliefs about the efficacy of some of these practices turns out to be false, then we may have good reason for dropping or modifying those practices. What *is* wrong is to forget that these practices, and their reception, the reactions to them, really *are* expressions of our moral attitudes and not merely devices we calculatingly employ for regulative purposes. Our practices do not merely exploit our natures, they express them. Indeed the very understanding of the kind of efficacy these expressions of our attitudes have turns on our remembering this. When we do remember this, and modify the optimist's position accordingly, we simultaneously correct its conceptual deficiencies and ward off the dangers it seems to entail, without recourse to the obscure and panicky metaphysics of libertarianism.

Chapter 2

Free Will and Rationality

A.J. Ayer

A.J. Ayer's central concern in this paper is with the relevance of the concept of desert for the rationality of our reactive attitudes. The concept of desert, as we ordinarily employ it, is one that 'sustains our actual attributions of moral responsibility and the whole range of attitudes which they enter'. On close analysis, however, we find that the concept of desert is 'empty'—there are 'no possible circumstances in which its application would be justified'. On this basis, Ayer concludes that since 'the concept of desert is empty, so is the concept of responsibility which is founded upon it'. It follows from this that our reactive attitudes, in so far as they rest on the concept of desert, must be judged irrational. *They are irrational because they involve beliefs that require 'the satisfaction of a concept that dissolves on analysis'. This leaves Ayer in a dilemma: On one hand he holds that attitudes that are irrational in this sense ought to be discarded; on the other hand, he shares Strawson's view that a world without any 'interpersonal attitudes' would be deeply unattractive.*

In his most interesting and influential essay on 'Freedom and Resentment'[1] Professor Strawson has done us a great service in drawing our attention to the very wide range of attitudes and judgements in which the notion of responsibility plays an essential part. Discussions of the perennial issue of Free-will and Determinism have tended to concentrate far too narrowly on the question of punishment. The result is that those who have sought to argue that we do not need to be free in order to be responsible, or that if we do it is not in any sense that is inconsistent with determinism, have had things made easier for them by the fact that the idea of retributive punishment has fallen rather into disrepute. This has helped to secure a more favourable reception for their contention that nothing of value will be lost if the notion of responsibility is analysed or revised in such a way that agents are held responsible, and therefore liable to be rewarded or punished, for their actions, only in cases where there is good reason to believe that the prospect and bestowal of rewards and punishments will so affect them and others as to increase the likelihood of their behaving in future in ways that are considered socially beneficial and decrease the likelihood of their behaving in ways that are considered socially harmful.

---

1 *Proceedings of the British Academy*, 1962. Reprinted in Sir Peter Strawson's *Freedom and Resentment and Other Essays* (1974). [Page references for "Freedom and Resentment" will, as previously stated, be to pages 19–36 of this volume, followed by (after the slash) the corresponding pages of Gary Watson (ed.), *Free Will* (1982). (Thus, for example, 'FR, 26/68' refers to this volume, p. 26/and *Free Will*, p. 68.) – the editors.]

Even in this relatively narrow area, I think that there has been a tendency to underrate the extent to which this purely utilitarian approach is at variance with our ordinary ways of thinking. Even those who are emotionally repelled by the association of punishment with the idea of revenge, or those who regard the notion of expiation as intellectually or morally indefensible, will still be found adhering to two principles which do not fit into the utilitarian pattern. These principles are first that persons ought not to be punished for offences which they have not committed; and secondly that they ought not to be punished for actions which it was not in their power to avoid. The second principle is subject to some elasticity. For instance, it may be that someone has reached a state in which it is not in his power to avoid acting as he does, but he is still held liable to punishment because his being in that state is thought to be the result of previous actions which it was in his power to avoid: or it may be that someone is exonerated for an action which he was thought capable of avoiding, but only at a price, such as the probable loss of his life, which it was not in the circumstances thought reasonable for him to pay.

I know that utilitarians have made an effort to accommodate at least the first of these principles within their theory. To my mind, this effort has not been successful. I think that their theory will still be found to authorize the taking of punitive action, as a purely preventive or deterrent measure, in circumstances where it would not, in the general view, be morally justified and would, indeed, do violence to their own moral sentiments, if these were not wholly subjugated to their theory. This is not, however, a question that I wish to argue here. I am not concerned to criticize our utilitarians for depriving us of our concept of justice or for their failure, if indeed it is a failure, to make the loss good. I want only to stress the fact that they do deprive us of it and the reasons for which they do so. They deprive us of it by severing the historical connection, which there undoubtedly has been and indeed continues to be for most minds, between the concept of justice and the concept of desert, and the reason why they do so is that, while wishing to preserve as much of the idea of justice as is capable of rescue, they believe that the concept of desert is empty, if not meaningless, in the light of the possibility that all human actions are determined.

The service which Strawson has rendered us is to draw out the full implications of this rejection of the concept of desert. As he rightly points out, it is not only the concept of justice that is affected but almost all the concepts that enter into our estimations of one's own and other people's worth. We do indeed feel admiration or distaste for people's natural endowments, their good or bad looks, their native intelligence or stupidity, the good or bad dispositions which seem to form part of their genetic inheritance. To a very much greater extent, however, our judgements of their merits and demerits, and the feelings with which these judgements are allied, relate to qualities and dispositions which we imply that the agent need not have developed and to behaviour which it was, or at least once had been, in his power to avoid. Strawson reminds us how often in our relations with one another we display and think that we have good reason to display such feelings as gratitude and resentment, how we take pride in our achievements and feel remorse for our misdeeds, how actions to which we are not a party can evoke our moral approval or indignation. In all these cases there is a tacit or explicit reference to the concept of desert. A person who does me a benefit deserves my gratitude because he could have withheld the favour. I feel remorse for my neglect of my friends, because I could have taken more trouble to please them. In my hatred of tyranny, wherever it is displayed, the idea is implicit that the tyrant could have restrained himself, or even if this is no longer possible, that he himself is at least partly to blame for having become the monster that he is. But how can any of these attitudes be justified if there is even any probability that determinism reigns over all actions, and if one of the consequences of determinism is that no one could ever have acted otherwise than as he did?

Strawson himself does not put the issue quite so sharply, partly no doubt because he begins by allying himself with those who say that they do not know what the thesis of determinism is. He can afford to adopt this standpoint because his ignorance of the exact content of determinism is not such as to preclude his knowing that it is a general thesis about the springs of human conduct, and the main point which his essay is intended to establish is that no thesis which applies to human conduct indiscriminately can pose such a threat as I have been describing. More concretely, if we follow him in speaking of the feelings and judgements, which carry the implication of desert, as entering into 'ordinary inter-personal relationships'[2] as well as into our assessments of moral worth, and if we follow him also in speaking of someone who judges or responds to human behaviour only from the point of view of its causes and effects as taking an 'objective attitude'[3] towards it, then his contention is first that 'it is practically inconceivable'[4] that the acceptance of the thesis of determinism, whatever it may turn out to be, would lead to a thoroughgoing substitution of 'objective attitudes' for those that currently figure in our moral assessments and our interpersonal relationships, and secondly that even if this substitution could actually be made, it would not be rational to make it.

So far as I can see, the only argument which Strawson advances in favour of the first of these contentions is that whenever we do adopt an objective attitude towards some agent, either in respect of some or all of his actions, it is always for a special reason. Our resentment of what we should otherwise regard as an injury is inhibited, even when it is the work of one whom we take to be a responsible agent, because we have reason to believe that in this particular case he did not intend it or was subject to some pressure which it would not have been reasonable to expect him to resist. In such circumstances his action does not qualify as an injury. In other cases the disqualification may attach to the agent, if we judge that through no fault of his own he wasn't fully in command of himself. These cases are episodic, but there is also an important sub-class of cases in which an agent is persistently absolved from responsibility, because we view him 'as psychologically abnormal—or as morally undeveloped'.[5] It is only in cases such as these that we tend to treat the person in question not as an appropriate object of our ordinary interpersonal attitudes, but 'as an object of social policy'; someone 'to be managed or handled or cured or trained'.[6] And the same considerations apply to what Strawson calls our vicarious moral

---

2 FR, 26/68.
3 FR, 27/69.
4 FR, 26/68.
5 FR, 24/66.
6 FR, 25/66.

judgements. It is only when for some special reason the agent is seen in an 'abnormal light' that we think it inappropriate to react to his behaviour in the ways that are characteristic of our regarding him as 'a member of the moral community'.[7]

The reason, then, why Strawson thinks it unnecessary for his purpose to explore the general thesis of determinism is that on the comparatively rare occasions on which we do adopt a purely objective attitude towards our fellow human beings, it is always the result of our detecting some special sort of abnormality in their natures or in the conditions under which they have acted, and that for the rest 'the human commitment to participation in ordinary inter-personal relationships is too thoroughgoing and too deeply rooted for us to take seriously the thought that a general theoretical conviction might so change our world that, in it, there were no longer any such things as inter-personal relationships as we normally understand them'.[8] Consequently, no matter what the general thesis of determinism turns out to be, and however strong the arguments in its favour, we can rely on the fact that 'a sustained objectivity of inter-personal attitudes, and the human isolation which this would entail, does not seem to be something of which human beings would be capable'.[9]

Now Strawson may very well be right in making this empirical conjecture. Many philosophers and scientists have accepted or believed that they accepted a general thesis of determinism, and no doubt many laymen have followed their lead, but I do not think that any scientific enquiry has yet been made into the effect that this has had upon their social outlook. There is indeed the example of Professor Skinner who has written of the general adoption of the objective attitude not only as a future possibility but as a condition of his picture of Utopia, but I do not know whether he consistently adheres to this position in his own private life. It would cast no deep shadow on his sincerity if he did not, since from his point of view it would prove no more than that his own conditioning had been imperfect. So far as my own observation goes, professing determinists are not the less likely to feel gratitude or resentment, or pride or remorse or moral indignation, or to avoid any of the other commitments which their theory might be expected to deny them. If this is generally true, it is a point in Strawson's favour. Even so, I think that he reaches his conclusion too easily, and my ground for this charge lies in his avoidance of any discussion of the general thesis of determinism. I hope to show that the content which it is reasonable to attach to the thesis is not so irrelevant to his argument as he supposes it to be.

Let me say at once that I do not myself propose to examine the thesis in depth. There are just two points about it that seem to me to have an important bearing upon the present question. The first of them is that the thesis is vacuous if it claims no more than that every human action is subject to law; for any collection of phenomena whatsoever can be made to fit some set of generalizations, if no restrictions are placed on the character of these generalizations or their complexity. The thesis is worth discussing only if it is interpreted as claiming that all human actions are subject to

---

7 FR, 30/73.
8 FR, 26/68.
9 FR, 27/68.

what I call manageable laws; that is to say, the generalizations have to be such that we could actually use them to explain every facet of human behaviour, and that not merely *ex post facto*; they would have to enable us to make consistently successful predictions. In this form, the thesis has surely not been proved to be true. On the other hand, I do not think that we have any *a priori* reason for rejecting it.

The second and more important point is linked to the first. The thesis owes its force in this context to its being taken to entail that no one could ever have acted otherwise than as he did. We need, therefore, to examine what this conclusion comes to. I think it useless to begin with the suggestion that 'he could have acted otherwise' means 'he would have acted otherwise, if he had chosen'. Not only is the equivalence open to doubt, but at best it only leads to the question whether he could have chosen otherwise, on which we gain no foothold with this approach. A more profitable course, as I see it, is to ask under what conditions we actually judge that a man could not have acted otherwise, or conversely that he could. And here the answer does not seem to me far to seek. The cases in which we judge that the man could not have acted otherwise are those in which our beliefs encompass a set of particular facts and a set of well-established hypotheses which together entail or at least make it highly probable that he acted as he did. I ignore for the sake of simplicity the class of cases in which we judge that an action was avoidable but that it would not have been reasonable in the circumstances to expect the agent to avoid it. Conversely, the cases in which we judge that the man could have acted otherwise are those in which we are not in a position to draw the inference that he acted as he did, whether the shortage lies in our command of the requisite facts or the well-established hypotheses, or both. Obviously, to escape making it trivially true that all actions which are known to have occurred were unavoidable, it has to be stipulated that the stock of particular facts to which appeal can be made does not include the fact that the action in question took place, or any fact which entails it without the assistance of some available hypothesis.

The consequence of this analysis is that the question whether or not a person could on some particular occasion have acted otherwise than as he did is made relative to the state of our knowledge. There might be thought to be a problem as to whose knowledge is at issue, but I think that this can be circumvented. We can regard the claim that a person could have acted otherwise in a given instance as an open challenge to produce the information which would meet the conditions laid down for judging that he could not, and so long as this information is not forthcoming the claim remains acceptable.

Now it is noteworthy that the exceptional cases in which, as Strawson recognizes, we tend to adopt an 'objective' rather than a 'personal' attitude towards a particular action, or towards the over-all behaviour of a particular type of agent, are those in which we do think that we command a set of scientific hypotheses from which, in conjunction with facts which are practically ascertainable if not already ascertained, the conclusion that the behaviour takes place can be derived with at least a high degree of probability and in quite a specific form, even if it does not reach down to every detail. It is indeed true that the actions of those whom we do include in the moral community, with all that Strawson takes this to imply, are not always or even very often such as greatly surprise us. Our friends and acquaintances form habits with which we become familiar. There are social norms with which we can usually trust them to comply. Our treating them as responsible agents is not just dependent on the greater difficulty that we have in predicting what they will say and do. The difference lies rather in the way that we arrive at these conclusions. Whatever justification we may have for attributing to them the personal character and the particular beliefs and intentions, in terms of which we account for their behaviour, the generalizations involved are not accorded the status of scientific laws. They are statements of tendency which are not thought to be sufficiently strong or far-reaching to make the actions which they govern unavoidable. They do not sustain the verdict that the agent could not have acted otherwise.

This does not mean that the actions which we are accustomed to view in this fashion are thought to be incapable of being explained scientifically. There have indeed been 'libertarians',[10] as Strawson calls them, who have regarded the ascription of free will to human beings as requiring that if the actions which they freely perform are caused, their causes must include as a necessary condition an exercise of the will which is itself spontaneous; and faced with this difficulty have opted for free will. One of the weaknesses of their position, as Strawson remarks, is that this notion of the spontaneous exercise of the will is very obscure. If what is meant is that there is a random factor in what we choose to do, then it does not seem that the libertarians will have gained their objective, even if they are right. For why should the extent to which our actions occur by chance make us any more responsible for them than we would be if they were causally determined?

The more common view nowadays is, however, one that sets no *a priori* limit in this domain to the extension of the empire of science. For instance, many philosophers hold that what we normally classify as mental events are factually identical with events in the subject's brain, and they think it likely that events in the brain are subject to causal laws. Even so, this belief does not appear to inhibit them from making moral judgements, of a not purely utilitarian kind or from entering, as Strawson puts it, into 'ordinary inter-personal'[11] relationships. Are we to infer from this that they are inconsistent, or that their materialistic beliefs are not entirely sincere? Is it simply a vindication of Strawson's thesis that the thoroughgoing adoption of an 'objective attitude' is practically inconceivable?

It is tempting just to say 'Yes' to all three of these questions, but I think that it would be wrong. I suggest that what saves these philosophers from inconsistency is that their theory of the physical determination of mental events is not a working theory. They may sincerely believe that some specific theory of this sort is true, but they do not in fact know how it operates. They are not in a position to put any such theory to any widespread practical use. Physiology does not yet provide us with a complete explanation of the transition from one particular brain-state to another, or with the means of identifying or even uniquely correlating particular mental with cerebral events. Possibly these theoretical advances will be made, but even if they are, there will still be some way to go before the theory can be put to much practical use. To make only one simple point, it is not easy to see how we are going to be

---

10 FR, 35/79.
11 FR, 30/73.

furnished with the requisite information about the current states of people's brains. Consequently, if my analysis is correct, a philosopher who believes that a given action was physically determined can still truly say that the agent could have acted otherwise. He can say so because we do not have the detailed scientific knowledge from which to derive the conclusion that the agent acted as he did.

But now suppose that this were altered. Suppose that the requisite physiological or psycho-physical theories were developed and that we could use them in everyday life to make mainly accurate predictions. Or if this be thought too fanciful, let us suppose that the theory of conditioning were developed to a point where it became possible to implant desires and beliefs and traits of character in human beings, to an extent that it could be deduced, at least in fairly general terms, how any person who had been treated in this way would most probably behave in a given situation, and that we lived under a regime in which these powers were exercised upon us, let us say from early childhood. It may be remarked that there have been, and are, regimes in which a very large measure of such control has been seriously attempted; and that the historical evidence tends to show that its effects are not so overwhelming as some behavioural psychologists would have us believe. This is not, however, the point at issue. We are once again postulating a scientific advance to which, so far as I can see, there is no objection of logical principle. We are supposing that the methods of conditioning, to whatever ends they may be directed, are both universally employed and almost totally effective and the question is whether our interpersonal attitudes would be likely to withstand them.

My own view is that they most probably would not, unless, what is also conceivable, the conditioning itself were directed towards their preservation. Otherwise, I think that if it were a matter of common knowledge that these methods were practised, and if we understood the ways in which they operated, or even just the nature of their effects, sufficiently well to be able to account by their means for almost everything that anybody said or did, we should be most strongly disposed to assume an objective attitude not only towards our fellow human beings but even towards ourselves. It would be as if we were spectators of a play in which we also participated with no other option than to enact the roles allotted to us. Even those who were charged with writing and directing the play would see themselves as guided to frame it along certain specific lines. We could still attach moral and aesthetic values to the ways in which the various characters performed, but the judgements and attitudes which depend on our seeing people as responsible agents would be missing.

Would such a point of view be rational? It might be argued that the question does not arise. If we have come to a point where we see everything as decided for us, we shall hardly be troubled with the question what decisions we ought to take. 'Things and actions are what they are and the consequences of them will be what they will be.'[12] We should no longer have the inclination to 'desire to be deceived'.[13] Once again, however, the position may not be quite so simple. For instance, if the general belief that we cannot act otherwise than as we do were derived not from the prevalence of conditioning but from the general acceptance of a working physiological theory,

---

12 Bishop Butler, *Fifteen Sermons*, No. 7, para. 16.
13 *Ibid.*

then the fact of our believing that a causal explanation of each of our choices was readily available might not preclude our seeing the choices as needing to be made. I think that it would make some difference here whether we knew that the result of our deliberation had actually been predicted, and one need not assume that this would always be the case. It is anyhow worth noting that our ability to explain such things as the drawing of inferences does not dispense them from their subjection to normative standards. However detailed our knowledge of the way in which a calculating machine works, we can still coherently raise the question whether its calculations are correct.

An easier course of argument, which will have the advantage of giving the question of rationality a keener point, is to suppose that we are at a stage where the development of efficient processes of over-all conditioning is admitted to be practically feasible, and the question which we have to decide is whether we should favour or oppose it. The possibility of there being a causal explanation for our coming to whatever decision we do is not a factor in this argument since we are still in a position in which, if I am right in my analysis, either decision is open to us. Let us suppose also that we are taking for granted the truth of the very dubious proposition that the policy to which the conditioning was adapted would be and remain beneficent, and that we see it as leading to the prevalence of objective attitudes. Would it be rational for us in this case to favour 'the march of mind'?[14]

Strawson's answer is that it would not. He views rational choice 'in the light of an assessment of the gains and losses to human life, its enrichment or impoverishment'[15] and considers that from this point of view a state of affairs in which objective attitudes were generally prevalent would be of less value than one in which our present commitments to interpersonal relations were maintained. So far as I can see, he offers no argument in favour of this conclusion, and indeed I think that we should not expect him to. He had taken the issue to a point where it becomes a matter of moral sentiment, and we have only, as William James once put it, 'to confess to each other the motives for our several faiths'.[16]

For my part, I am strongly inclined to side with Strawson on this matter, but I have a qualm which he does not seem to share. As he hints in a footnote,[17] there is another sense of 'rational' in which the rationality of an attitude is measured not by the probable consequences of adopting it but by the standing of the beliefs which enter into it. In this sense, an attitude is irrational if it rests on a belief which we have no good reason for accepting: more seriously so, if it rests on a belief which we have good reason to reject. Such reasons may be various: but one of them surely is that the belief requires the satisfaction of a concept which dissolves on analysis, where what I mean by its dissolving is that a dissection of it reveals no possible circumstances in which its application would be justified.

Now my trouble is that I believe this to be true of the concept of desert. I do not deny that the extension with which this concept is unwarrantably credited could be

---

14   See T.L. Peacock, *Crotchet Castle*.
15   FR, 28/70.
16   William James, *Essays in Radical Empiricism*, p. 276.
17   FR, 28/70.

roughly covered by a different concept of a utilitarian character; but that is beside the point. I am speaking of the concept that we actually employ, the one that sustains our actual attributions of moral responsibility and the whole range of attitudes into which they enter. Even in our present state of knowledge, without any forecast of further scientific developments and their probable consequences, I cannot discover any circumstances in which the application of *this* concept would be justified. Whether we conceive of human actions as subject to causal or statistical laws, or whether we explain them in terms of motives the emergence of which leaves room for the play of chance, there is, as Lord Melbourne said of the award of the Garter 'no damned merit about it'; and no demerit either. Our actual attributes of merit and demerit depend upon the use of a metaphysical idea of self-determination, which Strawson himself dismisses as inane.[18]

But if the concept of desert is empty, so is the concept of responsibility which is founded on it. The moral judgements, in which persons are credited with such responsibility, are consequently irrational, in the sense of the term with which we are now concerned, and so are all the attitudes that either involve such moral judgements or commit us to the same ascriptions of responsibility; in effect, all the attitudes that Strawson prizes.

I find myself, therefore, in a dilemma. I attach a strong value to being rational in this second sense. I am dismayed when any belief that I hold appears to me irrational, in the way that I have just defined irrational belief, and in such a case I think that I ought to discard the belief, so far as this seems to be within my power. Correspondingly, I see it as an objection to an attitude that it rests on any such irrational belief, and again I think that I ought to try to refrain from adhering to it, so far as I can. From this it appears to follow that I should set myself to cultivate an objective attitude towards myself and others, and to welcome an ordering of society in which it was generally prevalent. What should concern me morally would be just the beneficence of the conditioning. At the same time I have to confess that the prospect of any such Brave New World repels me. Why it should is not clear to me. I see no harm, but rather goodness, in the attempt to influence people by argument and precept. This too is a form of conditioning, though not in many cases as effective as one would like it to be. Why then should I recoil from the idea of our all being subject to forms of conditioning that really would be effective and beneficent? If I were pressed for an answer, I should probably be reduced to saying something to the effect that it seemed to me an infringement of liberty or an affront to the dignity of man. But what would this mean? It looks as if I half-consciously hold the metaphysical belief in self-determination which my reason repudiates.

This shows, it may be said, that I just am not able to be rational, in the way I think I ought to be, which should not prevent my looking forward hopefully to scientific advances that will cause such disabilities to be overcome. But there is more to it than that. The fact is that I hold strong moral convictions, and strong personal attachments and antipathies, in which the unredeemed concepts of merit and demerit play an essential part; and that the idea of replacing these feelings and convictions by objective attitudes is not, on balance, attractive to me, not only as applying to

---

18 FR, 35/79.

myself, but also as a matter of general policy. Like Strawson, I am disposed to see the outcome as an impoverishment of 'human life'.

I am inclined therefore to endorse Strawson's epigram that 'if such a choice were possible', as unlike him I think it quite easily might be, 'it would not necessarily be rational to choose to be more purely rational than we are'.[19] I wish only that I could accept it as blithely as he does; without my present feeling of intellectual discomfort.

---

19 FR, 28 n4/70n4.

Chapter 3

Accountability (II)

Jonathan Bennett

Strawson's great paper solves some seemingly intractable problems. To see how, one must grasp the three tightly linked theses that provide its structure and generate its energy. (1) When you judge someone to be accountable for something he has done, the fundamental reality is not your recognition of a fact about him but rather your willingness to relate yourself to him in one special way. (2) Facts can make it wrong to hold someone accountable for something he has done; but this is the wrongness of conduct that is stupid, coarse, clumsy, infantile, uncivilized, not *the wrongness of judging that the person has a property that he really lacks. (3) No facts can make it wrong—in that or any other way—*not *to hold someone accountable for something he has done. When we get those three straight in our minds, light comes flooding in.*

1. Introduction

I shall present a problem about accountability, and its solution by Strawson's 'Freedom and Resentment'.[1] Some readers of Strawson's paper don't see it as a profound contribution to moral philosophy, and I want to help them. It may be helpful to follow up Strawson's gracefully written discussion with a more staccato presentation. My treatment will also be angled somewhat differently from his, so that its lights and shadows will fall with a certain difference, which may make it serviceable even to the converted. Also, I shall point to some disputable things in 'Freedom and Resentment', and offer repairs.

So I wrote in the first published version of this paper.[2] I wanted not only to be useful to others but also to elicit Strawson's certificate of approval; and that hope was realized. In his 'Reply' Strawson wrote: 'Bennett in the first eleven sections of his essay sets out and elaborates the essence of my position with such thorough and sympathetic understanding as to leave me little to say.'[3]

I also tried, unsuccessfully, to analyze with more precision Strawson's concept of *reactive attitude*, and to explore the extent of and reasons for the incompatibility

---

[1] P.F. Strawson, 'Freedom and Resentment', first published in 1962 and reprinted in Gary Watson (ed.), *Free Will* (Oxford: Oxford University Press, 1982), pp. 59–80; second edition 2003. Page references will be to pages 19–36 of this volume, followed by (after the slash) the corresponding pages of Watson's (1982) first edition. (Thus, 'FR, 16/59' refers to this volume, p. 16/and to Watson (1982), p. 59.)

[2] Jonathan Bennett, 'Accountability', in Z. Van Straaten (ed.), *Philosophical Subjects: Essays Presented to P. F. Strawson* (Oxford: Clarendon Press, 1980), pp. 14–47.

[3] P.F. Strawson, 'Replies', *ibid.*, pp. 260–96, at p. 264.

between reactive attitudes and the objective attitude. I hoped that the display of my failures would induce Strawson to tackle the problems himself, with more success. No such luck! He wrote: 'Bennett seeks ... to produce a tighter and more unified organization of the phenomena ... than I achieved in "Freedom and Resentment"',[4] but he did not return to the fray. On the contrary: 'It does not seem to me to matter if a strict definition [of 'reactive'] is not to be had'; and he said nothing about reasons for the reactive/objective conflict.

In the present version of the paper, I expound 'Freedom and Resentment' much as before. Since my attempts to tighten and deepen the theory failed to hook Strawson, and are not of much intrinsic interest, I now omit them. I shall, however, add an application of the doctrines of 'Freedom and Resentment' to the most basic philosophical question regarding punishment.

2. Accountability

We welcome some events, and regret some. Among the kinds of events that may be welcomed or regretted are human actions. When we regret an action, we may blame the agent for it, resent his doing it, hold it against him, find fault with him, speak of or to him in a manner that is censorious or vilifying or abusive, seek revenge, demand punishment. These responses are all related to *blame*—not as a faulty compass may be blamed for an accident, but in the stronger sense in which the object of blame must be believed to be personal, and the attribution of blame is a censure or reproach, which could naturally carry with it thoughts about moral unworthiness. When we welcome an action, we may respond with praise, admiration, gratitude, thoughts of reward, or the like. These responses can be thought of as praise-related—not as one might praise a fine physique or beautiful hair, but rather as one might accompany praise with thoughts of moral worth.

I shall assume that blame-related and praise-related responses to actions constitute two classes of responses, each of which is unified enough for philosophy to be done about it. (If they do not, this essay will collapse; but so also will much of the literature.) Any unclarity about the borderlines of the two classes will be harmless, because my main points can be made in terms of responses that are well in from the boundaries.

Certain discoveries about why a regretted action was performed will lead any civilized person to regard blame-related responses as inappropriate. Suppose someone commits a murder, and it turns out that he had a brain tumor which had a crucial role in the causation of the murderous act: every victim of such a tumor would be virtually certain to commit hostile and violent acts and this man will become a mild and reliably law-abiding citizen once his tumor is removed. In that case, it would be inappropriate to respond to the murder with reproaches etc., or to seek revenge or demand punishment. This man is not blameworthy.

Similarly, if a welcome action is explicable in a certain way, praise-related responses are inappropriate. If a benefactor was manifesting an insane compulsion

---

4 *Ibid.*, p. 266.

to give things away, the beneficiary may welcome the gift but should not be grateful for it. This person is not praiseworthy.

It is widely believed, I think rightly, that what stops the performer of a regretted action from being blameworthy is just what stops the performer of a welcomed action from being praiseworthy. Anyway, the two sets of conditions have a large overlap, which is my topic.

By 'accountable' I shall mean 'blameworthy or praiseworthy': someone is 'accountable' for an action, in my usage, if a blame- or praise-related response to the action would not be inappropriate. And my concern is with a problem about the conditions for 'accountability' in this sense. Since appropriateness can be a matter of degree, so can accountability; but I shall mainly use all-or-nothing formulations, to keep things simple. What about actions that are not notably regrettable or welcomable? Their authors are not 'accountable' for them in my sense, which seems wrong. It does not matter. My concern is with cases where the question of accountability *comes up* in a natural way, namely ones that are regretted or welcomed, so that praise or blame may be appropriate.

3. A Problem

I cannot pretend to tell, even abstractly, the whole story about the conditions for accountability; but two of them suffice for my purposes. For someone to be accountable for an action, (1) the action must relate in a certain way to his decisions, and (2) his decision-making capacities must satisfy a certain condition. More specifically: he is accountable for doing A only if (1) he would not have done A if he had decided (or chosen or willed or wanted, etc.) not to do A; and (2) he could have decided not to do A. There is no special problem about 1: if it is not satisfied, then something prevents him from not doing A, or makes him do A; and it is unproblematic to accept that the agent is then not accountable for doing A. But condition 2, and especially its use of 'could have', raises a problem which I shall now present as abstractly as possible.

If determinism is true, then for any event E occurring at time T there obtained at an earlier time a state of affairs that causally sufficed for E's occurring at T and therefore causally ruled out E's not occurring at T. Now, it is not obviously absurd to think that 'An earlier state of affairs obtained which causally ruled out the non-occurrence of E' entails 'E could not have not occurred'; so it is not obviously absurd to think that determinism implies that nothing which did happen could have not happened, and thus implies that there is no accountability.

There are two ways of meeting this difficulty.

4. The Libertarian Answer

One is to suppose that determinism is false. So it probably is, in which case some events 'could have' not happened, in the sense of not being preceded by causally sufficient conditions for their occurrence. But this does not help to rescue accountability; for a chance event, whose occurrence is a matter of absolutely brute, inexplicable fact, is one for which obviously nobody is accountable. I am assuming that accountability requires intelligibility, and that something which is not caused cannot be rendered intelligible or removed from the 'brute fact' category. Causal explanation is not the only kind; but no explanation is possible for an event for which there is no causal explanation. For arguments directly in support of this, see Hobart's classic paper.[5] Indirect support comes from the plausibility of current philosophical theories that give the concept of cause a primary place in memory, personhood, action, and so on.

It is also instructive to look at actual attempts to base accountability on the falsity of determinism. For example, C.A. Campbell says that accountability belongs only to actions that arise partly from 'effort of will'; causes may limit what a man can do, but he is accountable only if causes leave open the question of whether the man will follow his baser desires or rather the call of 'duty', and this depends upon how much 'effort of will' he exerts towards doing what he conceives to be 'his duty'.[6] But Campbellian 'effort of will' cannot be what we ordinarily describe in terms of 'effort' or 'trying' or 'struggling to do one's best' or the like; for those expressions name phenomena with thick causal roots running back into the past. How hard someone tries to do his best can be affected by parental and other influences, and by his having resolved to do his best, meditated on the importance of morality, and so on. But such influences cannot bear upon Campbellian 'effort of will', which is a pure repository of uncaused determinants of action. So we don't know what Campbellian 'effort of will' is, and hence can have no reason to connect it in any way with accountability. I predict the same fate for any attempt to base accountability on uncaused inputs into action.

5. The Reconciling Answer

The other way of trying to rescue accountability is by arguing that any sense of 'could have' which makes it true that:

(1) If determinism is true, then it is never true of something that did not happen that it could have happened;

is stronger than any sense of 'could have' which makes it true that:

(2) An agent is accountable for an action only if he could have decided not to perform it.

I accept that there is this ambiguity and that the non-existence of accountability therefore does not follow from determinism; and this is the currently most popular view of the matter. But it needs to be stiffened by an account of what the sense

---

5 R.E. Hobart, 'Free Will as Involving Determination and Inconceivable Without It', *Mind* 43 (1934), pp. 1–27; reprinted under the author's real name, Dickinson Miller, *Philosophical Analysis and Human Welfare* (Dordrecht: Reidel, 1975), pp. 104–31.

6 C.A. Campbell, 'In Defence of Free Will', published in 1938 and reprinted in *In Defence of Free Will and Other Philosophical Essays* (London: Allen and Unwin, 1967), pp. 35–55; see especially pp. 42–5.

of 'could have' is that renders (2) true. The various attempts to explain this sense have in common something like this: An agent 'could have' decided differently if there was no impediment or obstacle to his doing so; the idea being that just as there are outer obstacles to executing one's will, there are also inner obstacles or impediments to the exercise of one's will. (It would be easy to restate this whole discussion in terms of 'compulsion' or 'coercion' of the will.) Now, of course, the problem has been relocated, and we must explain what an 'obstacle' is. There is no special problem about (outer) obstacles to the executing of one's will: they are just states of affairs which bring it about that one does not refrain from performing an A even if one chooses, decides, wants, etc. not to perform an A; and it is not puzzling that accountability should require the absence of such obstacles, for the blame- and praise-related responses are essentially directed to what agents willingly do.

But there is a double problem about obstacles to the exercise of the will. The item in question does not stand in opposition to the agent's will—so why is it an 'obstacle'? The action in question is performed willingly—so why is the person not accountable for it?

The former question might be answered by adducing facts about usage, exhibiting semantic principles according to which a brain tumor may count as an 'obstacle' while certain other causally sufficient conditions do not. But that will leave untouched the harder, deeper half of the problem: if tumors count as 'obstacles' or 'impediments' whereas some brain-structures do not—or if brainwashing counts as 'coercive' whereas normal education does not—then why does accountability depend upon facts about impediments or obstacles or coercion?

6. The Schlickian Rationale

Until 'Freedom and Resentment' appeared, the only answer to this question that the literature contained was the one offered by theories of accountability like Moritz Schlick's.[7] These focus on the notion of moral pressure, considered as a means for changing the likelihood that the person concerned (or others who know of the 'pressure') will act similarly on later comparable occasions. Moral pressures extend from faint expressions of (dis)approval through to dire punishments and munificent rewards—a mixed bag, but all capable of generating threats or inducements, i.e. of equipping someone with a thought of the form 'If I perform an A, the upshot is likely to be U', which may affect his decision whether to perform an A. (For brevity, I shall concentrate on deterrence, ignoring encouragement; and on deterrence of the protagonist, ignoring onlookers.) Now, if someone performs an A and would not have been deterred by threats, then on future closely similar occasions he will again be undeterred by them; and so it is not useful to apply them to him by morally pressuring him in respect of the A which he has performed. That, according to

---

[7] Moritz Schlick, *The Problems of Ethics* (trans. D. Rynin, New York: Prentice, 1939), Ch. 7. See also Hobart, *op. cit.*, pp. 24–7; P.H. Nowell-Smith, *Ethics* (London: Pelican, 1954), pp. 300–306; John Hospers, 'What Means this Freedom?', in Sidney Hook (ed.), *Determinism and Freedom in the Age of Modern Science* (New York: University Press, 1958), pp. 113–30, at pp. 115–19.

Schlickian theories, explains the extent of the concept of accountability: the man with the brain tumor, for example, is not accountable for what he did because it is so unlikely that the exerting of moral pressures would have deterred him from doing it. Similarly with the person who has been brainwashed. Quite generally—say the Schlickian theories—we do not hold babies, the insane, the intellectually handicapped, the tortured, accountable for bad things they do, because it is not useful to apply moral pressures to someone who is too young, too ill, too stupid, too hard-pressed, to be affected by them.

Accountability is strongly correlated with susceptibility to moral pressures, and so Schlickian theories draw the line—or locate the continuum—in about the right place. And they do not employ an unexplained 'could have', but only the relatively plain 'would have' which occurs in the form 'If he had thought ..., he would have decided ...'. Furthermore, they describe accountability in a way that offers to explain *why* the concept's limits lie where they do. Without that explanatory component, Schlickian theories would not be seriously interesting.

7. Why Schlickian Theories are Unacceptable

With it, however, they are in trouble: the Schlickian description of what accountability is—or of what the concept is for—is obviously incomplete and strikes most people as positively wrong. The latter will say that although a distinction based on the utility of a certain sort of therapy or behavior-control might coincide with accountability/non-accountability, it cannot give the latter's essence, and that the Schlickian rationale for the line misrepresents the real nature of our praise- and blame-related responses. When we express indignation for someone's cruelty, or admiration for his unselfishness, we usually are not engaged in any sort of therapy. Blame-related responses all involve something like hostility towards the subject; whereas a moral-pressure therapist, though he may have to feign ill-feeling for therapeutic purposes, can in fact be in a perfectly sunlit frame of mind. And—to move briefly to the 'welcome' side of the fence—one may apply moral pressures to encourage a welcomed kind of behavior while remaining in an ice-cold frame of mind, with no feelings of gratitude, admiration or the like.

Schlickians defend their omission, arguing that we ought to jettison blame-related responses and handle ill-doers purely with a view to producing the best possible outcome. But what about the praise-related responses? Schlickians never say that we should give up admiration and gratitude and settle for 'therapies' aimed at encouraging recurrences of the welcomed kind of behavior; but shouldn't they say just that? If blame-related responses are condemned just because we cannot explain the extent of accountability except by relating it to the relevance of a certain kind of 'therapy', then there is a strictly analogous case against the praise-related responses; but obviously we ought not to give up admiration and gratitude. So something has gone wrong.

We need to make room for at least part of what Schlickian theories omit, doing so in a manner that is not embarrassed by renewed difficulties over explaining why the line falls where it does. This double need is, in my view, satisfied by 'Freedom and Resentment'.

8. Reactive Feelings

According to Strawson, all that is omitted by Schlickian theories is the element of what he calls *reactive attitudes*, from which I shall at first lift out the component notion of a reactive *feeling*. Reactive feelings are ones that are prominent in blame, reproach, vilification, resentment, admiration, gratitude, praise and so on. (If I could define 'reactive' I would do so, rather than resorting to examples.) Clearly, Schlickian theories offer us a way of handling accountability, or some notion coextensive with it, in a manner that does not demand reactive feelings. It is a manner that does demand the *objective attitude* towards the person concerned. The phrase 'the objective attitude' is Strawson's, and the core of its meaning seems to be this: To adopt the objective attitude towards something is to inquire into how it is structured and/or how it functions.

Many people find that feelings such as those of resentment and gratitude, indignation and admiration, do not easily occupy the mind along with a thoroughgoing concern to study the subject's behavior patterns. That is why, as Strawson points out, one can dispel a hostile reactive feeling by cultivating objectivity of attitude towards the offender, e.g. dispelling indignation by viewing him as 'a case'.

In so far as reactive feeling won't mix with thorough objectivity, to that extent we must choose: we cannot always proceed as Schlick would have us do while also throwing in reactiveness for good measure. Now, really, all that Schlickian theory advocates is that we let our response to each welcomed or regretted action be guided by a concern for achieving the best over-all outcome. So if reactive feelings are to have a place in our lives, we cannot always ask ourselves 'What response to that action will be for the best in the long run?' Displays of indignation or of gratitude often produce good results; but such feelings cannot be motivated by the desire to produce good results, nor, it seems, are we able closely to control them by thoughts of what will bring the best results. So apparently reactive feelings can have a considerable place in our lives only at the risk of our sometimes not acting in the most fortunate manner; and that fact might be used in a Schlickian counter-attack. Strawson's defense is to maintain that it would be unfortunate if we were always guided by the thought of what would be most fortunate: the prospect of human life with continual Schlickian preoccupations and no reactive feelings, he says, is barely conceivable and wholly repellent. And so the practical question 'Should we try to rid ourselves of reactive feelings?' is given a suitably practical answer.

9. The Extent of Accountability: Strawson's Rationale

When should reactive feelings occur? Well, to start with, Strawson marks off the area in which they would be flatly inappropriate, as fear is in the absence of danger. We could call this the area of non-accountability. Strawson gives a non-Schlickian rationale for that line's falling where it does, i.e. for the *extent* of the concept of accountability (FR, 23–6/64–7). It has two parts, corresponding to the two main things Strawson says about the role of reactive feelings in our lives. (1) They get their value from their role in normal, adult, interpersonal relations; and so it is inappropriate to have such feelings towards someone whose youth, mental ill-health, etc. incapacitates him—whether temporarily or permanently—for such relations. (2) They are essentially expressions of one's caring about the attitudes of other people; and so they can be inappropriate because 'he didn't realize …', 'they couldn't help …', 'she didn't mean …' etc., where behavior does not really manifest attitudes which it superficially seems to manifest. Under both (1) and (2), incidentally, there is plenty of room for accountability to be a matter of degree.

Without denying that this is a therapeutically useful place to draw the line, therefore, Strawson can still maintain that utility is not the whole story since he has also a non-Schlickian explanation for the line's falling where it does.

10. The Topology of Blame

Within the area where reactive feelings are never flatly inappropriate, there may be sub-areas where they would predictably be so harmful that they should be systematically excluded from them: Strawson gives the example of the feelings of a psycho-analyst towards a patient. (Another plausible candidate is the applying of the penal code—a topic I shall discuss in my final sections.) However, to try always to keep reactive feelings within the bounds of prudence—avoiding every counter-productive fit of pique or surge of love—would involve keeping them continuously under objective-teleological control; and that seems to be impossible. If our lives are to have a measure of warmth and engagement and spontaneity, we must pay the price of sometimes not acting in the most prudent or fortunate way. This throws a new light on the conspicuous unruliness of our emotional lives. It is not merely true, but inevitable and acceptable, that the detailed facts about when a given person has feelings of indignation, admiration, resentment, gratitude, etc. partly reflect individual temperament, personal style, the mood of the moment, perhaps physiological accident.

A picture might help. There is a large 'accountability' circle within which reactive feelings are confined: it roughly coincides with the circle within which moral-pressure therapies have some chance of success. Inside that, there are smaller circles marking areas from which it is prudent to exclude reactive feelings because they are so counter-productive there. Their fully permissible range, then, consists of the area that lies inside the large circle and outside the smaller ones. They are free to roam through that area without further confinement: one cannot mark off further sub-areas within which reactive feelings are mandatory, or establish any rules of the form: if …, then it is wrong not to be indignant (grateful, resentful, etc.). In speaking of the ability to dispel a reactive feeling on a given occasion by cultivating thorough objectivity towards a person in question, Strawson says that we 'sometimes' have this option (FR, 25/67); but I think he would and should allow that that option is always theoretically open, i.e. that it is never just wrong—though it is sometimes psychologically impossible—to dispel one's reactive feelings by retreating into objectivity. We can regard someone as 'a case' without believing or pretending that he is mentally ill etc.; for it is just a matter of thoroughly viewing him, in a spirit of inquiry, as a natural object, and this can never be 'wrong in the nature of the case'.

This has an important upshot, which for brevity's sake I shall state only in terms of blame. Consider the proposition that someone 'is blameworthy'. Strawson has a sense for this if it means that it would *not be wrong to* blame the person, but not if it means that it would *be wrong not to* blame him. There is a way of thinking about accountability according to which a person's being 'to blame' implies that blame ought not to be withheld from him (though he may be spared its consequences because of forgiveness); but Strawson's account has nothing like this—no imperatives demanding indignation or any other reactive feeling, but only imperatives forbidding them in certain areas, and permissions to have them in the remaining areas.

This is one mark of the non-propositional nature of blaming, praising etc. in Strawson's account: feelings are made central, and are not tied systematically to any propositions about their objects. My feeling of indignation at what you have done is not a perception of your objective blameworthiness, nor is it demanded of me by such a perception. It expresses my emotional make-up, rather than reflecting my ability to recognize a blame-meriting person when I see one. The gap left by the Schlickian account is not to be filled by facts about desert or about the meriting of blame, facts that are acknowledged by the adoption of reactive attitudes; rather, in Strawson's words, 'it is just these attitudes themselves which fill the gap' (FR, 35/79).

Strawson says that his theory provides a basis for an understanding 'of what we mean, i.e. of *all* we mean, when, speaking the language of morals, we speak of desert, responsibility, guilt, condemnation, and justice' (FR, 35/78). I believe that his theory is more revisionary—or, rather, excisionary—than this implies, because I think that many people have a notion of accountability which incorporates the belief that desert or blameworthiness or accountability is strictly a matter of objective fact. Perhaps Strawson means to claim only to have provided for every *coherent* element in 'what we mean', so that what is offered is not a fully conservative theory but rather a maximal salvage. That claim would be correct, I think, but I cannot prove it is. I don't anticipate anyone's denying that Strawson's account is all right as far as it goes, but some may maintain that it is not the whole story. We can evaluate that claim when they tell us what the rest of the story is supposed to be.

11. An Impasse Explained

This work of Strawson's yields benefits that he does not explicitly point out. One is a satisfying way of settling (at last!) the old issue about determinism as a threat to accountability. Many careful and intelligent people are influenced by lines of thought in which a person is presented as a natural object whose structure and behavior ultimately results from nothing but the behavior of parts of the universe other than himself; and in which his behavior is presented as wholly predictable. Such lines of thought lead many people to say that the person is not really accountable for what he does—that his behavior results from his structure and his environment, both of which are ultimately hands that were dealt to him by God or nature, so that neither they nor anything resulting purely from them should be blamed upon the person himself. I call this position 'Spinozism'.

It is often said that Spinozism is a pure product of conceptual muddle: someone who thinks that determinism rules out accountability must be failing to grasp which sufficient conditions count as 'compelling', which relations to the universe count as 'victimhood', which sort of predictability defeats accountability, and so on. For example: 'We have here ... a persistent, an age-long deadlock due solely to the indisposition of the human mind to look closely into the meaning of its terms.'[8]

This cannot be the whole story; for many people, without being in the least muddled, hold that if a person is as God or nature made him, and if how he is determines what he does, then it is 'in some ultimate sense hideously unfair' that he should be blamed for bad things that he does. That phrase comes from Bernard Williams.[9] In the course of sketching Kant's theory of freedom, he offers something that could explain the power of determinism to create doubts about accountability. It is that one element in 'moral ideas influenced by Christianity' is the thought 'that moral worth must be separated from any natural advantage whatsoever', a thought that led Kant 'to the conclusion that the source of moral thought and action must be located outside the empirically conditioned self'.

One version of this frame of mind depends on the belief in a God who is ultimately responsible for every fact about the natural realm, and is also the arbiter and punisher of wrongdoing. This implies that there is something repellent about the idea of someone's being blameworthy for an action that is an inevitable consequence of earlier states of the universe. The God of Christianity, it seems, cannot justly blame us for anything unless he has given us some kind of agency that takes our actions right out of his field of operations. The causal order he has imposed on the universe must be incomplete, and we must be able to determine some of what happens in the gaps.

That, however, does not meet the need. When *in*determinism is taken seriously, it seems equally at odds with accountability. When we view a human action as *not* deterministically caused, so that the totality of its causal antecedents did not settle whether the person would act thus rather than so, his acting thus strikes us as random, a matter of luck, and our sense of him as possibly to blame for his behavior is again weakened. Some will say that this is because of another conceptual muddle: we have thought in terms of mere indeterminism instead of in terms of *agent causation*. How the person acted was not fully determined by antecedent states of the universe because it was partly determined by *him*. In the absence of an account of agent causation—I mean one that is coherent, detailed, and deep—this sounds like whistling in the dark. I do not think that many people would be attracted to it if they did not see it as their best chance of rescuing accountability. I shall offer something better.

First, I should mention the not unpopular view that both sides of the impasse are right: someone's being accountable for an action is incompatible *both* with its having been deterministically caused by antecedent states of the universe *and also*

---

8 Hobart, *op. cit.*, p. 107 in the reprint.
9 Bernard Williams, 'Morality and the Emotions', reprinted in his *Problems of the Self* (Cambridge: Cambridge University Press, 1973), pp. 207–29, at p. 228.

with its not having been so determined; from which it follows that our concept of accountability is inconsistent, making demands that the world could not possibly meet. This might be correct; I do not hold on principle that everything must be all right with our conceptual scheme. But it would be unphilosophical to leave it at that. If we have a logically unsatisfiable concept of accountability, why do we have it? It must be because we are pulled two ways; and we should ask what does the pulling. Strawson's work could enable us to answer that question; it could let us strengthen and complete the inconsistent-concept diagnosis of the impasse, by explaining what led us into that conceptual mishap. I shall present it, however, as doing something different, namely explaining the impasse without supposing any inconsistent concept to be involved. It matters little which of these we adopt.

The Strawsonian explanation for the impasse goes as follows. When we contemplate someone's action as the upshot of deterministic causes, we adopt the objective attitude towards him; our frame of mind encourages questions like 'What do we have here? How did this come about?' which naturally goes with the question 'How can we lessen (or increase) the chance that this will happen again?' That objectivity of attitude *dispels* reactive feelings, and their disappearance presents itself to us as the judgment that the person is not morally accountable.

When instead we contemplate the action as not arising inevitably from antecedent events, we again adopt an objective attitude towards him; we are again in the 'What do we have here?' frame of mind; and so again we are pushed out of reactive attitudes towards the person in respect of this action, and we think that this has involved our giving up the judgment that he is morally accountable.

What seemed to be this:

> The proposition *that P* conflicts with the attribution of moral accountability, and so does the proposition *that not-P*,

from which we might infer that the concept of accountability cannot be satisfied, is really this:

> By actively raising the question '*P or not-P?*'—i.e. by thinking objectively about the action—we get into a frame of mind in which we cannot have reactive feelings; and their absence makes us reluctant to describe or treat the person as morally accountable.

Rather than moral accountability's being *logically* inconsistent with each *answer* to the question, reactive feelings are *psychologically* immiscible with the frame of mind in which the question is *asked*. The answer does not matter: the objectivity of attitude that frames the question does the real work. Dostoyevsky described it memorably:

> But what can I do if I don't even feel resentment? ... My anger, in consequence of the damned laws of consciousness, is subject to chemical decomposition. As you look, its object vanishes into thin air, its reasons evaporate, the offender is nowhere to be found,

the affront ceases to be an offence and becomes destiny, something like toothache, for which nobody is to blame.[10]

The affront ceases to be an offence, not because of what you find when you look but just because *you look*.

In what follows, I shall use the phrase 'naturalistic thoughts about x' to mean 'intense thoughts about the causes, whether deterministic or not, of x's behavior'.

12. Dispelling and Disqualifying

The foregoing explanation requires (1) that when you are drawn by naturalistic thoughts about someone's actions towards the conclusion that he is not to blame for them, you are losing your feelings of indignation, etc.; and (2) that in such cases your feelings are being dispelled without being disqualified or shown to be inappropriate. Of these (1) seems clearly to be true: it fits what happens when people are swayed by Hospers's eloquent and persuasive Spinozist attack on accountability;[11] and I cannot imagine anyone thinking hard about the causation of behavior while continuing to boil with rage against the malefactor. As for (2): well, it would be absurd to accept that the feelings are being disqualified, in the absence of any account of how or why.

Admittedly, I cannot explain how an intellectual operation can dispel a feeling without disqualifying it; but that gap in my position still leaves me with a reason for saying that naturalistic thoughts do not disqualify indignation, etc. If they did, the conclusion must be that if men are fit subjects of such thoughts, then we oughtn't to have reactive feelings towards them. But they *are* fit subjects for such thoughts—*everything* is—yet if we try to imagine our lives without reactive feelings we find ourselves (here I follow Strawson) confronted by a bleak desolation. We cannot be obliged to give up something whose loss would gravely worsen the human condition, and so reactive feelings cannot be made impermissible by any facts, e.g. the fact that men are natural objects about which naturalistic thoughts are possible.

That argument presupposes that the question 'Ought we to give up reactive feelings?' is a *practical* one. Anyone who construes it as such will agree with Strawson that it is to be answered 'in the light of an assessment of the gains and losses to human life' (FR, 28/70); but is that the right way to construe it? It has usually been assumed that the decision about whether to permit ourselves indignation etc. must depend strictly upon whether our fellow humans are objectively (un)meritorious in some way which calls down blame or praise upon them. Even on the Strawsonian position which I am adopting, a theoretical question is involved: reactive feelings would be inappropriate if men couldn't enter into relations of love, hate, etc. But given that conduct lies within the large circle, the remaining question is a practical one which does not strictly depend upon the establishing of any further kind of fact about the present.

---

10 Fyodor Dostoyevsky, *Notes from Underground* (trans. J. Coulson, Harmondsworth: Penguin Books, 1972), p. 27 (Ch. 1, section 5).

11 Hospers, *op. cit.*, pp. 119–27.

Strawson does not prove this; nor can I. But the literature contains no coherent account of any relevant 'further kind of fact' and Strawson offers a liberating hypothesis which enables us to dispense with this elusive theoretical item. It is reasonable to adopt his hypothesis if it stands up while every rival falls flat.

The greatest single achievement of 'Freedom and Resentment', in my view, is its showing how the question 'Ought we to retain praise, blame, etc.?' could be a fundamentally practical one rather than having a strict dependence upon a perpetually troublesome theoretical question. Construed as practical, the question is easy to answer.

Strawson emphasizes—more than I would want to—that we could not possibly relinquish all reactive feelings. Still, ought we to try? Ought we to strive in that direction? We do have a live question about what course we should steer, and I have been expounding Strawson's answer to it.

13. Harmful Kinds of Reactive Feelings

Even if we should not set ourselves against all kinds of reactive feelings, perhaps some should not be retained. Some people think it would be better if we lacked resentment and anger, etc., while retaining gratitude and every sort of love, etc.

I have heard it argued that this semi-Spinozist ideal is self-defeating, because the non-adverse reactive feelings require the adverse ones. For instance: 'You can't really love someone with whom you never get angry.' Clearly, some people hold that view of love, but the mere existence of such certainties does not count for much: men have thought that you can't really love a woman whom you never beat. I don't advocate the semi-Spinozist ideal, but I offer it as needing discussion even if one follows Strawson in rejecting the complete Spinozist ideal of relinquishing all reactive feelings.

Strawson would reject the semi-Spinozist ideal, I believe. He characterizes reactive attitudes as essentially 'participant', and associates 'sustained objectivity' with 'isolation'; and this suggests that the semi-Spinozist ideal would involve our participating in personal relations only while they please us, and withdrawing into 'isolation' whenever others behave in ways we regret. Put like that, it sounds unattractive; but I reject this formulation of the issue because reactive attitudes should not be allowed to claim the whole territory of 'participant' relationships. A therapist and her client can be closely *involved* with one another, in a therapeutic programme in which they both *participate*; but that involvement might be untouched—at least on the therapist's side—by anything Strawson would call 'reactive'.

Some people may think that we should at least try to relinquish adverse reactive feelings about ourselves, especially guilt and remorse. This could be called the Yeatsian ideal:

> I am content to follow to its source
> Every event in action or in thought;
> Measure the lot; forgive myself the lot!
> When such as I cast out remorse

> So great a sweetness flows into the breast
> We must laugh and we must sing,
> We are blest by everything,
> And everything we look upon is blest.[12]

What is in question in the third line is not the 'reactive' kind of forgiveness that Strawson discusses (FR, 22/63), but rather the kind that consists in opting out of blame and into objectivity of attitude, into 'measuring the lot'—the sort that supplies whatever truth there is in *Tout comprendre, c'est tout pardonner*. Yeats's rejection of remorse was part of his fight against 'emotions ... in which there is not an athletic joy'; this was not a rejection of all adverse reactive feelings, for 'indignation is a kind of joy'. Remorse, he rightly thought, isn't.

This Yeatsian (or demi-semi-Spinozist) ideal need not make us complacent about our past wrongdoings and failures: complacency can be warded off by self-criticism, which is consistent with perfect objectivity of attitude. To be self-critical and self-corrective, we need standards by which to judge our behavior; but neither the Yeatsian ideal nor the all-in Spinozist one offers the slightest impediment to our judging some actions to be good or right or successful and others to be bad or wrong or failures. Without having any tendency to remorse or guilt, I may resolve not to harm other people, and when I do harm someone I may regret this very much, and be concerned to find out what went wrong—'measure the lot'—and correct it.

I don't endorse the Yeatsian ideal either; but like the semi-Spinozist one it is worth thinking about.

14. The Other Two Categories

Strawson's account starts with 'personal' reactive attitudes and then adds to them self-reactive attitudes and impersonal or moral ones. Let us examine these two additions.

First, I should say more about how personal reactive attitudes are introduced. Having instanced some of 'the many different kinds of relationship which we can have with other people', Strawson remarks that 'in general, we demand some degree of goodwill or regard on the part of those who stand in these relationships to us' (p. 63); and he represents personal reactive attitudes as essentially a person's response to the goodwill, indifference, etc. of those with whom he is suitably interrelated. These two elements—kinds of relationship, and demands for goodwill within them—generate the two parts of Strawson's line around accountability: the agent is not to blame because he is incapable of entering into relationships of the relevant kind, or because his action did not really manifest a lack of goodwill. That collaboration between the two elements is a smoothly efficient affair, increasing one's confidence that Strawson has them right.

Confidence wanes, however, when one looks at the extension of the account from personal reactive attitudes to impersonal and self-directed ones (FR, 28–31/70–74).

---

12 W.B. Yeats, 'A Dialogue of Self and Soul', in his *Collected Poems* (London: Macmillan, 1952) at p. 267.

Here, Strawson makes one of the two elements do all the work. He connects personal reactive attitudes with the demand that others show goodwill towards oneself, impersonal ones with the demand that others show goodwill towards men in general, and self-directed ones with the demand upon oneself that one show goodwill towards others. Nothing is said about any interpersonal relations within which such demands arise; and indeed Strawson says explicitly that the moral reactive attitudes 'permit ... a certain detachment' (FR, 21/62) and remarks on their not needing to include 'antecedent personal involvement' (FR, 31/73). The impression is conveyed that to have impersonal or self-directed reactive attitudes is just to 'acknowledge the claims' of men upon men or of others upon oneself. Strawson does not quite say this, but it is suggested by his silence regarding what else is involved in these two kinds of reactive attitude.

But there must be more to them than that. I might 'acknowledge' your 'claim' to my goodwill, and thus regret my failures to give it to you, yet handle these lapses through self-criticism and self-amendment with no tincture of guilt or remorse; in which case I acknowledge the claims but do not have the corresponding kind of reactive attitude (unless Strawson counts self-criticism as 'reactive', in which case I am lost). Analogously, I might hold strongly that people should show goodwill towards one another, yet not be indignant when they fail to do so; for I may adopt a non-reactive, clinical, corrective, objective attitude to every instance I encounter of man's inhumanity to man. I submit that the answers to the questions: 'Why does he regret [welcome] that action?' and 'Is his response reactive?' are logically independent of one another. If they are, then impersonal and self-directed reactive attitudes cannot be fully explained in terms of the acknowledging of claims: those 'acknowledgements' explain welcomes and regrets, but cannot explain the reactiveness.

In his Reply Strawson wrote: 'I freely admit that "acknowledgment of claims" is too weak a phrase.'[13]

15. Relocating One Element

Personal reactive attitudes are introduced, as I have noted, through the notions of claim-to-goodwill and interpersonal relation. Now, Strawson speaks of the goodwill that is demanded in certain relations; but isn't it also demanded outside of them? And cannot the latter demands also generate reactive attitudes? And, to take in some of the territory not covered by 'claim', cannot gratitude, for instance, occur without any antecedent personal involvement? 'But in all these cases'—you might say—'there is the "involvement" created by the very behavior to which the reactive attitude is a response.' That is true, but Strawson is not thinking of kinds of involvement or 'interpersonal relation' that could be created just by kicking somebody or throwing him a coin. A large theme in 'Freedom and Resentment' is the contrast between the involvements that go with reactive attitudes and the 'isolation' that would be entailed by their absence, as well as the 'relief from the strains of involvement'

---

13 Strawson, 'Replies', *op. cit.*, p. 266.

(FR, 27/69) that comes from replacing reactive attitudes by the objective one; and all of that is reduced to nonsense if one construes 'involvement' etc. so as to include mere helpings and harmings.

As for the converse: Strawson clearly implies that the fact that ill-will occurs within a relationship of the emphasized sort does not guarantee that the response to it will be reactive.

One might conclude that the notion of interpersonal relation is not supposed to help explain what a personal reactive attitude is, and is offered only as part of the natural history of reactive attitudes—a mere description of their place in our lives. But that is hard to reconcile with the amount of weight Strawson seems to lay upon such expressions as 'participant' and 'non-detached'. Fortunately, there is another way out.

It is to give the notion of an interpersonal relation (of the relevant kind) a role in the analytic or explanatory part of the account, but not quite the role initially allotted to it by Strawson. What should be emphasized, I suggest, is not the relations *within* which reactive attitudes arise, but rather the relations *towards* which they point. If I resent someone's treatment of me, there may have been antecedently no special kind of relation between us; but my very resentment creates one, or sets the stage for one. I cannot say precisely what the 'special kind' is: that belongs to the problem of *defining* 'reactive', which I kicked around in the original version of this paper and now set aside. But any attempt to solve that problem, provide that definition, should be helped by the point I am now making: the participations and involvements that Strawson emphasizes should be seen not primarily as the ground in which reactive attitudes grow but rather as embodied in or consequential upon them; not as required in the past or present, but as implied or suggested or invited for the future.

This idea, though implicit throughout most of 'Freedom and Resentment', needs more explicit emphasis than Strawson gives it. It could lead to a tightening of the curiously loose and structureless paragraph in which 'reactive attitudes' are first introduced (FR, 21–2/62–3). It could also let us strengthen a soft spot in Strawson's rationale for the line around the concept of accountability. The reason why 'seeing someone [as] deranged or compulsive' tends to 'set him apart from normal participant reactive attitudes' (FR, 25/66) is that those attitudes connect with normal interpersonal relations. Connect how? If reactive attitudes essentially embody or point towards or prepare for interpersonal relations, then it is clear how someone's incapacity for the latter makes it inappropriate to have reactive attitudes towards him. But if the connection is just that reactive attitudes (should?) arise out of events between people who are interrelated, it is not clear how the argument runs. It would apparently have to put 'He is deranged' on a par with 'He is a stranger to me'; in each case there is no significant relationship between us, and so (for some still unclear reason) it would be inappropriate for me to have a reactive attitude towards him. Things go better when reactive attitudes are seen as pointing towards possible or imagined future interpersonal relations, rather than as growing out of past ones. (That view of them, incidentally, agrees with the etymological roots of 'attitude', which run back to the Latin *aptus*—apt or fit for a given kind of action.)

By relocating the notion of interpersonal relation in this way, we get good help with Strawson's extension of his account to cover the other two categories of reactive attitudes. A self-reactive attitude does involve an important 'interpersonal' relation: remorse, for instance, can be represented as a confrontation—with an accusing glare on one side and downcast eyes on the other—between one's present self and some past self. I offer this as a realistic view of what self-reactive attitudes are like, though admittedly a still incomplete one; and as better than an account that focuses on the acknowledging of claims.

Similarly with impersonal reactive attitudes: moral indignation—we can now say—involves actually or imaginatively putting oneself into, or readying oneself for, a special kind of relation, with the person towards whom the indignation is directed.

This in turn throws light on Strawson's view that 'moral' reactive attitudes are significantly more 'detached' than personal ones are. In my revised version, the important kind of 'interpersonal relation' is equally present in both categories. Often in moral cases the attitude is only an entertaining of an imagined relation, but the same is true in many personal cases, e.g. gratitude to a dead benefactor, anger at an unidentified thief, resentment towards an oppressor whom one hopes never to see again. There is this much in Strawson's thesis: a reactive attitude of the kind he calls 'personal' is a response to someone's attitude towards oneself, and so personal reactive attitudes must be in that sense self-involving. But I see no reason to think that they must pertain to the important kinds of interpersonal relation to a greater degree than the 'moral' ones do.

This presumably connects with Strawson's suggestion that 'the tension between objectivity of view and the moral reactive attitudes is perhaps less than the tension between objectivity of view and the personal reactive attitudes' (FR, 31/73). I can find no reason to agree with this. (Indeed, a blaming attitude seems to be more easily banished by severe objectivity than is a resentful one; but the evidence for this might be reinterpreted as showing that objectivity is harder to achieve where one's own interests are concerned. So that is a stand-off.) I can only conjecture that Strawson was guided here by the idea that moral reactive attitudes are significantly more 'detached' than personal ones are; so this is another burden which is lifted from our shoulders if the notion of interpersonal relations is relocated in the manner I have advocated.

The relocation may also contribute a little towards explaining why reactive attitudes will not mix with the objective attitude. (Some people claim that the two can cohabit in *their* minds, where reactivity persists even when they 'look' with Dostoyevsky or 'measure the lot' with Yeats. This conflict of testimony could reflect our unclarity as to what the issue is; but the phenomenon may be subject to real interpersonal variation. Still, something needs explaining here.) Strawson does not discuss why there should be any conflict or tension, merely emphasizing how *different* the objective attitude is from reactive ones; but why does that set them against one another? Is it just a matter of the limits on how much mental variety one can manage at a single time—limits that a virtuoso of the inner life might transcend through practice? I tentatively suggest a different account. Reactive attitudes essentially prepare for personal interaction of a certain kind, while the objective attitude prepares for inquiry, and these two sorts of activity are somehow incompatible. If that is right, the two sorts of attitude are derivatively in conflict, like simultaneously readying oneself for a sexual encounter and for giving an after-dinner speech. Even if that is right, however, more work has to be done to make this matter clear.

16. Generalizing the Other Element

The relocation of the notion of interpersonal relation frees us to reconsider the demand-for-goodwill element in the account. It is salutary to be reminded of how much we care about the attitudes of others towards ourselves and towards one another; but I contend that this 'caring' belongs to the natural history of reactive attitudes rather than to the elucidation of 'reactive attitude'. We can make sense of the idea of your being genuinely morally indignant over my attitude to natural beauty, for instance; so moral indignation does not have to be a response to someone's attitude towards people. If nothing else really merits moral indignation, that is a matter of substantive morality rather than a fact about the concept of moral indignation.

The same basic point holds for non-moral reactive attitudes, but here there is a terminological snag. Strawson assumes—rightly, in my view—that an attitude counts as 'moral' only if it rests on a general principle, or anyway on something that does not essentially refer to any particular item. So an attitude of mine is not moral if its basis *essentially* involves myself: I am morally indignant at your contemptuous attitude towards a benefactor, but I resent your contemptuous attitude towards me. But the basis for an attitude might lack generality—thus depriving the attitude of the status of 'moral'—in some quite different way. For a bit of behavior might enrage me on a particular occasion, although it neither infringes any general principle that I hold nor essentially involves myself. For instance, I take no general stand on attitudes to natural beauty, but on this one occasion it just makes me angry to see a man walk unheedingly past the masses of Alpine Lilies and Indian Paintbrush. Or I have an unreasoned 'thing' about Bruckner, which leads me to feel something like gratitude towards anyone who loves his music. That anger and the 'gratitude' are both reactive, I suppose; but they are not 'moral', since one concerns a particular occasion and the other a particular person, and neither rests on general principles. But neither of them fits comfortably under Strawson's label 'personal reactive attitude', since that label so naturally suggests an attitude which responds to someone's attitude to oneself.

I suggest, therefore, that the two basic categories of reactive attitudes are 'non-principled' and 'principled' (or 'moral'), with 'personal' as an important species within the former.

As for self-reactive attitudes: some of them are principled and some are not; for an attitude of self-censure or self-congratulation may, but need not, rest upon some principle that one holds. Strawson focuses primarily on the principled ones—which rest on one's acknowledgement of others' claims on one's goodwill—and perhaps they matter most. But there are others, such as self-reproach for having made a fool of oneself in public. Incidentally, Strawson's use of the word 'moral' is unsatisfactory on any showing, for his 'moral' category positively excludes self-reactive attitudes. Admittedly, what is 'moral' must have a general basis; but that is no obstacle to allowing that self-reactive attitudes can be moral. My remorse over my cruelty is as principled as my indignation over yours. Strawson has written that I am 'certainly right' about this.[14]

So much for taxonomy and terminology. Returning now to the substantive point: I suggest that although it is all right to tie reactive attitudes to responses to *somebody's attitude*, it is unduly narrowing to tie them to responses to *somebody's attitude towards somebody*. The '... towards somebody' bit looms large in the natural history—and perhaps also in the ethics—of reactive attitudes, but not in the account of what reactiveness is.

When the account is thus generalized, it covers cases that are untouched by Strawson's treatment. Also, as I have shown, it forces us to make independently worthwhile revisions in the taxonomy and terminology. And, finally, it makes no difference to the relevant part of Strawson's rationale for the line around accountability. For that concerns cases where, despite appearances to the contrary, 'the agent's attitude and intentions [are] what we demand they should be' (p. 65); and this need not draw on the idea that the relevant 'attitude' must be towards one or more people.

17. A Problem About Punishment

This work of Strawson's supplies a basis for clearing up some long-standing troubles concerning the justification of punishment.[15]

Here is a convict; how should we treat him? There are two ways of coming at an answer to this. (1) The forward-looking way says that we must consider only what treatment will maximize utility, that is, do the most over-all good. For present purposes it does not matter how that good is distributed between reforming the convict, deterring him and others, placating victims and their kin, and so on. (2) The partly backward-looking way says that we must also take into account a fact about the past, namely the fact that he did commit a crime together with the facts about how grave a crime it was.

Those who confine themselves to approach (1)—'utilitarians', for short—are accused of neglecting the facts about guilt or innocence. When someone has been *wrongly* convicted of a crime, it may be best over-all if he is nevertheless treated in a punishing way. This offends our sense of justice, as does the related possibility that someone who is guilty of a minor crime may on utilitarian grounds be assigned a harsh punishment. (In this context, the relevance of whether there was a crime stands or falls with the relevance of how grave a crime it was. I find it helpful to think of innocence as committing a crime with gravity = 0, and to think of not being punished as receiving punishment with severity = 0.) The utilitarian can argue that it is not so easy to describe a case where utility really *would* be maximized by a deliberate injustice—penalizing an innocent person, or punishing a guilty one with a harshness disproportionate to the gravity of his crime; and we can trade intuitions about cases. For most of us, though, the question of whether and how gravely the person has

---

14 Strawson, 'Replies', *op. cit.*, p. 266.

15 The ideas sketched in this section and the next are developed more fully in Jonathan Bennett, 'Punishment', forthcoming.

offended is *directly* relevant to whether and how he should be punished; which is to say that we favor approach 2.

The word *desert* and its kin naturally come in here: the facts missed by utilitarianism relate to what the person in the dock *deserves* to have done to him. This, however, does not explain much. To say that offenders deserve to be punished is to imply that their guilt is a reason—a direct, immediate reason—why it is all right to punish them. We can agree with this while still wanting to know why it is so, wanting to get this judgment from something deeper and/or more general; and the mention of 'desert' does not supply it.

Indeed, desert is not much of a concept: I can find almost no serious attempts to explain or analyze it, and I have never seen it being *used* in an argued defense for either answer to the most important question involving it:

> If someone deserves to be punished in a certain way, does it follow that he *ought* to be punished in that way, even if the over-all consequences would be better if he were punished less severely or not at all?

More briefly:

> Do facts about someone's desert ever imply that he should be punished against utility?

In the literature we find confident affirmative answers, and equally robust negative ones. The latter come mostly from people who acknowledge that desert theorists used to answer that yes, people ought to be punished as they deserve, even against utility, but assert that in these more enlightened times nobody believes this any more. These pronouncements, pro and con, are never accompanied by arguments in which the concept of desert is at work—or indeed by arguments of any other kind. This is a striking manifestation of the concept's theoretical poverty.

As a matter of morality, I take my stand with those who say not merely that we are never morally required to punish against utility but that we are morally required not to do so, but I also hold that the maximizing of utility is not the whole basis for a system of punishment. I want a *basis* for that pair of moral intuitions—something deeper and more general from which they follow. That is what can be found in Strawson's 'Freedom and Resentment'.

18. Outline of a Theory of Punishment

A defensible penal action does over-all good by means that bring suffering to one person. Not being outright utilitarians, we are not always willing to avail ourselves of opportunities to do this. Suppose that ceremonially hurting one randomly chosen person would be sure—through some mysterious but well-tested mechanism—to reduce the incidence of some really nasty disease. Most of us would be reluctant to go through with the ceremony, even if we judged that this one person's suffering would be less bad than a state of affairs in which the disease is endemic.

Why? We are moved by sympathy for the one person—a fellow-feeling for someone in distress—but sympathy should have a place on the other side of the equation as well. Why does it not? Or why, at any rate, does it function differently there? Well, for most of us, harm to an identified person outweighs help—or lessened harm—to an unidentified group. Even when punishing a particular criminal will certainly bring benefits, we may be unable to point to any particular people as the beneficiaries. There may indeed *be* no people of whom it is determinately the case that *they* would benefit from this convict's being punished. This seems to affect our moral thinking. We serenely launch building projects in which probably some workers will die; compare that with how we react when a particular child is trapped in a well.

There are other possible contributors to our unwillingness to hurt one in the interests of many, though they do not do much credit to our intelligences. Anyway, we *are* in general reluctant to harm one person in the interests of many, and that reluctance seems unbudgeable. I shall take it as a given and work on from there.

Now, *punishing a criminal* should be seen, I submit, as a species of *hurting one person in the interests of many*. The moral or emotional obstacle to doing that is less in this species than throughout the rest of the genus; the fact that the one has committed a crime makes a difference. 'Because criminals deserve punishment', some will say. I agree, but I cannot make attributions of desert *explain* anything.

The best answer I can find looks not to our moral principles but rather to an aspect of our nature lying deeper than our moral principles and helping to produce them and—insofar as anything can—to justify them. In blaming a convict for his behavior, we do not assent to a proposition about him but rather adopt towards him the reactive attitude that Strawson calls 'vicarious resentment', or resentment on behalf of his victims; this essentially involves at least incipient hostility or ill-will towards its object; and this makes us less unwilling for its object—in our present case, the convict—to be hurt in the interests of the greater good. We already have indignant, offended or resentful feelings towards him, and these reduce our unwillingness that he should be made to suffer for the general good. Thus Adam Smith: 'Gratitude and resentment ... are the sentiments which most immediately and directly prompt to reward and to punish ... That action must ... surely appear to deserve punishment which everybody who hears of it is angry with, and upon that account rejoices to see punished.'[16]

That underlies the common idea that *it is all right to punish the guilty*. From a starting-point that differs from utilitarianism because it involves a reluctance, in many cases, to do good by inflicting suffering on one person, we introduce resentment and its vicarious analogue, blame, to lessen that reluctance and bring us closer to utilitarianism. Why is it generally wrong to punish the innocent? Because the explanation of why it is right to punish *anybody* applies only to the guilty.

This account of punishment has two desirable features. (1) It does not morally permit us—let alone require us—to punish someone more harshly than would maximize utility. The source of that feature of the account is not a mere add-on, but rather the account's driving force, namely the thesis that punishment is to be engaged in only as a way of doing good. And room is made for this by a basic

---

16 Adam Smith, *The Theory of Moral Sentiments*, ed. D.D. Raphael and A.L. Macfie (Oxford: Clarendon, 1976), pp. 69, 70.

fact about reactive attitudes, namely that they are sometimes permissible *and never required*. That secures that nothing in the nature of things can require us to punish someone if considerations of utility go against our doing so.

It is also a merit in this account that it provides a *direct* relevance between gravity and severity—doing this right out to the end of the scale where innocence is directly a reason for not punishing the person at all. We are initially morally reluctant to punish anyone, and for an innocent person nothing overcomes that reluctance. Similarly, nothing much overcomes it in the case of a mild offender. In this theory of punishment, innocence and degrees of severity are relevant not only because of the traces they will leave in the future but also directly.

This account puts an openly retributivist element into punishment: in it, the willingness to punish someone arises *directly* from the belief that he has committed a crime. Some defenders of retribution have taken pains to prevent it from brushing up against the idea of revenge, which they think would taint it. I have no such scruple. While I do not find it helpful to describe the crucial reactive attitude as 'vengeful', it certainly has the same human roots as the desire for vengeance.

Although my account is retributivist, it frames punishment within utilitarian considerations, not allowing any punishment that goes against utility. Sher writes: 'To assert that we can justify punishment only by showing that it brings advantages is to beg the question against retributivism.'[17] Though that is plausible, I have shown it to be false. Griffin writes:

> What would be entirely wrong would be to try to introduce utilitarian reasons into desert. As we have seen, it destroys a response to inject extraneous considerations into it, and utilitarian reasons are extraneous. Authenticity is not merely the best or purest form of responses such as admiration, gratitude, or appreciation; it is the only form.[18]

That looks like a partial list of reactive attitudes, and I suppose that Griffin would include resentment in it (though he does not mention Strawson's work). I agree that one cannot adopt a reactive attitude for a purpose: there cannot be contrived or considered or judicious resentment. But that does not place such a high barrier between punishment and utility as Griffin apparently wants to erect there. Reactive attitudes are essentially spontaneous, adopted without the guidance of a *telos*; but one can—and civilized people do—have goal-directed policies for delimiting areas of life within which they will deny themselves the luxury of reactivity.

In a more complex way, it is open for us to give play to our generalized vicarious resentment of criminal behavior by endorsing a system of punishment, expressing our resentment in our willingness to put the offender at the disposal of the legal system; while at the same time resolving that this should be enacted only in cases where it has a good enough chance of doing some good. The permissive framework is set by utility; the punishment within that framework expresses our reactive, retributive, anger or resentment. Thus, a genuinely retributive element in punishment cohabits with severe utilitarian constraints.

---

17 George Sher, *Desert* (Princeton: Princeton University Press, 1987), p. 74.
18 James Griffin, *Well-Being, Its Meaning, Measurement, and Moral Importance* (Oxford: Oxford University Press, 1986), p. 259.

Chapter 4

The Importance of Free Will[1]

Susan Wolf

Why do people care so much about whether we have free will? More precisely, why would the impossibility of free will be a problem? This paper considers several attempts to answer these questions, ultimately agreeing with Strawson that the absence of free will would give us no reason at all to give up either our practices of reward and punishment or the reactive attitudes that these practices ordinarily express. Despite this, however, the paper argues that it would still be reasonable to be upset if free will turned out to be impossible, due to the way free will is connected to the meaning of our lives and the realization of our values.

The assumption that we have free will is generally thought to lurk behind the justifications of many of our current practices. That is, it is generally thought that only if we have free will can it be appropriate for us to engage in these practices, and that, if we should conclude that we don't have free will, we would have reason to give these practices up. The importance of the problem of free will in philosophy is often thought to depend on its relation to the justification of these practices. Thus, if an adequate justification of these practices were to be found, it may be thought that either the free will problem would thereby be solved or that, at least, it would thereby cease to be of interest.

In this paper, I shall argue that the justification of these practices need not rest on the assumption that we do have free will, and that the conclusion that we don't have free will gives us no reason at all to abandon these practices. My argument, however, seems to me to leave both the problem and its importance intact. The thought that our wills may not be free is no less disturbing even when all ties to the justification of our practices are completely and irrevocably severed.

Of course, there are some for whom the problem of free will was never disturbing in the first place. This paper is not likely to provide them with any new reason to be disturbed. Moreover, to those who have been and continue to be disturbed by the problem, this paper is not likely to offer much solace. Still, my paper is primarily addressed to this latter group, for, if it cannot provide solace, it may still provide insight into why—and why not—such solace is needed.

I shall begin by outlining a naive attempt at expressing the fears of those who find the problem of free will upsetting, and a naive response by those who think that the problem of free will gives us nothing to worry about. This expression of fear and

---

1 More people have benefited me by their comments and criticisms of drafts of this paper than I am able to acknowledge here. Of the many whom I am grateful, special thanks are due to Jonathan Bennett and Martha Nussbaum.

the response to it constitute a first stage of debate, which focuses on the justification of our practices of overt reward and punishment. The inadequacies at this stage of the argument suggest a way of advancing to a deeper stage, which focuses not on the overt practices themselves, but on the attitudes these practices typically express. Proceeding by way of two analogical cases, I shall argue that these attitudes, too, are safe from the threat of being undermined by reason and metaphysics. Nonetheless, I think that feelings of dissatisfaction may reasonably remain. I shall finally attempt to express what I take to be the appropriate focus of these feelings.

The Justification of Reward and Punishment

I shall hereafter refer to the group who find the problem of free will upsetting as 'the pessimists'. In this, I follow P.F. Strawson in his article "Freedom and Resentment".[2] The pessimists include all those who believe, first, that whether or not we have free will depends on which metaphysical hypotheses are true, and, second, that it is not unlikely that the wrong metaphysical hypotheses are true. Perhaps the most common pessimists are those who believe that the thesis of determinism is both incompatible with free will and very likely true. However, they are also pessimists who believe that indeterminism is both incompatible with free will and, at least, very possibly true. And there are some, who may be said to be more pessimistic still, who believe that both determinism and indeterminism are incompatible with free will. For the remainder of this paper, I shall address myself to the first sort of pessimist, but it should be obvious how what I have to say to him can, with minimal adjustments, be addressed as significantly to the concerns of the other sorts of pessimist as well.

The opposing group, the optimists, are likely to doubt that the question of whether or not we have free will can profitably be said to depend on the truth of 'hypotheses', metaphysical or otherwise, at all. But, in any case, they believe that in so far as free will does depend on the truth of hypotheses, the facts already known to us are sufficient to guarantee that the appropriate hypotheses are true.

Of course, in calling the group who believes that we probably lack free will pessimistic, I adopt their accompanying view that the absence of free will would be a very bad thing. Unfortunately, when it comes to explaining why it would be a very bad thing, the pessimists tend to be distressingly obscure. Of the practices they feel to be potentially undermined by the absence of free will, those associated with attributions of moral responsibility are most often cited. That is, they seem to think that the practices of praising and blaming people, punishing and rewarding them on the basis of the moral quality of their actions would be irrational, inappropriate, and unjustifiable if the thesis of determinism were true.

If this is all that the pessimists are worried about, however, the optimists have a ready reply. For they can provide a justification of the allegedly threatened practices

---

2 P.F. Strawson, "Freedom and Resentment", in his *Freedom and Resentment and Other Essays* (Methuen & Co., 1974). I am indebted to this brilliant article for many of the ideas in this paper. [Page references for "Freedom and Resentment" are to pages 19–36 of this volume, followed by (after the slash) the corresponding pages of Gary Watson (ed.), *Free Will* (1982). Thus, 'FR, 16/59' refers to this volume, p. 16/and *Free Will*, p. 59—the editors.]

that is in no way invalidated by the truth of determinism. They can argue, in particular, that the way in which we justify—or at least, the way in which we ought to justify—the application of these practices is one that depends on the consequences of engaging in them. We should praise or blame an individual, they may argue, if and only if by doing so we shall improve the moral quality of actions in the future. Or they may argue that we should praise or blame an individual if and only if by doing so we shall be obeying rules the institution of which will improve the moral quality of actions in the future. The hypotheses on which both these justifications of moral praise and blame rest are guaranteed to be true by the facts we already possess. We already know that we can improve the moral quality of actions by maintaining institutions of punishment that serve functions of rehabilitation and deterrence. We already know that we can improve the moral quality of actions by maintaining institutions of reward that provide incentives. Thus, we know that our practices of reward and punishment are justified whether or not the thesis of determinism is true.

I take it that this forward-looking, consequentialist type of justification of the practices of overt moral praise and blame is a good one, and therefore I take it that the intelligent pessimist will think it a good one as well. But in conceding this, the pessimist is likely to withdraw not his fear of determinism, but only his account of it. For the pessimist is likely to feel that the optimist's response somehow misses the pessimist's point. There is a striking difference between the type of justification of moral praise and blame that the optimist offers and a type of justification on which we ordinarily rely. It is in this difference that the pessimist's point, on a revised account, may be said to lie.

The justification of praise and blame the optimist suggests is one that emphasizes the fact that we can view praising and blaming as kinds of action, which, like any other actions, may or may not be sensible conclusions of practical reasoning. Whether or not to engage in these practices is on this view to be decided, like many other practical questions, according to whether engaging in these practices is a good way of achieving other desired ends. But we do not ordinarily praise and blame other persons because, as a result of engaging in practical deliberation, we have reached the conclusion that it would be in our interests to do so. Rather, we praise and blame persons as natural expressions of natural responses to what we see people do. We do not ordinarily *decide* whether a word of praise or a public scolding would be a useful directive to future behavior. Rather, we find ourselves *reacting* to the actions and characters of others, approving of some, disapproving of others. Unless there is reason to restrain ourselves, we simply express what we feel.

In other words, although moral praising and blaming *can* be considered as kinds of actions, our ordinary experience of these phenomena encourages us to consider them as expressions of a kind of judgment. Accordingly, although one *can* justify these practices in a way that is analogous to justifications of other kinds of action, one can also try to justify these practices in a way that is analogous to justifications of other kinds of judgment. In particular, one can try to justify them by showing how the relevant judgments are fitting for, appropriate to, or, most aptly, *deserved by* the relevant objects of these judgments—in this case, human agents.

To justify praise and blame in the way the optimist suggests is to leave out of account such judgments of individual desert. It is to leave out of account any question of whether it is an individual's fault that he has done something wrong or whether it is to the individual's credit that he has done something right. In short, to justify the praise and blame of persons in the way the optimist suggests is to justify these practices in the same way that we justify the praise and blame of lower animals—in the same way, that is, that we justify the reward and punishment of pets, of pigeons in the laboratory, of monkeys in the circus. It is to justify these practices only as a means of manipulation or training.

The pessimist's fear may now be expressed as the fear that if determinism is true, this consequentialist justification of praise and blame is the only kind of justification that would be available to us. If determinism is true, the pessimist fears, the type of justification of praise and blame that rests on judgments of individual desert can never be appropriate or valid. He fears that if we discover that determinism is true, we will be rationally obliged to give up making and relying on such judgments—and, more important perhaps, we will be rationally obliged to give up the attitudes which are essentially tied to these judgments.

It is notoriously difficult to give any precise characterization of these attitudes, to do more than be merely suggestive about their range and significance. The attitudes I have in mind include admiration and indignation, pride and shame, respect and contempt, gratitude and resentment. P.F. Strawson, in the article I mentioned earlier, has called this set of attitudes 'the reactive attitudes'. They are attitudes one has toward individuals only in so far as one views these individuals as persons. In contrast to the reactive attitudes, we may take what Strawson calls 'the objective attitude' toward the individuals with whom we interact. This is the attitude we do take—or at least, the attitude we rationally ought to take—toward most animals, present-day machines, and very young children.

The Justification of the Reactive Attitudes

What the pessimist really fears, then, is that if determinism is true, we must give up not the practices of praise and blame themselves, but the attitudes and judgments these practices typically express. We must give up all reactive attitudes, and adopt the objective attitude toward ourselves and each other, as we do toward everything else. It may be thought that in restating the pessimist's concerns, the scope and importance of his fears have considerably shrunk. The changing of attitudes seems to be such a private and insubstantial affair that it might be thought to make very little difference in the world. On second glance, however, we can see that the abandonment of all the reactive attitudes would make a very great difference indeed. To replace our reactive attitudes with the objective attitude completely is to change drastically—or, as most would say, reduce—the quality of our involvement or participation in all our human relationships.

Imagine for a moment what a world would be like in which we all regarded each other solely with the objective attitude. We would still imprison murderers and thieves, presumably, and we would still sing praises for acts of courage and charity. We would applaud and criticize, say 'thank you' and 'for shame' according to whether our neighbours' behavior was or was not to our liking. But these actions and words would have a different, shallower meaning than they have for us now. Our praises would not be expressions of admiration or esteem; our criticisms would not be expressions of indignation or resentment. Rather, they would be bits of positive and negative reinforcement meted out in the hopes of altering the character of others in ways best suited to our needs.

An act of heroism or of saintly virtue would not inspire us to aim for higher and nobler ideals, nor would it evoke in us a reverence or even admiration for its agent. At best we would think it a piece of good fortune that people occasionally do perform acts like this. We would consider how nice it must be for the beneficiaries and decide to encourage this kind of behavior. We would not recoil from acts of injustice or cruelty as insults to human dignity, nor be moved by such acts to reflect with sorrow or puzzlement on the tide of events that can bring persons to stoop so low. Rather, we would recognize that the human tendency to perform acts like this is undesirable, a problem to be dealt with, like any other, as scientifically and efficiently as possible.

The most gruesome difference between this world and ours would be reflected in our closest human relationships—in the relations between siblings, parents and children, and especially spouses and companions. We would still be able to form some sorts of association that could be described as relationships of friendship and love. One person could find another amusing or useful. One could notice that the presence of a certain person was, like the sound of a favorite song, particularly soothing or invigorating. We could choose friends as we now choose clothing or home furnishings or hobbies, according to whether they offer, to a sufficient degree, the proper combination of pleasure and practicality. Attachments of considerable strength can develop on such limited bases. People do, after all, form strong attachments to their cars, their pianos, not to mention their pets. Nonetheless, I hope it is obvious why the words 'friendship' and 'love' applied to relationships in which admiration, respect, and gratitude have no part, might be said to take on a hollow ring. A world in which human relationships are restricted to those that can be formed and supported in the absence of the reactive attitudes is a world of human isolation so cold and dreary that any but the most cynical must shudder at the idea of it.

It is such a world in which the pessimist fears we would be rationally obliged to live if we came, once and for all, to the conclusion that the thesis of determinism was true. It is such a world, so much bleaker and more barren than our present world, to which the pessimist fears the truth of determinism would rationally force us. Once the optimist recognizes just what it is that the pessimist fears is at stake, however, the optimist once again has a ready reply. One thing he can point out is that even if the truth of determinism would give us some *reason* to regard ourselves differently, we would be psychologically incapable of changing our attitudes in the appropriate way. Another is that even if the truth of determinism would give us *some* reason to regard ourselves differently, we would have an overriding reason to keep the attitudes we currently hold. The overriding reason, of course, is that were we to give up our reactive attitudes, we would drastically reduce our sense of the meaning and value of our lives.

In light of the magnitude of this potential loss, it seems to me not irrational for the pessimist once again to concede the optimist's point. Once again, however, in conceding this, the pessimist is likely to withdraw not his fear of determinism but only his account of it. In other words, the pessimist might accept the optimist's argument—but he will accept it with despair. For with the first of his arguments, the optimist does not even attempt to allay the pessimist's fear that we will be forced to the conclusion that our attitudes toward ourselves are unjustified. Rather, he only seeks to show the pessimist how impotent this conclusion, if reached, would be. With the second of his arguments, the optimist suggests a way to avoid the feared conclusion. However, in so far as the optimist's justification takes the form of providing reasons that *override* other reasons, the justification can be only as satisfying as the acceptance of the lesser of two evils can be. How satisfying that is depends, in turn, on how evil is the evil we are forced to accept. Thus, it is worthwhile to get clear about the evil with which the pessimist now thinks we are left—the reason, in other words, for giving up the reactive attitudes which the optimist's argument must override.

Recall, then, that for the pessimist, whether or not we have free will is a matter of metaphysical fact. If determinism is true, then we do not have free will—that is, we are not free and responsible beings. In so far as we take reactive attitudes towards ourselves and each other, however, we regard ourselves as free and responsible beings. If determinism is true, then by continuing to take these attitudes, we live in a way that is discordant with the facts.[3]

The reason for giving up our reactive attitudes, then, is that by doing so we will be living in accordance with the facts. We will be accepting our status as creatures who are no more responsible for their lives and characters than are animals and machines. We will be accepting our status as agents to whom notions of personal credit, discredit, and desert fail to apply. If, despite the knowledge that this is our status, we choose to retain our reactive attitudes, we choose to live as if we were a kind of being that we know we are not. In doing this, we choose something akin to self-deception.[4]

As I said earlier, I believe such a choice may be rational. With Strawson, I think that it may be rational to choose *not* 'to be more purely rational than we are'.[5] It may be rational for a man to choose not to face the fact that he has a terminal illness or for a woman to try to avoid discovering that her husband is having an affair. If the costs would be high enough, it may be rational to override the reason for a course of action that is given by the acknowledgment that only that course of action would constitute living in accordance with the facts. To override this reason, however, is not just to choose to leave a desire unsatisfied. It is to choose to leave a value unrealized, a

---

3 Discordance with the facts is weaker than logical inconsistency. It is logically consistent to take attitudes that are essentially subject to certain standards of justification while at the same time believing that no such justifications are possible.

4 On this I part company with Strawson. For an excellent alternative account of these matters more faithful to Strawson's own views, see Jonathan Bennett, "Accountability", in Zak Van Straaten (ed.), *Philosophical Subjects: Essays Presented to P. F. Strawson* (Clarendon Press, 1980).

5 FR, 28 n4/70n4.

value, moreover, which is arguably one of considerable depth and importance.[6] To choose to act against, or contradict, a value as deep as this one, is inevitably to suffer a significant loss. It should not be surprising if the conviction that such a choice may be rational fails to bring the pessimist peace of mind.

Even to this last account of the pessimist's fear, I believe that the optimist has a reply which should make the pessimist withdraw his attempt to express and explain the threat of determinism yet another time. For I believe that even if determinism is true, and even if this implies that as a matter of metaphysical fact we are not free and responsible beings, this gives us *no reason at all* to regard ourselves as unfree, unresponsible beings. That is, we have no reason at all to abandon our reactive attitudes and to adopt the objective attitude in their place. If we have no reason at all to abandon these attitudes, then we have nothing we need to override, no value we need to contradict in choosing to keep these attitudes. Our retention of the reactive attitudes need not be viewed as a choice between the lesser of two evils.

At first glance, it may appear that *this* conclusion must finally put the pessimist's mind at ease. We shall return to this claim later. First we must understand why this conclusion is warranted.

The case of the addict

Let us consider a hypothetical but not unrealistic situation: the situation of a drug addict who cannot help but take the drug to which he is addicted regardless of the attitude or value or second-order desire he has concerning his addiction. Let us further assume that in other respects our addict is a normally functioning, intelligent human being. Then the degree to which we hold this individual responsible for his drug-taking actions will vary in proportion to the degree to which we think he approves of—or, at least, doesn't disapprove of—the fact that he takes these actions. If the addict, with apparent sincerity, says and shows that he is relatively content to be an addict, that he sees no sufficient reason for trying to resist his addiction, then he is, in effect, accepting responsibility for taking the drug. He is affirming the fact that his efforts to obtain and to take the drug are *his actions*, that they affect and contribute to his character and his life in a way that may fairly enter into an assessment of what kind of person he is. It is therefore rational for us to regard him as responsible for taking the drug. If, on the other hand, the addict says and shows that he repudiates his addiction, that he makes all possible efforts to resist taking the drug, then he effectively removes himself from responsibility for taking the drug. He shows that he takes the drug only because he is addicted and that he would not take the drug if he could help it. It is therefore rational for us to regard him as not responsible for taking the drug. In other words, the addict's own attitude toward taking the drug gives us a reason (perhaps *the* reason) by which to establish ours—that is, it gives us the means by which to decide whether we ought to regard him as responsible for taking the drug.

---

6 For a good account of the distinction between values and other desires, see Gary Watson, "Free Agency", *The Journal of Philosophy*, lxxii (24 April 1975), pp. 205–20.

The addict's actions are not free because he will take the drug whether or not he chooses to take the drug because he is compelled to do so. However, the addict's responsibility for his actions turns on the truth or falsity of an independent claim: namely, that whether or not the addict is compelled to take the drug, he will take the drug because he chooses to do so.[7] The addict, then, in taking an attitude toward his unfree actions, can thereby claim or disclaim responsibility for them. But whichever attitude the addict does take, the addict, in taking *an* attitude, asserts himself as a free and responsible being. By this I mean that if the addict accepts responsibility for taking the drug, he claims in effect that as a free and responsible being he chooses to take it, and if the addict rejects responsibility for taking the drug, he claims in effect that as a free and responsible being he does not choose to take it. The fact that we take the addict's own attitudes to his drug-taking actions seriously—that is, the fact that his attitudes count as a reason for us to hold him more or less responsible for these actions—rests on our belief that the addict, qua attitude-taker, *is* a free and responsible being. If we believed that the addict's approval or disapproval of his actions were itself determined by the influence of the drug, we would not regard his attitude as giving us a reason by which to establish ours.

The case of the robot

Let us turn now to a second case which takes us into the realm of science fiction. Let us imagine an individual who has been and continues to be very completely and elaborately programmed. He is programmed not only to make various choices and perform various actions, but also to engage in various thought processes, to form various second-order volitions and so forth, in coming to perform these actions. Indeed, this individual is programmed in such a way as to appear to be an ordinary human being in every respect. If no one were informed that this individual was programmed, he would appear both to us and to himself to be 'one of us'. I shall hereafter refer to this individual as a robot, but I believe that whether he is a member of the human species or not is irrelevant to the case.

Let us further assume that the robot's programming is not of any normal or familiar kind. In particular, let us assume it is not the case that any complete program is installed in the robot before he is, as it were, released into the world. Rather, let us assume that the robot is programmed on a day-to-day or moment-to-moment basis: the programmer implants the robot's responses to situations as these very situations arise. One might imagine the relation between robot and programmer to be very much like a possible relation between author and character; or, perhaps even better, one might imagine the relation to be like the relation between a magician and a human being over whose thoughts and bodily movements the magician has complete control.

---

7 I take it that I am agreeing here with Harry Frankfurt in "Freedom of the Will and the Concept of a Person", *The Journal of Philosophy*, lxviii (14 January 1971), pp. 5–20. My description of the addict was suggested by his discussion of three kinds of addict—the willing addict, the unwilling addict, and the wanton, who has no attitude or second-order desire concerning his addiction. I am concerned only with the first two kinds.

In light of the nature of the robot's programming, I believe that the only way of living in accordance with the facts would be by regarding the robot solely with the objective attitude.[8] That is, I believe that the robot is not a free and responsible being in whatever sense of 'free and responsible' the objects of our reactive attitudes are ordinarily assumed to be. Were we to be purely rational, we would allow ourselves to feel some emotions toward the robot, but we would not feel those emotions or sentiments constitutive of our reactive attitudes. For though the robot might choose to perform the actions he performs, he chooses to perform them only because he is programmed to so choose. Though his decisions and judgments may be preceded by thoughts which look or sound like reasons, he cannot be said to reason to these conclusions in the way we do. He is not in ultimate control of his values, his personality, or his actions. He is, properly speaking, only a vehicle for carrying out the plans (if plans there be) of his programmer.

Were such a robot to live within our society, it may well be that we would not ultimately regard him in the way that I have suggested it would be purely rational for us to regard him. The sheer difficulty of keeping in mind the fact that the robot is programmed (along with all its implications) may make it psychologically impossible for us to take the objective attitude towards him consistently. Moreover, we might decide that, though there is some reason for us to treat the robot objectively, there are overriding reasons to treat him as a normal member of the community. Or perhaps we would take some sort of middle ground. (For example, we might treat him as if he had some of the rights of a normal person, but we would shrink from allowing one of our daughters to marry him.)[9] All that is important for my purposes is that we take it to be purely rational to regard the robot objectively. For this should carry at least some weight in determining how we ought ultimately to regard him.

Let us now assume that, after years of thinking himself to be like other human beings, the robot comes to believe that he is completely programmed. If at this point we were to adopt the robot's interests as our own, would it be rational for us to urge (to the programmer, presumably) that the robot take the objective attitude toward himself?

By this question I mean to approach the question: 'Would it be rational for the robot to adopt the objective attitude toward himself?' as closely as my standards of conceptual coherence allow. I am not sure that we can make sense of the question 'What would it be rational for the robot to do?', because the attempt to answer it seems to require that we imaginatively endow the robot with the powers of a free and responsible being while, at the same time, remaining convinced that the robot lacks these same powers. However, I see nothing to prevent us from reasoning

---

8 Some philosophers will resist this conclusion, and the few remarks I add (directly below) by way of support may be insufficient to convince them. However, I believe the pessimist would think that this conclusion is correct, and it is with the pessimist's position that I am primarily concerned.

9 This recalls a scene from a play by Woody Allen: Two characters in the play appeal for help in their dialogue from the members of the audience. An attractive woman comes to their aid, with whom one of the characters begins to fall in love. The other character, trying to discourage the romance, asks his friend, 'What kind of children would you have? She's Jewish, you're fictional!'

on the robot's behalf. Thus, to repeat my question, I ask, if we were to adopt the robot's interests as our own, would it be rational for us to urge that the robot take the objective attitude towards himself?

Well, I can imagine some situations in which it might be. If, for example, the robot were an individual unusually tormented by an awareness of his limitations, the belief that he was not responsible for the meagreness of his abilities might be a source of some comfort to him. Or, if the members of the robot's community did take the purely rational attitude toward the robot, the robot's own adoption of the objective attitude toward himself might allow him to take this treatment less personally. (Of course, here as always, it will ultimately be up to the programmer whether the robot's adoption of the objective attitude would serve the purposes that I have suggested they might serve. But let us assume at this point that the programmer is cooperative.)

In so far as we argue that the robot should adopt, or try to adopt, the objective attitude toward himself for reasons such as these, however, we are not arguing for the adoption of this attitude simply on the grounds that the attitude is appropriate. That is, we are not arguing that the robot should take this attitude simply because of his (and our) value in living in accordance with the facts. Our reasons for urging that the robot should take the objective attitude are, rather, utilitarian ones: his life will be less painful if he takes the objective attitude toward himself.

Furthermore, if the robot were programmed to take this attitude, he would not really be taking an attitude that would be in accordance with the facts. In believing that reactive attitudes toward himself are inappropriate, he would not be accepting all the implications of the fact that he is programmed; he would not be denying his freedom and responsibility completely. For the robot, in taking an objective view of himself, necessarily leaves a part of himself out of this view—specifically, he leaves out that part of himself which is taking the objective attitude. The robot perhaps takes comfort in the fact that *he*—as it were, 'his self'—is not responsible for his meager abilities; or, the robot takes comfort in thinking that he is not responsible for the fact that he is merely a robot. But the robot's alienation from his abilities on the one hand, or from his robotness on the other, presupposes a self from whom these things are alienated, a self whose fault these things are not. And of course, in this example, the robot's self is itself the result of his programming. To the extent that being programmed justifies a denial of responsibility for *any* feature of the robot's existence, it justifies—indeed, demands—a denial of responsibility for *every* feature of his existence—including, in particular, his denial of responsibility for every other feature.

We can bring this out by comparing the case of the robot to that of the addict. For, recall that the addict, in taking any attitude toward his addiction, asserts himself as a free and responsible being. If he accepts responsibility for taking the drug, he claims that as a free and responsible being he chooses to take it. If he rejects responsibility for taking the drug, he claims that as a free and responsible being he does not choose to take it. Similarly, the robot in taking an attitude toward himself, asserts himself as a free and responsible being. But unlike the addict, the robot is not a free and responsible being in any respect whatsoever. He is in a position analogous to that of the addict whose attitude toward his addiction is itself determined by the influence of the drug. Thus, the robot's own attitude toward himself cannot have any weight for us. If the robot, as a matter of metaphysical fact, is an unfree, unresponsible being, then *his* acceptance of this fact gives us no extra reason to regard him as such.

The case of our (determined) selves

We may finally turn to the question of what it would be purely rational for us to do if we came to believe that the thesis of determinism was true and that this implied that, as a matter of metaphysical fact, we were not free and responsible beings. Perhaps the pessimist thinks that if determinism is true, then the whole world is in a position analogous to that of the robot—that, in other words, the thesis of determinism is not different in any relevant respect from the thesis that the whole world is, like the robot, completely programmed. In this case, would it be rational for us to take the objective attitude toward ourselves? Again, we might answer, as we did when reasoning on behalf of the robot, that we can imagine some situations in which it might be. In particular, it would be rational for us to take this attitude if by doing so we would become, on the whole, better off. But considerations of the sort I suggested earlier make this possibility seem very unlikely. It is hard to believe that more of our desires (all orders inclusive)[10] would be satisfied if we ceased to take the reactive attitudes and adopted the objective attitude in their place. Still, among our desires, we must include the often very strong desire to live in accordance with the facts. Indeed, as I said earlier, this is not just a desire, but a value of considerable depth and importance. If, by taking the objective attitude toward ourselves, we would better realize this value, then, regardless of our ultimate decision, we would have at least some reason to adopt the objective attitude.

It should now be clear, however, that we would *not* be realizing this value by adopting the objective attitude. If we were to view ourselves objectively, we would, like the robot, necessarily leave a part of ourselves out of this view. In taking any attitude toward ourselves, including the attitude that we are not free or responsible beings, we would be asserting ourselves *as* free and responsible beings.[11] Any attitude we take, then, would involve a false step—any attitude would be unjustified. Thus, it seems that the only way we could live in accordance with the facts would be by ceasing to have any attitudes at all—by ceasing, that is, to make or rely on any judgments about an individual's responsibility or lack of it at all.

The truth of determinism, then, gives us no reason at all to replace our present reactive attitudes with the objective attitude. Some might think, however, that it gives us reason to do something even more drastic—namely, to give up the taking of attitudes altogether. For I have said that we place a considerable value in living in accordance with the facts. And I have also said that if determinism were true, and if this implied that, as a matter of metaphysical fact, we were not free and responsible beings, then the only way in which we would be living in accordance with the facts would be by giving up the taking of attitudes altogether.

---

10 The idea of higher-order desires is taken from Harry Frankfurt, *ibid.*

11 Perhaps this claim can be taken as a reformulation of the liar paradox: 'Do not take me seriously.'

Of course, in answer to the question: 'Would it be rational for us to give up all our attitudes?', pragmatic replies of the sort I suggested earlier will be all the more poignant. That is, even if determinism gave us some *reason* to give up all our attitudes, we would be psychologically incapable of meeting this demand. And even if determinism gave us *some* reason to give up our attitudes, we would have overriding reason to retain them.

If our sense of the value and meaning of our lives would be sharply reduced in a world without reactive attitudes, it would be altogether eliminated in a world in which no attitudes were taken at all. For the only way we could give up taking either the attitudes that regard others as responsible for their actions or the attitude that regards others as not responsible for their actions would be by giving up thinking in terms of the notions of responsibility and desert at all. Giving this up, I believe, would require in turn that we give up a great deal more. We would have to stop thinking in terms of what ought and ought not to be. We would have to stop thinking in terms that would allow the possibility that some lives and projects are better than others.[12] Were we to make ourselves into the kind of creatures that ceased to think in these terms, we would lose the distinction between desires and values and, therefore, our distinction as valuing creatures. We would lose our ideals, our sense of self, and, I think, our status as persons. A world without reactive attitudes would be a tragic world of human isolation; a world without reactive attitudes or the objective attitude would be a bleak, blank world of human brutes.

Thus, as I said, in answer to the question 'Would it be rational for us to give up all our attitudes?', pragmatic replies will be all the more poignant. If the optimist's arguments stopped here, however, the pessimist could still sigh and point out once again that pragmatic replies are merely pragmatic. As such, they can be only as satisfying as the acceptance of the lesser of two evils can be. However, I believe that the optimist's arguments need not stop here, with the merely pragmatic. If we *had* some reason to give up all our attitudes, we would have overriding reason to retain them. But, in fact, I believe, we have no reason at all to take this very drastic step. We have no reason at all to fulfill our desire to live in accordance with the facts, when the facts in question are facts such as these. In other words, the desire is itself irrational in relation to facts such as these. If the facts are that we are, in all relevant respects, like the robot, there is no point to living in accordance with them.

Unfortunately, it is not at all clear what the point of this desire normally is. The desire to live in accordance with the facts is more easily felt than explained. It is this desire, I take it, that people sometimes express when they say that they want to live in the Real World. It is this desire that makes people shudder at the thought of passing their days hooked up to a pleasure machine. This desire shows up in more realistic situations when we consider how important it is to us that we not only feel ourselves to be loved, but that we truly be loved, or when we see how important it is

---

12 Here I assume that 'ought' and 'better' have the force of objective reason. Once the thought that some things ought to be is allowed, so is the thought that some things ought to be done (by oneself, for instance). And this, I think, leads inevitably to the thought that one is, *ceteris paribus*, responsible for doing them.

to us that we not only believe that our efforts to achieve something in the world have succeeded, but that they really have succeeded.

Why is it so important to us that our conception of our lives correspond to some more objective fact? Why does it matter so much that the world we live in is the Real World? I can think of two possible answers.

First, I think it plausible that we place a primitive, unanalyzable value on 'getting things right'. Perhaps, that is, we value being right for its own sake. From this value, the value of living in accordance with the facts would follow as a direct corollary. If so, it should at least give us pause to notice that living in accordance with the fact that we are not free and responsible beings would require us to give up our value in being right. For living in accordance with the fact that we are not free and responsible beings would require us to give up all our values. More important, if we were to live in accordance with the fact that we are not free and responsible beings by giving up the taking of attitudes altogether, we would not even realize our (past) value in getting things right. We would admittedly cease to be getting some things wrong, for we would cease to regard ourselves as free and responsible beings. But we would do this at the cost of ceasing to regard ourselves as anything at all.

On the other hand, our desire to live in accordance with the facts—our desire, that is, to live in the Real World—may rest essentially on the belief that it is the Real World, and the beings within it, that matter. In other words, we may want to live in accordance with the facts because we want ourselves to matter in the right sort of way, to make the right sort of difference to the world and the beings who do matter and to whom we might matter. But all the beings that could possibly be encompassed by these concerns must themselves be within the grasp of the same determinism as ourselves.[13] If the point of living in accordance with the facts is to make the right kind of difference to the right kind of beings, then it cannot possibly be an achievement to eliminate the right kind of beings *en masse*.

It might be rational for the robot to commit a kind of suicide of self as a result of the realization that he is, unlike the rest of us, a robot. For it seems plausible that the realization that you cannot, and/or rationally ought not, matter to the people or to the world that matters to you—indeed, to the people or to the world that matter independently of you—might give you a reason to commit suicide.[14] But the realization that you are determined because your whole world is determined cannot generate such a reason. For us, either this world matters or none at all. If this world matters, then it would be irrational to destroy it. And if this world does not matter, then it certainly doesn't matter that we do or do not choose to destroy it.

Thus, we reach the conclusion that the truth of determinism gives us no reason at all to give up our reactive attitudes. Let me briefly review the argument.

---

13 As perhaps all the people a person in a dream can concern himself with are themselves dream-people. Perhaps, one might think, we can also concern ourselves with the programmer (or God), if there is one, and this individual would not be in the grasp of the same determinism as ourselves. Even if this were correct, however, we could in no way improve our status with such a being by living in accordance with the facts.

14 Douglas MacLean once suggested to me that Kafka's *Metamorphosis* might be interpreted as an illustration of just this point.

We first considered the suggestion that the recognition that, as a matter of metaphysical fact, we were not free or responsible beings would give us a reason to regard ourselves as unfree, unresponsible beings—it would give us a reason, that is, to replace our present reactive attitudes with the objective attitude toward ourselves and each other. But we saw that this change would fail to achieve its purpose; it would not satisfy the desire to live in accordance with the facts. For it is only rational to take some particular attitude toward ourselves, in the context of the belief that we are, at least in our capacity as attitude-takers, free and responsible beings. Therefore, we would be no less irrational if we chose to take the objective attitude than if we chose to take the other alternative.

Second, we considered the suggestion that the desire to live in accordance with the facts might give us a reason to cease to take attitudes altogether. But we saw that if living in accordance with the facts required this change, we would have no reason to live in accordance with them. For there seemed to be two possible sources of our desire to live in accordance with the facts. According to the first, this desire rests on the belief that by living in accordance with the facts we will promote our ability to get things right. According to the second, this desire rests on the belief that living in accordance with the facts would put us in the world that is most worth living in—the world, that is, with valuable and valuing selves. But if determinism is true, and if this implies that we are not free and responsible beings, then neither of these beliefs is justified. On neither of these accounts would it be rational to live in accordance with the fact that determinism is true.

Thus, the truth of determinism gives us no reason at all to choose to take one attitude rather than another. And the truth of determinism gives us no reason at all to choose to take no attitude rather than some.

Since the truth of determinism gives us no reason at all, we must look elsewhere for reasons by which to decide which attitudes, if any, it would be best for us to take. Presumably, we would have to look at the consequences of these various decisions—and, looking at these, we would, presumably, choose to keep our present reactive attitudes. This brings us to the apparently optimistic conclusion that, even if determinism were true, and even if this implied that, as a matter of metaphysical fact, we were not free or responsible beings, it would still be rational—and without impurification—to retain our present reactive attitudes.

The Importance of Free Will

Some might think that this conclusion must finally silence the pessimist. For it should convince him that no answer to the problem of free will can have any practical, pessimistic consequences whatsoever. But here again, I believe the pessimist might withdraw not his fear of determinism, but only his account of it. If the argument I have presented as the justification of our attitudes is the only justification we can have, the pessimist again, might accept this justification—but he will accept it with despair. For the position I have outlined might be said to reduce, in effect, to something like this: 'Even if we are puppets on the strings of the hands of God, there is nothing at all we can do about it. It would therefore not be rational to try to do anything about it, nor would it be rational, because of *this*, to commit suicide. Since there are no rational options by which to respond to this possibility, the option we do take cannot be irrational. So we are rationally permitted—perhaps, even obliged—to go on living our (possibly puppet-) lives.'

This argument, unfortunately, takes nothing away from the fact that we don't *want* to be puppets. We don't want to be, or to be no better than, objects of someone else's manipulation. Of course, it is nice to know that, whatever the facts, the rationality of our practices is not open to criticism. It is nice to know that, whatever the facts, we are not making fools of ourselves. It is also nice to know that, as new facts come to light, nothing can happen that will generate, or that even ought to generate, a practical crisis. We will not have to choose between the lesser of two evils; we will not have to choose self-deception. But the guarantee that we are not behaving irrationally or serving as the unwitting agents of our own humiliation and error—the guarantee, in other words, that *we* cannot be faulted for taking an inappropriate attitude towards ourselves and our place in the world—is not the only guarantee that one can reasonably wish for. And the onset of a practical crisis, of the recognition of the need to confront an inconsistency in ourselves and to change our personalities and practices in undesirable ways, is not the only state of affairs that one can reasonably fear.

The pessimist fears that if determinism is true, then we are no better off than puppets. And the lives of puppets, the pessimist thinks, are meaningless and absurd. No one would dream of faulting the puppets for this—the thought that puppets are blameworthy for not recognizing their puppethood and integrating their recognition into the way they live their lives is at worst incoherent and at best simply false. Nonetheless, the puppets' lives are meaningless, and, from the puppets' point of view, that would be too bad. The pessimist fears that if determinism is true, then we are no better off than puppets. Naturally, from the pessimist's point of view, if determinism were true, that would be too bad. The fact that we don't have to *change* our values is of little solace if it may be the case that we are, now and forever, incapable of *realizing* our values. The fact that we don't have to think that our lives are meaningless is of little comfort if, for all that, our lives may actually *be* meaningless.

Thus, the apparently optimistic conclusion that it is completely rational for us to regard ourselves as free and responsible beings must, in order to silence the pessimist, be reached in a more optimistic way. No position which allows that as a matter of metaphysical fact we might not be free and responsible beings—even if this gives us no reason at all to regard ourselves as such—can properly be called optimistic. The pessimist will only give up his pessimism if the possibility of this state of affairs is directly refuted. In other words, for the pessimist, who asks for a justification of the fact that we treat ourselves as free and responsible beings, only one kind of justification will do—a justification, in particular, which relies on the fact that we *are* free and responsible beings.

Chapter 5

On "Freedom and Resentment"

Galen Strawson

This paper questions whether P.F. Strawson's paper "Freedom and Resentment" really succeeds in undercutting the traditional debate about free will and suggests that the deepest source of our commitment to belief in free will lies not, as Strawson suggests, in our personal-reactive attitudes to others, but in our experience of our own agency. It continues with a general examination of the "cognitive phenomenology" of freedom, i.e. of our overall lived experience of being free agents, pointing up both its naturally compatibilist and naturally incompatibilist elements, and concludes with a Buddhism-inspired speculation about the extent to which it might be possible for us to give up our commitment to belief in freedom and the reactive attitudes.

I. Feelings, Attitudes, Practices, Concepts and Beliefs

I wish to consider P.F. Strawson's commitment theory of freedom, which stresses our commitment to certain *attitudes* and *practices* which appear to presuppose belief in true responsibility, rather than directly stressing our commitment to belief in true responsibility.[1] I will first suggest that it cannot by appealing to the notion of commitment show the worries of incompatibilist or "hard" determinists to be wholly misconceived or groundless. Then I will suggest that it may mislocate the true centre of our commitment in our interpersonal rather than in our self-regarding attitudes.

In so far as it holds the truth or falsity of determinism to be irrelevant to the question of whether or not we can correctly be said to be free, Strawson's view counts as a variety of compatibilism, and one may therefore avail oneself of the assumption that determinism is true in putting it to the test. There is, however, a determinism-independent argument for the impossibility of self-determination, or for "non-self-determinability", which poses exactly the same problem for freedom as determinism does.[2] Although I will speak in a traditional fashion of determinism and the problems that it poses, I could equally well (if more laboriously) speak of the problems posed for freedom by the impossibility of self-determination or by non-self-determinability. The basic question is this: can a commitment theory of

---

[1] "Freedom and Resentment", in P.F. Strawson, *Freedom and Resentment and Other Essays* (Methuen & Co., 1974). [As previously noted, page references for "Freedom and Resentment" will be to pages 19–36 of this volume, followed by (after the slash) the corresponding pages of Gary Watson (ed.), *Free Will* (1982). Thus, "FR, 16/59" refers to this volume, p. 16/and *Free Will*, p. 59—the editors.]

[2] Cf. my *Freedom and Belief* (Oxford: Oxford University Press, 1986), Ch. 2, esp. 2.1.

freedom really avoid the problems that seem to be posed by determinism (or non-self-determinability)?

Consider a man who becomes a determinist. He is often pictured as being faced first and foremost with the problem of what he is to make of other people, given his new belief. But of course his judgement of determinedness extends also, and far more immediately, to himself. He cannot see himself as an ordinary (and ordinarily responsible) man in an otherwise determined world. Or if he does—as he may, if the self-regarding aspects of commitment to belief in freedom are indeed less easy to renounce than the interpersonal ones—he should not. His first problem is himself.

But still, what should he make of other people? It seems that most people would find abandonment of the ordinary, strong notion of responsibility intolerable, not to say practically speaking impossible, from a social point of view. It would undermine the foundations of their conception of what human life is. For it is not as if one can excise one's inclination to praise and blame people while leaving all one's other attitudes to them untouched. If determinism is called upon to justify any such excision, one whole central range of what Strawson calls "personal-reactive" or "reactive" feelings and attitudes is thereby put at risk: attitudes and feelings, both moral and non-moral, to and about oneself and others; feelings, more or less considered and complicated, of condemnation and approbation, of gratitude and resentment, of despite and scorn; certain feelings of admiration for people's achievements and creations; certain aspects of feelings of hatred, anger, love, affection, and so on; feelings of guilt and remorse, pride and shame with regard to oneself and one's doings.

Such feelings and attitudes, and associated practices like praising and blaming, are all similarly threatened to the extent that their propriety depends in some way on our supposing that people are truly responsible for what they do. The connection of dependence seems very clear in the majority of cases even if, irrational and anthropomorphistic, some of our feelings for and attitudes to non-human and even inanimate entities go by the same name. It is also clear we are deeply committed to the belief that people can be truly responsible for what they do—just as it is clear that determinism (or non-self-determinability) raises a major prima-facie doubt about the validity of this belief.

Can appeal to the undeniable fact of our commitment to these personal-reactive attitudes and practices show this doubt to be unwarranted? One argument that it can, might go as follows: there is indeed a clear connection between (*a*) the personal-reactive attitudes and practices and (*b*) belief in true responsibility. Indeed one can argue *from* the fact of our practically speaking unrenounceable commitment to these (at least partly) non-epistemic things, these feelings, attitudes, and practices, *to* the conclusion that no claim that the belief in true responsibility is false needs to be taken seriously. For if the truth of the belief in true responsibility is indeed *in some sense* a necessary condition of the justifiability of these attitudes and practices, the justifiability of these attitudes and practices is by the same token a sufficient condition of the truth of the belief. So if these attitudes and practices are independently justifiable, in some sense of "justifiable"—if they are justifiable without appeal to the belief in responsibility, perhaps just by appeal to the fact that it is an absolutely fundamental natural fact about us that we are deeply and perhaps unrenounceably committed to them—then they can plausibly be taken to uphold the belief in responsibility, when pressure is put upon it. Instead of being supported by it, they can support it, being supported in turn by the ground-floor fact of our unrenounceable commitment.

Strawson does not offer precisely this argument. But he does claim, in a comparable way, that we are *non-rationally* committed to the personal-reactive attitudes and practices—and, hence, presumably, to belief in the applicability of the concepts of responsibility and freedom—in such a way that it cannot be right to suppose that to give them up would be the correct or rational thing to do if determinism were shown to be true. In fact, he suggests, we are in any case incapable of giving them up, practically speaking. We could not at will adopt a completely "objective" attitude to people (including ourselves), never praising or blaming them, never, in short, treating them as if they were properly responsible agents.

Feelings, attitudes, practices, concepts, and beliefs are all different things, and Strawson is mainly concerned with certain of the personal reactive *feelings*, *attitudes*, and *practices*—those which have in common that they involve reacting to people as if they were genuinely self-determining and truly responsible agents. He has less to say about the more problematic-seeming questions that arise about the applicability of the related *concepts* of responsibility and freedom, and about the truth or falsity of *beliefs* in responsibility and freedom. But, considering the concept of moral responsibility in § 6, he does link attitudes and practices to concepts and beliefs. He suggests that the "pessimist" (or incompatibilist) about freedom is wrong to think that one cannot by appealing to the personal-reactive attitudes and practices "fill the gap" in the "optimist's" (or conventional compatibilist's) account of the concept of responsibility.

I take this suggestion to involve the claim (*a*) that the concepts of, and belief in, moral responsibility and freedom are *in some sense* shown to have application, and to be justified, respectively, by the mere fact of the existence of our commitment to the personal-reactive attitudes and practices; and (*b*) that the concepts of responsibility and freedom that are in this way shown to have application are in *some* way essentially stronger or richer concepts than those that can be admitted by conventional compatibilists. For they "fill the gap" in the conventional compatibilist account.

It may be, though, that Strawson's argument is best understood simply as an attempt to draw attention to, and connect up, the two following things: the viability of (1) the conventional compatibilist account as far as it goes, and (2) the natural fact of our commitment to personal reactive attitudes, emotions, and practices. They connect up in that reference to the latter fills the gap that the pessimists discern in the former. But, on this view, reference to (2) does not fill the gap in (1) in the sense that it supports and straightforwardly justifies belief in the proper applicability of a notion of responsibility that is essentially stronger than that allowed for in (1). It fills the gap in (1) only in the sense that it supplements (1) with an account of the primordially important role in human thought and action of a belief in a kind of responsibility that (1) can never show to be justified: it fits this belief into, and illuminates it in its proper place in, the general human "form of life". And, once placed in its true (and, essentially, partly non-rational) context, the belief can be seen to be immune, in some vital respect, to attack by any argument from determinism (or non-self-determinability). One could put this in a Humean way: belief in responsibility is "more properly an act of the sensitive, than of the cogitative part of our natures".[3] So the products of the pessimists' excogitations, although properly called beliefs, simply fail to connect with our *non*-cogitatively natural belief in responsibility in such a way that they and it can be assessed (with negative result) for mutual consistency.

This is an attractive reconciliation. One thing that someone who adopts such a position may simply underestimate, however, is the equal naturalness of the pessimists' position, when they insist that determinism is incompatible with freedom. Secure in theoretical indefeasibility, the reconciler may tend to mistake for a failure of subtlety in his opponent what is in fact a proper sensitivity to the power of the basic incompatibilist intuition that determinism is incompatible with freedom. The fact that the incompatibilist intuition has such power for us is as much a natural fact about cognitive beings like ourselves as is the fact of our quite unreflective commitment to the reactive attitudes. What is more, the roots of the incompatibilist intuition lie deep in the very reactive attitudes that are invoked in order to undercut it. The reactive attitudes enshrine the incompatibilist intuition. The notion of true responsibility comes easily to the non-philosophizing mind, and is not found only in (or behind) what Strawson calls the "panicky metaphysics" of philosopher libertarians.[4]

On balance, then, it is not clear that Strawson's appeal to commitment can undercut the pessimists' demand for an account, incompatible with determinism, of what it is that actually makes us truly responsible. Nor can it clearly assuage the pessimism of those who think that no such account can possibly be given.

II. Commitment and Rationality

Strawson suggests that a question (1) "about what it would be *rational* to do if determinism were true, a question about the rational justification of ordinary inter-personal attitudes in general", could (2) seem "real only to one who had failed to grasp the purport" of the point about "our natural human commitment to ordinary inter-personal attitudes. This commitment is part of the general framework of human life, not something that can come up for review ... within this general framework."[5] It is (3) "*useless* to ask whether it would not be rational for us to do what it is not in our nature to (be able to) do".[6] If (4) "we could imagine what we cannot have, viz.

---

3 Hume, D. *A Treatise of Human Nature*, ed. L.A. Selby-Bigge, 2nd edn (Oxford: Clarendon Press, 1978), 1.4.1.8/183. [*The editors:* The now standard edition is that edited by D.F. Norton and M.J. Norton (Oxford: Oxford University Press, 2000). Following the convention given in the Nortons' *Treatise*, citations are provided as follows: "Book. Part. Section. Paragraph, followed by page references to the Selby-Bigge/Nidditch edition". Thus, *Treatise*, 1.4.1.8/183 indicates that the above quotation comes from the *Treatise*, Book 1, Part 4, Section 1, paragraph 8/Selby-Bigge/Nidditch page 183.]

4 By "libertarian" I mean someone who believes that we are free, and that freedom is incompatible with determinism, and that determinism is therefore false.

5 FR, 28/70.

6 FR, 31/74.

a choice in this matter [a choice in the matter of our commitment to the ordinary interpersonal attitudes], then we could choose rationally only in the light of the gains and losses to human life, its enrichment or impoverishment; and the truth or falsity of a general thesis of determinism could not bear on the rationality of *this* choice".[7]

He concludes, (5), that "the question ... of the connection between rationality and the adoption of the objective attitude to others is misposed when it is made to seem dependent on the issue of determinism"; and, (6), that "it would not necessarily be rational to choose to be more purely rational than we are ... if such a choice were possible".[8]

With regard to the first three quotations: one might again object, that while we have a deep and perhaps ineracinable commitment to the reactive attitudes and practices, it is also in our nature to take determinism to pose a serious problem for our notions of responsibility and freedom. (This is so even if we grant that indeterminism cannot help.) Our commitments are complex, and conflict. Although our thoughts about determinism appear in actual fact quite impotent to disturb our natural and unconsidered reactive attitudes and feelings (this reveals one commitment), it also seems very difficult for us not to acknowledge that the truth of determinism or of non-self-determinability brings the propriety of the reactive attitudes seriously into doubt (this reveals the other commitment). Defenders of the reactive attitudes may be unwise to seek to strengthen their position by appealing to the fact that commitment to the reactive attitudes is, unlike the opposed commitment, *practically* basic. For the incompatibilist "pessimists" may then reply that, while the commitment they are concerned to stress is of an essentially more theoretical character, it appears to represent the simple *truth*. There is a very real conflict of commitment.

At one point in his characterization of the nature of our commitment to the reactive feelings and attitudes, Strawson compares it to our commitment to belief in the validity of inductive procedures. This commitment to inductive belief-formation is "original, natural, non-rational (not *ir*rational), in no way something we choose or could give up".[9] It cannot be supposed to be purely rational, as Hume showed. Yet it can plausibly be said to be a commitment we are not wrong to have—it is quite implausible to say that it is simply irrational. It is very hard, furthermore, to see how we could give it up. And it seems absurd to suppose that it might be rational to do so, or more rational to do so than not to do so.

The claim implicit in the comparison appears to be this: that our commitment to the reactive attitudes and, derivatively, to belief in responsibility, is similarly non-rational in such a way that it is something that we are not wrong to have in the face of determinism (or non-self-determinability). But there appears to be an important difference. The correct sceptical objection to commitment to the validity of inductive belief-formation is not that it involves a demonstrably false belief, but only that it involves a belief that cannot be shown to be true, and in that sense cannot be justified, although it may in fact be true (it may in fact be true that there is a

---

7   FR, 28/70.

8   FR, 28n4/70. For a more recent statement of his position, see *Skepticism and Naturalism: Some Varieties* (New York: Columbia University Press, 1985), pp. 31–8.

9   FR, 35n7/79.

real material world governed by certain fundamental forces that are intrinsic to the very constitution of matter, a world in which everything takes place in accordance with what one may perfectly well call "natural necessity"). The sceptical objection to belief in true responsibility, however, is that it is a belief that is apparently demonstrably false. This objection is then extended into a criticism of the reactive attitudes as demonstrably inappropriate given their essential dependence on a belief that is demonstrably false.

Even if the two commitments are of the same depth and strength just *qua* commitments, then, there is a respect in which they are different in nature. But are they in fact of the same depth and strength? They may resemble each other in this, that it would no more be right or rational to (try to) give up the reactive attitudes than it would be to (try to) give up reliance on inductive belief-formation. But merely placing them side by side does not show that this is so; and it does not seem so inconceivable that we should weaken in our commitment to the reactive attitudes as it does that we should weaken in our commitment to inductive belief-formation. (One possibility not allowed for by this all-or-nothing view of our commitment to the reactive attitudes is that of local erosions, within the general framework of human life, of certain facets of this commitment.)

On balance, it does not seem that the question about what it would be rational to do if determinism were true can yet be rejected as an unreal one. It is in our nature to be deeply committed to the reactive attitudes. But it is also in our nature to take determinism (non-self-determinability) to pose a serious problem for the notions of freedom and responsibility.

Quotations (4)–(6) have roughly the same import, but they merit separate comment. Consider a man who is an incompatibilist, and who comes to believe that determinism is true. He has a great love of truth, or, rather, a great desire to be correct in all things, to have justified attitudes. Surely he can act rationally in choosing to (try to) adopt the objective attitude to people, in the light of this desire and belief in determinism? The quotations suggest that the truth or falsity of determinism is never relevant to such a choice, and that the nature of human commitment to the reactive attitudes is such that one can legislate quite generally about what constitute gains and losses to human life, without considering the widely differing aims and preferences of individuals. But even if most people agree that the truth of determinism does not give them good reason to try to adopt the objective attitude, given other considerations about gains and losses to human life, the egregious lover of truth just mentioned, who now believes in determinism and so feels that his reactive attitudes are not justified, can reasonably claim that it is rational for him to try to adopt more objective attitudes. It is true that belief in determinism cannot *by itself* make it rational to adopt the objective attitude. But this is merely because no non-evaluative belief of this kind can ever provide a reason for action by itself.

In general, it simply is not clear that the fact of commitment makes it a mistake to suppose that the truth of determinism renders one's personal-reactive attitudes unjustified in some way.[10] Nor is it clear that the fact of commitment makes it

---

10 This may be so even if assuming the falsity of determinism is of no help in an attempt to demonstrate their appropriateness. (Those who agree that indeterminism is no better than

impossible for us as we are to adopt universally objective attitudes to people.[11] And it surely cannot make it impossible for us to *try* to adopt the objective attitude (though in section V, I will suggest that newly fledged incompatibilist determinists may find themselves unable to adopt any rational plan of action at all, given their belief in determinism).

In the other case imagined by Strawson, that of choosing between our actual world and a world in which everyone adopts the objective attitude, we would, certainly, make our choice "in the light of the gains and losses to human life". But again this is not to say that there is a single rational choice. For it depends on what the chooser wants or thinks best, and there is a crucial sense in which desires and values are simply not comparable in respect of rationality.[12] Most would opt for the actual world. But a utilitarian who believed that personal-reactive-attitude-involving human relations cause more suffering than happiness overall would think it right or rational for us to choose to be more purely rational than we are, given the choice, in order to cancel the balance of suffering.[13]

In conclusion: it does not follow, from the fact that the truth of determinism cannot by itself make it rational to try to adopt the objective attitude, or from the fact that there is no single rational choice to be made in this case, that the correctness of the objective attitude does not in some sense follow from the truth of determinism. It does seem to be true that praising, blaming or resenting what other people do is in some sense completely inappropriate, given the truth of determinism, even if it is odd to talk of "correct" attitudes. (For if determinism is true, then to pass moral judgments on people, and to say that they acted morally rightly or wrongly, is, in a crucial respect, exactly like saying they are beautiful, or ugly—something for which they are not responsible.) And it seems that this is so whatever one's desires are, and whatever one thinks one should do. Finally, while there may indeed be no single right answer to the question of what it would be rational to do if determinism were

---

determinism, so far as the prospects for freedom are concerned, can replace "(the truth of) determinism" by "the way things are" throughout sections I–II).

11 It is conceivable that one could have a choice in the matter—it could be a simple matter of wiring up one's brain and pushing a button.

12 If I desire something impossible—to grow parsley on the moon—I am not *in any way* irrational, only unlucky; and I am not irrational, only subject to conflict of desire, if I desire to achieve something the achievement of which is incompatible with achievement of my other desires. One's fear of (English) spiders may be said to be irrational because it is only rational to fear what one believes to be harmful; and such irrationality may be supposed to infect one's corresponding desire not to come into contact with spiders. But even if one's desire is wholly derived from a fear that can properly be called irrational, it is not in itself irrational; one can have the same desire without the fear. (Derek Parfit has argued convincingly that certain patterns of preference may be intrinsically irrational; see *Reasons and Persons* [Oxford: Oxford University Press, 1984], § 46. But his unusual cases do not affect the present point.)

13 A man might rate more highly than anything else a diminution in the rate of *crimes passionnels*; he might find this kind of killing far more terrible than any other kind. Confident that this would diminish drastically upon universal adoption of the objective attitude, he might regard all the other effects of its adoption as a price well worth paying.

shown to be true, the question has not been shown to be unreal. I will now consider it further, in conjunction with some more strictly phenomenological themes.

III. Feelings and the Causality of Reason: Doings and Happenings

Many of our ordinary "personal-reactive" attitudes and feelings seem to be somehow inappropriate or incorrect, given the truth of determinism (or of non-self-determinability). It is true that feelings and attitudes are correct or incorrect, if at all, only in some derivative sense—only in so far as they are tied to beliefs. Nevertheless, it seems reasonable to say that if determinism is true (or since true self-determination is impossible), the attitudes and feelings currently in question can be shown to be appropriate only by appeal to beliefs which are in fact incorrect; it seems that they stand in a sufficiently close relation to certain beliefs to depend for their correctness or appropriateness on the correctness of those beliefs. Accordingly, there appears to be room for the exercise of reason in thinking through the consequences of one's beliefs for one's attitudes and feelings. It does not seem that the bare fact of one's commitment to these attitudes and feelings renders any such exercise of reason simply pointless.

How might such reasoning go? Well, just as believing "if p then q" and coming to believe p is likely to *cause* one to come to believe that q, according to what one could call the "natural causality of reason", so, similarly, if one genuinely believes that the propriety of certain of one's feelings presupposes the correctness of certain beliefs, and if one then comes to think that these beliefs are false, then this may understandably cause one to cease to have these feelings; it may cause them to change or weaken, at least. On the other hand, if the feelings are linked to inherently non-rational emotions and desires, the natural "causality of reason" will be impeded. Clearly it will vary in its operation with the individual case.

But does this have any consequences for the question of what one should *do*? If a change in one's feelings and attitudes were produced in this way by one's coming to believe in determinism, this would be something that happened to one, not something one did.[14] And the difficulties that attend Strawson's question about what it might be rational to do if one came to believe, say, that both incompatibilism and determinism were true are not diminished by the fact that there is a real and unproblematic question about what might *happen* to one in such a case.

So: what should one do—if anything? What might one do, in any case?

One can hardly decide to take no notice of what one now believes—that people, including oneself, are, in some unequivocal sense, in no way responsible for their actions. But if one's reaching this theoretical conclusion (many have) has not in fact caused one's reactive attitudes to change in any way (this has often been the case),

---

14 This is part of a general point about reasoning. One does not really act at all, in reasoning. Rather one "sees"—one realizes—that this follows from that. Reasoning is more like sensation (or perception) than action: the action in reasoning is at most the getting of the premisses together, and the bringing of the mind to bear on them, if it is anything. It is not the reasoning as such; that is what happens when you do these other things. The same goes for thinking in general.

is one then bound to try to stop treating people as proper objects of gratitude and resentment, praise and blame, and to undertake some course of action to that end? Say one doesn't want to. Isn't that a sufficient reason not to?

It is not clear that it is; or rather, it is not clear that these questions really arise. For it is of course true that if one believes that there are okapi in San Diego zoo, but has not been to check, there is no reason why one should check if one doesn't want to. But the present case is different. One has formed a belief, and there is in a clear sense nothing hidden from view that remains to be actively checked. To claim that one need not try to take into account the apparent fact that people are not proper objects of reactive attitudes if one doesn't want to seems rather like claiming that one need not believe something one believes if one doesn't want to. But one doesn't have such a choice; belief is not subject to the will in this way.[15]

All this may be true; and yet it is also true that the theoretical incompatibilist determinists' reactive attitudes are very unlikely to have been much perturbed by their theoretical views. But can they reasonably tolerate this? Shouldn't they do something about it? It seems that we have to ask once again whether the fact of non-rational commitment can somehow justify, as well as explain, their imperturbability; or whether, alternatively, it can somehow pre-empt the need for any such justification.

The problem is important, because it is not just a problem for incompatibilist determinists. The fact of the impossibility of true self-determination threatens to propel us all into this difficulty—whatever we believe about determinism. People do not make themselves to be the way they are. And this gives rise to a vital sense in which they are not ultimately responsible for what they do. But they go on thinking of themselves as if they were thus responsible.

It is no good saying "I am determined to go on having these feelings and attitudes". To suppose that this dissolves the problem is to make the mistake of fatalism (the mistake of thinking that nothing one can do can change what will happen). It may be true that one is so determined that one does make this mistake. But it is also true— even if everyone is determined to believe everything that he, or she, believes—that it is a mistake, and that people who think clearly will not make it.[16] And if such people are not convinced that appeal to the fact of non-rational commitment can justify as well as explain our reactive feelings and attitudes, or decisively pre-empt the demand for justification, then they cannot really avoid the problem of what now to think, what now to do.[17]

---

15 Although one could hire a hypnotist to wipe out one's belief.

16 Here I am assuming the invalidity of the argument that one cannot believe in determinism because this belief undercuts one's right to appeal to the notions of truth and falsity altogether, cf. J.R. Lucas, *The Freedom of the Will*, § 21; cf. also *Freedom and Belief*, and D. Wiggins, "Freedom, Knowledge, Belief and Causality" in G. Vesey (ed.), *Knowledge and Necessity* [London: Macmillan, 1970].

17 "Carelessness and in-attention alone can afford us any remedy. For this reason", Hume says: "I rely entirely upon them" (*Treatise*, 1.4.2.57/218).

IV. Determinism, Action, and the Self: A Thought Experiment

Reflections such as these can start up odd intellectual fatigues, veering sleights of mind, or a deep and almost contemptuous rejection of the apparently manifest demands of reason. One's commitment to the reactive attitudes is instrumental in this; largely, I suggest, because one's deepest commitment is not to belief in the appropriateness of the interpersonal reactive attitudes, but to belief in the appropriateness of certain self-concerned reactive attitudes. One's deepest commitment is to the view of oneself as truly responsible, both in general and in particular cases of action. The sleights of mind begin because the biggest problems raised by the apparent demands of reason concern oneself. Trying to think through the consequences of these demands, it seems that one risks thinking oneself out of existence, as a *mental someone*. ("A mental someone" is a good description of one absolutely central way in which we think of ourselves. Here as elsewhere I am concerned only with this fact of "cognitive phenomenology", and not at all with the question of what if anything a "mental someone" could possibly be, factually or metaphysically speaking.)

Why does one risk thinking oneself out of existence as a mental someone? Because what one naturally takes oneself to be, *qua* mental someone, is a truly self-determining agent of the impossible kind.[18] One takes it (however unreflectively) that this is an *essential* aspect of what one is, mentally considered: given the way I am, mentally considered, I could not continue to exist and lack this property. So the risk is not merely that a process of tenacious concentration on the thought of determinism (or non-self-determinability) might force me to cease to believe that I had a certain property—true responsibility—whose possession meant a lot to me. It is rather that there might remain nothing that was recognizable as me at all; nothing recognizable as me, the "agent-self", but only a bare consciousness-function, a zombie.

Perhaps the best way to see the force of this suggestion is by means of the following thought-experiment, for it may seem rather vague and farfetched. It is not particularly vague, in fact. What may be true, though, is that one really does have to stop and think about it for oneself with concentration and imagination.

The thought-experiment consists simply in the rigorous application of the belief in determinism to the present course of one's life: one does one's best to think rapidly of every smallest action one performs or movement one makes—or indeed everything whatsoever that happens, so far as one is oneself concerned—as determined; as not, ultimately, determined by oneself; this for a minute or two, say.

This should have the effect of erasing any sense of the presence of a freely deciding and acting "I" in one's thoughts; for—so it seems—there is simply no role for such an "I" to play. It may even be strangely, faintly depressing; or it may give rise to a curious, floating feeling of detached acquiescence in the passing show of one's own psychophysical being; a feeling, not of impotence, but of radical uninvolvement. Or

---

18 The fact that one also takes oneself to be an embodied agent capable of physical action is not at present relevant.

alternatively the feeling may be: I am not really a person; there isn't really anyone there at all.[19]

I take this effect to indicate that one's sense of self is of a profoundly libertarian cast; and to indicate that one naturally and unreflectively conceives of oneself, *qua* the mental planner of action, as standing in some special impossible relation of true-responsibility-creating origination to one's choices and actions. One disappears in the thought experiment because it reveals that one is not possible, so conceived.

At the same time, of course, one does not—cannot—disappear just like that. One's thought naturally and inevitably occurs for one in terms of "I",[20] and one's conception of this "I" remains a conception of a truly responsible self-determining someone. So while one's attempts to grasp the consequences of determinism fully may succeed in bursts, they will in the longer term always break up on one's rock-hard commitment to a self-conception which is wholly incompatible with fully fledged, continually applied belief in determinism.[21]

When this happens, one may continue to have and to try to apply, the thought that everything about one is determined; but it will not be striking with its full force. And when it is striking with less than its full force the thought of one's total determinedness will probably not make it seem that one does not really exist at all (as a mental someone), but, rather, that although one does somehow or other exist (as a mental someone), and although one does continue to act in various ways, still one cannot truly be said to do anything oneself, because determinism gobbles up everything, revealing everything one does to be not really *one's own doing*. (Remember that this is a claim about how things will appear to someone who takes the problem of free will seriously and pursues the thought experiment; as such it is not a rejection of theoretical compatibilism.)

I suggest, therefore, that there are two principal poles around which one's thought is likely to oscillate when one is trying to apply the thought that one is totally determined. At one pole, the freely deciding and acting "mental someone" somehow goes out of existence altogether. At the other pole, the mental someone continues to exist, but one can no longer see oneself as a freely deciding and acting being in any way. One's thought is likely to oscillate around this second pole when the thought-experiment has not been engaged with full force, and is not having its full effect of strangely dissolving the (sense of) self.[22]

---

19 The thought-experiment might make a good meditation exercise for certain schools of Buddhism—see further section VIII below.

20 This is why Lichtenberg's famous objection to Descartes—that he should not have affirmed the certainty of "I think" but only of "It thinks" or "It's thinking" (on the analogy of "It's raining")—is wrongly put. The correct point is simply that when one makes Descartes' move one should not suppose that any conclusion about one's substantial nature follows from the certainty of "I think".

21 Hardened conventional compatibilists are likely to have the most trouble with the thought-experiment, for they are not likely to confuse their theoretical opinions (or prejudices) with their real everyday attitudes to themselves and their actions—in a way that makes it difficult to see the problem.

22 It is at the second pole that we may most vividly encounter what Thomas Nagel calls "the ... erosion of what we do by the subtraction of what happens". See his "Moral Luck",

This is not likely to convince anyone who does not seriously attempt the thought-experiment; and such an appeal to thought-experiment is likely to encounter scepticism. But I do not think that the point can be made adequately in words.

It may be claimed that the thought-experiment is not practicable: the "I" as it occurs in thought[23] can never fully attain the thought that it is itself just part of the determined world, because it can never quite catch up with itself: any judgment of determinedness on its part necessarily involves its taking an eternal view of the object of the judgment, which it cannot have of itself *qua* the thinking subject at present making the judgment. But this is no real problem. Even if one were to become aware of this point,[24] it would not check the *general* effect that would be produced in one by thinking of everything one is and does as totally determined—the effect of seeming to erase the "I" as ordinarily conceived. Suppose one did think about one's thinking in particular as a completely determined phenomenon. Then whatever thought one had, one would, pursuing the thought-experiment, think of that thought too as determined. And, this being so, no thought would ever be able to emerge as the true product of the familiar "I", the putative true originator of thoughts, decisions, and actions that is not a merely determined phenomenon: this "I" would perpetually evanesce, however far one pursued the possible regress of thoughts about thoughts about thoughts. (This is just one way among others in which the thought-experiment could develop.)

In fact the idea that one cannot be supposed to be a truly responsible originator of one's thoughts or ideas can acquire experiential (as opposed to merely theoretical) impact without recourse to the tricky rigours of this thought-experiment. The point is a familiar one (already touched on in note 14). Thoughts simply "occur" to one; one just "has" ideas, they simply "come to one"—whether they are philosophical, mathematical, or scientific (in which case the occurrence of one's thoughts and ideas is somehow controlled by one's wish to arrive at the truth) or whether they are musical, fictional, or poetical (in which case their occurrence may be controlled by many things). There is a commonly felt sense in which one has no real responsibility for any of them.[25] I think it is helpful to dwell on this (it is part of doing philosophy).

---

in *Mortal Questions* (Cambridge: Cambridge University Press, 1979), esp. pp. 37–8. Cf. also Bernard Williams' paper on "Moral Luck", in *Moral Luck* (Cambridge: Cambridge University Press, 1981), to which Nagel's paper was a response.

23 Here again I am concerned only with the *character* of our thought, not with the idea that there could be some special mental entity called the "I" or the "self".

24 Discussed by Ryle in "The Systematic Elusiveness of 'I'", *The Concept of Mind* (Harmondsworth: Penguin, 1969), Ch. 6, § 7.

25 It is worth quoting Rimbaud's well-known remarks in full: "C'est faux de dire: Je pense: on devrait dire on me pense ... Je est un autre. Tant pis pour le bois qui se trouve violon" (letter to Georges Izambard, 13 May 1871); and again "Les romantiques ... prouvent si bien que la chanson est si peu souvent l'oeuvre, c'est à dire la pensée ... *comprise* du chanteur .... Car Je est un autre. Si le cuivre s'éveille clairon, il n'y a rien de sa faute. Cela m'est évident: J'assiste à l'éclosion de ma pensée [I am a spectator at the unfolding of my thought]: je la regarde, je l'écoute .... " (Letter to Paul Demeny, 15 May 1871; *Oeuvres Completes* [Paris: Gallimard, 1972]).

And it is worth reflecting on Hume's famous claim, that when one earnestly inspects one's own mind for the "I", the self, one never finds anything there.[26]

Serious incompatibilist determinists (or non-self-determinationists, i.e. those who believe that true self-determination is necessary for freedom and that it is impossible) should try the thought-experiment; for them, after all, undertaking it involves nothing more than dwelling with special concentration on something they already believe to be true. Those who learn to maintain the state of mind induced by the thought-experiment will be well on the way to a truly thoroughgoing, truly lived, or as I shall say *genuine* belief in determinism or non-self-determinability. (They may be on the way to nirvana.) But it is important to be clear what this involves. A person may *theoretically* fully accept that he, or she, is wholly a product of his or her heredity and environment—many of us do—and yet, in everyday life, have *nothing like* the kind of self-conception that is here required of the genuine incompatibilist determinist (non-self-determinationist). In fact such a self-conception seems scarcely possible for human beings. It seems to require the dissolution of any recognizable human sense of self. Certainly one cannot adopt such a radically "objective" attitude to oneself at will.

Perhaps this is not very clearly expressed. But I think the general idea will become clear to most of those who concentrate on the problem, or undertake the thought-experiment. Those who disdain the thought-experiment, or claim that it does not work, may fail to grasp the general idea. It does work; and this is a very important fact about us.

V. What Might Happen

These considerations suggest that there may after all be a sense in which the question (considered in section II) about what it would be rational to do if determinism were true is an "unreal" question. For it may be an unreal question for anyone who has become a *genuine* incompatibilist determinist (non-self-determinationist) in the present sense—for anyone who has gone beyond merely theoretical acceptance of determinism (or non-self-determinability).

Consider a man who is an incompatibilist and who has just come to believe that determinism is true, and who is struggling to attain a true perspective on his situation. How is he to think of himself as he sits back, rubs his eye, looks for a book in the bookshelves, debates whether to give more money to famine relief, thinking perhaps, of each of his thoughts and movements that it is determined, and thinking that his thinking this is determined in turn, and so on?

We may suppose that he does not make the fatalist mistake—the mistake (for example) of ceasing to try to get what he wants because he thinks it is already determined whether he will get it or not, in such a way that he can do nothing about it. He knows perfectly well that his own planning and action are real and effective parts of the continuing deterministic process. It is rather that when he does something intentionally which he feels to be reprehensible (say), he may then think to himself:

---

26 Hume, *Treatise*, 1.4.6.3/252.

that was determined to happen, and yet if I had not done it that too would have been determined to happen. This is a very ordinary thought in philosophy. But what is it like to take it seriously in life, trying to apprehend every detail of one's life as determined?

He may find that he feels that *he* (i.e. he the truly responsible agent, he as he automatically conceives of himself in his natural, unreconstructed thought about himself) can do nothing at all. Here he is at the second of the two main poles of serious self-applied determinism: he feels he exists, but that he cannot really *act* at all. This is how he puts it, at least. Or rather, this is how he would put it, were it not for the fact that, relaxing his application of the thought of determinism to himself, and being an as yet unreconstructed incompatibilist determinist, he still feels completely responsible for what he has done. He feels he simply knows that he knew at the time of action that he could have done otherwise. He is unable to accept that he is exempt from responsibility or blame, or indeed from praise, because it was determined to happen as it did. (Perhaps he followed his desires and neglected his duty.) Yet he also now believes that the way he is, and his decision, are things for which he is ultimately in no way responsible. And when, see-sawing back, he concentrates again on this thought, he finds, again, that he can no longer make sense of the idea of his performing an action that is truly *his* action. For the sense of self he naturally has (and which is expressed here by the italicization of "he" and "his") is irremediably incompatible with any deep acceptance of the idea that all he is and does is determined.[27]

He may think as follows: that to choose to (try to) abandon his personal reactive attitudes is not really possible, because only a free agent, which he does not now consider himself to be, can really have a reason for action which is really its own reason. There may be a train of practical deliberation going on in his head, but he feels that it is not really *his* thought at all (although it feels just like it, as soon as he stops concentrating on his determinedness), but (because) a determined process. He thinks that he cannot reason or deliberate in a way that culminates in a decision which is truly his, and which is such that the ensuing action is something for which he is truly responsible; or indeed something that *he* really did. For he knows that what he thinks of as his choice is determined, however much he may hesitate or contrasuggestibly change his mind. And so, stuck with his unreconstructed sense of self, he cannot think of it as really *his* choice. To talk of freedom here, as compatibilists do, is, he thinks, to talk of the freedom of the turnspit, or of the self-sealing tank.[28] It is the "wretched subterfuge" of compatibilism, a "petty word-jugglery".[29] It is "so much gobbledegook".[30] It is not really to talk of freedom at all.

---

27 With suitable minor adjustments, the same story can be told of a non-self-determinationist.

28 Cf. Kant in the *Critique of Practical Reason*, trans. L.W. Beck (London: Longmans, 1898), p. 191 (*Ak. V.* 97); and D. Davidson in "Freedom to Act", in T. Honderich (ed.), *Essays on Freedom of Action* (London: Routledge & Kegan Paul, 1973), p. 141.

29 Kant, *Critique of Practical Reason*, pp. 189–90 (*Ak. V.* 96).

30 G.E.M. Anscombe, "Causality and Determination", *Metaphysics and the Philosophy of Mind* (Oxford: Blackwell, 1981), p. 146.

So the whole picture of the thoughtful incompatibilist determinist coming to believe in determinism, and then raising the question of what to do about it, may be ill-conceived. The question may be completely unreal for him, so long as he concentratedly applies the thought of determinism to himself. For he may then feel that he cannot really choose to do, or do, anything, in the way he thought. This rejection of the possibility of real choice or action is, certainly, a piece of reasoning on his part. But it too cannot be thought to have any practical consequences, or to rationalize any decision—such as a decision not to choose or decide anything on the grounds that it is strictly speaking impossible to do so. One cannot decide not to decide anything on the grounds that one cannot decide anything.

But nor can he decide to abandon himself to his determinedness, for that too would be something determined, hence not something he really did, in the vital sense. He cannot think "I find that these reasons to do X occur to me, and *since* X now appears to me (determinedly, I know) to be the best thing to do, I will do X", as if he thus had access to a further reason to do X—the knowledge that reasons to do X have determinedly outweighed reasons to do anything else (or, worse, as if ability to take account of what was determinedly the case, so far as his reason-state was concerned, somehow gave him access to a secret, undetermined fulcrum point of free decision). These would be simple mistakes. Correcting himself, and foreseeing the paralytic regresses that threaten, he may tell himself not to think about the nature of his practical reasoning any more than he used to. But this too will involve a decision—a decision to try to think nothing. So it will not really be his decision, in his view.

This is a strange drama, an enactment of the deep problem of free will. In the end only the exigencies of everyday life will carry him forward. The continual tendency of his unreconstructed thought will be to reinsert him, conceived as a truly self-determining mental someone, into his thought and deliberation. And continually he will correct this tendency. For nothing, he realizes, can be done by him, so conceived. Nothing can be done by him in the sense that matters to him; things can only happen. Whatever he starts to plan and do, it is whipped away from him, only to appear as not really his own, by the thought that it is entirely determined.

It seems, then, that a genuine belief in determinism or non-self-determinationism, uneasily coupled with an unreconstructed conception of self, may produce a *total paralysis* of all purposive thought as it is ordinarily conceived and experienced. To experience things in this way is not to make the mistake of fatalism. It is simply to experience the clash between determinism (non-self-determinationism) and our ordinary conception of freedom in a particularly vivid manner. (It is useful to think of morally weighted choices here.)

There are certainly other more compatibilistic ways of thinking and theorizing about deliberation and action, some of which will be discussed in the next section, and which are of such a kind that when we employ them, we may find that we are quite untroubled by the thought of determinism. But it does not follow that the present story is not accurate as a story of what might happen to a newly fledged, thoughtful incompatibilist determinist (non-self-determinationist). What may follow is that we are deeply inconsistent in our characteristically very vague thought about freedom, action, deliberation, and ourselves. (Seasoned philosophical compatibilists are likely to find it much harder than most to appreciate the force of these points. Perhaps they should imagine facing the following choice: if you agree to submit to twenty years of torture—torture of a kind that leaves no time for moral self-congratulation—you will save ten others from the same fate. [Perhaps they should agree to be hypnotized into believing that they really are facing such a choice—hypnotized in such a way that, afterwards, they remember exactly what it felt like.])

This story is not just a curiosity, for although determinism is unverifiable even if it is true, the non-self-determinationist position—according to which true self-determination is (a) necessary for true responsibility and (b) provably impossible—appears to be correct.[31] It is therefore worth considering some other suggestions about what might happen to a new incompatibilist determinist or non-self-determinationist.

One possibility is this. One might simply cease to believe that the specifically moral reactive attitudes and practices of praise and blame were justified or appropriate, and losing this belief might cause one to cease to be moved to praise and blame. Generally, believing determinism to be true and just· being generally speaking very rational*istic* might cause a man to come to have more objective attitudes, without his trying to *do* anything. And this might occur despite the fact that he felt that the quality of his life suffered greatly as a result. On the other hand, his moral and non-moral reactive attitudes might be quite unaffected by his new theoretical belief, given the strength of his commitment to them. (This is what usually happens.) We are all effortlessly capable of the magnificent inconsistency of beliefs and attitudes that this appears to involve. And this, of course, is something that gives extremely powerful support to the commitment theorists' claim about the unrenounceability of the commitment.

Perhaps one may picture the reactive feelings and attitudes as composing a spectrum. At one end—this is very rough—there are the most basic feelings and sentiments of pleasure and "unpleasure", aggression, animal attraction, fear, anger, and so on—the "true" passions, those most clearly undergone or suffered. At the other end there are the most purely moral sentiments and feelings of approval and disapproval, praise and blame. Resentment and gratitude may be seen as lying somewhere near the centre of the spectrum, distanced from the basic passions by their appearing to involve a considerable degree of mental sophistication, but distanced also from the most purely moral feelings and sentiments—for resentment and gratitude could survive recognition of inappropriateness where tendencies to praise and blame succumbed: "I realize it's absurd to blame him (the lunatic), but I can't help feeling resentful"; "I know it's only an android robot, but I can't help feeling grateful."

There are different ways of categorizing emotions and feelings, but this ranking according to basicness seems to match closely the ordering which may be derived by comparing their dependence for appropriateness upon certain beliefs, such as belief in true responsibility, and the relative likelihood of their alteration given change in these beliefs. Dependence upon beliefs varies inversely with basicness. For example: a tendency to get angry with people is less likely to diminish in response to belief in

---

31 Cf. *Freedom and Belief*, 2.1.

determinism than a tendency to blame them (inanimate objects can make one angry, and it does not seem that this is irrational, whereas blaming them is.)

Any individual's case will be far more complicated than this schema suggests, however. In a particular case there will doubtless be special non-rational dependencies, formed as a result of traumatic experiences, for example, or a religious upbringing. And then, some people are naturally far more quick to anger—and to forgive—than others. One man's anger at people might turn to anger at the whole creation by his acquiring a belief in determinism—this would be a case of a "basic" feeling responding to a change in belief. Alternatively, he might hold that a natural and ultimate feature of creation was a rigid code of punishment, and thus retain his practice of moral judgment even after coming to believe in determinism: "It is perhaps a terrible fault in creation, but you have done wrong and are to blame." This would be a case of a more purely moral sentiment failing to respond to change in belief. Calvinists do not hold (earthly) punishment to have a purely pragmatic justification.

What would happen generally is unpredictable. But it does seem conceivable that a highly rationalistic and generally un-neurotic man, low on non-rational dependencies, might lose (not actively abandon) only those attitudes which were in his view justifiable only by his discarded belief in true responsibility; being one in whom, as one might say, the causality of reason was strong, and non-rational commitment to belief in true responsibility weak. But he could not simply lose them by choice. Nor does calling him "rationalistic" carry any implication that others would be rational to set about trying to abandon these attitudes. Nor do I think that we can fully imagine what it would be like to be him, if he did lose all the attitudes in question.[32]

VI. Natural Compatibilism

Our sense of self and of freedom is in many respects profoundly libertarian in character. But it is also naturally and unhesitatingly compatibilistic in many other respects. And since this natural compatibilism is part of what underlies our commitment to belief in freedom, it deserves some consideration at this point. (A full treatment of it would be a lengthy matter; but Hume made some of the relevant points in the *Enquiry*, and many others have been made by compatibilists since.)[33]

---

32 The quite remarkable readiness with which human beings slip into adopting apparently true-responsibility-presupposing attitudes (like blame, resentment, and gratitude) to many classes of objects—animals, stones, cars, aeroplanes, computers, the world in general—that they would not in their cooler moments dream of classifying as free agents can be interpreted in more than one way. It can be seen simply as further evidence of how profoundly we are committed to true-responsibility-presupposing feelings and attitudes. Or (less usefully) it can be seen as casting doubt on the extent to which these attitudes are essentially true-responsibility-presupposing. The truth is that they are true-responsibility-presupposing; it is just that we are even more irrational than we think.

33 D. Dennett's *Elbow Room: The Varieties of Free Will Worth Wanting* (Oxford: Clarendon Press, 1985) is among other things a contribution to the description of the extent of our natural compatibilism.

The principal idea is this: so far as many aspects of our general sense of ourselves as free agents are concerned, we are not inclined to think that they are put in question *in any way* by the truth of determinism or non-self-determinability. Sometimes this is a reasonable attitude on our part; sometimes it is not. It depends on what aspect of our sense of freedom is in question. But in either case it is a natural compatibilist attitude, in the present sense of the phrase.

1. Thus—for example—many people are naturally (pre-philosophically) inclined to accept accounts of how they came to be as they are that simply rule out any kind of true self-determination; and they can in addition easily be brought to see that true self-determination is not really possible. (To say this may seem inconsistent with the account of our natural sense of self given above; but the inconsistency is in our view of ourselves, not in the account given of our view of ourselves.) Many people accept that they are, ultimately, entirely determined in all aspects of their character by their heredity and environment. But it follows from this that, whether the heredity-and-environment process that has shaped them is deterministic or not, they cannot themselves be truly or ultimately self-determining in any way. And yet they do not feel that their freedom is put in question by this—even though they naturally conceive of themselves as free in the ordinary, strong, true-responsibility-involving sense. To this extent they are natural compatibilists. This is a very common position.

Those who occupy this position cannot have thought about the matter very hard, you may say. That may be so. But very many thoughtful and intelligent people occupy exactly this position. Even those who are, as philosophers, revisionary compatibilists who hold that our ordinary strong notion of freedom is indefensible, reveal unmistakably, in the everyday conduct of their lives, that they too occupy it.

2. To this one may add the fact that we are neither inclined to suppose that we can be self-determining with respect to (the particular content of) our beliefs (for we simply desire that what we believe should be determined in a reliable, truth-inducing manner by the way things are), nor inclined to suppose that we can be radically self-determined with respect to our desires—or, generally, with respect to all those things other than beliefs that motivate our actions. It is true, as remarked, that we can cultivate tastes and traits; but we readily recognize that, if we do so, we do so because we are motivated to do so by certain desires and attitudes that we already have; or by certain beliefs about what is true or right that we already have, beliefs with respect to which we have our normal attitude: that of supposing that they are true, and, briefly, that we have in coming to hold them been determined to do so simply by the way things are. That is, in our ordinary thought we recognize, more or less explicitly, that true self-determination is impossible—even independently of acknowledging the truth of physical determinism or heredity-and-environment determinism. But we also feel that the fact that it is impossible poses no threat at all to our freedom. And in this we are again natural compatibilists.

It is true that one reason why we feel that this impossibility poses no threat to freedom is that we naturally credit ourselves with an *in*compatibilistically conceived power of free decision that we see as rendering us somehow independent of our ultimately non-self-determined beliefs, desires, and so on (cf. *Freedom and Belief*, 2.9, 3.4). But we also naturally accept that explanations in terms of ultimately non-self-determined beliefs and desires can be *full* explanations of our actions, without our freedom being threatened; and it is this that makes it reasonable to see the present point about beliefs and desires as illustrating part of our natural compatibilism.

3. The above description of natural compatibilism involves reference to determinism, and in particular to heredity-and-environment determinism, and it may be questioned to what extent it can be said to articulate a *natural* (unreflective, pre-philosophical) compatibilistic outlook. The claim that it is natural can be defended by appeal to the idea that even if people do not ordinarily think at all about heredity and environment, or about how or why they are free, still there are certain things that they—we—would naturally be led to say if asked certain questions about freedom. Presented with objections to their initial responses (questioned further in a genially aporetic manner) there are certain further moves that they would also be naturally inclined to make. All these can be supposed to form part of natural compatibilism as currently understood.

As remarked, a full discussion of natural compatibilism would be a lengthy business. Here, by way of example, I propose to consider just one natural compatibilist aspect of the general phenomenology of freedom: a point about our attitude to our desires or non-epistemic motives generally considered. (Note that the phenomenology of freedom is not restricted to description—to saying what our sense of freedom is like. It can also offer explanations—explanations of why we have the sort of sense of freedom we do have.)

4. For any desire with which we are concerned at some particular time, we are not usually in the least concerned to be able to say that we are, somehow, the originators of the desire—whatever sense can be made of this. Our unreflective attitude to it is that it is simply there, in the way that a chair, a feature of the world, is simply there. I don't and I can't choose my desires. And I don't have to choose them for them to be mine (or to be free when they move me to act). They are just a part of me. This is how I am. One's desires are not of course publicly observable in the way that chairs are. The point of the analogy is rather one's desires are or can be as much a fact about the world that one confronts as the fact of a chair's being there. I like loganberries, the chair is there in front of me. A desire can be importunate, I can bump into a chair. There are of course important differences in the "being-there" of desire and of chair—in the experience one has, with respect to both desire and chair, of being passive with respect to the fact of their existence or presence. But there are also important similarities.[34]

One might say that some desires are more like the fact of having a body of a particular sort than they are like chairs in particular places, in that they are part of oneself, and are more permanently "just there", and are unthinkingly taken into account in one's thought and action (as is one's body both by proprioceptive and kinasesthetic sense, and by one's less immediate sensory and cognitive awareness of it). This point does not displace the point about the chair-like objectivity of some desires; however, it only complicates it. For it remains true that many desires are in an important sense apprehended by us as just being there; as being in a sense external

---

34 Moral beliefs also characteristically have this sort of just-thereness; one confronts the chair, one confronts one's belief that one ought to do X.

to the mental self that confronts them. And it remains true that their just-thereness is not seen as posing any sort of threat to freedom. And this fact forms part of the explanation of part of our natural compatibilism. It forms part of the explanation of why we may be naturally quite unworried when confronted by philosophers with the thought that our desires can be said to be determined in us in the sense of not having been freely adopted during some process of self-determination: we never really thought they were the result of self-determination anyway, or that they had to be if we were to be free.[35]

But it also forms part of the explanation of our natural *in*compatibilism. (This is a typical complication in the phenomenology of freedom.) For it also forms part of the explanation of the strength of our tendency to conceive of ourselves as possessed of a self separate from, and somehow irreducibly over and above, all its particular desires, pro-attitudes, and so on. And in this respect it turns out to be central to the naturally occurring libertarian notion of the truly self-determining "agent-self" that is in its choice of action potentially completely independent of any of its particular (determined or not self-determined) desires, pro-attitudes, and so on. This is just one more instance in which naturally compatibilist and naturally incompatibilist (and indeed libertarian) elements in our thought about freedom share common roots.

5. The principal idea behind the suggestion that there is a sense in which we are naturally compatibilist in our thought about freedom is, as remarked, simply this: there are a great many aspects of our experience of ourselves as free agents which, *either for good or for bad reasons*, we do not feel to be threatened in any way by the truth of determinism or non-self-determinability. Most presentations of natural compatibilism have been undertaken by philosophers who are themselves compatibilists, and who wish to show that compatibilism is true. They are therefore only interested in the good reasons. But uncommitted phenomenology of freedom takes the bad reasons with the good, and finds them of equal interest in giving an account of the ways in which we are naturally compatibilist.

In conclusion, let me mention something which has intentionally been ignored until now, and which not only provides one of the strongest arguments in favour of compatibilism considered as a philosophical theory, but is also one of the principal features of natural compatibilism. It is this. Behind the whole compatibilist enterprise lies the valid and important insight that, from one centrally important point of view, freedom is nothing more than a matter of being able to do what one wants or chooses or decides or thinks right or best to do, *given* one's character, desires, values, beliefs (moral or otherwise), circumstances, and so on. Generally speaking, we have this freedom. For determinism does not affect it at all, and it has nothing whatever to do with any supposed sort of ultimate self-determination, or any particular power to determine what one's character, desires, and so on will be. It is true that the fact that we generally have this freedom provides no support for the idea that we are or can be "truly" self-determining in the way that still appears to be necessary for true responsibility. But we can indeed be self-determining in

---

[35] It is *also* arguable, however, that there is a (rather slippery) sense in which we conceive our relation to our desires, pro-attitudes and so on as if they were things we were somehow or in some degree responsible for. See the next section. Both arguments may be correct.

the compatibilist sense of being able by our own action, and in the light of our necessarily non-self-determined characters and desires, to determine to a very considerable extent what happens to us.

Compatibilists who stress this point have a powerful question to ask: "What else could one possibly suppose, or reflectively require, that freedom could or should be, other than this?" But the old incompatibilist answer remains. This account of freedom does nothing to establish that we are truly responsible for our actions, nor, in particular, to establish that we are or can be truly *morally* responsible for our actions, in the ordinary, strong, desert-entailing sense. Nor, correspondingly, does it provide any reason for thinking that people either are or can be free or truly responsible in a way that could render the "personal-reactive" attitudes truly appropriate. It seems that nothing can do this. But this still seems to be what we want.

So much for natural compatibilism; it can be developed much further. I wish now to say something more about our natural incompatibilism, and in so doing to return to the question of the nature of our commitment to belief in freedom.

VII. The True Centre of Commitment

If our commitment to belief in freedom and responsibility were entirely (or even only primarily) grounded in our experience of other people, then I think we would lack a truly satisfactory explanation of its strength. Such an explanation is swiftly forthcoming when it is realized that it is grounded primarily in our experience of our own agency, and only secondarily in our experience of other people as proper objects of the reactive attitudes. The true centre of one's commitment to the notion of human freedom lies in one's attitude to and experience of oneself. The notion is integral to one's deepest sense of oneself as a self-determining planner and performer of action, someone who can create things, make a sacrifice, and do a misdeed.

To say that the true centre of one's commitment lies in one's attitude to and experience of oneself is not to deny that one's attitude to and experience of oneself is deeply determined by one's interaction with others, and, in particular, by the kind of interaction necessary for acquisition of language (though it will be argued later that a solitary being could have an ordinarily strong sense of self as truly responsible). So far as human beings are concerned, it is simply to consider two things that develop in us in the course of our necessarily social development—our sense of ourselves as truly responsible and our sense of others as truly responsible; to claim that the nature and causes of these two things can profitably be distinguished, in certain respects at least; and to claim that the former is more important than the latter, so far as our general commitment to belief in true-responsibility-creating self-determination is concerned.

A naturalistic explanation of this sense of self-determination would connect it tightly with our sense, massively and incessantly confirmed since earliest infancy, of our ability to do what we want to do in order to (try to) get what we want, by performing a vast variety of actions, great and small, walking where we want, making ourselves understood, picking up this and putting down that. We pass our days in more or less continual and almost entirely successful self-directing intentional activity, and we know it.[36] Even if we don't always achieve our aims, when we act, we almost always perform a movement of the kind we intended to perform, and in that vital sense (vital for the sense of self-determining self-control) we are almost entirely successful in our action.

This gives rise to a sense of freedom to act, of complete self-control, of responsibility in self-directedness, that is in itself compatibilistically unexceptionable, and is quite untouched by arguments against true responsibility based on the impossibility of self-determination. But it is precisely this compatibilistically speaking unexceptionable sense of freedom and efficacy that is one of the fundamental bases of the growth in us of the compatibilistically speaking *im*permissible sense of true responsibility. To observe a child of two fully in control of its limbs, doing what it wants to do with them, and to this extent fully free to act in the compatibilist sense of the phrase, and to realize that it is precisely such unremitting experience of self-control that is the deepest foundation of our naturally *in*compatibilistic sense of true-responsibility-entailing self-determination, is to understand one of the most important facts about the genesis and power of our ordinary strong sense of freedom.

One reason why we advance from the permissible to the impermissible sense of freedom is perhaps a merely negative one, remarked on by Spinoza: ignorant of the causes of our desires, we do not normally experience our character, desires, or pro-attitudes as determined in us in any way at all; let alone in any objectionable way. We don't think back behind ourselves as we now find ourselves. It can happen that we do so, of course. But even if it does happen—even if some particular desire is experienced, in its importunacy, as somehow foreign, imposing itself from outside the self, as it were—this probably only serves, by providing a contrast, to strengthen our general sense that our desires and pro-attitudes are not determined in us. For if a desire is experienced as importunate, as imposing itself on one, as unwanted, then there must be present some other desire or pro-attitude in the light of which the first one is experienced as unwanted or as imposing itself. And the second desire or pro-attitude will presumably not also be experienced as an imposition, as alien. It will presumably be a pro-attitude which one "identifies" with, and apprehends as part of oneself, and acquiesces in.

A great deal is locked up in this acquiescence. (It is here that our naturally incompatibilist thought appears to run directly counter to our naturally compatibilist acceptance of the "just-thereness" of desires discussed in the last section.) For although it is unlikely to involve any explicit sense that one has been in any way actively self-determining as to character, it does nevertheless seem to involve an implicit sense that one is, generally, somehow in control of and answerable for how one is; even, perhaps, for those aspects of one's character that one doesn't particularly like.[37] As for those pro-attitudes and aspects of one's character that are welcome to one, it is as if the following ghostly subjunctive conditional lurks in

---

36 Most of these actions are routine or trivial, more or less thoughtlessly performed. But this in no way diminishes the importance of the experience of their performance as a source of the sense of self-determinability that we ordinarily have.

37 Consider the sense of sin. People who see themselves as sinners do not only feel guilty about giving in to bad aspects of their character; they also feel guilty about (responsible for having) these bad features in the first place.

one's attitude to them: if *per impossibile* I were to be (had been) able to choose my character, then these are the features I would choose (would have chosen).[38] This, I suggest, contributes importantly to the impermissible sense of true responsibility for themselves that most people have, more or less obscurely, more or less constantly.[39]

But it is not the principal reason for which we have the impermissible sense of true responsibility. The principal reason, I think, concerns the nature of our experience of choice. It is simply that we are, in the most ordinary situations of choice, unable not to think that we will be truly or absolutely responsible for our choice, whatever we choose. Our natural thought may be expressed as follows: even if my character is indeed just something given (a product of heredity and environment, or whatever), I am still able to choose (and hence act) completely freely and truly responsibly, given how I now am and what I now know; this is so whatever else is the case—determinism or no determinism.

This thought is reinforced by the point just considered: according to which something that is in itself negative—the absence of any general sense that our desires, pro-attitudes, character, and so on, are *not* ultimately self-determined—is implicitly taken as equivalent to some sort of positive self-determination. Certainly we do not ordinarily suppose that we have gone through some sort of active process of self-determination at some particular past time; but it seems accurate to say that we do unreflectively experience ourselves rather as we would experience ourselves if we did believe that we had engaged in some such activity of self-determination.

There are many complexities here. But the main causes of the development of our sense of true responsibility out of our unremitting and compatibilistically speaking unexceptionable sense of complete self-control may perhaps be summarized as follows.

1. We tend to think that we have a will (a power of decision) distinct from all our particular motives.
2. In all the ordinary situations of choice, we think that we are absolutely free to choose *whatever* else is the case (even if determinism is true, for example), and are so just because of the fact of our full appreciation of our situation. (Our experience of freedom is of course particularly vivid in cases of morally significant decisions.)
3. In some vague and unexamined fashion, we tend to think of ourselves as in some manner responsible for—answerable for—how we are.[40]

---

38 It is hardly surprising that the subjunctive conditional as it were confirms the central, acceptable *status quo*; for the "I" that features in the conditional is in a sense actually constituted, as something with pro-attitudes that imagines choosing its pro-attitudes, by the very pro-attitudes that it imagines choosing.

39 To say this is not to say that people cannot occasionally—or even chronically—be disgusted by themselves. There are many complications here. Some of them are illustrated by H. Frankfurt in *The Importance of What We Care About* (Cambridge: Cambridge University Press, 1988), Chs 2, 4, 5.

40 For these points, see *Freedom and Belief*, 2.8, 3.4, 3.6. E.H. Carr asserts that "normal adult beings are morally responsible for their own personality" (*What Is History?*, p. 89); Kant

All these aspects of the sense of true responsibility directly concern only one's experience of oneself and one's own agency.[41]

Various other ways of bringing out the independence of the sense of oneself as truly responsible from the sense of other people as so responsible suggest themselves. For example: surely one could come to be a sceptic about other minds and still continue to believe as strongly as ever in one's own freedom?

To this it may be objected that belief in the existence of other minds is at least a genetic condition of acquisition of commitment to belief in freedom. But the objection can be met as follows: (a), belief in other minds, may perhaps be a genetic condition of—or at least an invariable concomitant of—(b), the acquisition of a sense of self, and of (c), language-acquisition (and indeed of (d), acquisition of the intellectual complexity necessary for conceiving explicitly of, and then doubting the existence of, other minds). And (b) and even perhaps (c) may be conditions of the possibility of (e), the acquisition of a sense of oneself as truly responsible. But a genetic-condition claim of this sort is simply not a claim of the right kind to provide grounds for an objection to the view that one could come to doubt the existence of other minds without this affecting one's conviction as to one's own freedom in any way; and there does not seem to be any special, independent connection between (a) and (e), such as might be shown to hold if it could be shown that possession of other-reactive attitudes were actually essential for possession of the notion of true responsibility.[42]

---

wrote of "man's character, which he himself creates" (*Critique of Practical Reason*, trans. L.W. Beck, p. 101); Sartre talked of "le choix que tout homme me fait de sa personnalité".

41 There are a number of other familiar things that prevent us from experiencing ourselves and the world as determined in a way that might undermine our sense of freedom. For example: there is the fact that a person's own future choices and decisions are "unpredictable in principle" for that person (cf. e.g. D.M. MacKay, "On the Logical Indeterminacy of a Free Choice", *Mind* 69 [1960], and D.F. Pears, "Predicting and Deciding", in *Questions in the Philosophy of Mind* [London: Duckworth, 1975]). There is the experiential quality of uncertainty and dithering indecision: it seems that things could so easily go either way (cf. Hume, *Treatise*, 2.3.2.2/408): it seems absurd to say that it is entirely determined which way they do go. There is the fact that even if determinism is true, what happens in the world in general does not produce any sense in us that it is deterministic in character (though we may be convinced materialists and believe firmly in the existence of deterministic laws of nature). For there are so many things that "could so easily have happened" that did not happen in fact (or vice versa). One might so easily not have met one's lover, husband, or wife. Glancing at a newspaper left on the underground train, one may pick it up and read an announcement that changes one's life. Most lives contain many events of this sort. What happens seems to us to have an essentially fluid and open character. Perhaps we are not sufficiently reflective, but it is hard for us, in such circumstances, to be very *impressed* by the thought that our choices and actions may be entirely determined phenomena.

42 Furthermore: although unreflective belief in the existence of other minds is doubtless an invariable concomitant of language-learning here on earth, and as things are, it seems quite possible that a child might learn a language from other people (or even from actually experienceless robots), a constant theme of whose everyday conversation (or "conversation") was that there was nothing it was like to be them. Although this might not at first make much sense to the child, and although it might at first suppose them to be like itself, it could

More simply: it seems possible that a being might develop a strong sense of freedom (a sense of freedom that was in all essentials the same as ours) in a world in which there were no other creatures like itself, and no creatures which were such as to cause it to come to suppose that they were free—although there were, we may suppose, creatures which were such as to cause it to form the belief that they had experiences and pursued goals. The solitary being's sense of freedom might derive from its having to make difficult choices, life-determining choices, perhaps, about which of several equally attractive but very different and not co-attainable ends to pursue. It would not have to have any sense of moral good and bad. It might simply have a powerful sense that it was entirely up to it what it did. (This said, it must be granted that a sense of moral right and wrong acts powerfully in fostering a sense of true responsibility, as Kant saw.)[43]

It may be objected that the solitary being would have to be linguistically endowed, and self-conscious, in order to be free—that these may be necessary conditions of free agenthood. If so, it might be said, it would need company, in order to acquire a language. However, logical possibility provides for the idea that it may just be created self-conscious and already possessed of a language, or at least the capacity for language-like thought.[44] Alternatively, it may be brought up by other members of its own species to a point at which it is fully possessed of language, and then left to fend for itself after all memory of the existence of other sentient beings has been wiped from its mind. Surviving and flourishing, making difficult choices, it may develop or retain a strong sense of freedom of choice without any thought of others at all.

Suppose that this solitary being is persistently but by no means always hindered by constraining circumstances in the execution of its intentions. This being so, it may

---

presumably grow up into the firm (and possibly true) belief that there was nothing it was like to be any of its interlocutors. Growing up in this way, it could acquire a normally powerful sense of its actions being up to it in some absolute fashion.

43 Here there is a complication worth noting. It is true that the general experience of difficult choice contributes vitally to the "impermissible" sense of true responsibility, in the ordinary case. But the phenomenology of making a difficult (and let us say non-moral) choice in which one believes that there is a *right* and a *wrong* decision, if only one could work out which was which, need involve nothing at all that conflicts with a wholly compatibilistic view of things. In this case one considers and reconsiders the pros and the cons, and what one wants is simply that it should become clear which is the right choice. One wants to come to see which is best; and there is nothing in this experience that either involves or gives rise to any sense of true responsibility—any more than there is in considering which of a number of melons is ripest, or in wanting to be able to read the words on a sign that is just too far away. In cases like this the phenomenology of difficult choice is essentially that of wanting to form a true belief, and, so far at least, need involve nothing of the sense of radical freedom that may be produced by facing a dramatic conflict of duty and desire, or an important, life-determining choice between two very different morally neutral options which are in one's opinion equally attractive all things considered (between which there is "nothing to choose").

44 Possessed, that is, of at least the following: a disposition to have just the same sorts of experience, qualitatively speaking, that a solitary Robinson Crusoe who had forgotten that other people existed might have, so far as those of his experiences that he himself would be inclined to classify as experiences of thinking or speaking in language were concerned.

acquire a sense of freedom of *action*—that which it feels when unhindered—which is importantly different from the sense of freedom of *choice* just mentioned. Neither of these senses of freedom depends essentially on interaction with other people, or upon preparedness to attribute freedom to others, but only on the private experience of deliberation and action. One's belief that others are free has the power it has because it is, first and foremost, a belief that they are like one finds oneself to be. We attribute to others the same sort of consciousness of responsibility for, and hence freedom of, choice and action that we cannot but attribute to ourselves. It is not as if adversion either to the circumstances of our learning the word "free", as members of a linguistic community, or to the dubiety of the "argument from analogy", can undercut this point. On the contrary: the availability of this point, and others like it, illustrates the risk of exaggerating both the consequences of Wittgenstein's "private language" argument and the error allegedly involved in putting forward the argument from analogy in answer to certain skeptical puzzles.

Certainly our acquisition of an understanding of the words "free" and "truly responsible" proceeds in such a way that we are, ordinarily, *as* prepared to apply these words to others as we are to ourselves. And certainly we are, in being committed to the reactive attitudes to other people, committed to the belief that they are truly responsible agents. This is not denied. The claim is merely that the deepest point of attachment of one's commitment to belief in true responsibility lies in the experience one comes to have, *as* a social, linguistic being, of one's own agency. Even if it were true that a being could not develop in such a way as to come to attribute true responsibility to itself without having been participant in a social and linguistic community, this fact would provide no basis for an objection to the above claim, which is merely a claim about the deepest foundation of our present commitment to belief in true responsibility, not about the conditions of our past acquisition of such a belief.

It is not the "general framework" of social life, then, that is currently in question. It is the agent's private experience of agency. It is one's commitment to belief in one's own efficacy, control, self-determination, and total responsibility (in normally unconstrained circumstances), rather than one's commitment to holding others responsible and treating them as proper objects of reactive attitudes, that is primarily unrenounceable.

It only remains to say that, to the extent that it is primarily in one's attitudes to and conception of oneself that the roots of one's commitment to belief in true (moral) responsibility lie, the problems which determinism (and non-self-determinability) raises for that belief are particularly acute in one's own case. What on earth is one to think that one is, or is doing, if one thinks that one cannot really be responsible at all for what one does? Those who have fully understood what the application of the thought of determinism to themselves involves should be bewildered by this question (recall the thought-experiment in section V).

But it is likely to leave them undisturbed. And it is this equanimity in the face of the problem, this equanimity with which we continue to discuss the problem of freedom and determinism, that is perhaps the best indication of the strength of our commitment to belief in freedom.

VIII. Satkāyadṛṣṭi

The suggestion that one's commitment to belief in freedom and the reactive attitudes may be of such a kind that its abandonment is practically speaking impossible has not so far been challenged. But it has been suggested that one might be able to engineer (or might simply undergo) partial but not total erosions of this commitment; and that it is perhaps not equally unrenounceable in all areas. For example: one's commitment to belief in one's own responsibility for action seems to be more deeply founded than one's commitment to belief in the responsibility of others, even if this difference is not revealed in a difference of surface strength in everyday life; and so it seems correspondingly more likely that one might cease to be moved to blame others, on account of belief in determinism or non-self-determinability, than that one might cease to feel guilty about what one took to be one's own miscreance.

But perhaps one can raise a more general doubt about arguments for unrenounceable commitments to attitudes or beliefs that appear to be false from some natural point of view. Consider certain Buddhist philosophers who argue, on a variety of metaphysical grounds, that our natural notion of the persisting individual self is a delusion. Having reached this conclusion, they set themselves a task: that of overcoming the delusion.

There are several routes to the doctrine of *satkāyadṛṣṭi*, the "false view of individuality".[45] Which one is taken is of no present importance. The Buddhists presently in question hold that (a), the false sense or conception of self, leads to (b), suffering because it is essentially bound in with, as a necessary condition of, (c), the having of desires and aversions, which is itself a condition of the possibility of suffering.[46] To realize that there is no such thing as the individual self, to undermine the false view of individuality in oneself, is to cease to be bound by desires, cravings, and aversions, and hence to achieve liberation from suffering. It is, ultimately, to achieve the "blowing out" of self in nirvana, and thereby to cease to suffer and to fear old age, sickness, and death.

These Buddhists not only have theoretical reasons for believing that their natural sense or conception of self is delusory; they also have powerful practical reasons for trying to improve their grasp on the fact of its delusoriness. They recognize, however, that one cannot simply abolish one's sense of individuality, by some sort of effortless, rationally motivated, self-directed intellectual fiat. Delusions delude, after all; and the ordinary, strong sense of self (and hence of self-determination) is a particularly powerful delusion. They therefore recommend the adoption of a certain

---

45 *An-ātman*, or "no-soul", denotes the corresponding positive doctrine that there is no soul or self; and the experiential or phenomenological correlate of the factual or metaphysical error involved in *satkāyadṛṣṭi* is called *asmimāna*, or the "'I am' idea". See *Selfless Persons*, by S. Collins (Cambridge: Cambridge University Press, 1982), pp. 94, 100.

46 (b) requires (c) and (c) requires (a); So to eliminate (a) is to eliminate (b). Obviously the unselfconscious—dogs, bats, and so on—can also suffer. The point is made in this particular way because it is the basis of a practical recommendation for human beings.

practice—that of meditation—the eventual effect of which, they claim, is to cause the delusion to dislimn.[47]

Now a decision to adopt such a practice of meditation is presumably motivated by some desire. It can be simply a desire for an undeluded view of things—a love of truth or of correct attitude. In the Buddha's case, the originally predominant motive was his desire to overcome his horror of old age, sickness, and death: suffering, decrepitude and death are fearful only to a man who has desires and aversions of such a kind that he confronts himself as an object to worry about, and who has a sense of himself as a continuing entity, a person.[48]

What is curious about this general project is that if one attains nirvana, or at least a state of desirelessness, then one's desire for truth or correctness of attitude, or one's wish to escape from one's fear of mortal ills, lapses with all other desires, so that it is no longer there to be finally fulfilled by the course of action that it set in motion. Thus a man who attains nirvana, or a state of desirelessness, can never give any current reason—if this involves adducing a present desire presently satisfied—for being the way he is. Nevertheless, given his love of truth or of correctness of attitude, or his fear of old age and death, his adoption of the practice of meditation *was* rational, even if he is now (practically speaking) non-rational, and is so as a result of that practice.

The foregoing enables one kind of person, at least, to answer the question of what it would be rational to do given belief in determinism and incompatibilism (or in non-self-determinability): someone who had such a belief, and wished to lose any sense of self as free or truly self-determining in any way, in order to achieve a more correct attitude to the world, would do well to adopt the allegedly self-dissolving practice of meditation. A sense of self is not only a necessary condition of fear for one's future; it is also, obviously, a necessary condition of possession of the allegedly illegitimate sense of oneself as a truly self-determining planner and performer of action.

A more general point is this. There appear to be powerful lines of reasoning available, within what Strawson calls our "general framework" of attitudes and ideas, which question the correctness of the framework—or of paramount aspects of it—from within. There are, to say the least, some major tensions in it. No doubt a decision to adopt the "objective" attitude to oneself and others cannot be implemented overnight, given the nature and strength of the framework and our commitment to it. But there is no such difficulty with a decision to initiate some practice which may more gradually undermine or alter the supposedly inflexible constraints of the framework. And, if we admit the possibility of partial alterations in attitudes or habits of thought to which we are, as things are, deeply committed, then this points to the possibility of a progressive abandonment of these attitudes or habits of thought which, gradually achieved, amounts to a total abandonment relative to

---

47 Perhaps we may suppose that their goal is to achieve some kind of affectively speaking selfless but cognitively speaking fully self-conscious state of mind. See however *Freedom and Belief*, Appendix E, § III.

48 If there is, in a sense, no "I", then there is nothing to fear in death and dissolution, and there is no one there to feel fear in any case. For it is precisely the "I's" dissolution that is feared, and it is precisely the "I" that does the fearing.

the original position. It is not implausible to suppose that Buddhist monks and other mystics have succeeded in altering quite profoundly their experience of themselves (and others) as acting, thinking, and feeling beings.

And—finally—it is not implausible to say that they have in so doing achieved what is in certain respects a more correct view of the world, precisely to the extent that they have ceased to regard themselves and others as truly self-determining sources of actions, and have thereby come to adopt the objective attitude.[49] Having done so, they are certainly inhuman, in some way. And, as remarked, I do not think that we can really imagine what it might be like to be them. But there is no reason to think that they need be inhuman in any pejorative sense; and whatever nirvana is supposed to be like, it is clear that adoption of the objective attitude is in no way incompatible with compassion.

---

49 It is arguable that philosophers who believe that true responsibility is impossible, and who see themselves as committed to the pursuit of truth, ought to undertake some practice of meditation. For it may enable them to come to appreciate the truth of their theoretical conclusion in a way of which they are presently incapable.

Chapter 6

Responsibility and the Limits of Evil
Variations on a Strawsonian Theme[1]

Gary Watson

Examples of extreme evil bring to the fore certain tensions in our thought about responsibility. On a Strawsonian framework, being open to moral blame presupposes our capacity to participate in moral discourse, which requires a capacity to respond to moral reasons. And yet some evil bespeaks a deep insensitivity to such reasons. In what sense can a deeply cruel man respond to reasons of kindness? An apparent paradox looms: extreme evil seems to disqualify us for blame. Furthermore, being responsible is understood in the Strawsonian framework as being the appropriate object of reactive attitudes, which are said to track the quality of will manifested in action. But very often people of ill will are victims of childhood abuse, a fact that Strawson treats as a potential excusing or exempting condition. It is unclear, though, how to accommodate such historical considerations without going significantly beyond the resources of the quality of will thesis. This paper explores these questions.

Responsibility is ... one aspect of the identity of character and conduct. We are responsible for our conduct because that conduct is ourselves objectified in actions.
— John Dewey, *Outlines of a Critical Theory of Ethics*

There is nothing regrettable about finding oneself, in the last analysis, left with something which one cannot choose to accept or reject. What one is left with is probably just oneself, a core without which there could be no choice belonging to the person at all. Some unchosen restrictions on choice are among the conditions of its possibility.
— Thomas Nagel, *The Possibility of Altruism*

Our practices do not merely exploit our natures, they express them.
— Peter Strawson, "Freedom and Resentment"

Introduction

Regarding people as responsible agents is evidently not just a matter of belief. So regarding them means something in practice. It is shown in an embrace or a thank you, in an act of reprisal or obscene gesture, in a feeling of resentment or sense of obligation, in an apology or demand for an apology. To regard people as responsible agents is to be ready to treat them in certain ways.

---

1   To Sally Haslanger and Brian Skyrms, I am grateful for discussing bits and pieces of this material with me; to Ferdinand Schoeman, for comments on an earlier draft.

In "Freedom and Resentment",[2] Peter Strawson is concerned to describe these forms of treatment and their presuppositions. As his title suggests, Strawson's focus is on such attitudes and responses as gratitude and resentment, indignation, approbation, guilt, shame, (some kinds of) pride, hurt feelings, (asking and granting) forgiveness, and (some kinds of) love. All traditional theories of moral responsibility acknowledge connections between these attitudes and holding one another responsible. What is original to Strawson is the way in which they are linked. Whereas traditional views have taken these attitudes to be secondary to seeing others as responsible, to be practical corollaries or emotional side effects of some independently comprehensible belief in responsibility, Strawson's radical claim is that these "reactive attitudes" (as he calls them) are *constitutive* of moral responsibility; to regard oneself or another as responsible just is the proneness to react to them in these kinds of ways under certain conditions. There is no more basic belief which provides the justification or rationale for these reactions. The practice does not rest on a theory at all, but rather on certain needs and aversions that are basic to our conception of being human. The idea that there is or needs to be such an independent basis is where traditional views, in Strawson's opinion, have gone badly astray.

For a long time, I have found Strawson's approach salutary and appealing. Here my aim is not to defend it as superior to its alternatives, but to do something more preliminary. A comparative assessment is not possible without a better grasp of what Strawson's theory (or a Strawsonian theory)[3] *is*. As Strawson presents it, the theory is incomplete in important respects. I will investigate whether and how the incompleteness can be remedied in Strawsonian ways. In the end, I find that certain features of our practice of holding responsible are rather resistant to such remedies, and that the practice is less philosophically innocent than Strawson supposes. I hope that the issues uncovered by this investigation will be of sufficient importance to interest even those who are not as initially sympathetic to Strawson's approach as I am.[4]

Strawson's Theory

Strawson presents the rivals to his view as responses to a prima facie problem posed by determinism. One rival—consequentialism—holds that blaming and praising judgments and acts are to be understood, and justified, as forms of social regulation. Apart from the question of its extensional adequacy, consequentialism

---

2 *Proceedings of the British Academy*, 1962, reprinted in Gary Watson (ed.), *Free Will* (Oxford: Oxford University Press, 1982), pp. 59–80; second edition (2003), pp. 72–93. [Hereafter, references for "Freedom and Resentment" will be to pages 19–36 of this volume, followed by (after the slash) the corresponding pages of Watson (1982) (the first edition). Thus, 'FR, 19/59' refers to this volume, p. 19/and *Free Will*, p. 59—the editors.]

3 My interpretation of Strawson's essay will be in many places very conjectural, and I will sometimes signal this fact by speaking of a "Strawsonian" theory.

4 I have learned much from the penetrating exploration of Strawson's essay by Jonathan Bennett: "Accountability", in *Philosophical Subjects*, Zak van Straaten (ed.), (Oxford: Clarendon Press, 1980), pp. 14–47.

seems to many to leave out something vital to our practice. By emphasizing their instrumental efficacy, it distorts the fact that our responses are typically personal reactions to the individuals in question that we sometimes think of as eminently appropriate reactions quite aside from concern for effects. Rightly "recoiling" from the consequentialist picture, some philosophers have supposed that responsibility requires a libertarian foundation, that to bring the "vital thing" back in, we must embrace a certain metaphysics of human agency. This is the other rival.

What these otherwise very different views share is the assumption that our reactive attitudes commit us to the truth of some independently apprehensible proposition which gives the content of the belief in responsibility; and so either the search is on for the formulation of this proposition, or we must rest content with an intuition of its content. For the social-regulation theorist, this is a proposition about the standard effects of having and expressing reactive attitudes. For the libertarian, it is a proposition concerning metaphysical freedom. Since the truth of the former is consistent with the thesis of determinism, the consequentialist is a compatibilist; since the truth of the latter is shown or seen not to be, the libertarian is an incompatibilist.

In Strawson's view, there is no such independent notion of responsibility that explains the propriety of the reactive attitudes. The explanatory priority is the other way around: It is not that we hold people responsible because they *are* responsible; rather, the idea (*our* idea) that we are responsible is to be understood by the practice, which itself is not a matter of holding some propositions to be true but of expressing our concerns and demands about our treatment of one another. These stances and responses are expressions of certain rudimentary needs and aversions: "it matters to us ... whether the actions of other people ... reflect attitudes toward us of good will, affection, or esteem on the one hand or contempt, indifference, or malevolence on the other" (FR, 22/63). Accordingly, the reactive attitudes are "natural human reactions to the good or ill will or indifference of others toward us (or toward those we care about) as displayed in *their* attitudes and actions" (FR, 25/67). Taken together, they express "the demand for the manifestation of a reasonable degree of good will or regard, on the part of others, not simply towards oneself, but towards all those on whose behalf moral indignation may be felt ... " (FR, 29/71).

Hence, Strawson accuses rival conceptions of "overintellectualizing" our practices. In their emphasis on social regulation, consequentialists lose sight of sentiments these practices directly express, without which the notion of moral responsibility cannot be understood. Libertarians see the gaping hole in the consequentialist account, but rather than acknowledging that "it is just these attitudes themselves which fill the gap" (FR, 35/79), they seek to ground these attitudes in a metaphysical intuition—"a pitiful intellectualist trinket for a philosopher to wear as a charm against the recognition of his own humanity" (FR, 35/79). Holding responsible is as natural and primitive in human life as friendship and animosity, sympathy and antipathy. It rests on needs and concerns that are not so much to be justified as acknowledged.

Excusing and Exempting

To say that holding responsible is to be explained by the range of reactive attitudes, rather than by a commitment to some independently comprehensible proposition about responsibility, is not to deny that these reactions depend on beliefs and perceptions in particular contexts. They are not mere effusions of feeling, unaffected by facts. In one way, Strawson is anxious to insist that these attitudes have no "rationale", that they neither require nor permit a "rational justification" of some general sort. Nevertheless, Strawson has a good deal to say about the particular perceptions that elicit and inhibit them. Reactive attitudes do have internal criteria, since they are reactions to the moral qualities exemplified by an individual's attitudes and conduct.[5]

Thus, reactive attitudes depend upon an interpretation of conduct. If you are resentful when jostled in a crowd, you will see the other's behavior as rude, contemptuous, disrespectful, self-preoccupied, or heedless: in short, as manifesting attitudes contrary to the basic demand for reasonable regard. Your resentment might be inhibited if you are too tired, or busy, or fearful, or simply inured to life in the big city. These are causal inhibitors. In contrast, you might think the other was pushed, didn't realize, didn't mean to, and so on. These thoughts would provide reasons for the inhibition of resentment. What makes them reasons is, roughly, that they cancel or qualify the appearance of noncompliance with the basic demand.[6]

In this way, Strawson offers a plausible account of many of the "pleas" that in practice inhibit or modify negative reactive attitudes. One type of plea is exemplified by the aforementioned reasons for inhibited sentiments. This type of plea corresponds to standardly acknowledged *excusing* conditions. It works by denying the appearance that the other failed to fulfill the basic demand; when a valid excuse obtains, the internal criteria of the negative reactive attitudes are not satisfied. Of course, justification does this as well, but in a different way. "He realized what he was doing, but it was an emergency." In general, an excuse shows that *one* was not to blame, whereas a justification shows that one was not to *blame.*

Strawson distinguishes a second type of plea. These pleas correspond roughly to standard *exempting* conditions. They show that the agent, temporarily or permanently, globally or locally, is appropriately exempted from the basic demand in the first place. Strawson's examples are being psychotic, being a child, being under great

---

[5] Reactive attitudes thus permit a threefold classification. Personal reactive attitudes regarding others' treatment of oneself (resentment, gratitude, etc.); vicarious analogues of these, regarding others' treatment of others (indignation and approbation); self-reactive attitudes regarding one's own treatment of others (and oneself?) (guilt, shame, moral self-esteem, feeling obligated). Many of the reactive attitudes reflect the basic demand (on oneself and others, for oneself and others), whereas others (for example, gratitude) directly express the basic concern.

Contrary to some of Strawson's discussion, responsibility does not concern only other-regarding attitudes. You can hold yourself responsible for failing to live up to an ideal that has no particular bearing on the interests or feelings of others. It may be said that others cannot *blame* you for this failure; but that would be a moral claim.

[6] Below, this remark is qualified significantly.

strain, being hypnotized, being a sociopath ("moral idiot"), and being "unfortunate in formative circumstances". His general characterization of pleas of type-2 is that they present the other either as acting uncharacteristically due to extraordinary circumstances, or as psychologically abnormal or morally undeveloped in such a way as to be incapacitated in some or all respects for "ordinary adult interpersonal relationships".

In sum, type-2 pleas bear upon the question of whether the agent is an appropriate "object of that kind of demand for goodwill or regard which is reflected in ordinary reactive attitudes" (FR, 24/65). If so, he or she is seen as a responsible agent, as a potential term in moral relationships, as a member (albeit, perhaps, in less than good standing) of the moral community. Assuming the absence of such exemptions, type-1 pleas bear upon the question of whether the basic demand has been met. These inhibit negative reactive attitudes because they give evidence that their internal criteria are not satisfied. In contrast, type-2 pleas inhibit reactive attitudes because they inhibit the demand those attitudes express (FR, 30–31/73).

When reactive attitudes are suspended on type-2 grounds, we tend to take what Strawson calls an "objective view". We see individuals not as ones to be resented or esteemed but as ones to be controlled, managed, manipulated, trained .... The objective view does not preclude all emotions: "It may include repulsion and fear, it may include pity or even love", though not reciprocal adult love. We have the capacity to adopt an objective view toward competent agents as well; for certain kinds of therapeutic relationship, or simply to relieve the "strains of involvement", we sometimes call upon this resource.

As we have seen, one of Strawson's concerns is to deny the relevance of any theoretical issue about determinism to moral responsibility. In effect, incompatibilists insist that the truth of determinism would require us to take the objective attitude universally. But in Strawson's view, when we adopt the objective attitude, it is never because of a theoretical conviction in determinism, but either because one of the exempting pleas is accepted, or for external reasons—fatigue, for example, or relief from the strain of involvement. No coherent thesis of determinism entails that one or more of the pleas is always valid, that disrespect is never meant, or that we are all abnormal or undeveloped in the relevant ways. Holding responsible is an expression of the basic concern and the basic demand, whose "legitimacy" requires neither metaphysical freedom nor efficacy. The practice does not involve a commitment to anything with which determinism could conflict, or which considerations of utility could challenge.

Blaming and Finding Fault

This is the basic view as Strawson presents it. For convenience, we may call it the expressive theory of responsibility. With certain caveats,[7] the expressive theory may

---

7 The term "compatibilism" denotes the view that determinism is compatible with responsibility. Hence it may presuppose that determinism is an intelligible thesis. Since Strawson seems skeptical about this presupposition, he might refuse this appellation.

be called a nonconsequentialist form of compatibilism; but it is not the only such form. It can be clarified by contrasting it with another.

Consider the following common view of blame and praise: To blame someone morally for something is to attribute it to a moral fault, or "shortcoming", or defect of character, or vice,[8] and similarly for praise. Responsibility could be construed in terms of the propriety conditions of such judgments: that is, judgments to the effect that an action or attitude manifests a virtue or vice.[9]

As I understand the Strawsonian theory, such judgments are only part of the story. They indicate what reactive attitudes are reactions *to* (namely, to the quality of the other's moral self as exemplified in action and attitude), but they are not themselves such reactions. Merely to cite such judgments is to leave out something integral to the practice of holding responsible and to the concept of moral responsibility (of being one to whom it is appropriate to respond in certain ways). It is as though in blaming we were mainly moral clerks, recording moral faults, for whatever purposes (the Last Assizes?).[10] In a Strawsonian view, blaming is not merely a fault-finding appraisal—which could be made from a detached and austerely "objective" standpoint—but a range of responses to the agent on the basis of such appraisals.[11] These nonpropositional responses are constitutive of the practice of holding responsible.

I will have something to say later about the nature of these responses. Clearly they make up a wide spectrum. Negative reactive attitudes range from bombing Tripoli to thinking poorly of a person. But even those at the more covert and less retributive end of the spectrum involve more than attributions of defects or shortcomings of moral character. Thinking poorly (less well) of a person is a way of regarding him or her in view of those faults. It has subtle implications for one's way of treating and interacting with the other. (Where the other is dead or otherwise out of reach, these

---

8   See Robert Nozick, *Philosophical Explanations* (Harvard University Press, 1981), p. 396.

9   Such a view is hinted at by James Wallace: "Answers to (the question of when an action is fully characteristic of an excellence or a vice) are fundamental for an account of the conditions for the appropriateness of praise, blame, reward and punishment and for an account of the derivative notion of responsibility" (*Virtues and Vices*, Cornell University Press, p. 43). This also seems to be R. Milo's view in *Immorality* (Princeton University Press, 1984). I don't say that such a view is necessarily compatibilist—it could be insisted that conduct fully exemplifies a virtue or a vice only if determinism is false (this is clearly the Abélardian view, discussed below)—but it is clear how a compatibilist version would go.

10 Consider Jonathan Glover's remark: "Involved in our present practice of blame is a kind of moral accounting, where a person's actions are recorded in an informal balance sheet, with the object of assessing his moral worth" (*Responsibility*, Routledge and Kegan Paul, 1970, p. 64).

11 "Blaming is a type of response to faults in oneself or in others", Robert Adams, "Involuntary Sin", *Philosophical Review*, January 1985, p. 21. Adams does not tell us what kind of response it is. Since he thinks that thinking poorly of someone *is* a form of unspoken blame (*ibid.*), he must think that thinking poorly of someone is more than noting a moral fault. I think this is correct.

implications will be only dispositional or potential.) It is the sort of attitude that is forsworn by forgiveness, which itself presupposes the attribution of (former) fault.

Some Critical Questions

I turn now to certain hard questions for the expressive theory. It accounts nicely for "excusing conditions," pleas of type-1; but exactly—or even roughly—what is its account of type-2 pleas? The "participant" reactive attitudes are said to be "natural human reactions to the good or ill-will or indifference of others as displayed in their attitudes and actions" (FR, 25/67); but this characterization must be incomplete, for some agents who display such attitudes are nevertheless exempted. A child can be malicious, a psychotic can be hostile, a sociopath indifferent, a person under great strain can be rude, and a woman or man "unfortunate in formative circumstances" can be cruel. Evidently reactive attitudes are sensitive not only to the quality of others' wills, but depend as well upon a background of beliefs about the objects of those attitudes. What are those beliefs, and can they be accommodated without appealing to the rival accounts of responsibility that Strawson sets out to avoid?

Strawson says that type-2 pleas inhibit reactive attitudes not by providing an interpretation which shows that the other does not display the pertinent attitudes, but by "inhibiting" the basic demand. It would seem that many of the exemption conditions involve *explanations* of why the individuals display qualities to which the reactive attitudes are otherwise sensitive. So on the face of it, the reactive attitudes are also affected by these explanations. Strawson's essay does not provide an account of how this works or what kinds of explanations exempt.

The problem is not just that the theory is incomplete, but that what will be necessary to complete it might undermine the theory. Strawsonian rivals will rush to fill the gap with their own notions. So it will be said that what makes some of these explanations exempting is that they are deterministic; or it will be said that these conditions are exempting because they indicate conditions in which making the basic demand is inefficacious. To the extent that some such account seems necessary, our enterprise is doomed.

In the following sections, I investigate a Strawsonian alternative. Following Strawson's idea that type-2 pleas inhibit reactive attitudes *by* inhibiting the basic demand, I propose to construe the exempting conditions as indications of the constraints on intelligible moral demand or, put another way, of the constraints on moral address.

I shall not attempt anything like a comprehensive treatment of the type-2 pleas mentioned by Strawson. I discuss, first and rather briefly, the cases of being a child and being under great strain. I then turn to a more extended discussion of "being unfortunate in formative circumstances", for this looks to be entirely beyond the resources of the expressive theory.

Demanding and Understanding

As Strawson is fully aware, being a child is not simply exempting. Children "are potentially and increasingly capable both of holding, and being objects of, the full range of human and moral attitudes, but are not yet fully capable of either" (FR, 32/75). Children are gradually becoming responsible agents; but in virtue of what are they potentially and increasingly these things? A plausible partial answer to this question is "moral understanding". They do not yet (fully) grasp the moral concepts in such a way that they can (fully) engage in moral communication, and so be unqualified members of the moral community.

The relevance of moral understanding to the expressive theory is this: The negative reactive attitudes express a *moral* demand, a demand for reasonable regard. Now a very young child does not even have a clear sense of the reality of others; but even with this cognitive capacity, children may lack an understanding of the effects of their behavior on others. Even when they understand what it is to hurt another physically, they may lack a sense of what it is to hurt another's feelings, or of the various subtle ways in which that may be done; and even when these things are more or less mastered, they may lack the notion of *reasonable* regard, or of justification. The basic demand is, once more, a moral demand, a demand for reasonable regard, a demand addressed to a moral agent, to one who is capable of understanding the demand. Since the negative reactive attitudes involve this demand, they are not (as fully) appropriately directed to those who do not fully grasp the terms of the demand.

To be intelligible, demanding presumes understanding on the part of the object of the demand. The reactive attitudes are incipiently forms of communication, which make sense only on the assumption that the other can comprehend the message.

No doubt common views about the moral capacities of children are open to challenge, and the appeal to the notion of understanding itself raises important issues.[12] However, what is important here is whether these views can be understood by the Strawsonian theory, and it seems the ordinary view that reactive attitudes make less sense in the case of children is intelligible in Strawsonian terms; this exemption condition reflects constraints arising from the notion of moral demand.

In a certain sense, blaming and praising those with diminished moral understanding loses its "point". This way of putting it smacks of consequentialism, but our discussion suggests a different construction. The reactive attitudes are incipient forms of communication, though not in the sense that resentment *et al.* are

---

12 Do *we adults* fully comprehend the notions of justification and reasonable regard? Does understanding presuppose a disputable cognitive view of morality? Certainly conceptions of children are subject to cultural variation. William Blackstone discusses the case of an eight-year old boy who was tried for setting fire to some barns. Because he was found to exhibit "malice, revenge, and cunning, he was found guilty, condemned and hanged accordingly". (In *Commentaries on the Laws of England* (1765–67), as quoted by Jennifer Radden, *Madness and Reason*, George Allen and Unwin, 1985, p. 136.)

It is doubtful that diminished moral understanding is the only relevant factor here. Surely various capacities of concentration and "volitional" control are relevant as well. How the expressive theory could account for these factors requires further discussion.

usually communicated; very often, in fact, they are not. Rather, the most appropriate and direct expression of resentment is to address the other with a complaint and a demand. Being a child exempts, when it does, not because expressing resentment has no desirable effects; in fact, it often does. Rather, the reactive attitudes lose their point as forms of moral address.[13]

Not Being Oneself

Let's consider whether this kind of explanation can be extended to another of Strawson's type-2 pleas: "being under great strain". Strawson includes this plea in a subgroup of exemptions that include "he wasn't himself" and "he was acting under posthypnotic suggestion". His statement of the rationale in the case of stress is somewhat cryptic:

> We shall not feel resentment against the man he is for the action done by the man he is not; or at least we shall feel less. We normally have to deal with him under normal stresses; so we shall not feel towards him, when he acts under abnormal stresses, as we should have felt towards him had he acted as he did under normal stresses (FR, 24/65–6).

I take it that what leads Strawson to group these cases together is that in each case the agent, due to special circumstances, acts *uncharacteristically*.

When you learn that someone who has treated you extremely rudely has been under great strain lately, has lost a job, say, or is going through a divorce, you may reinterpret the behavior in such a way that your erstwhile resentment or hurt feelings are inhibited and now seem inappropriate. How does this reinterpretation work? Notice, again, that unlike type-1 pleas, the new interpretation does not contradict the *judgment* that the person treated you rudely; rather, it provides an explanation of the rudeness.

What Strawson says about this case seems plausible. What seems to affect your reactive attitudes is the thought that she's not herself, that the behavior does not reflect or fully reflect the person's moral "personality". The following remark indicates the same phenomenon: "He was drunk when he said that; I wouldn't hold it against him". (There is room here for disagreement about the bounds of the moral self. Some parts of folk wisdom have it that one's "true self" is revealed when drunk.

---

13 Reactive attitudes are even more clearly pointless in the case of a radically disintegrated personality, one that has no coherent moral self to be addressed. The case of the sociopath is much more complicated, but arguably something similar may be said here. Those who deal with sociopaths often lose the sense that such characters have a moral self at all; despite appearances, there is "no one home".

For case studies and psychiatric commentary, see Hervey Cleckley, *The Mask of Sanity*, C.V. Mosby (1941). For philosophical discussion, see Herbert Fingarette, *On Responsibility*, Ch. 2; Vinit Haksar, "The Responsibility of Psychopaths", *The Philosophical Quarterly*, Vol. 15 (1965); M.S. Pritchard, *On Becoming Responsible* (Lawrence, Kan.: University Press of Kansas, 1991); Antony Duff, "Psychopathy and Moral Understanding", *American Philosophical Quarterly*, Vol. 14 (1977); and Jeffrie Murphy, "Moral Death: A Kantian Essay on Psychopathy", *Ethics*, Vol. 82 (1972).

To my knowledge, this has never been claimed about stress.) Again, what is the Strawsonian rationale?

Perhaps this type of case can also be understood in terms of the conditions of intelligible moral address. Insofar as resentment is a form of reproach addressed to an agent, such an attitude loses much of its point here—not, as before, because the other does not fully understand the reproach, but because *he* or *she* (the true self) repudiates such conduct as well. Unlike the case in which the agent acts rudely in the absence of "strain", here the target of your resentment is not one who "really" endorses the behavior you are opposing. You see the behavior as not issuing from that person's moral self, and yet it is the person, qua moral self, that your resentment would address.

The point can be put more generally in this way: Insofar as the negative reactive attitudes express demands (or in some cases appeals) addressed to another moral self, they are conceptually conditioned in various ways. One condition is that, to be fully a moral self, the other must possess sufficient (for what?) moral understanding; another is that the conduct in question be seen as reflecting the moral self. Insofar as the person is subject to great stress, his or her conduct and attitudes fail to meet this latter condition.

I am unsure to what extent these remarks accord with Strawson's own views. They are in any case exceedingly sketchy, and raise problems I am unable to take up here. For one thing, the notion of moral address seems essentially interpersonal, and so would be unavailing in the self-reflexive case. We have negative reactive attitudes toward and make moral demands upon ourselves. To determine whether this is a fatal asymmetry, we would have to investigate the reflexive cases in detail. For another thing, the notion of moral self is certainly not altogether transparent. Why are our responses under stress not reflection of our moral selves—namely, reflections of the moral self under stress? Clearly then, the explanation requires development.

It will be recalled, however, that I am not trying to determine whether a Strawsonian account of the exemption conditions is the *best* account, but to indicate what such an account might be. It will be enough for my purposes here if we can be satisfied that a Strawsonian theory has the resources to provide *some* explanation.

To recapitulate, then, the thesis is this: First, type-2 pleas indicate in different ways limiting conditions on moral address. These are relevant to reactive attitudes because those attitudes are incipiently forms of moral address. This thesis makes sense of Strawson's remark that pleas of this type inhibit reactive attitudes by inhibiting moral demand. Second, given that those conditions are satisfied, type-1 pleas indicate that the basic demand has not been flouted, contrary to appearances (though here again, we must distinguish excuse from justification).

On this account, the practice of holding responsible does indeed seem metaphysically modest, in that it involves no commitments to which issues about determinism are relevant. In a subsequent section I will consider some more bothersome features of our practice; but first I want to call attention to some general issues raised by the account given so far.

Evil and the Limits of Moral Community

To understand certain exempting and extenuating considerations, I have appealed to the notion of the conditions in which it makes sense morally to address another. I suggested that in different ways these conditions are not (fully) satisfied by the child and the person under severe stress. In the case of children, it seemed plausible to speak of a lack of understanding. What is involved in such understanding is a complex question. Obviously we do not want to make *compliance* with the basic demand a condition of moral understanding. (After all, for the most part, children *do* "comply", but without full understanding.) For the negative reactive attitudes come into play only when the basic demand has been flouted or rejected; and flouting and rejecting, strictly speaking, require understanding.

These remarks raise a very general issue about the limits of responsibility and the limits of evil. It is tempting to think that understanding requires a shared framework of values. At any rate, some of Strawson's remarks hint at such a requirement on moral address. He writes that the reactive attitudes essentially involve regarding the other as "a morally responsible agent, as a term of moral relationships, as a member of the moral community" (FR, 30/73). This last phrase suggests shared ends, at some level, or a shared framework for practical reasoning. Thus, co-members of the moral community are potential interlocutors. In his discussion of Strawson's essay, Lawrence Stern suggests this point:

> ... when one morally disapproves of another person, it is normal to believe that he is susceptible to the appeal of the principles from the standpoint of which one disapproves. He either shares these principles or can come to share them.[14]

Does morally addressing another make sense unless we suppose that the other can see some reason to take us seriously, to acknowledge our claims? Can we be in a moral community with those who reject the basic terms of moral community? Are the enemies of moral community themselves members? If we suppose that moral address requires moral community, then some forms of evil will be exempting conditions. If holding responsible requires the intelligibility of moral address, and if a condition of such address is that the other be seen as a potential moral interlocutor, then the paradox results that extreme evil disqualifies one for blame.

Consider the case of Robert Harris:

> On the south tier of Death Row, in a section called "Peckerwood Flats" where the white inmates are housed, there will be a small celebration the day Robert Alton Harris dies.
>
> A group of inmates on the row have pledged several dollars for candy, cookies and soda. At the moment they estimate that Harris has been executed, they will eat, drink and toast to his passing.
>
> "The guy's a misery, a total scumbag; we're going to party when he goes", said Richard (Chic) Mroczko, who lived in the cell next to Harris on San Quentin Prison's Death Row for more than a year. "He doesn't care about life, he doesn't care about others, he doesn't care about himself."

---

14 "Freedom, Blame, and Moral Community", *Journal of Philosophy*, February 14, 1974, p. 78.

"We're not a bunch of Boy Scouts around here, and you might think we're pretty cold-blooded about the whole thing. But then, you just don't know the dude."

San Diego County Assistant Dist. Atty. Richard Huffman, who prosecuted Harris, said: "If a person like Harris can't be executed under California law and federal procedure, then we should be honest and say we're incapable of handling capital punishment."

State Deputy Atty. Gen. Michael D. Wellington asked the court during an appeal hearing for Harris: "If this isn't the kind of defendant that justifies the death penalty, is there ever going to be one?"

What crime did Robert Harris commit to be considered the archetypal candidate for the death penalty? And what kind of man provokes such enmity that even those on Death Row ... call for his execution?

On July 5, 1978, John Mayeski and Michael Baker had just driven through [a] fast-food restaurant and were sitting in the parking lot eating lunch. Mayeski and Baker ... lived on the same street and were best friends. They were on their way to a nearby lake for a day of fishing.

At the other end of the parking lot, Robert Harris, 25, and his brother Daniel, 18, were trying to hotwire a [car] when they spotted the two boys. The Harris brothers were planning to rob a bank that afternoon and did not want to use their own car. When Robert Harris could not start the car, he pointed to the [car] where the 16-year-olds were eating and said to Daniel, "We'll take this one".

He pointed a ... Luger at Mayeski, crawled into the back seat, and told him to drive east ....

Daniel Harris followed in the Harrises' car. When they reached a canyon area ..., Robert Harris told the youths he was going to use their car in a bank robbery and assured them that they would not be hurt. Robert Harris yelled to Daniel to get the .22 caliber rifle out of the back seat of their car.

"When I caught up", Daniel said in a recent interview, Robert was telling them about the bank robbery we were going to do. He was telling them that he would leave them some money in the car and all, for us using it. Both of them said that they would wait on top of this little hill until we were gone, and then walk into town and report the car stolen. Robert Harris agreed.

"Michael turned and went through some bushes. John said: 'Good luck', and turned to leave."

As the two boys walked away, Harris slowly raised the Luger and shot Mayeski in the back, Daniel said. Mayeski yelled: "Oh, God", and slumped to the ground. Harris chased Baker down a hill into a little valley and shot him four times.

Mayeski was still alive when Harris climbed back up the hill, Daniel said. Harris walked over to the boy, knelt down, put the Luger to his head and fired.

"God, everything started to spin", Daniel said. "It was like slow motion. I saw the gun, and then his head exploded like a balloon, ... I just started running and running .... But I heard Robert and turned around."

"He was swinging the rifle and pistol in the air and laughing. God, that laugh made blood and bone freeze in me."

Harris drove [the] car to a friend's house where he and Daniel were staying. Harris walked into the house, carrying the weapons and the bag [containing] the remainder of the slain youths' lunch. Then, about 15 minutes after he had killed the two 16-year-old boys, Harris took the food out of the bag ... and began eating a hamburger. He offered his brother an apple turnover, and Daniel became nauseated and ran to the bathroom.

"Robert laughed at me", Daniel said. "He said I was weak; he called me a sissy and said I didn't have the stomach for it."

Harris was in an almost lighthearted mood. He smiled and told Daniel that it would be amusing if the two of them were to pose as police officers and inform the parents that their sons were killed. Then, for the first time, he turned serious. He thought that somebody might have heard the shots and that police could be searching for the bodies. He told Daniel that they should begin cruising the street near the bodies, and possibly kill some police in the area.

[Later, as they prepared to rob the bank], Harris pulled out the Luger, noticed blood stains and remnants of flesh on the barrel as a result of the point-blank shot, and said: "I really blew that guy's brains out." And then, again, he started laughing.

... Harris was given the death penalty. He has refused all requests for interviews since the conviction.

"He just doesn't see the point of talking", said a sister, ... who has visited him three times since he has been on Death Row. "He told me he had his chance, he took the road to hell and there's nothing more to say."

... Few of Harris' friends or family were surprised that he ended up on Death Row. He had spent seven of the previous 10 years behind bars. Harris, who has an eighth-grade education, was convicted of car theft at 15 and was sentenced to a federal youth center. After being released, he was arrested twice for torturing animals and was convicted of manslaughter for beating a neighbor to death after a dispute.

Barbara Harris, another sister, talked to her brother at a family picnic on July 4, 1978. He had been out of prison less than six months, and his sister had not seen him in several years.

... Barbara Harris noticed his eyes, and she began to shudder ...."I thought, 'My God, what have they done to him?' He smiled, but his eyes were so cold, totally flat. It was like looking at a rattlesnake or a cobra ready to strike. They were hooded eyes, with nothing but meanness in them."

"He had the eyes of a killer. I told a friend that I knew someone else would die by his hand."

The next day, Robert Harris killed the two youths. Those familiar with the case were as mystified as they were outraged by Harris' actions. Most found it incomprehensible that a man could be so devoid of compassion and conscience that he could kill two youths, laugh about their deaths and then casually eat their hamburgers ...

... Harris is a dangerous man on the streets and a dangerous man behind bars, said Mroczko, who spent more than a year in the cell next to Harris' ....

"You don't want to deal with him out there", said Mroczko .... "We don't want to deal with him in here."

During his first year on the row, Mroczko said Harris was involved in several fights on the yard and was caught trying to supply a prisoner in an adjacent yard with a knife. During one fight, Harris was stabbed and the other prisoner was shot by a guard. He grated on people's nerves and one night he kept the whole cell block awake by banging his shoe on a steel water basin and laughing hysterically.

An encounter with Harris always resulted in a confrontation. If an inmate had cigarettes, or something else Harris wanted, and he did not think "you could hold your mud", Mroczko said, he would try to take them.

Harris was a man who just did not know "when to be cool" he said. He was an obnoxious presence in the yard and in his cell, and his behavior precipitated unwanted attention from the guards ....

He acted like a man who did not care about anything. His cell was filthy, Mroczko said, and clothes, trash, tobacco and magazines were scattered on the floor. He wore the same clothes every day and had little interest in showers. Harris spent his days watching television in his cell, occasionally reading a Western novel.[15]

On the face of it, Harris is an "archetypal candidate" for blame. We respond to his heartlessness and viciousness with moral outrage and loathing. Yet if reactive attitudes were implicitly "invitations to dialogue" (as Stern puts it), then Harris would be an inappropriate object of such attitudes. For he is hardly a potential moral interlocutor, "susceptible to the appeal of the principles from the standpoint of which one disapproves". In this instance, an invitation to dialogue would be met with icy silence (he has "nothing more to say") or murderous contempt.

However, not all communication is dialogue. Harris refuses dialogue, and this refusal is meant to make a point. It is in effect a repudiation of the moral community; he thereby declares himself a moral outlaw. Unlike the small child, or in a different way the psychopath, he exhibits an inversion of moral concern, not a lack of understanding. His ears are not deaf, but his heart is frozen. This characteristic, which makes him utterly unsuitable as a moral interlocutor, intensifies rather than inhibits the reactive attitudes. Harris's form of evil *consists* in part in being beyond the boundaries of moral community. Hence, if we are to appeal to the constraints on moral address to explain certain type-2 pleas, we must not include among these constraints co-membership in the moral community or the significant possibility of dialogue—unless, that is, evil is to be its own exemption. At these outer limits, our reactive attitudes can be nothing more (or less) than a denunciation forlorn of the hope of an adequate reply.

The Roots of Evil

I said that Harris is an archetypal candidate for blame—so, at least, we react to him. Does it matter to our reactions how he came to be so? Strawson thinks so, for, among type-2 pleas, he includes "being unfortunate in formative circumstances". We must now investigate the relevance of such historical considerations to the reactive attitudes. As it happens, the case of Robert Harris is again a vivid illustration.

> [During the interview] Barbara Harris put her palms over her eyes and said softly, "I saw every grain of sweetness, pity and goodness in him destroyed .... It was a long and ugly journey before he reached that point."
>
> Robert Harris' 29 years ... have been dominated by incessant cruelty and profound suffering that he has both experienced and provoked. Violence presaged his birth, and a violent act is expected to end his life.
>
> Harris was born Jan. 15, 1953, several hours after his mother was kicked in the stomach. She was six-and-a-half months pregnant and her husband, an insanely jealous man, ... came home drunk and accused her of infidelity. He claimed that the child was not his, threw her down and kicked her. She began hemorrhaging, and he took her to the hospital.

---

15 From Miles Corwin, "Icy Killer's Life Steeped in Violence", *Los Angeles Times*, May 16, 1982. Copyright, 1982, *Los Angeles Times*. Reprinted with permission. For the length of this and the next quotation, I ask for the reader's patience. It is very important here to work with realistic and detailed examples.

Robert was born that night. His heartbeat stopped at one point ... but labor was induced and he was saved. Because of the premature birth, he was a tiny baby; he was kept alive in an incubator and spent months at the hospital.

His father was an alcoholic who was twice convicted of sexually molesting his daughters. He frequently beat his children ... and often caused serious injury. Their mother also became an alcoholic and was arrested several times, once for bank robbery.

All of the children had monstrous childhoods. But even in the Harris family, ... the abuse Robert was subjected to was unusual.

Before their mother died last year, Barbara Harris said, she talked incessantly about Robert's early years. She felt guilty that she was never able to love him; she felt partly responsible that he ended up on Death Row.

When Robert's father visited his wife in the hospital and saw his son for the first time, ... the first thing he said was: "Who is the father of that bastard?" When his mother picked him up from the hospital ... she said it was like taking a stranger's baby home.

The pain and permanent injury Robert's mother suffered as a result of the birth, ... and the constant abuse she was subjected to by her husband, turned her against her son. Money was tight, she was overworked and he was her fifth child in just a few years. She began to blame all of her problems on Robert, and she grew to hate the child.

"I remember one time we were in the car and Mother was in the back seat with Robbie in her arms. He was crying and my father threw a glass bottle at him, but it hit my mother in the face. The glass shattered and Robbie started screaming. I'll never forget it", she said ....

"Her face was all pink, from the mixture of blood and milk. She ended up blaming Robbie for all the hurt, all the things like that. She felt helpless and he was someone to vent her anger on."

... Harris had a learning disability and a speech problem, but there was no money for therapy. When he was at school he felt stupid and classmates teased him, his sister said, and when he was at home he was abused.

"He was the most beautiful of all my mother's children; he was an angel", she said. "He would just break your heart. He wanted love so bad he would beg for any kind of physical contact."

"He'd come up to my mother and just try to rub his little hands on her leg or her arm. He just never got touched at all. She'd just push him away or kick him. One time she bloodied his nose when he was trying to get close to her."

Barbara Harris put her head in her hands and cried softly. "One killer out of nine kids .... The sad thing is he was the most sensitive of all of us. When he was 10 and we all saw 'Bambi', he cried and cried when Bambi's mother was shot. Everything was pretty to him as a child; he loved animals. But all that changed; it all changed so much."

... All nine children are psychologically crippled as a result of their father, she said, but most have been able to lead useful lives. But Robert was too young, and the abuse lasted too long, she said, for him ever to have had a chance to recover.

[At age 14] Harris was sentenced to a federal youth detention center [for car theft]. He was one of the youngest inmates there, Barbara Harris said, and he grew up "hard and fast".

... Harris was raped several times, his sister said, and he slashed his wrists twice in suicide attempts. He spent more than four years behind bars as a result of an escape, an attempted escape and a parole violation.

The centers were "gladiator schools", Barbara Harris said, and Harris learned to fight and be mean. By the time he was released from federal prison at 19, all his problems were accentuated. Everyone in the family knew that he needed psychiatric help.

The child who had cried at the movies when Bambi's mother dies had evolved into a man who was arrested several times for abusing animals. He killed cats and dogs, Daniel said, and laughed while torturing them with mop handles, darts and pellet guns. Once he stabbed a prize pig more than 1,000 times.

"The only way he could vent his feelings was to break or kill something", Barbara Harris said. "He took out all the frustrations of his life on animals. He had no feeling for life, no sense of remorse. He reached the point where there wasn't that much left of him."

... Harris' family is ambivalent about his death sentence. [Another sister said that] if she did not know her brother's past so intimately, she would support his execution without hesitation. Barbara has a 16-year-old son; she often imagines the horror of the slain boys' parents.

"If anyone killed my son, I'd try my damnedest, no matter what it took, to have my child revenged" Barbara Harris said. "I know how those parents must suffer every day.

But Robbie in the gas chamber .... " She broke off in mid-sentence and stared out a window. "Well, I still remember the little boy who used to beg for love, for just one pat or word of kindness .... No I can't say I want my brother to die."

... Since Harris has been on Death Row, he has made no demands of time or money on his family. Harris has made only one request; he wants a dignified and serene ceremony after he dies—a ceremony in marked contrast to his life.

He has asked his oldest brother to take his ashes, to drive to the Sierra, hike to a secluded spot and scatter his remains in the trees.[16]

No doubt this history gives pause to the reactive attitudes. Why does it do so? "No wonder Harris is as he is!" we think. What is the relevance of this thought?

Note, to begin with, that the story in no way undermines the judgments that he is brutal, vicious, heartless, mean.[17] Rather, it provides a kind of explanation for his being so. Can the expressive theory explain why the reactive attitudes should be sensitive to such an explanation?

Strawson's general rubric for type-2 pleas (or the subgroup in which this plea is classified) is "being incapacitated for ordinary interpersonal relationships". Does Harris have some independently identifiable incapacity for which his biography provides evidence? Apparently, he *is* incapacitated for such relationships—for example, for friendship, for sympathy, for being affected by moral considerations. To be homicidally hateful and callous in Harris's way is to lack moral concern, and to lack moral concern is to be incapacitated for moral community. However, to exempt Harris on these grounds is problematic. For then everyone who is evil in Harris's way will be exempt, independently of facts about their background. But we had ample evidence about *this* incapacity before we learned of his childhood misfortunes, and that did not affect the reactive attitudes. Those misfortunes affect our responses in a special and nonevidential way. The question is why this should be so.

---

16 Miles Corwin, *op. cit.* Copyright, 1982, *Los Angeles Times*. Reprinted by permission.

17 Although, significantly, when his past is in focus, we are less inclined to use certain *reactive* epithets, such as "scumbag". This term is used to express an attitude about the appropriate treatment of the individual (that he is to be thrown in the garbage, flushed down the toilet, etc.). Some other reactive terms are "jerk", "creep", "son of a bitch".

This would seem to be a hard question for compatibilist views generally. What matters is whether, in one version, the practice of holding responsible can be efficacious as a means of social regulation, or whether, using the expressive theory, the conditions of moral address are met. These questions would seem to be settled by how individuals *are*, not by how they came to be. Facts about background would be, at most, evidence that some other plea is satisfied. In themselves, they would not seem to matter.

A plea of this kind is, on the other hand, grist for the incompatibilists' mill. For they will insist on an essential historical dimension to the concept of responsibility. Harris's history reveals him to be an inevitable product of his formative circumstances. And seeing him as a product is inconsistent with seeing him as a responsible agent. If his cruel attitudes and conduct are the inevitable result of his circumstances, then he is not responsible for them, unless he was responsible for those circumstances. It is this principle that gives the historical dimension of responsibility and of course entails the incompatibility of determinism and responsibility.

In this instance, however, an incompatibilist diagnosis seems doubtful. In the first place, our response to the case is not the simple suspension of reactive attitudes that this diagnosis would lead one to expect, but ambivalence. In the second place, the force of the example does not depend on a belief in the *inevitability* of the upshot. Nothing in the story supports such a belief. The thought is not "It had to be!" but, again, "No wonder!"

Sympathy and Antipathy

How and why, then, does this larger view of Harris's life in fact affect us? It is too simple to say that it leads us to suspend our reactive attitudes. Our response is too complicated and conflicted for that. What appears to happen is that we are unable to command an overall view of his life that permits the reactive attitudes to be sustained without ambivalence. That is because the biography forces us to see him as a *victim*, and so seeing him does not sit well with the reactive attitudes that are so strongly elicited by Harris's character and conduct. Seeing him as a victim does not totally dispel those attitudes. Rather, in light of the "whole" story, conflicting responses are evoked. The sympathy toward the boy he was is at odds with outrage toward the man he is. These responses conflict not in the way that fear dispels anger, but in the way that sympathy is opposed to antipathy. In fact, each of these responses is appropriate, but taken together they do not enable us to respond overall in a coherent way.

Harris both satisfies and violates the criteria of victimhood. His childhood abuse was a misfortune inflicted upon him against his will. But at the same time (and this is part of his very misfortune) he unambivalently endorses suffering, death, and destruction, and that is what (one form of) evil is. With this in focus, we see him as a victimizer and respond to him accordingly. The ambivalence results from the fact that an overall view simultaneously demands and precludes regarding him as a victim.

What we have here is not exactly a clash between what Thomas Nagel has called the objective and subjective standpoints.[18] It is not that from the more comprehensive viewpoint that reveals Harris as a victim, his responsibility is indiscernible. Rather, the clash occurs within a single point of view that reveals Harris as evil (and hence calling for enmity and moral opposition) and as one who is a victim (calling for sympathy and understanding). Harris's misfortune is such that scarcely a vestige remains of his earlier sensibilities. Hence, unless one knew Harris as a child or keeps his earlier self vividly in mind, sympathy can scarcely find a purchase.

Moral Luck and Moral Equality

However, what is arresting about the Harris case is not just the clash between sympathy and antipathy. The case is troubling in a more personal way. The fact that Harris's cruelty is an intelligible response to his circumstances gives a foothold not only for sympathy, but for the thought that if *I* had been subjected to such circumstances, I might well have become as vile. What is unsettling is the thought that one's moral self is such a fragile thing. One tends to think of one's moral sensibilities as going deeper than that (though it is not clear what this means). This thought induces not only an ontological shudder, but a sense of equality with the other: I too am a potential evildoer.[19]

This point is merely the obverse of the point about sympathy. Whereas the point about sympathy focuses on our empathetic response to the other, the thought about moral luck turns one's gaze inward. It makes one feel less in a position to cast blame. The fact that my potential for evil has not been nearly so fully actualized is, for all I know, something for which I cannot take credit. The awareness that, in this respect, the others are or may be like oneself clashes with the distancing effect of enmity.

Admittedly, it is hard to know what to do with this conclusion. Equality of moral potential does not, of course, mean that Harris is not actually a vile man; on the contrary, it means that in similar circumstances I would have become vile as well. Since he is an evil man, we cannot and should not treat him as we would a rabid dog. The awareness of moral luck, however, taints one's own view of one's moral self as an achievement, and infuses one's reactive attitudes with a sense of irony. Only those who have survived circumstances such as those that ravaged Harris are in a good position to know what they would have done. We lucky ones can only wonder. As a product of reflection, this perspective is, of course, easily lost when the knife is at one's own throat.

---

18 In *The View from Nowhere*, Oxford University Press, 1986.

19 In "Determinism and Moral Perspectives" (*Philosophy and Phenomenological Research*, September 1960), Elizabeth Beardsley calls attention to the perspective evoked by such cases as Harris, though she links this perspective too closely, in my opinion, to the notion of determinism.

Determinism and Ignorance

Nothing in the foregoing reflections is necessarily inconsistent with the expressive theory. The ways in which reactive attitudes are affected by sympathy and moral luck are intelligible without appealing to any of the conceptions of responsibility that Strawson eschews. Nevertheless, our attitudes remain puzzling in a number of respects.

Earlier we questioned an incompatibilist diagnosis of our example on the grounds that the historical explanation need not be construed as deterministic. Horrid backgrounds do not inevitably give rise to horrid people. Some manage somehow to survive a similar magnitude of misfortune, if not unscathed, at least as minimally decent human beings. Conversely, people are sometimes malicious despite a benign upbringing. What do we suppose makes the difference?

Strictly speaking, no one who is vicious in *just* the way we have interpreted Harris to be could fail to have had an abusive childhood. For our interpretation of who Harris is depends upon his biography, upon our interpretation of his life. Harris's cruelty is a response to the shattering abuse he suffered during the process of socialization. The objects of his hatred were not just the boys he so exultantly murdered, but the "moral order" that mauled and rejected him. (It is significant that Harris wanted to go out and kill some cops after the murder; he wanted not just to reject authority, but to confront it.) He defies the demand for human consideration because he has been denied this consideration himself. The mistreatment he received becomes a ground as well as a cause of the mistreatment he gives. It becomes part of the content of his "project".

Thus, someone who had a supportive and loving environment as a child, but who was devoted to dominating others, who killed for enjoyment, would not be vicious in just the way Harris is, since he or she could not be seen as striking back at "society"; but such a person could be just *as* vicious. In common parlance, we sometimes call such people "bad apples", a phrase that marks a blank in our understanding. In contrast to Harris, whose malice is motivated, the conduct of "bad apples" seems inexplicable. So far, we cannot see them as victims, and there is no application for thoughts about sympathy and moral luck.

However, do we not suppose that *something* must have gone wrong in the developmental histories of these individuals, if not in their socialization, then "in them"—in their genes or brains? (Suppose a certain kind of tumor is such that its onset at an early age is known to be strongly correlated with the development of a malicious character. This supposition is no doubt bad science fiction; that a complex and articulated psychological structure could be caused by gross brain defect seems antecedently implausible.) Whatever "nonenvironmental" factors make the difference, will they not play the same role as Harris's bad upbringing—that is, will they not have victimized these individuals so that thoughts about sympathy and moral luck come into play? Or can evil be the object of unequivocal reactive attitudes only when it is inexplicable?

If determinism is true, then evil is a joint product of nature and nurture. If so, the difference between any evil person and oneself would seem to be a matter of moral luck. For determinism seems to entail that if one had been subjected to the internal and external conditions of some evil person, then one would have been evil as well. If that is so, then the reflections about moral luck seem to entail that the acceptance of determinism should affect our reactive attitudes in the same way as they are affected in Harris's case. In the account we have suggested, then, determinism seems to be relevant to reactive attitudes after all.

This conclusion does not follow, though, without special metaphysical assumptions. For the counterfactuals that underlie thoughts about moral luck must be constrained by the conditions of personal identity. It may be that no one who had been exposed to just the internal and external conditions of some given individual could have been me. To make sense of a counterfactual of the form, "If i had been in C, then i would have become a person of type t," C must be supposed to be compatible with i's existence as an individual (i must exist in the possible world in which C obtains). For example, it is widely held that genetic origin is essential to an individual's identity. In that case, the counterfactual, "If I had had Harris's genetic origin and his upbringing, then I would have been as evil as he", will not make sense. Now it might be that Harris's genetic origins are among the determinants of his moral development. Thus, even if this is a deterministic world, there may be no true counterfactual that would support the thought that the difference between Harris and me is a matter of moral luck. There is room for the thought that there is something "in me" by virtue of which I would not have become a vicious person in Harris's circumstances. And if that factor were among my essential properties, so to speak, then that difference between Harris and me would not be a matter of moral luck on my part, but a matter of who we essentially were. That would not, of course, mean that I was essentially good or Harris essentially evil, but that I would not have been corrupted by the same circumstances as those that defeated Harris. To be sure, to suppose that this difference is in itself to my moral credit would be odd. To congratulate me on these grounds would be to congratulate me on being myself. Nevertheless, this difference still might explain what is to my credit, such moral virtues as I may possess. This will seem paradoxical only if we suppose that whatever is a ground of my moral credit must itself be to my credit. But I see no compelling reason to suppose this.

Historical Responsibility

Libertarians believe that evil is the product neither of nature nor of nurture, but of free will. Do we understand what this might mean?

It is noteworthy that libertarians will be able to agree with much of what we have said about moral luck. Harris's history affects us because it makes us wonder how *we* would have responded, and thus shakes our confidence that we would have avoided a pernicious path in those circumstances. But this effect is perfectly compatible with Harris's responsibility for how he did respond, just us we would have been responsible for how we would have responded. The biography affects us not because it is deterministic, libertarians can say, but because it shakes our confidence that we would have exercised that freedom rightly in more dire straits. We are not, of course, responsible for our formative circumstances—and in this respect we are morally lucky and Harris is unlucky—but those circumstances do not determine our responses to them. It is the individual's own response that distinguishes those who become evil from those who do not.

This idea is nicely captured by Peter Abélard: "Nothing taints the soul but what belongs to it, namely consent."[20] The idea is that one cannot simply be caused to be morally bad by the environment. So either Harris's soul is not (morally) marred, or he has been a willing accomplice to the malformation of the self. His evil means that he has consented to what he has become—namely, one who consents to cruelty. Thus, Abélardians try to fill the statistical cracks with the will. The development of the moral self, they will say, is mediated by consent.

We should be struck here by the a priori character of libertarian convictions. How is Harris's consent to be construed, and why *must* it have occurred? What evidence is there that it occurred? Why couldn't Harris just have become that way? What is the difference between his having acquiesced to what he became and his simply having become that way? The libertarian faces the following difficulty: If there is no such difference, then the view is vacuous, for consent was supposed to explain his becoming that way. If there is a difference, what evidence is there that it obtains in a particular case? Isn't there room for considerable doubt about this, and shouldn't libertarians, or we, insofar as we are libertarians, be very doubtful about Harris's responsibility—and indeed, on the Abélardian thesis, even about whether Harris is an evil man, whether his soul is morally marred? (Notice that the tumor case is a priori impossible on that thesis, unless we think of the tumor somehow as merely presenting an occasion for consent—as inclining without necessitating.) One suspects that the libertarian confidence in their attributions of historical responsibility is rooted in a picture according to which the fact that Harris became that way *proves* that he consented. Then, of course, the appeal to consent is explanatorily vacuous.

Epistemology apart, the attempt to trace the evil self to consent at an earlier stage is faced with familiar difficulties. If we suppose (fancifully) that Harris, earlier on, with full knowledge and deliberation, launched himself on his iniquitous career,[21] we would be merely postponing the inquiry, for the will which could fully and deliberately consent to such a career would have to have its roots in a self which is already morally marred—a self, therefore, which cannot itself be seen simply as a product of consent. Are we instead to suppose that at some earlier stage Harris slipped heedlessly or recklessly into patterns of thought and action which he ought to have known would eventuate in an evil character? (This seems to have been Aristotle's view in *Nicomachean Ethics*, Book III.5.) In that case, we would be tracing his present ways to the much less egregious faults of negligence.[22]

---

20 Peter Abélard, *Ethics* (c. 1139), in *Ethical Writings* (Indianapolis: Hackett, 1995), p. 10.

21 If such a thing ever occurred, it must have occurred at a stage when Harris clearly would have fallen under the exemption condition of "being a child".

22 Adams makes this point; *op. cit.*

Responsibility for Self

Strawson and others often charge libertarians with a metaphysically dubious conception of the self. The foregoing reflections indicate a basis for this charge. Libertarianism combines the Abélardian view about consent (or something like it) with the principle (or something like it) that to be responsible for anything, one must be responsible for (some of) what produces it. If we think of agents as consenting to this or that *because* they are (or have?) selves of a certain character, then it looks as though they are responsible for so consenting only if they are responsible for the self in which that consent is rooted. To establish this in each case, we have to trace the character of the self to earlier acts of consent. This enterprise seems hopeless, since the trace continues interminably or leads to a self to which the individual did not consent. The libertarian seems committed, then, to bearing the unbearable burden of showing how we can be responsible for ourselves. This burden can seem bearable only in a view of the self as an entity that mysteriously both transcends and intervenes in the "causal nexus", because it is both product and author of its actions and attitudes.

Must libertarians try to bear this burden? Perhaps the idea that they must rests upon a view of the self to which libertarians need not be committed. Perhaps the trouble arises in the first place from viewing the self as a thing standing in causal relation to acts of consent. The libertarian might say that to talk about the (moral) self is not to talk about an entity which necessitates specific acts of consent, but to talk about the sorts of things to which an individual tends to consent. To speak of Harris's moral self is not to explain his conduct, but to indicate the way he is morally. What we are responsible for are the particular things we consent to. We need not consider whether we are responsible for the genesis of the entity whose characteristics necessitate those acts of consent, for there is no such entity. In a way, of course, one is derivatively responsible for one's self, since one's moral self is constituted by the character of what one consents to, and one is responsible for what one consents to.[23]

The historical dimension of the concept of responsibility results from the principle that one is not responsible for one's conduct if that is necessitated by causes for which one is not responsible. This leads to a problematic requirement that one be responsible for one's self only if one thinks of the self as an entity that causes one's (its) actions and willings. Libertarians can reject this view. What they must affirm is that we are responsible for what we consent to, that consent is not necessitated by causes internal or external to the agent, and that if it were, we could not properly hold the individual responsible for what he or she consents to. These claims are far from self-evident. But they hardly amount to a "panicky metaphysics" (FR, 36/80).[24]

---

[23] It is noteworthy that Harris himself seems to accept responsibility for his life: "He told me he had his chance, he took the road to hell and there's nothing more to say." (From the end of the first excerpt from the Corwin article.)

[24] For an attempt at libertarianism without metaphysics, see David Wiggins, "Towards a Credible Form of Libertarianism", in Watson 2003. Wiggins responds specifically to Strawson at pp. 117–20.

In the end, however, I do not think that libertarianism can be so readily domesticated. The idea that one is responsible for and only for what one consents to is not of course distinctive of libertarianism; that idea has no historical implications. What is distinctive is the further requirement that consent be undetermined. I do not think the idea that consent is undetermined is in itself particularly problematic. The trouble begins only when we ask why this is *required*. The ground of this requirement is the intuition that unless consent were undetermined, we would not truly be *originators* of our deeds. We would be merely products, and not, as it were, producers. It is this intuition to which the libertarian finds it so difficult to give content. "Being an originator" does not mean just "consenting to", for that is already covered by the first thesis. Nor is this notion captured simply by adding the requirement of indeterminism; that is a merely negative condition. Attempts to specify the condition in positive terms either cite something that could obtain in a deterministic world, or something obscurely transcendent.

I suspect, then, that any metaphysically innocuous version of libertarianism must leave its incompatibilist component unmotivated.

Ignorance and Skepticism

I have been exploring some ways in which the expressive theory might explain the relevance of certain historical considerations. Whatever the best explanation may be, the remarkable fact is that we are, for the most part, quite ignorant of these considerations. Why does our ignorance not give us more pause? If, for whatever reason, reactive attitudes are sensitive to historical considerations, as Strawson acknowledges, and we are largely ignorant of these matters, then it would seem that most of our reactive attitudes are hasty, perhaps even benighted, as skeptics have long maintained. In this respect, our ordinary practices are not as unproblematic as Strawson supposes.

It might be thought that these suspicions about reactive attitudes have no bearing on responsibility, but on the expressive theory, that thought cannot be easily maintained. As we normally think of the matter, not all considerations that affect reactive attitudes are strictly relevant to responsibility. For example, if one shares a moral fault with another, one may feel it inappropriate to blame the other. Here the point is not that the other is not responsible or blameworthy, but that it is not *one's* business to blame. One should tend to one's own faults first.[25] Thoughts about moral luck seem to be continuous with this ordinary phenomenon. The thought is not that the other is not blameworthy, but that one may be no better, and that indignation on one's part would be self-righteous and indulgent. By calling our attention to our general ignorance of historical considerations, the skepticism we have just been considering is merely an extension of these reflections.

---

25 Montaigne would not agree: "To censure my own faults in some other person seems to me no more incongruous than to censure, as I often do, another's in myself. They must be denounced everywhere, and be allowed no place of sanctuary."("On the Education of Children", in *Essays*, Penguin Classics, 1971, p. 51.)

With an expressive theory, however, it is not clear that a general skepticism about the propriety of the reactive attitudes can be separated from skepticism about responsibility. For the latter concept *is* the concept of the conditions in which it is appropriate to respond to one another in reactive ways. In a Strawsonian view, there is no room for a wedge between the practices that evince the reactive attitudes and the belief in responsibility. In a particular case, one may believe another to be responsible without actually responding to him or her in reactive ways (due to strains of commitment and so on), because one may regard the other as blameworthy, as an appropriate object of the reactive attitudes by others in the moral community. But if one thinks that *none* of us mortals is in a position to blame, then it is doubtful that any sense can be given to the belief that the other is nonetheless blameworthy. One can still attribute cowardice, thoughtlessness, cruelty, and so on, to others; but as we have seen, these judgments are not sufficient in a Strawsonian view to characterize the practice of holding responsible. We might try to appeal to the reactive attitudes of a select group of actual or hypothetical judges, but then the connection to reactive attitudes becomes so tenuous or hypothetical that the attitudes lose the central role they are given in "Freedom and Resentment", and the expressive theory loses its distinctive character. It then collapses into the view discussed above (at pp. 119–21) in the section called "Blaming and finding fault".

Objectivity and Isolation

It remains unclear to what extent our ordinary practices involve dubious beliefs about ourselves and our histories. To acknowledge the relevance of historical considerations is, on any account, to acknowledge a potential source of skepticism about those practices; moreover, in a Strawsonian account (though not in a libertarian account), such skepticism cannot be readily separated from skepticism about responsibility itself. In this respect, Strawson is inordinately optimistic about our common ways.

However, these practices are vulnerable to a different kind of suspicion. This suspicion is related to Strawson's conception of the place of "retributive" sentiments in those practices, and to his claim that that practice, so conceived, is not something that is optional and open to radical criticism, but rather is part of the "framework" of our conception of human society. One could agree that the expressive theory best gives the basis and content of the practice of holding responsible and still maintain that abandoning this practice is not only conceivable but desirable, for what it expresses is itself destructive of human community. I conclude with some comments on this further issue.

Consider some remarks by Albert Einstein:

> I do not at all believe in human freedom in the philosophical sense. Everybody acts not only under external compulsion but also in accordance with inner necessity. Schopenhauer's saying: "A man can do what he wants, but not want what he wants", has been a very real inspiration to me since my youth; it has been a continual consolation in the face of life's hardships, my own and others', and an unfailing well-spring of tolerance. This realization mercifully mitigates the easily paralysing sense of responsibility and prevents us from

taking ourselves and other people all too seriously; it is conducive to a view of life which, in particular, gives humor its due.[26]

Significantly, in the same place Einstein speaks of himself as a "lone traveler", with a "pronounced lack of need for direct contact with other human beings and human communities", who has

> never belonged to my country, my home, my friends, or even my immediate family, with my whole heart; in the face of all these ties, I have never lost a sense of distance and a need for solitude—feelings which increase with the years.

The point that interests me here is not that these remarks confute Strawson's claim that reactive attitudes are never in practice affected by an acceptance of determinism, but that they corroborate his central claim about the alternative to the reactive, participant stance. The "distance" of which Einstein speaks is just an aspect of the "detachment" Strawson thinks characterizes the objective stance. At its extremes, it takes the form of human isolation. What is absent from Einstein's outlook is something that, I suspect, Strawson cherishes: the attachment or commitment to the personal, as it might be called.[27]

Whatever its grounds, Einstein's outlook is not without its appeal. Perhaps part of its appeal can be attributed to a fear of the personal, but it is also appealing precisely on account of its repudiation of the retributive sentiments. In another place, Einstein salutes the person "to whom aggressiveness and resentment are alien".[28] Can such an ideal of the person be pursued only at the cost of the attachment to the personal? Must we choose between isolation and animosity?

Some of Strawson's remarks imply that we must:

> Indignation, disapprobation, like resentment, tend to inhibit or at least to limit our goodwill towards the object of these attitudes, tend to promote at least partial and temporary withdrawal of goodwill .... (These are not contingent connections.) But these attitudes ... are precisely the correlates of the moral demand in the case where the demand is felt to be disregarded. The making of the demand *is* the proneness to such attitudes .... The holding of them does not ... involve ... viewing their object other than as a member of the moral community. The partial withdrawal of goodwill which these attitudes entail, the modification they entail of the general demand that another should if possible be spared suffering, is ... the consequence of *continuing* to view him as a member of the moral community: only as one who has offended against its demands. So the preparedness to acquiesce in that infliction of suffering on the offender which is an essential part of punishment is all of a piece with this whole range of attitudes ... (FR, 34/77).

---

26 Albert Einstein. *Ideas and Opinions* (Crown Publishers, 1982), pp. 8–9.

27 To what extent Einstein lived up to this outlook, I am not prepared to say. Some other writings suggest a different view: "External compulsion can ... reduce but never cancel the responsibility of the individual. In the Nuremberg trials, this idea was considered to be self-evident .... Institutions are in a moral sense impotent unless they are supported by the sense of responsibility of living individuals. An effort to arouse and strengthen this sense of responsibility of the individual is an important service to mankind" (*op. cit.*, p. 27). Is Einstein taking a consequentialist stance here?

28 Ibid.

This passage is troubling. Some have aspired to rid themselves of the readiness to limit goodwill and to acquiesce in the suffering of others not in order to relieve the strains of involvement, nor out of a conviction in determinism, but out of a certain ideal of human relationships, which they see as poisoned by the retributive sentiments. It is an ideal of human fellowship or love which embodies values that are arguably as historically important to our civilization as the notion of moral responsibility itself. The question here is not whether this aspiration is finally commendable, but whether it is compatible with holding one another morally responsible. The passage implies that it is not.

If holding one another responsible involves making the moral demand, and if the making of the demand *is* the proneness to such attitudes, and if such attitudes involve retributive sentiments and hence[29] a limitation of goodwill, then skepticism about retribution is skepticism about responsibility, and holding one another responsible is at odds with one historically important ideal of love.

Many who have this ideal, such as Gandhi or King,[30] do not seem to adopt an objective attitude in Strawson's sense. Unlike Einstein's, their lives do not seem characterized by human isolation: They are often intensely involved in the "fray" of interpersonal relations. Nor does it seem plausible to suppose that they do not hold themselves and others morally responsible: They *stand up* for themselves and others against their oppressors; they *confront* their oppressors with the fact of their misconduct, *urging* and even *demanding* consideration for themselves and others; but they manage, or come much closer than others to managing, to do such things without vindictiveness or malice.

Hence, Strawson's claims about the interpenetration of responsibility and the retributive sentiments must not be confused with the expressive theory itself. As these lives suggest, the retributive sentiments can in principle be stripped away from holding responsible and the demands and appeals in which this consists. What is left are various forms of reaction and appeal to others as moral agents. The boundaries of moral responsibility are the boundaries of intelligible moral address. To regard another as morally responsible is to react to him or her as a moral self.[31]

Postscript to "Responsibility and the Limits of Evil"

Robert Harris, often described in the media as the "laughing killer", didn't get the last laugh. That went to some of the witnesses of his execution at San Quentin Prison on 21 April 1992. Michael Kroll described what he saw that morning for *The Nation* magazine (6 July, 1992). Calling himself "a close friend [of Harris] for nearly a decade", Kroll records that as Harris was finally fastened to the chair in the gas chamber, he looked around and, recognizing the father of one of his victims, mouthed the words: "I'm sorry". Sixteen minutes after the cyanide was released, an official pronounced Harris dead. The scene that prompted the laughter, according to Kroll,

---

29 Rather than attempting to separate retribution from responsibility, one might try to harmonize retribution and goodwill. This possibility seems to me worth exploring.

30 For these examples, and the discussion in this section, I am indebted to Stern (*op. cit.*).

31 We have, of course, seen reasons why these boundaries require further delineation.

was this: for seven minutes, Harris "writhed ..., his head falling on his chest .... He lifted his head again and again .... His heart ... kept pumping for nine more minutes." In this way, the state of California enacted the reactive attitudes of its citizens.

Kroll writes:

> We were in the middle of something indescribably ugly. Not just the fact of the cold-blooded killing of a human being, and not even the fact that we happened to love him—but the ritual of it, the witnessing itself of this most private and personal act. It was nakedly barbaric. Nobody could say this had anything to do with justice, I thought. Yet this medieval torture chamber is what a larger majority of my fellow Californians ... believe in. The implications of this filled me with fear ... while my friend was being strangled slowly to death in front of me.

One thing is clear from this report that was not obvious at the time of the killings: in his last years Harris either remained, or became once again, capable of friendship and remorse. His crimes were monstrous, but he was not a monster after all. He was one of us.

Chapter 7

Strawson's Way of Naturalizing Responsibility

Paul Russell

P.F. Strawson interprets the "Pessimist" as one who claims that if determinism is true then the attitudes and practices associated with moral responsibility cannot be justified and must be abandoned altogether. Against the Pessimist Strawson argues that no reasoning of any sort could lead us to abandon or suspend our "reactive attitudes". He claims that responsibility is a "given" of human life and society—something which we are inescapably committed to. In this article I argue that Strawson's reply to the Pessimist is seriously flawed. In particular, he fails to distinguish two very different forms or modes of naturalism and he is constrained by the nature of his own objectives (i.e. the refutation of Pessimism) to embrace the stronger and less plausible form of naturalism.

> Where Nature thus determines us, we have an original non-rational commitment which sets the bounds within which, or the stage upon which, reason can effectively operate.
> – P.F. Strawson, Skepticism and Naturalism

In this article I am concerned with a central strand of Strawson's well-known and highly influential essay "Freedom and Resentment".[1] One of Strawson's principal objectives in this work is to refute or discredit the views of the "Pessimist". The Pessimist, as Strawson understands him, claims that the truth of the thesis of determinism would render the attitudes and practices associated with moral responsibility incoherent and unjustified. Given this, the Pessimist claims that if determinism is true, then we must abandon or suspend these attitudes and practices altogether. Against the Pessimist Strawson argues that no reasoning of any sort could lead us to abandon or suspend out "reactive attitudes". That is to say, according to Strawson responsibility is a "given" of human life and society—something which we are inescapably committed to.[2] In this article I will argue that Strawson's

---

1   Page references to "Freedom and Resentment" will be to pages 19–36 of this volume, followed by (after the slash) the corresponding pages, 59–80, of Gary Watson (ed.), *Free Will*. Thus, for example, 'FR, 26/68' refers to this volume, p. 26/and *Free Will*, p. 68. References to P.F. Strawson, *Skepticism and Naturalism* (London: Methuen, 1985) will be abbreviated as SN—the editors.

2   This is a theme that Strawson emphasizes repeatedly, both in "Freedom and Resentment" and his more recent work *Skepticism and Naturalism*. Whatever we may think of this claim, it cannot be dismissed as an unnecessary or inessential aspect of Strawson's general position. On the contrary, as I will show, it plays a crucial role in Strawson's effort to refute or discredit the views of the Pessimist. In a highly sympathetic discussion of "Freedom

reply to the Pessimist is seriously flawed. More specifically, I argue that Strawson fails to distinguish two very different forms or modes of naturalism and that he is constrained by the nature of his own objectives (i.e., the refutation of Pessimism) to embrace the stronger and far less plausible form of naturalism. On this basis I conclude that while there is something to be said for Strawson's general approach to these matters, we nevertheless cannot naturalize responsibility along the specific lines that he suggests.[3]

I.

Strawson develops his analysis of the nature and conditions of moral responsibility on the basis of what he takes to be a "commonplace" observation: the attitudes and intentions which individuals manifest to each other are of great importance to human beings, and we react to each other accordingly (FR, 21–2/62–3). Strawson claims that perplexity has been generated on the subject of moral responsibility largely because philosophers have been unable or unwilling to recognize or acknowledge the significance of "reactive attitudes and feelings" in this sphere. (Hereafter, I will refer simply to "reactive attitudes".) More specifically, it is our reactive attitudes, Strawson claims, which are essential to, or constitutive of, the whole framework or fabric of moral responsibility. It seems clear, then, that we must consider the arguments of the Pessimist from this general perspective.

There are two different claims which are constitutive of the Pessimist's outlook.[4] The Pessimist maintains, first, that if the thesis of determinism is true, then we have

---

and Resentment" Jonathan Bennett has distanced himself, in this respect, from Strawson's position. Bennett claims that Strawson places too much emphasis on the claim "that we could not possibly relinquish all reactive feelings" (Jonathan Bennett, "Accountability", in *Philosophical Subjects*, ed. Zak van Straaten [Oxford: Oxford University Press, 1980], p. 30). Whatever Bennett's views on this subject may be, however, Strawson does not show any sign of withdrawing any emphasis on this claim. See, for example, Strawson's remarks to the contrary in his reply to Bennett: "What I was above all concerned to stress ...." (P.F. Strawson, "Replies", in van Straaten (ed.), p. 265). More critical discussions of Strawson's views, closer to my own position in this article, can be found in A.J. Ayer, "Free Will and Rationality," in van Straaten (ed.), pp. 1–13 (reprinted in this volume, pp. 37–46) and in Thomas Nagel, *The View from Nowhere* (Oxford: Oxford University Press, 1986), Ch. 7, sec. 4.

3 On my interpretation, the core of Strawson's naturalism in regard to responsibility is contained in the claim that moral responsibility is in some way a "given" or inescapable feature of human life and existence—and it is this claim that I am especially concerned with. However, the naturalistic approach may be described in more general terms, as involving two closely related principles. First, it insists upon an empirical, descriptive approach to this issue—one that has an informed and plausible moral psychology. Second, the naturalistic approach emphasizes the role of emotion or feeling in this sphere. Clearly, the narrower claim has its foundations in the more general principles guiding the naturalistic approach.

4 There is, of course, a large literature defending the Pessimist outlook—particularly from a libertarian perspective. The classic statement in this century is given by C.A. Campbell: "Is 'Freewill' a Pseudo-Problem?", reprinted in *Free Will and Determinism*, ed. Bernard Berofsky (New York: Harper & Row, 1966), pp. 112–35. Strawson's asides concerning "contra-causal

reason to reject and repudiate the (established) attitudes and practices associated with moral responsibility on the ground that they are incoherent and unjustified. Beyond this, the Pessimist supposes that if we have reason to suspend or abandon the attitudes and practices associated with moral responsibility, then we are, psychologically or practically speaking, capable of doing so. Strawson rejects both Pessimist claims. In reply to the Pessimist he weaves together two quite distinct lines of argument, each of which corresponds to the two key claims of the Pessimist noted above. I will distinguish these lines of argument as the "rationalistic strategy" and the "naturalistic strategy". Strawson believes that his anti-Pessimist strategies, although independent of each other, are, nevertheless, consistent and mutually supportive. I will show that their relations with each other are not as straightforward as Strawson supposes.

Let us consider these strategies in more detail. The Pessimist believes that if determinism is true, excusing considerations will (somehow) apply to all human action and thus hold universally. It follows that in these circumstances no individual is ever responsible for anything. Strawson's rationalistic strategy counters by way of an analysis of excusing considerations. Under what circumstances, he asks, do we "modify or mollify" our reactive attitudes or withhold them altogether? There are, he maintains, two different sorts of excusing consideration (FR, 23–5/64–6). The first sort—which I will refer to as "specific" considerations—in no way suggests that the agent is (either temporarily or permanently) an inappropriate object of reactive attitudes or one of whom it is not reasonable to demand some degree of goodwill and regard. Rather, in these cases (e.g., accident, ignorance, etc.) "the fact of injury [is] quite consistent with the agent's attitude and intentions being just what we demand they should be". By contrast, the second part of excusing consideration—which I will refer to as "global" consideration—invites us to withdraw entirely our reactive attitudes in regard to the agent on the ground that the individual is not one of whom we can make the usual demand of goodwill. Such individuals may be placed in abnormal circumstances (e.g., stressed, drugged, etc.) or, more important, they may be either psychologically abnormal or morally underdeveloped. In situations such as these we must adopt what Strawson describes as the "objective attitude". "To adopt the objective attitude to another human being is to see him, perhaps, as an object of social policy; as a subject for what, in a wide range of sense, might be called treatment; as something ... to be managed or handled or cured or trained ... *But it cannot include the range of reactive feelings and attitudes which belong to involvement or participation with others in inter-personal human relationships*" (FR, 25/66; my emphasis). It is important to be very clear about how the objective attitude relates to excusing considerations. The following distinction is especially important. (a) Where excusing considerations of the second sort apply ("abnormality", etc.) we must – that is, we are rationally and morally required to – adopt the objective attitude (FR, 24–6/66–8 and SN, 39–40). In other words, as Strawson's rationalistic strategy would have it, there are circumstances in which the objective attitude is not merely an option for us, regarding certain individuals but it is, rather, demanded of

---

freedom" suggest that he has Campbell primarily in mind; cf. FR, 35/79 with Campbell's remark that "moral responsibility implies a contra-causal type of freedom" (p. 126).

us (at least, insofar as we are "civilized"; cf. FR, 26–7/68–9)[5] (b) There are other circumstances, it is argued, when the objective attitude is an available option, which we may choose to adopt if we wish, though we are not required to do so. That is to say, the objective attitude may sometimes be adopted even when we are dealing with "the normal and mature" because we want, for example, to use it as a "refuge from the strains of involvement" or an "aid to policy" (FR, 25–6, 26, 27, 30–31/67, 68, 69, 73; and SN, 34). However, in these cases (i.e., circumstances where we are dealing with normal adults) there are strict limits to the extent to which we can adopt the objective attitude. More specifically, being human, Strawson says: "we cannot *in the normal case*, do this for long or altogether" (FR, 25/67; my emphasis).

In what way are Strawson's observations concerning excusing considerations supposed to refute the Pessimist? Strawson maintains that nothing about the thesis of determinism implies that we always act accidentally, or in ignorance, or without forethought. Nor does the thesis suggest that we are all (somehow) rendered psychologically abnormal or morally undeveloped. In short, considerations of determinism, however they are interpreted, do not, as such, provide us with any reason to modify or suspend our reactive attitudes. The grounds on which we do suspend or alter our reactive attitudes are of a wholly distinct and independent nature (FR, 25–6, 31/67–8, 74). We have, accordingly, no reason whatsoever to suspend or abandon our reactive attitudes entirely even if the thesis of determinism is true. This is the essence of Strawson's rationalistic reply to the Pessimist.

The rationalistic strategy does not, by itself, convey the real force or power of Strawson's position. The most interesting and most controversial aspect of Strawson's reply to the Pessimist is contained in the naturalistic strategy. The heart of the naturalistic strategy is the claim that it is psychologically impossible to suspend or abandon our reactive attitudes entirely. Our "human commitment" to the whole framework of reactive attitudes is so "thoroughgoing and deeply rooted" in our nature that it is "practically inconceivable" (though perhaps not self-contradictory) that we should simply "give them up" or entirely abandon them. A sustained objectivity of attitude to all people through time "does not seem to be something of which human beings would be capable, *even if some general truth were a theoretical ground for it*" (FR, 27/68). Our "commitment" to reactive attitudes is, on this account, insulated from skeptical doubts by our inherent nature or constitution. It is, therefore, "useless" and "idle" to ask whether or not it would be rational to suspend or abandon our reactive attitudes if the thesis of determinism is true. On any interpretation, no such option is available to us. If reason were to point us in this direction, Strawson argues, we would be constitutionally incapable of following its lead. Clearly, then, we cannot expect to follow reason in an area where it is nature that must be our guide (FR, 31, 34–5/74, 78–9).[6] Contrary to what Strawson seems to suppose, there

---

5   Strawson, it should be noted, speaks of the objective attitude as being a consequence of viewing the agent as one in respect of whom global excusing considerations apply (FR, 26–7/68–9). This indicates the strength of the demand that we withdraw reactive attitudes in these circumstances.

6   The same themes are pressed by Strawson with, perhaps, even greater vigor in *Skepticism and Naturalism*. Arguments and counterarguments concerning whether it would

are, I suggest, significant strains between his two anti-Pessimist strategies. That is to say, on the face of it, the naturalistic strategy appears to imply that the rationalistic strategy, considered as a response to the Pessimist, is fundamentally mistaken or misguided. To reason with the Pessimist, to endeavor to meet his arguments with counterarguments, is, according to the naturalistic strategy, to share the Pessimist's mistaken views about the nature of our commitment to reactive attitudes. That is, insofar as the rationalist strategy is understood as an effort to show that we have no reason to suspend or abandon our reactive attitudes (if the thesis of determinism is true), it suggests that without some adequate philosophical or rational defense our reactive attitudes may indeed (have to) be abandoned altogether. From the point of view of the naturalistic strategy, such an approach is wholly mistaken. This observation suggests that something has gone amiss in Strawson's twofold reply to the Pessimist. A more detailed analysis of Strawson's specific arguments will reveal where the trouble lies.

II.

Lying at the heart of Strawson's naturalistic strategy is, I have argued, the claim that it is psychologically impossible to suspend or abandon our reactive attitudes altogether (i.e., such reactions are an inescapable feature of human life). This claim is, of course, intimately bound up with the related but distinct claim that responsibility must be understood or interpreted in terms of our emotional reactions or responses to the attitudes and intentions which we manifest to one another. Strawson speaks of "reactive attitudes and feelings" but he points out that the phrase "moral sentiments" would be a good name for the network of emotions that he is concerned with (FR, 35/79). When we recognize the parallels between our reactive attitudes and other emotions, it seems that much of what Strawson is claiming falls into place. The fact that the whole framework of reactive attitudes "neither calls for nor permits, an external 'rational' justification" is easily understood once we recognize that the reactive attitudes (or moral sentiments) are simply a species of emotion. No species or type of emotion requires an external rational justification. Nor is there any question of us suspending, abandoning, or giving up the various emotions (e.g., love, hate, fear, grief, etc.) of which we are susceptible. Within the framework of these emotions there may be, as Strawson suggests, considerable scope for criticism, modification, redirection, and justification. Clearly, however, "questions of justification are internal to the structure [of any particular species of emotion] or relate to modifications internal to it." It is, as Strawson suggests, useless

---

be rational for us to suspend the whole framework of our reactive attitudes (given the truth of some general metaphysical thesis) are both, equally "inefficacious and idle". Such arguments are beside the point because our reactive attitudes are "neither shaken by skeptical argument nor reinforced by rational counter-argument" (SN, 39). In other words, reason simply does not operate at this level of moral life. In respect of these matters, Strawson claims to follow "Hume the naturalist against Hume the skeptic". "According to Hume the naturalist", Strawson says: "skeptical doubts are not to be met by argument. *They are simply to be neglected*" (SN, 12–14, 38–9; my emphasis).

to ask whether it would or would not be rational to "suspend" a particular species or type of emotion. Someone who presses such a question reveals that he or she has failed to grasp the fact that our "commitment" to a given kind of emotion is simply founded upon human nature. Further, someone who presses this sort of question reveals that he has failed to grasp the role which reason plays in justifying our emotions. Our questioner has, as Strawson puts it, "over-intellectualized" the facts and, consequently, her whole line of questioning proceeds from presuppositions which are themselves seriously mistaken.

Consider, for example, the emotion of fear.[7] When we are afraid, there are many considerations which may be brought to our attention which will "modify or mollify" this emotion (i.e., particular instances or given tokens of this emotion). Sometimes, for example, we may recognize, in the light of new information, that our being afraid is unjustified or unreasonable. At other times, we may recognize that we actually have good reason for being afraid. Clearly, then, we all recognize in day-to-day life that this emotion may be deemed reasonable or unreasonable, justified or unjustified, depending on the circumstances. Thus, on any particular occasion, if relevant considerations are brought to our attention, we may either cease to be afraid or become afraid. Beyond this, however, the question of justifying the fact that we are susceptible to this species of emotion does not arise. The whole framework of the emotion of fear, obviously, comes with our human nature. Nor is there any question of us giving a reason for the fact that this species of emotion is "retained". We no more need to, or can, justify the fact that we are susceptible of fear than we need to, or can, justify the fact that the human being is born with a heart and two kidneys.[8] In short, an appreciation of the parallels between reactive attitudes and other emotions provides considerable support for the view that reactive attitudes require no external, rational justification and are, at least in some sense, a given of our human nature.[9]

---

7 The analogy between reactive altitudes and fear is suggested by Strawson; see his "Replies", p. 265.

8 Consider what may happen if we fail to grasp this point: namely, that the emotion of fear requires no external rational justification. More than likely, some philosopher (e.g., a "one-eyed utilitarian") will suggest that this emotion is justified by its social utility. Without fear, it may be argued, man would not respond so effectively in dangerous situations and this would threaten our species. Thus, it may be suggested that this emotion can be "justified" in terms of considerations regarding our individual well-being and the interests of human society. It is, I think, obvious that this line of reasoning is mistaken. Were we to discover, e.g., that the emotion of fear is of little value to man, we could hardly reason ourselves into "abandoning" this emotion altogether (although, no doubt, we would do our best to inhibit it).

9 The inclination to justify the fact that we are susceptible to various species or types of emotion is perhaps encouraged by certain theological doctrines. In particular, once it is assumed that God made humans the way we are with some reason or purpose in mind, then it is not entirely unnatural to ask for a general, external rationale for the emotion in question. Thus Bishop Butler, e.g., in his sermon "Upon Resentment", asks: Why, for what end, is "so harsh and turbulent" a passion as resentment "given" to man? Butler argues that the passion, "as implanted in our nature by God", has a good influence "upon the affairs of the world". Men, he suggests: "are plainly restrained from injuring their fellow-creatures by fear of resentment; and it is very happy that they are so, when they would not be restrained by a principle of virtue" (Joseph Butler, *Fifteen Sermons*, [London: Bell & Sons, 1949], p.

Strawson, as I have indicated, believes that these naturalistic observations constitute an effective way of refuting or discrediting Pessimism. I believe that he is mistaken about this. Consider, again, the parallels between reactive attitudes and the emotion of fear. Suppose that we encounter a pessimist with respect to fear—the counterpart of the Pessimist with respect to reactive attitudes. There are, I suggest, two very different sorts of pessimism that we may be presented with. The first, type-pessimism, focuses on the supposed need for an (external, rational) justification for the fact that we are susceptible or liable to fear. Having failed to identify any satisfactory justification of this nature, the fear-type-pessimist maintains that we can and must free ourselves of this (irrational) disposition to fear. The appropriate response to this mode of pessimism is provided, in general terms, by the naturalistic argument or observations outlined above. Let us refer to this response as type-naturalism. Type-naturalism claims that our liability to fear is natural to humans and requires no general justification of any sort. It is not possible for us to disengage from fear at this level.

The fear-pessimist may reply, at this point, that his concerns have been misunderstood. The fear-pessimist should be interpreted as claiming only that given our circumstances we are never justified in being afraid (i.e., we are never justified in entertaining any tokens of fear). This claim may be in itself highly implausible, but it cannot be dismissed on the ground that it commits the fear-pessimist to type-pessimism (i.e., the demand for external, rational justifications, etc.). On the contrary, the fear-pessimist, on this account, insists on being interpreted as a token-pessimist and rightly points out that this is consistent with being a type-naturalist. In other words, it is at least consistent to maintain that while we may be (naturally) prone or liable to fear, we are nevertheless capable of altogether ceasing to feel or experience fear if and when we judge that, given our circumstances, this emotion is never justified.

What, then, is the appropriate (naturalistic) reply to this distinct form of pessimism? The most obvious strategy is to establish that, contrary to what has been claimed, we regularly and inevitably encounter circumstances in which fear is entirely appropriate or reasonable and, hence, feelings or experiences of fear will continue to be an inescapable part of human life. It is important to note, however, that this reply turns, crucially, on the claim that we do regularly and inevitably encounter the relevant or appropriate circumstances or conditions required to render fear reasonable or appropriate. The naturalist of a Strawsonian disposition may regard such a response as conceding too much to the fear-pessimist. Accordingly, a stronger line may be pursued. It may be argued that no reasoning of any sort could ever lead us to cease altogether entertaining or feeling this emotion. That is to say, on this strong naturalistic account, it is claimed that no reasoning or theoretical considerations of any sort can prevent us entirely from having or experiencing tokens of fear. Whatever considerations are brought to our attention regarding our

---

131 [Sermon 8]). The important point here is that while it, perhaps, makes some sense to ask for God's justification for "giving" man some species of emotion, it is senseless for men to demand of each other that they justify their own emotional make-up as if they created themselves *ex nihilo*.

circumstances—whatever reason may suggest to us—we will nevertheless continue to experience fear as an active force in our lives. No matter what arguments the fear-token-pessimist may present us with in an effort to show us that fear is never in order or called for, the fact is that we will continue to feel and experience fear. Nature, according to the token-naturalist, insulates us from the skeptical arguments of the token-pessimist no less than it insulates us from the skeptical arguments of the type-pessimist. We do not need to reason against token-pessimism any more than we need to reason against type-pessimism. Fear is natural to human beings not only in the sense that we are inescapably liable to this emotion but in the further, stronger, sense that we will inescapably or inevitably continue to entertain or feel this emotion, whatever reason suggests to us.

In respect of fear-pessimism, both type- and token-pessimism are equally implausible—but they are implausible for very different reasons. Type-pessimism, as I have suggested, misrepresents the way in which our disposition to fear is embedded in our human nature. There is no scope for skeptical anxieties at this level. Things are very different, however, with regard to token-pessimism. What is implausible about token-pessimism is the claim that circumstances are never such that fear is in order or justified. Clearly, we have good reason to be skeptical about this claim. Note, however, that if the token-pessimist were right about this, then it is not implausible to suggest that in these circumstances we should cease, and are capable of altogether ceasing, to entertain or feel (tokens of) fear. From this perspective it seems evident that the token-naturalist (unlike the type-naturalist) puts forward the wrong sort of reply to his pessimist counterpart. More specifically, the token-naturalist, in an effort to discredit the token-pessimist, makes claims that seem suspect in point of fact and which, in any case, do nothing to lift or remove the wholly legitimate concerns of the token-pessimist (i.e., that in the circumstances fear is inappropriate and uncalled for). The claims advanced are suspect in point of fact because it is far from obvious—indeed, it seems simply untrue—that we are constitutionally incapable of entirely ceasing to entertain or feel fear in circumstances where we believe that it is never appropriate or called for. Similarly, the claims advanced by the token-naturalist do nothing to lift or remove the (wholly legitimate) concerns of the token-pessimist because they do not even address the justificatory issue which is the focus of the token-pessimist's concerns.

The parallels between pessimism in respect of fear and pessimism in respect of reactive attitudes are, I believe, quite straightforward. The crucial question, therefore, is, What sort of naturalism does Strawson embrace? and—on the other side of the same coin—what sort of pessimism is he trying to discredit? Given our analysis of fear-pessimism it seems clear that Strawson's position is much more plausible if he is interpreted as a type-naturalist who is seeking to discredit type-pessimism in respect of reactive attitudes. Much of what Strawson says suggests that this is how he understands his own position (insofar as he draws the distinction at all). On this view of things the Pessimist who is the target of Strawson's remarks in "Freedom and Resentment" is a type-pessimist—one who believes that if determinism is true, then we are not justified in being disposed or prone to reactive attitudes and that we must, therefore (somehow) rid ourselves of this type or species of emotion.

This interpretation of the Pessimist's position, I believe, misrepresents the nature and character of her concerns. That is to say, the Pessimist may argue that the issue which ought to concern us is whether (granted our liability to reactive attitudes) we can or cannot reasonably or appropriately entertain or engage these attitudes. Strawson acknowledges that we may find ourselves in circumstances where our reactive attitudes are not called for or are inappropriate. Accordingly, at this level—the level of entertaining or engaging our reactive attitudes—emotional reactions of this nature can and must be withdrawn or suspended altogether when this is required of us. Clearly, then, while we may remain prone to reactive attitudes, they are, with us, in these circumstances, wholly inactive and disengaged (because they are acknowledged to be inappropriate and uncalled for). These straightforward observations—which Strawson readily accepts in the context of his rationalistic strategy—may be further extended by the Pessimist and applied to the question of determinism. The Pessimist does not (or need not) claim that we are capable of suspending or abandoning our disposition or liability to reactive attitudes—much less that the thesis of determinism requires us to do so. This is not the level at which her concerns arise. Rather, the Pessimist claims only that we can and must cease to entertain reactive attitudes toward any and all individuals who are morally incapacitated and that we are capable of ceasing altogether to engage or entertain reactive attitudes insofar as we have reason to believe that everyone is incapacitated in the relevant ways. If the thesis of determinism is true, the Pessimist argues, then we are, indeed, all morally incapacitated.[10] It is important to note that the Pessimist may be wrong in claiming or supposing that determinism implies that we are all so incapacitated and yet, nevertheless, still right in maintaining that if the truth of determinism does have these implications, then we are capable of ceasing altogether to entertain or engage out reactive attitudes. In order to assess independently Strawson's (distinct) rationalistic and naturalistic arguments, it is crucial that we distinguish these issues. The Pessimist, then, should be interpreted as claiming only that if the thesis of determinism is true, then (disposed as we may be to reactive attitudes) the fact is that our circumstances are such that we are never justified in entertaining or feeling (tokens of our) reactive attitudes. Moreover, in these circumstances, the Pessimist claims, we both can and must cease altogether to entertain such emotions. Clearly, then, so interpreted, the Pessimist is a token-Pessimist.

This analysis indicates that, from any perspective, Strawson's naturalistic reply to the Pessimist is seriously flawed. That is to say, if Strawson is embracing type-naturalism, then he does nothing to refute or discredit the Pessimist. If, on the other hand, he is embracing token-naturalism, then, worse still, he is embracing a position that is committed to suspect and disturbing factual claims and which, moreover, does not even address itself to the (legitimate) concerns of the Pessimist. The most plausible interpretation of Strawson's remarks in "Freedom and Resentment" (and *Skepticism and Naturalism*), I suggest, is that Strawson is putting forward both type-

---

10 The relevant capacity, according to libertarian-Pessimists at any rate, is "free will" or "contra-causal freedom" (see n. 4 above). Strawson objects to this aspect of the (libertarian) Pessimist's position on the ground that it involves "obscure and panicky metaphysics" (FR. 36/80; cf. sec. 6. *passim*). I will return to this issue below.

and token-naturalism (but fails entirely to distinguish adequately between them). Indeed, it seems clear that Strawson has to be arguing for (stronger) token-naturalism given his objectives. Strawson is fundamentally concerned to deny the Pessimist's supposition that we are capable of adopting the "objective attitude" toward everyone all of the time. To take up the objective attitude, as Strawson understands it, involves ceasing to entertain (tokens of) reactive attitudes toward some or all individuals. It does not, clearly, involve giving up our disposition or proneness to such attitudes (i.e., objectivity does involve giving up our "commitment" to this type of emotion). Only token-naturalism, therefore, stands opposed to the Pessimist's claim that we are capable of taking up the "objective attitude" toward everyone. That is to say, while a universal objectivity of attitude is compatible with type-naturalism, it is not compatible with token-naturalism. Strawson, then, can discredit the Pessimist's position by means of token-naturalism alone. If he withdraws from his token-naturalist claims, then he has no effective naturalistic reply to the Pessimist at all (keeping in mind that the Pessimist can readily embrace type-naturalism). In this way, we may conclude that Strawson is constrained by the nature of his own objectives to embrace token-naturalism and that this approach to the problem of responsibility entirely misfires.

In light of these observations it seems clear why the Pessimist finds Strawson's naturalistic reply both misguided and disturbing. What is particularly disturbing about Strawson's naturalistic strategy, expressed in more general terms, is that it casts doubt on our ability, or capacity to curb or control our emotional life according to the dictates of reason. More specifically, it seems clear that, despite disclaimers to the contrary, Strawson's naturalistic strategy invites us to accept or reconcile ourselves to reactive attitudes (and their associated retributive practices) even in circumstances when we have reason to repudiate them.[11] Given this, it seems evident that we have good reason to reject Strawson's suggestion that we dismiss the Pessimist and refuse to take her arguments seriously. We have, on the contrary, every reason to take the Pessimist seriously, and this puts greater weight on Strawson's rationalistic strategy. I will argue, however, that Strawson's rationalistic strategy, as he presents it, cannot bear this weight.

---

11 According to Strawson, our reactive attitudes and retributive practices are intimately (i.e., naturally or "humanly") connected. In FR, however, Strawson has very little to say about the problem of punishment as it arises within the framework of his naturalistic account of responsibility. (See FR, 34/77). More specifically, Strawson does nor consider in any detail to what extent, or in what way, our retributive practices are a "given" of human nature. Nor does he explain the relationship between justificatory issues as they arise for our reactive attitudes and as they arise for our retributive practices. Suffice it to say that I believe that Strawson's position encounters a number of (further) difficulties in this area. These matters are explored and discussed in some detail in my "Hume on Responsibility and Punishment", *Canadian Journal of Philosophy* 20 (1990): 539–64 (esp. sec. 3).

III.

Strawson's effort to discredit Pessimism by means of naturalistic claims leads, or compels, him, I maintain, to embrace an implausibly strong form of naturalism. The Pessimist cannot, I have argued, be refuted or discredited by means of a strategy or approach of this nature. It may be, however, that it is possible to refute or discredit the Pessimist's position by means of the rationalistic strategy which Strawson independently advances. More specifically, it may be argued that the Pessimist is mistaken in claiming that if the thesis of determinism is true, then we are all morally incapacitated. If this can be established, and the Pessimist's anxieties can be shown to be groundless, then there is no reason to accept the related claim which the Pessimist puts forward to the effect that if determinism is true, our reactive attitudes are never justified or appropriate. Strawson believes that the rationalistic arguments which he puts forward serve to discredit and refute Pessimism in just this way.

The rationalistic strategy, as I have noted, distinguishes between two different sorts of excusing considerations: specific and global considerations. Strawson maintains that the truth of the thesis of determinism does not, as such, imply that either specific or global excusing considerations apply universally. I am concerned with Strawson's specific argument(s) purporting to show that the truth of the thesis of determinism cannot lead to the conclusion that global excusing considerations apply to everyone. Strawson states: "The participant attitudes, and personal [and moral] reactive attitudes in general, tend to give place, and it is judged by the civilized should give place, to objective attitudes, just in so far as the agent is seen as excluded from ordinary adult human relationships by deep-rooted psychological abnormality—or simply by being a child. *But it cannot be a consequence of any thesis which is not itself self-contradictory that abnormality is the universal condition*" (FR, 26/68; my emphasis).[12] This argument is crucial to the success of Strawson's rationalistic strategy. Strawson, that is, must establish, against the Pessimist, that determinism does not (or cannot) imply that everyone is "abnormal". Failing this, the rationalistic strategy would collapse. Nevertheless, the argument that Strawson puts forward is wholly inadequate. Throughout these crucial sections Strawson's argument turns (repeatedly) on a conflation or equivocation between being "abnormal" and being "incapacitated". Contrary to the general drift of Strawson's remarks, it is not abnormality, as such, which excuses but, rather, incapacity. Strawson appears to be aware of the difficulty: "Now it is certainly true that in the case of the abnormal, though not in the case of the normal, our adoption of the objective attitude is a consequence of our viewing the agent as incapacitated in some or all respects for ordinary inter-personal relationships" (FR, 27/69; Strawson's emphasis).[13] While it is incapacity that lies at the heart of our concerns in these circumstances, Strawson

---

[12] Strawson seems to be aware that these remarks are not altogether satisfactory. He continues: "Now this dismissal might seem altogether too facile; and so in a sense it is".

[13] The inappropriate and misleading nature of Strawson's talk of "abnormality" in the context is revealed by its awkward coupling with references to children and those who are "morally underdeveloped". What is relevant here, clearly, is incapacity and not "abnormality".

has, nevertheless, developed his reply to the Pessimist in terms of the language of "abnormality" (see esp. FR, 23–4, 26/65, 68, where Strawson places particular emphasis on this terminology). This terminology, as I will show, has considerable significance for Strawson's argument.

If we replace Strawson's references to "the abnormal" and "abnormality" with references to "the incapacitated" and "incapacity", his reply to the Pessimist, quite simply, collapses. Obviously, it is not inconceivable or self-contradictory to suggest that there could be a world, or things might develop, such that everyone is or becomes incapacitated. Imagine, for example, the spread of some terrible disease or genetic mutation which affects the brain and thereby destroys our relevant capacities. Clearly, in this situation there is no correspondence or extensional equivalence between the "abnormal" and the "incapacitated". On the contrary, the "normal" person will be incapacitated and the "abnormal" person (if there is one) will have the requisite capacities. Given this, our reactive attitudes will be inappropriate in the normal case and appropriate in the abnormal case. These observations plainly indicate that it is misleading and mistaken to place any emphasis on considerations of "abnormality" and the like in this context. Strawson has identified the wrong grounds on which global excuses are founded.

In light of this, let us consider the Pessimist's position once again. The Pessimist, clearly, should not be understood as claiming that if determinism is true, we are all (psychologically) abnormal. Rather, the Pessimist claims only that if the thesis is true, then we are all morally incapacitated (and thus inappropriate objects of reactive attitudes). There is, I have pointed out, nothing self-contradictory about a thesis which suggests that incapacity is the universal condition. The relevant capacity, according to the (libertarian) Pessimist, is "free will" or "contracausal freedom". Against this aspect of the (libertarian) Pessimist's position, Strawson repeats a charge often heard: that is, that libertarian notions of "free will" and "contra-causal freedom" involve "obscure and panicky metaphysics". The force of these remarks, in other words, is that (libertarian) Pessimists are insisting on a condition of responsibility "which cannot be coherently described".[14] I have considerable sympathy with these claims. Moreover, observations of this general nature certainly succeed in casting doubt on one interpretation of what the relevant capacities are supposed to be. It is far from obvious, however, that in itself this establishes that the truth of the thesis of determinism poses no threat to our moral capacities and hence to our reactive attitudes. On the contrary, no conclusion of this nature can be drawn until we have some alternative characterization of the relevant capacities in question. Strawson has suggested what these capacities do not involve (i.e., free will, etc.), but he has little or nothing to say about what they do involve, or how they should be understood. The reason for this is that he thinks that he can circumvent this difficult and complicated issue by showing, simply, that no thesis can imply that we are all morally incapacitated (and hence determinism cannot pose a threat of this nature to our moral capacities and reactive attitudes). The specific argument that Strawson puts forward in this direction fails and, hence, as things stand, he has not established

---

14 Strawson, "Replies", p. 265.

that it is impossible that we are all morally incapacitated.[15] Given this, we obviously need to identify and describe the nature of the capacities in question so that the Pessimist's claims (i.e., that the truth of the thesis of determinism would leave us all morally incapacitated, etc.) can be properly evaluated. In other words, without some (more plausible) alternative characterization of the nature of these moral capacities, we cannot say with any assurance whether the truth of determinism would or would not affect their functioning. While it may be that something of an appropriate nature can be said on behalf of the rationalistic strategy in this regard, we cannot find it in Strawson's remarks on this subject.[16] In short, while Strawson claims to have shown that determinism cannot (logically) imply that we are all morally incapacitated, he has failed to do so. He has, rather, succeeded only in repeating the standard objection that libertarian notions of "free will" and "contra-causal freedom" are obscure and unhelpful accounts of the capacities required of moral agents. In light of this, I think that we must conclude that Strawson's rationalistic reply to the Pessimist is, as it stands, at best incomplete. No satisfactory reply to the Pessimist can avoid addressing itself to the question regarding the nature of the moral capacities required of individuals who are deemed appropriate objects of reactive attitudes.[17]

---

15 It is certainly true that were we to find ourselves in circumstances where everyone were morally incapacitated, and thus our reactive attitudes were never called for or in order, then, as Strawson suggests, in these circumstances we may well have an overwhelming sense of "human isolation" (FR, 26/68). Contrary to what is implied by Strawson's remarks (FR, 27–8, 31/69–70, 74), however, forward-looking considerations concerning "the gains and losses to human life, its enrichment or impoverishment" cannot serve to justify us in treating the incapacitated as if they were not incapacitated. In this respect I find myself in particular disagreement with Bennett. He states: "If we try to imagine our lives without reactive feelings we find ourselves ... confronted by bleak desolation. We cannot be obliged to give up something whose loss would gravely worsen the human condition, and *so reactive feelings cannot be made impermissible by any facts*" (Bennett, p. 29; my emphasis). If the force of these remarks is that no facts of any sort can render our reactive attitudes altogether inappropriate or uncalled for, then Bennett is, I believe, clearly mistaken.

16 The sorts of (alternative) capacities that I am thinking of have been widely discussed in more recent literature. See, in particular, papers by ... and Charles Taylor, "Responsibility for Self" in Watson (ed.) (1982; n. 1 above); and also Daniel Dennett, *Elbow Room* (Oxford: Oxford University Press, 1984), esp. Chs 2–5. All these authors, in different ways, emphasize our capacity to reflect upon our desires and restructure our will (i.e., those desires that lead to action) on this basis.

17 Throughout FR Strawson tends to assume that all Pessimists are libertarians and that they are, accordingly, motivated by libertarian metaphysical assumptions (FR, 20, 32–3, 34–5, 36/60–61, 75–6, 78–9, 80). It is not evident, however, that this needs to be the case. A Pessimist who accepts the two principal theses that Strawson is attacking (as described in Sect. I above) may also be what Strawson describes as a "moral skeptic": i.e., someone who believes that the attitudes and practices associated with moral responsibility are "inherently confused and that we can see this to be so if we consider the consequences either of the truth of determinism or its falsity" (FR, 19/59; cf. Ayer's position in "Free Will and Rationality" [n. 2 above]). Clearly, in dealing with the moral skeptic's claim that our reactive attitudes are never appropriate or called for, it will not suffice to argue that libertarian notions of "free will" are obscure and unhelpful. This is a point which the moral skeptic will readily concede.

IV.

Throughout this article my principal concern has been Strawson's naturalistic reply to the Pessimist.[18] Strawson, I point out, fails to distinguish between type- and token-naturalism. Token-naturalism is implausibly strong in both its nature and intent, and it serves only to discredit the naturalistic approach. The plausible and valuable element in the naturalistic approach is to be found in type-naturalism. Given his commitment to token-naturalism, we cannot naturalize responsibility along the lines that Strawson suggests. Nevertheless, when all vestiges of token-naturalism are removed, it is possible that we can construct a coherent and plausible (type) naturalistic framework within which some relevant rationalistic reply to the Pessimist may be developed. An approach of this nature does not encourage us to accept or reconcile ourselves to reactive attitudes (and their associated practices) irrespective of whether or not we have reason to repudiate them. On the contrary, this approach leaves our reactive attitudes where we want them: within the bounds of reason.

---

18 It is worth emphasizing the point that in this article I have not been concerned with each and every (controversial) aspect of Strawson's discussion and approach. There remain, therefore, a number of interesting matters that I have not pursued in this context. Some critics of Strawson's may argue that there are (other) weaknesses or shortcomings of FR that require further attention and discussion. In contrast with this, those who are more sympathetic with Strawson's approach will no doubt argue that, criticism aside, there is more to be said for Strawson's approach than my criticisms suggest. I believe that there is some truth in both these views. Nevertheless, for our present purposes the important point to note is that both critic and sympathizer alike will have to take note of the specific objections which I have raised against Strawson's line(s) of argument.

Chapter 8

Emotions, Expectations and Responsibility

R. Jay Wallace

In these passages from his book Responsibility and the Moral Sentiments *R. Jay Wallace develops a general interpretation of the reactive attitudes, and draws on this interpretation to develop an account of what we are doing when we hold people morally responsible. The interpretation of the reactive sentiments takes as central the phenomena of resentment, guilt, and indignation. These attitudes, Wallace argues, are distinguished by their constitutive connection to the stance of holding someone to an expectation or demand. To adopt this stance toward someone is to be disposed to experience the reactive emotions in case the person should violate the expectation or demand in question, or to believe that their so acting would make it fitting that one experience an emotion from this class. Building on this account, Wallace then argues that to hold someone morally responsible is to hold them to a certain class of expectations—i.e. moral obligations that one accepts—in this way that is distinctively connected to the reactive emotions.*

Emotions and Expectations

On P.F. Strawson's view, emotions such as guilt, resentment, and indignation—what Strawson calls the reactive attitudes—provide the key to understanding moral responsibility and its conditions. I intend to develop this idea by working out an account of the stance of *holding* someone responsible, in terms of the reactive emotions. Before this can be done, however, it will first be necessary to get clear about the nature of the reactive emotions. What are the essential features of these emotions? What distinguishes them from other forms of moral and non-moral sentiment, and holds them together as a class? Answering these questions will provide the foundation for the account of responsibility and its conditions that follows.

A venerable approach to the reactive emotions holds that they are distinguished by the moral beliefs that give rise to them. Thus Joseph Butler suggested that deliberate resentment is excited by the belief that an injury has been done, where injury is construed as a moral concept, to be distinguished from mere suffering or harm or loss.[1] More recently, John Rawls has maintained that the moral sentiments are emotions whose explanation requires the invocation of a moral concept.[2] In these

---

[1] Joseph Butler, *Fifteen Sermons Preached at the Rolls Chapel* (London: Bell & Sons, 1949), sermon 8, "Upon Resentment".

[2] John Rawls, *A Theory of Justice* (Cambridge, MA: Harvard University Press, 1971), sec. 73.

terms, the reactive attitudes of guilt, resentment, and indignation are set apart by the *kind* of moral concept that figures in their explanation; specifically, explanation of these reactive emotions must invoke the concept of the right, as distinguished from that of the good. The appeal of these suggestions is the connection they postulate between the reactive attitudes and a certain kind of belief. The emotions of resentment, indignation, and guilt all have a propositional content—one feels indignant *about* something, or guilty *for* something one has done. It is tempting to characterize these contents in moral terms, by holding (for instance) that the reactive emotions must be caused by the belief that an injustice or an injury has been done. But the temptation should be resisted. It amounts to an excessive moralization of the reactive attitudes; for though these attitudes are often—perhaps even standardly—caused by distinctively moral beliefs, they do not have to be so caused. It is notoriously the case that one can feel guilt, for instance, without sincerely believing oneself to have done anything that would amount to a moral injury or an infraction of right.

Reflection on such cases has led some philosophers to sever altogether the connection of reactive emotions with beliefs. But if Butler and Rawls go too far in the direction of moralizing the reactive emotions, this alternative approach deprives us of the resources for acknowledging something that is characteristic of the reactive emotions as a class. For by severing their essential connection with beliefs, the alternative approach deprives the reactive emotions of their propositional content. If it seems plausible that guilt may be experienced in the absence of the belief that one is at fault, it seems equally plausible that a state that lacks a propositional object would not really be a genuine state of guilt at all. We need a way of explaining the distinctive propositional content of the reactive emotions, without characterizing that content in exclusively moral terms. This is particularly important if we are to improve on Strawson's account of responsibility in terms of the reactive emotions: a successful interpretation of what it is to hold someone responsible, that draws on the reactive emotions, must credit those emotions with propositional objects—something Strawson's own account does not clearly manage to do.

My own account of the reactive emotions aims to solve this problem. My main contention is that there is an essential connection between the reactive attitudes and a distinctive form of evaluation, or quasi evaluation, that I refer to as holding a person to an expectation (or demand). This form of evaluation is not conceptually prior to the reactive attitudes, but rather is defined in terms of them: to hold someone to an expectation, I maintain, is to be susceptible to the reactive attitudes in one's relations with the person. If this is right, then the task of characterizing the reactive attitudes must go hand in hand with the task of characterizing this distinctive form of quasi evaluation, for the two can only be understood in terms of each other. Among other things, pursuing the connection between reactive attitudes and expectations should help us to account for the characteristic propositional content of the reactive attitudes, without falling into the trap of overmoralizing them from the start. To be in a state of reactive emotion, one must believe that a person has violated some expectation that one holds the person to; and in terms of this belief, we can give an account of how the reactive emotions have the kind of propositional content that distinguishes them from other emotional states. But it need not be the case that the expectation that gives the content of a reactive emotion is a moral one, or even that it is an expectation one sincerely endorses. (This is why I refer to the attitude of holding a person to an expectation as a form of quasi evaluation.)

The Approach Sketched

To start with, note that there is one way of expecting a thing to happen that does not have any special connection with morality, or with the moral emotions. This is the sense in which to expect something to happen is simply to believe there is a high probability that the expected event will occur. Thus when I hit the appropriate button on the remote control, I expect my television to turn on; as the summer draws to a close, I expect that classes will soon begin; and when I assign the *Prolegomena* to my beginning students, I expect that they will not understand it on their own. Expectations in this sense are often associated with emotions of various kinds. For example, my expectation about the start of classes may be suffused with a feeling of anxiety that has its roots in my childhood experiences of school; the failure of my TV to go on as expected when I activate the remote control may provoke a fit of rage and frustration. But it is not in general the case that expectations of this sort—that is, beliefs about the future—are presumptively associated with any particular attitude. I may equally contemplate the expected start of classes with depression, enthusiasm, or with complete indifference, and none of these emotional responses would necessarily be more fitting than the others.

There is, however, a different way of expecting something to occur that is essentially tied to particular emotional responses. This is the sense in which, as we might say, we "hold someone to an expectation", or in which we demand of people that they act as we expect them to. In the case of my students, for instance, I not only expect, in the first sense, that they will not understand the *Prolegomena*, I also hold them to the expectation that they will not lie, cheat, attempt to blackmail me or their fellow students, and so on. In holding them to these various expectations, I often believe that the expectations will be fulfilled. Thus I generally believe that my students will not in fact attempt to blackmail me. But even when a belief of this sort is present, it does not capture what is centrally involved in holding a person to an expectation, or in making a demand of the person. The crucial element, I would suggest, is attitudinal: to hold someone to an expectation is essentially to be susceptible a certain range of emotions in the case that the expectation is not fulfilled, or to believe that the violation of the expectation would make it appropriate for one to be subject to those emotions. For reasons that will become clear in the course of my discussion, we may refer to this stance of holding someone to an expectation as a "quasi-evaluative" stance.

Emotions that are constitutively linked to expectations, in this sense of holding someone to an expectation, are the reactive attitudes, as I will interpret them. Take the central examples of resentment, moral indignation, and guilt. These are not mere feelings that one might happen to be subject to in any circumstances whatsoever. I may dislike my television set or be frustrated and annoyed when it fails to turn on; but insofar as I do not hold the TV to expectations, I cannot, properly speaking, be said to resent it or to be indignant at it. Resentment, indignation, and guilt are essentially tied to expectations that we hold ourselves and others to; susceptibility to these emotions is what constitutes holding someone to an expectation. This mutual dependence of emotion and expectation distinguishes the reactive attitudes, on the account of them I defend—a class of attitudes that includes a central group of moral emotions, but that also includes some nonmoral emotions as well.

Before we can develop this suggestion, however, a word or two of clarification is in order. So far I have used the terms "expectation" and "demand" in sketching the stance that is constitutively connected with the reactive attitudes. I have chosen these terms because they point at once in two different directions, in a way that is appropriate to the psychological phenomena I wish to call attention to.[3] Thus a demand is both a psychological stance we might adopt toward someone and that which we demand of the person when we adopt the stance. Strictly speaking, however, when I write of "holding someone to a demand or expectation", "demand" and "expectation" are to be taken in the latter sense: that which we demand or expect of the person. They are thus equivalent ways of expressing the notion of a practical *requirement* or *prohibition* in a particular situation of action. So construed, expectations must in principle be capable of being formulated linguistically, though for my purposes it will not be important to settle on a canonical formula for expressing such expectations in words. We might express an expectation by using the concepts of prohibition or requirement explicitly, say as an operator on sentences that describe kinds of action in a particular situation (for instance: "It is prohibited that you should break the promise you made to your sister"). Alternatively, expectations might be expressed by imperatives ("Do not break the promise you made to your sister").

However we choose to express expectations, when so construed there are several further points about them that must be noted. First, it is important that expectations should be capable of being supported by practical reasons. It is not necessary that expectations, to count as such, should either be or be believed to be supported by such reasons; as I will show, it is an important fact about us that we often hold ourselves and others to expectations that are supported by no justification that we may accept. But expectations can be supported by justifications that the agent accepts, and in the favorable cases they are supported in this way, so the possibility of such support needs to be left open. Second, though expectations must be capable of linguistic formulation, it is not required that the agents who hold themselves and others to such expectations should always be in a privileged position to produce such a formulation. Thus an agent might not be aware that she holds other people to a given demand, and might only come to grasp that demand discursively by inference from patterns in her emotional life (involving, for instance, the kinds of situations that move her to resentment). Finally, we should allow the possibility that expectations may conflict, so that in a given situation there are mutually inconsistent kinds of action that one is required to perform. At least, nothing in the very concept of an expectation, as I construe it, should rule out the possibility of such conflicts.

Something must now be said about the connection between expectations, construed in this way, and the reactive emotions. In characterizing this connection, I have used a disjunctive formulation: to hold someone to an expectation, I suggested,

---

3   The terms will be used interchangeably in the text that follows.

is to be susceptible to a certain level of emotions if the expectation is violated or to believe that it would be appropriate for one to feel those emotions if the expectation is violated. This disjunction is to be understood nonexclusively. Thus there are three different ways in which one might count as having the attitude of quasi evaluation that I have referred to as "holding someone to an expectation": (1) one simply finds oneself reacting with the emotions of resentment, indignation, or guilt in respect to the violation of a certain set of expectations, and it is part of the explanation of the emotions to which one is thus subject that one believes the expectations in question have been breached; (2) one is not consistently subject to these various emotions oneself on occasions when a given set of expectations has been violated, but one believes that it would be appropriate for one to react to their violation with this range of emotions, and one thinks that what would make these emotional reactions appropriate is the fact that the expectations have been breached; (3) one feels the emotions of resentment, indignation, and guilt on occasions when the expectations have been violated *and* one believes that these are appropriate emotions for one to feel on such occasions, because the expectations have been breached.

Holding someone to a demand, in any of these ways, can be either a long-term or a short-term condition. One might hold a person to a given demand only long enough to feel momentary resentment toward the person, or one might hold the person to a range of demands over a period of many years. Notice, too, that beliefs figure prominently and variously in my explanation of the stance of holding someone to a demand. There is, first, the belief that someone's violation of a demand would make one of the reactive emotions appropriate. Having such a belief is not necessary to count as holding the person to the demand (compare case 1), but even in the absence of the appropriate reactive emotion, this belief would be sufficient to qualify one as holding the person to the demand (case 2).

Moreover, when one is subject to a state of reactive emotion, the preceding account entails that a different kind of belief will figure in the explanation of the emotion. This is the belief that some demand has been breached. Even if we choose to express demands as imperatives, and hence as lacking truth-conditions, there will still be room for the belief that a demand has been violated. Furthermore, some belief of this kind must be present whenever an agent is in a particular state of reactive emotion, and must contribute to explaining why one is in this state.[4] This explanatory role of beliefs in accounting for particular states of reactive emotion is extremely important, since it will eventually provide the key to understanding the propositional content characteristic of the reactive emotions as a class. For the present, though, it will suffice to make the following observations. The *stance* of holding someone to a demand, as I interpret it, does not have explanatory priority

---

[4] By "belief" here, I mean an exclusively cognitive state whose propositional content is directly assessable as true or false. In these terms, a state in which one entertains a proposition one does not fully accept—to which one assigns an extremely low probability, for instance—may be allowed to count as a belief, at least in a degenerate sense. For the suggestion that the content of many emotions can best be understood in terms of beliefs of this degenerate sort, see P.S. Greenspan, *Emotions and Reasons: An Inquiry into Emotional Justification* (New York: Routledge, Chapman and Hall, 1988).

vis-à-vis the reactive emotions: to be subject to the reactive emotions is to take this stance toward a person, and to adopt this stance is in turn to be subject to the reactive emotions. At the same time, the nature of the connection between the reactive emotions and this stance is such that particular states of reactive emotion must always be explicable in terms of some belief concerning the violation of a demand. In this way, beliefs about the violation of demands have a kind of priority in accounting for particular states of reactive emotion.

Regarding particular states of reactive emotion, it should be further noted that I have not provided, and do not intend to provide, a complete analysis of what it is to be in such an emotional state. For purposes of discussion, we may assume that each of the reactive emotions is associated with a distinctive syndrome of sensory, behavioral, and linguistic dispositions. The state of guilt, for instance, is associated with characteristic patterns of salience and attention, dispositions to action, expectations regarding the reactions of others, susceptibilities to feel certain sorts of sensation, and so on.[5] Such syndromes may be taken to provide a rough characterization of the various emotional states. But it is not clear that these characterizations can be regarded as complete analyses of the various emotional states, in the sense of providing a specification of sufficient conditions for being in those states. For my purposes, it is not important that we have an analysis in this sense available.

What I do wish to insist on is that there is one characteristic that is essential to the reactive emotions, and that may be taken to distinguish them as a class from other types of attitudes. This is their connection to expectations, the connection I have described in terms of the quasi-evaluative stance of holding someone to an expectation. To pursue this strategy for understanding the reactive attitude is to define them together with the stance of quasi evaluation. The quasi-evaluative stance of holding someone to an expectation is characterized in terms of a susceptibility to the reactive emotions. And those emotions in their turn are characterized in terms of this evaluative stance, as the emotions one is susceptible to in virtue of holding someone to an expectation. Since neither of these items is taken to be conceptually prior, the strategy will only be illuminating if they can both be characterized together in ways that differentiate them from other evaluative stances, and that help us to mark important and recognizable distinctions between the reactive attitudes and other kinds of (moral and nonmoral) emotions.

Reactive and Nonreactive, Moral and Nonmoral

The reactive attitudes of resentment, indignation, and guilt all seem to have fairly complex propositional objects: one feels resentful or indignant *about* something that somebody has done, or guilty *for* having done something oneself. To account adequately for this aspect of the reactive emotions, we must suppose them to have a cognitive dimension; in particular, it seems that a person subject to a reactive emotion must have some kind of evaluative belief, one that figures in the explanation

---

5   See, for example, Rawls, *A Theory of Justice*, sec. 73.

of the emotional state. Reactive attitudes are also often moral sentiments, in that the evaluative beliefs that give rise to them are often beliefs that some moral transgression has been committed (by oneself or some other party), and yet they are not the only moral sentiments to which people are subject, nor are they exclusively moral sentiments. We need an account of the cognitive dimension in reactive attitudes that will enable us to draw the right kind of line: between the moral and the nonmoral reactive attitudes, and between moral reactive attitudes and other kinds of moral sentiment.

The approach I have sketched suggests a straightforward characterization of the cognitive dimension of reactive attitudes. On that approach, reactive attitudes as a class are distinguished by their connection with expectations, so that any particular state of reactive emotion must be explained by the belief that some expectation has been breached. It is the explanatory role of such beliefs about the violation of an expectation that is the defining characteristic of the states of reactive emotion as a class, and that provides them with their distinctive propositional objects; beliefs of this sort will therefore always be present when one is in one of the reactive states. Take indignation: a particular state of indignation will be focused on a specific propositional object; there must be something *about* which one is indignant, if the emotional state one is in is to count as indignation at all. According to the approach I have sketched, this propositional object of indignation can be specified by the belief that some expectation one holds people to has been breached. And what entitles us to suppose that this belief specifies the propositional content of the emotional state is the fact that it explains why one is in the emotional state.

Of course, it is possible to have the belief that an expectation has been violated without being in one of the reactive states, and so such beliefs will not always be sufficient conditions, by themselves, to produce a state of reactive emotion. One might believe that a demand has been violated that one does not hold people to oneself, in the sense I have been trying to characterize, and in this case the belief that the demand has been violated would not give rise to one of the reactive emotional states. How then, to characterize the difference between the agent for whom beliefs about the violation of prohibitions or requirements suffice to produce states of reactive emotion, and the agent for whom they do not? It is tempting to say that the difference consists in the *stance* of the two agents toward the expectations in question: the first agent adopts a stance toward the expectations, in virtue of which we can say that she holds people to them in a way that the second person does not. This is so far correct, but it should be borne in mind that the relevant stance is not necessarily something distinct from a susceptibility to states of reactive emotion when the expectations in question are breached. For this reason we should not say that the stance together with an agent's belief that an expectation has been breached—*explains* the agent's state of reactive emotion. Rather, that the agent has the stance *displays* itself in the fact that beliefs about the violation of certain expectations give rise to states of reactive emotion.

If this account of the cognitive element in reactive emotions is right, it suggests a natural way of distinguishing between moral and nonmoral reactive attitudes as well as a way of distinguishing the moral reactive attitudes from other kinds of moral emotions. I will start with the distinction within the category of reactive attitudes, between the moral and the nonmoral cases. Whether a reactive emotion is or is not a moral one would seem to depend on the kind of belief that gives rise to it, and hence the kind of propositional content that it has. At least on the face of it, there is no reason to suppose that all of the expectations we hold people to are distinctively moral in character, and so we might distinguish between the belief that a moral expectation has been violated and the belief that some nonmoral expectation has been violated. In these terms, a moral reactive emotion (say, resentment) would be one that is explained by a belief of the first type and therefore has a distinctively moral content, while nonmoral resentment would have a content specified by beliefs of the second (nonmoral) type.

This strategy for distinguishing between moral and nonmoral reactive attitudes may usefully be compared with Strawson's way of carving up the reactive attitudes, which also differentiates between moral and nonmoral varieties. Strawson identifies three different kinds of reactive attitudes. What he calls personal reactive attitudes are "the non-detached attitudes and reactions of people directly involved in transactions with each other", where one demands of others a degree of consideration toward oneself; resentment is the primary example here, but Strawson also mentions gratitude, love, forgiveness, and hurt feelings.[6] The distinctively moral reactive attitudes, Strawson seems to think, are not these personal attitudes, but vicarious analogues of them, such as moral indignation or disapprobation, where one holds people to standards of behavior and attitude, not specifically in relation to oneself, but in regard to others.[7] Finally there are self-reactive attitudes, associated with demands made on oneself in one's conduct with others; examples include guilt, remorse, shame, and the sense of obligation.[8]

Taken literally, however—and ignoring for the moment Strawson's inclusive interpretation of reactivity—this approach has some peculiar consequences. It would rule out the possibility of agent's feeling moral resentment on her own behalf, about the violation of moral expectations by other people in their behavior toward the agent; resentment about being treated unfairly, for instance, would not count as a moral sentiment. More strangely still, Strawson's approach classifies guilt as an exclusively nonmoral sentiment, since it involves the imposition of demands

---

6 P.F. Strawson, "Freedom and Resentment", reprinted in *Freedom and Resentment and Other Essays* (London: Methuen, 1974), pp. 1–25, and also in Gary Watson (ed.), *Free Will* (Oxford: Oxford University Press, 1982), pp. 59–80. Page references will be to pages 19–36 of this volume, followed by (after the slash) the corresponding pages, 59–80, of Gary Watson (ed.), *Free Will*. Thus, for example, this reference, 'FR, 21–2/62' refers to this volume, pp. 21–2, and to p. 62 of Watson's *Free Will*.

7 FR, 28–9/70–71. Strictly speaking, Strawson says only that the moral reactive emotions must be "capable" of being vicarious; but he does not explain how a nonvicarious emotion might be potentially vicarious. My alternative account of moral reactive emotions suggests a natural unpacking of this idea: a personal emotion may be capable of being vicarious if the demand it rests on is supported by reasons that generalize to cases that do not directly involve the agent subject to the emotion.

8 FR, 28–30/71–2.

on oneself rather than on other parties.[9] We get a more recognizable division of the reactive attitudes into moral and nonmoral varieties if we follow the suggestion I have made, that what makes a reactive attitude a moral one is not its vicarious quality but the *kind* of expectation it is essentially bound up with. The most plausible development of this suggestion would begin by noting that many expectations we hold people to are supported by justifications, which identify reasons for complying with the expectations. Moral expectations can then be defined as expectations that are justifiable in terms of distinctively moral reasons.[10] I will refer to expectations that admit of this kind of moral justification as *obligations*.

I propose that reactive emotions be classified as moral when they are connected with moral obligations in this sense. More precisely, we should count reactive emotions as moral when they are linked to obligations for which the agent is herself able to provide moral justifications; these justifications identify reasons that explain the agent's own efforts to comply with the obligations in question, and they provide moral terms that the agent is prepared to use to justify such compliance on the part of others, whom the agent holds to the obligations.[11] When they are linked with obligations of this kind, it is natural to treat reactive emotions as moral sentiments, since their explanation essentially requires moral beliefs, namely beliefs about the violation of what the agent himself correctly regards as moral obligations. The explanatory role of such moral beliefs gives these emotional states a distinctively moral content. And in fact we commonly do regard resentment, indignation, and guilt to be moral emotions when they are incited by beliefs about the violation of moral obligations.[12]

It is a further consequence of this general approach, however, that not all reactive attitudes need be distinctively moral in this way. Insofar as some of the expectations to which we hold ourselves and others are not moral obligations (that is, expectations supported by moral justifications), the reactive emotions to which they give rise will

---

9 A similar point is made by Jonathan Bennett, who suggests that the two basic categories of reactive attitudes are the "principle" and the "nonprincipled" ("Accountability", in *Philosophical Subjects*, ed. Zak van Straaten [Oxford: Oxford University Press, 1980], pp. 45–7). ... In his "Reply to Ayer and Bennett", Strawson admits that it was an error "so to use the word 'moral' as to exclude self-reactive attitudes from its scope" (in van Straaten (ed.), p. 266). But he, like Bennett, does not seem to acknowledge that personal reactive attitudes might also be moral sentiments, depending on the character of the expectations with which they are connected.

10 It is not necessary to opt here for a particular account of what makes reasons moral. For purposes of discussion in this book, however, I shall assume that moral reasons need not be impersonal or "agent-neutral" but may also be "agent-relative" (containing an essential reference to the particular agent who has the reasons). On the distinction between agent-neutral and agent-relative reasons, and the implications of the distinction for issues of objectivity in ethics, see Thomas Nagel, *The View from Nowhere* (New York: Oxford University Press, 1986), Chs 8–9.

11 The moral obligations in question would thus be ones that the agent *accepts* ....

12 Many of the demands we hold people to are supported by both moral and nonmoral reasons. In these cases we might say that the emotions caused by the violation of the demands are moral insofar as the reasons that support those demands are moral.

not have a distinctively moral content. There is nothing peculiar in the supposition that we might resent a breach of etiquette in the behavior of another person toward us,[13] or that we might feel guilty about our failure to measure up to expectations that we have taken over from our parents or our church but that we do not consider to be supported by any justifications at all. In both cases, however, it is required that there be some belief about the breach of an expectation that figures in the explanation of the reactive emotion. In this way we can begin to move away from the excessive moralization of the reactive attitudes, without denying them the kind of propositional content that sets them apart from other emotional states.

It remains to say something about the distinction between moral reactive attitudes and other types of moral sentiment. Here again it would seem that the beliefs that give rise to the emotions of various kinds may provide the key. Thus moral reactive attitudes are explained by the belief that some moral obligation has been violated. But this is not the only kind of moral belief that we entertain. Consider the various modalities of moral value, such as the values of kindness or consideration or benevolence or even justice. Such values often coincide with our moral obligations. Just as we demand, for example, that people keep their promises, or help others in extreme distress, so may we value acts of fidelity and benevolence, regarding them as good and admirable. But moral values can also diverge from moral obligations, construed as strict prohibitions and requirements. For instance, we may think that a certain sort of character is especially virtuous, even though we do not, strictly speaking, demand of people that they exhibit a character of that sort; or we might think that a particular action displays a degree of beneficence or consideration that goes well beyond what we actually demand of each other in our normal interactions. In all of these cases—the cases in which moral values coincide with our moral obligations, and the cases in which they exceed those obligations—there are often characteristic moral sentiments that are caused by evaluative moral beliefs. In addition to feeling guilt about my failure to act in accordance with the demands to which I hold myself, I may feel moral shame because I lack the moral excellences that I aspire to. And I may feel gratitude toward someone whose actions toward me are unusually beneficent or admire someone whose character is virtuous to an exemplary degree. Thus we may distinguish moral reactive emotions from other moral sentiments in terms of the kinds of moral beliefs that give rise to the moral sentiments, and that fix the content of those sentiments: the reactive attitudes are explained exclusively by beliefs about the violation of moral obligations (construed as strict prohibitions or requirements), whereas other moral sentiments are explained by beliefs about the various modalities of moral value.[14]

---

13 Some such breaches of etiquette will be resented, because they violate a distinctively moral obligation of respect or consideration. But I am imagining a case in which resentment is occasioned solely by the belief that a requirement of etiquette has been violated, not by a distinct moral belief.

14 Compare Rawls, *A Theory of Justice*, p. 484: "In general, guilt, resentment, and indignation invoke the concept of right, whereas shame, contempt, and derision appeal to the concept of goodness."

In the previous section I suggested that it is at least conceivable that there might be cultures whose members do not have the stance of holding people to expectations in their repertoire. The distinction just drawn between moral reactive attitudes and other kinds of moral emotions may help to flesh out this suggestion. The nonreactive moral emotions, I have suggested, are connected with beliefs about the various modalities of moral value. A shared set of such values might conceivably have sufficient structure to constitute an ethical system for regulating social interactions within a culture, and yet the members of that culture might not be subject to the distinctively reactive emotions at all. Perhaps they respond to their own failure to live up to their values with shame rather than guilt, and hold others who similarly fall short of such standards in contempt or derision, rather than resenting them or feeling indignation; a susceptibility to these nonreactive emotions might be sufficient to guide their conduct and to provide a framework for some kind of common ethical discourse.

It has frequently been claimed that there are "shame cultures" of this kind, whose members lack the characteristic emotional resources of guilt and the other reactive attitudes. Whether such claims are true is not a question that needs to be decided here. For my purposes it is sufficient to note the following points. First, there seems to be nothing in the very idea of the reactive emotions that rules out the possibility of shame cultures. The distinctive features of resentment, indignation, and guilt do not seem to be given along with the bare facts of human social life, and so one can see how there might be human communities whose members are not subject to these emotions.[15] Second, a shame culture would not necessarily be one in which there are no recognizable ethical norms, construed as norms that make social cooperation possible; nor would it be the case that the members of such a culture would not internalize these norms, in the sense of having incentives for compliance with the norms whose effectiveness is potentially independent of externally administered sanctions and rewards. On the contrary, the plausibility of the claim that there are shame cultures seems to me to rest crucially on the assumption that conformity with ethical norms can be sustained by emotional resources that do not include the

---

15 The claim that there are, in fact, cultures without the reactive emotions presupposes that such emotions cannot be understood in exclusively biological terms, but that they are instead somehow culturally constituted. For a summary discussion of endogenous (biological) and exogenous (cultural) accounts of emotions, see Paul Heelas, "Emotions across Cultures: Objectivity and Cultural Divergence", in S.C. Brown (ed.), *Objectivity and Cultural Divergence, Philosophy* (supp.) 17 (1984), pp. 21–42. The idea that reactive emotions are culturally constituted presupposes that susceptibility to say, guilt requires the ability to make attributions of guilt; but it does not presuppose the stronger and less plausible claim that one can only be in a state of guilt if one believes of oneself that one is in such a state at the time. Allan Gibbard seems to slide between these two claims when discussing what he calls "attributional" accounts of emotion in his book *Wise Choices, Apt Feelings: A Theory of Normative Judgment* (Cambridge, MA: Harvard University Press, 1990), pp. 141–50. (The less plausible claim has been advocated by Stanley Schachter, in *Emotion, Obesity, and Crime* (New York: Academic Press, 1971). For a criticism of Schachter's interpretation of his experimental results, see Robert M. Gordon, *The Structure of Emotions: Investigations in Cognitive Philosophy* (Cambridge: Cambridge University Press, 1987), Ch. 5.)

distinctively reactive emotions—that conformity can be sustained by the internal sanctions of shame and anger, for instance, rather than those of guilt and indignation.[16] This assumption may be empirically ungrounded, but there seems to be no reason to reject it on conceptual grounds alone. This is what I meant in saying that nothing in the very idea of the reactive emotions rules out the possibility of shame cultures.

But even if it should turn out that there are in fact no pure shame cultures, we should still distinguish the different ways in which emotions contribute to sustaining social cooperation. What I have called the reactive emotions differ from such emotions as shame and anger in their presumptive connection with the kind of prohibitions or requirements that I have referred to as moral obligations. These emotions help to define what Bernard Williams has called "the morality system", to mark a contrast between a conception of the moral and its demands that is especially prominent in modern, Christianized cultures and other aspects or forms of ethical life.[17] Though I do not share Williams's evident hostility toward the morality system so construed, I agree that it represents a distinctive interpretation of ethical prohibitions and requirements, and in the next chapter I shall argue that the special connection it postulates between moral obligations and the reactive emotions is the key to understanding what it is to hold someone morally *responsible*.

Responsibility

The question of what we are doing when we hold people responsible has not been adequately treated in discussions of freedom and responsibility. A common assumption is that moral responsibility can be understood primarily in terms of moral blame and sanction, so that to hold people morally responsible is to be prepared to blame or sanction them for their moral offenses, where the sanctions tend, at the limit, toward punishment. This is all right, so far as it goes, but philosophers have not yet given us a satisfactory interpretation of the stance that issues in these forms of treatment.

I take up this problem below, developing an approach to moral responsibility that builds on the account of the reactive emotions defended in the preceding chapter. According to that account, the reactive emotions of resentment, indignation, and guilt are distinguished by their connection with expectations (construed as prohibitions or requirements); so that to hold someone to such an expectation is to be susceptible to

---

16 The distinction between shame and guilt cultures does not necessarily carry with it the implication that shame cultures are psychologically and morally primitive, by comparison with guilt cultures. Indeed, shame-based moralities have recently been defended as superior to systems centered around the reactive emotions: see Bernard Williams, *Shame and Necessity* (Berkeley: University of California Press, 1993), Ch. 4; and, in a similar vein, Annette C. Baier, "Moralism and Cruelty: Reflections on Hume and Kant", *Ethics* 103 (1993), pp. 436–57. I take issue with some of Williams's and Baier's criticisms of guilt-based moralities in the chapters to follow; but they are surely correct to challenge the complacent "progressivism" that characterized many earlier discussions of the distinction between guilt and shame cultures.

17 See Bernard Williams, *Ethics and the Limits of Philosophy* (Cambridge, MA: Harvard University Press, 1985), Ch. 10.

the reactive emotions in the case that the expectation is breached, or to believe that the reactive emotions would be appropriate in that case. To hold a person morally responsible, I now want to argue, is to hold the person to moral expectations that one accepts. This approach correctly treats holding people responsible as a basic stance that we take toward them, that cannot be reduced to a behavioral disposition to sanction them for what they do. Furthermore, it connects the practice of holding people morally responsible with the notions of moral obligation, moral right, and moral wrong, which form the nexus of concepts in which responsibility would seem to belong. At the same time, the interpretation I offer suggests an appealing explanation of how moral blame and the various sanctioning responses hang together as a class: to blame someone is to be subject to one of the reactive emotions in terms of which the stance of holding people responsible is essentially defined, and these emotions are *expressed* by the sanctioning behavior to which the stance of holding people responsible inclines us. This point is developed below in the section, "The Reactive Account and Moral Judgment", which considers the question of how judgments of moral responsibility may be understood to go beyond mere descriptions of what an agent has done, and explains how we may hold someone responsible for a moral wrong without actually being subject to an episode of reactive emotion.

Responsibility and the Reactive Emotions

Above I argued that the reactive emotions of resentment, guilt, and indignation should be understood in terms of the quasi-evaluative stance of holding people to expectations. I now want to suggest that this stance provides the key to understanding what we are doing when we hold people morally responsible.

Holding someone to an expectation has been characterized in terms of the reactive emotions: to hold someone to an expectation is to be susceptible to the reactive emotions, or to believe that it would be appropriate for one to feel the reactive emotions, in the case that the expectation is violated. Now it would seem that when we hold people morally responsible we are similarly susceptible to the reactive emotions, if those held responsible breach our expectations, that we believe it would be appropriate for us to feel the reactive emotions in those cases. This suggests that moral responsibility might be analyzed in terms of the quasi-evaluative stance of holding people to expectations. To hold a person responsible, we might suppose, is simply to hold the person to expectations in the way that is connected with the reactive emotions.

This is a promising suggestion. The reactive emotions of indignation, resentment, and guilt seem to be natural candidates for the attitudinal component of moral blame, and with this component in place, one could understand the various moral sanctions to be unified by their common function of expressing the reactive emotions. But as formulated so far, this account cannot be correct, for two reasons. First when we hold people morally responsible, we are interested in whether their behavior does or does not comply with distinctively moral requirements. But it is possible to hold people to expectations that are not supported by specially moral justifications; in these cases, then, the stance of holding someone to an expectation would seem to range more widely than the stance of holding someone morally responsible. A second and more important possibility of divergence between the two stances is presented by cases of irrational guilt and resentment. As explained in Chapter 2, such cases should be understood as cases where one holds oneself or others to expectations that one does not fully accept, for purposes of practical deliberation and normative discussion. But if we do not accept a given set of expectations, I do not think that we would hold ourselves or others morally responsible for the failure to comply with them. A person who feels irrational guilt, for instance about the violation of a parental prohibition on going to the movies, is not apt to blame herself for the action that prompts the guilt, but to view the guilt as a symptom to be treated and cured. Moral responsibility seems to be tied to distinctively moral expectations, which are supported by reasons that we ourselves accept as a basis for practical deliberation and normative criticism and discussion.

This suggests the following revision of the initial account: to hold someone morally responsible is to hold the person to moral expectations that one accepts. The set of moral expectations that one both accepts and holds people to is basically the class of what I earlier called *moral obligations*. Restricting the set of expectations to moral obligations that the agent accepts focuses the analysis correctly on the range of cases in which moral responsibility would seem to come into play. To see this, recall that the notion of an expectation, as introduced in Chapter 2 (not included in this collection), was meant to capture the idea of a *prohibition* or *requirement*. Hence the moral obligations that one accepts, and that one holds oneself and others to, mark out a class of distinctively moral prohibitions or requirements. This class of moral prohibitions and requirements that one both accepts and holds people to constitutes a special sphere within our ethical concepts. It is the sphere of moral rightness or wrongness—a sphere that is narrower than the sphere of morality as a whole, but broader than the sphere of justice and injustice. The sphere is narrower than the sphere of morality as a whole, because there are moral considerations that confer value on actions and character traits without being strictly matters of moral obligation, right, or wrong. For instance, a person who is superlatively beneficent will act in ways that go beyond our moral expectations but that are still morally valuable; this is the sphere of the supererogatory. At the same time, the sphere of moral right and wrong encompasses more than considerations of justice and injustice alone, since there are things that it would be morally wrong to do, such as causing others unnecessary suffering, that may not strictly violate requirements of justice. The term "obligation", as I have introduced it, captures the set of moral requirements of right that an agent accepts.[18]

---

18 In using "obligation" to refer to all the requirements of right, I depart from some other conventions that have been adopted. Rawls, for instance, restricts the term to requirements on individuals that derive from voluntary acts whereby those individuals benefit from a just institution or practice; see John Rawls, *A Theory of Justice* (Cambridge, MA: Harvard University Press, 1971), sec. 18. By contrast, "obligation" as I shall use it ranges over all the requirements of right on individuals, including what Rawls calls natural duties, as well as obligations in his sense.

The account I am developing thus situates our practice of holding people morally responsible within a distinctive nexus of moral concepts, namely those of moral obligation, moral right, and moral wrong. This seems to be the context in which moral responsibility properly belongs, for judgments of responsibility, with their characteristic connection to moral blame and moral sanction, would appear to come into play primarily in cases where people have violated the moral obligations we hold them to. The special connection between moral obligation and moral responsibility and blame has been remarked by G. E. M. Anscombe and Bernard Williams, both of whom trace the strict notion of moral obligation to theological ideas that no longer have a secure place within contemporary moral life.[19] Anscombe contends that the notion of moral obligation is only intelligible within the context of a divine law conception of ethics, which we do not now accept, and Williams suggests that the notion of obligation is the central normative concept of "the morality system", which he takes to be a simplifying and aggressive interpretation of our ethical ideas under pressure of recognizably Christian concerns.

But even if Anscombe and Williams are correct in thinking that the notion of moral obligation was originally part of a distinctively theological conception of ethics, it does not follow that it is only intelligible within the context of religious ideas. Whether it is or is not depends on whether we can find an interpretation of moral obligation, right, and wrong and, I should add, the associated ideas of moral responsibility, blame, and sanction that relates them to a secular understanding of human nature and practical reason (a project begun, though hardly completed, by the moral philosophers of the modern period, from Hobbes through Kant). So the genealogical association of moral responsibility with theological assumptions does not necessarily call into question the modern practice of moral responsibility. If the genealogical proposal is correct, however, it implies that the members of societies that never had the relevant theological ideas could not, strictly speaking, be said to hold each other morally responsible. This seems peculiar, since it is natural to think of such people (the Athenian contemporaries of Plato and Aristotle, far example) as having had available to them the responses of blame and moral sanction.[20] What are we to make of this thought?

The genealogical suggestion seems to me to go together with the idea, broached in the preceding chapter, that there might be shame cultures whose members do not have the reactive emotions in their repertoire. The moral reactive emotions will only be available where the moral notions of obligation, right, and wrong are in place, and if Anscombe and Williams are correct, those ideas are historically and culturally local, linked to theological outlooks that are far from universal. But to suppose that there are cultures without the reactive emotions is not to suppose that the members of

---

19 G.E.M. Anscombe, "Modern Moral Philosophy", as reprinted in *Ethics, Religion and Politics*, vol. 3 of *The Collected Philosophical Papers of G. E. M. Anscombe* (Oxford: Basil Blackwell, 1981), pp. 26–42; Bernard Williams, *Ethics and the Limits of Philosophy* (Cambridge, MA: Harvard University Press, 1985), especially Ch. 10.

20 Aristotle's famous discussion of the voluntary, for instance, seems to presuppose a form of moral assessment that is "deep", in that it goes beyond mere evaluative description of what an agent has done; see *The Nicomachean Ethics*, bk. 3, Chs 1 and 5.

those cultures are altogether lacking in moral emotions. On the contrary, the idea of cultures without the reactive emotions seems plausible only on the assumption that other moral emotions are available in such cultures, such as shame and anger, and that these emotions are capable of providing internal sanctions sufficient to motivate general compliance with a system of ethical norms. But if the members of a shame culture are susceptible to motivating emotions of this sort, we can understand how something analogous to our practice of moral responsibility might emerge in such a culture. The analogous practice, like ours, would involve the responses of blame and moral sanction, but these responses would be understood in terms of the different moral emotions that facilitate social cooperation within the shame culture: blame would involve the emotions of shame and anger, rather than the reactive emotions of resentment, indignation, and guilt, and moral sanctions would serve to express these nonreactive emotions.[21] This approach postulates a generic stance of holding people morally responsible that is defined in terms of whatever moral sentiments prevail within a given culture, and so is available even where the theological ideas identified by Anscombe and Williams may not have left their traces. *Our* practice of holding people morally responsible, centered as it is around the notions of moral obligation, right, and wrong, would then be distinguished by its connection to a specific subset of moral sentiments, namely the reactive emotions of resentment, indignation, and guilt.[22] In this way, we preserve the privileged connection between our practice of holding people responsible and the notions of obligation, right, and wrong, while allowing that cultures without these moral ideas could have analogous patterns of response to moral offenses.

What is immediately striking about this approach is the role it ascribes to the moral emotions. The approach says that we hold people morally responsible for complying with moral obligations only if we *hold them to* those obligations. Since holding people to an expectation is in turn understood in terms its connection with the reactive emotions, the strategy essentially links moral responsibility to the moral reactive emotions. Specifically, one may say that the basic stance of holding someone morally responsible involves a susceptibility to reactive emotions if the person breaches moral obligations that we accept, or the belief that it would be appropriate for us to feel those emotions if the person should violate those obligations.[23] Because

---

21 Bernard Williams has defended the idea that the ancient Greeks had a sophisticated conception of moral responsibility—analogous to distinctively modern conceptions, and in many ways superior to such conceptions—even without such reactive emotions as guilt; see his *Shame and Necessity* (Berkeley: University of California Press, 1993), especially Ch. 3.

22 I should emphasize that I have not taken a stand on the genealogical hypotheses of Anscombe and Williams, or on the related idea that there are shame cultures that lack the reactive emotions of resentment, indignation, and guilt. My aim has rather been to explore the implications of these proposals for the account of moral responsibility I have been developing. If the proposals should turn out to be incorrect, then what I have called the "generic" stance of holding people morally responsible would include only the familiar modern form of responsibility, connected with the reactive emotions.

23 Of course, *which* reactive emotions would be appropriate depends on who has violated the obligations, and how the act that violates the obligations is related to the subject of the emotions. Guilt is appropriate to one's own violations, indignation to violations by others, and

of the central role this account ascribes to the reactive emotions, I will refer to it as the reactive account of moral responsibility.

By connecting moral responsibility to the reactive emotions in this way, the reactive account promises to improve on the economy of threats approach .... It treats the stance of holding people responsible essentially in terms of attitudinal conditions, and so avoids the behavioristic danger of associating responsibility too exclusively with moral sanctions. To hold myself responsible for a moral wrong for example, it is sufficient that I should feel guilt about my violation of a moral obligation that I accept, or at least believe that that violation would make it fitting for me to feel guilt; these conditions could of course be satisfied without my expressing my guilt to myself or anyone else, and certainly without my sanctioning myself. Furthermore, the reactive emotions seem to have the right kind of content to capture the attitudinal dimension of moral blame. On the account of them I have offered, resentment, indignation, and guilt are backward-looking emotions, responses to the actions of a particular agent (or agents); they are essentially *about* such actions, in a way that exactly captures the backward-looking focus of moral blame. In addition, the actions to which the reactive emotions are responses are violations of expectations we accept, and this correctly connects blame with the moral notions of obligation, right, and wrong.

Once blame is understood in terms of the reactive emotions, however, we also have a natural and appealing explanation to hand of what unifies the sanctioning responses to which the stance of holding people responsible disposes us (such as avoidance, censure, denunciation, reproach, and scolding). These can all plausibly be understood as forms of behavior that serve to express the reactive emotions to which we are subject when we blame people for their moral failings ....

For all of these reasons, the reactive account seems a promising interpretation of the stance of holding people morally responsible. But does ... the account yield a way of understanding the practice of holding people responsible as something other than an expression of cruelty and vengeance? It is difficult to answer this question without knowing what cruelty and vengeance consist in, and I do not have a general account of these things to offer; but to start with, it should be noted that not all actions that aim to inflict harm are necessarily cruel—if, for example, I deliberately harm someone who has attacked me, as a strategy of self-defense, what I have done is not cruel. What matters is the goal that the infliction of harm is designed to achieve. Thus we might take as a paradigm of cruelty behavior that aims to inflict suffering (physical or psychic) as a way of subordinating the sufferer to one's will.[24] The

---

resentment others' failure to comply with moral obligations in their relations with oneself. I shall henceforth take these qualifications as understood when I refer either to the susceptibility to reactive emotions or to the belief that those emotions would be appropriate.

24 Compare Judith N. Shklar's definition of cruelty, in *Ordinary Vices* (Cambridge, MA: Harvard University Press, 1984), p. 8: "the willful inflicting of physical pain on a *weaker being* in order to cause anguish and fear" (my italics). The mistaken restriction of cruelty to cases involving physical pain is corrected by Shklar on p. 37 of *Ordinary Vices*, where she acknowledges a species of moral cruelty that involves deliberate humiliation without physical pain. The references to the weakness and humiliation of the victim of cruelty capture the element of subordination and domination made central in my paradigm of cruelty.

worry will then be that the blame and sanctioning responses characteristic of holding people responsible are responses that of their nature approximate to this paradigm, so that they are *essentially* cruel and vengeful.

No doubt many things have been done in the name of blame and moral sanction that are cruel and vengeful in this way—the history of punishment in the law provides a host of familiar and sobering examples.[25] But the issue is whether approximation to the paradigm of cruelty is essential to the practice of holding people responsible, and the reactive account suggests that it is not. Granted, blame and moral sanction often cause suffering for the person at whom they are directed. But it need not be the case that they aim to cause suffering, as part of a strategy of subordinating the sufferer to one's will. What is essential to the harmful moral sanctions, on the reactive account, is their function of expressing the emotions of resentment, indignation, and guilt; this is the real point of such responses as avoidance, denunciation, reproach, censure, and the like, and what holds them together as a class. Sanctioning behavior belongs to the syndrome of responses to which the reactive emotions dispose those who are subject to them, because the connection with reactive emotions is part of the conventional meaning of such behavior.[26] We learn the concepts of indignation, resentment, and guilt in part by learning to see their connection to sanctioning behavior, and the adequate expression of those emotions often requires such behavior. Insofar as it plays this expressive role, however, sanctioning behavior would not seem to be essentially cruel or vengeful, for the expressive role does not require the deliberate infliction of suffering as a means to the domination of another; it is one thing to inflict harm with the aim of subordinating a person to one's will, and quite another to inflict harm with the aim of expressing a moral emotion to which one is subject.

Of course, if the emotions expressed by sanctioning behavior were themselves emotions of blind hatred or anger, involving a desire to inflict harm on their object as an end in itself, the expressive function of that behavior might not rescue it from the charge of cruelty. But the reactive emotions expressed by moral sanctions are not of this kind. Rather, they are focused emotional responses to the violation of moral obligations that we accept. In expressing these emotions, then, we are not just venting feelings of anger and hatred, in the service of an antecedent desire to inflict harm for its own sake; we are demonstrating our commitment to certain moral standards, as regulative of social life. Once this point is grasped, blame and moral sanction can be seen to have a positive, perhaps irreplaceable contribution to make to the constitution and maintenance of moral communities: by giving voice to the reactive emotions, these responses help to articulate, and thereby to affirm and deepen, our commitment to a set of common moral obligations.[27]

---

25 Consider also Nietzsche's bad conscience and Freud's unconscious sense of guilt .... These are cases where guilt has a sado-masochistic aspect, being experienced as part of a strategy for inflicting torment on oneself.

26 Perhaps this is what P.F. Strawson means when he writes that a preparedness to acquiesce in the infliction of suffering is "all of a piece" with the reactive emotions (FR, 33–4/77).

27 See Joel Feinberg, "The Expressive Function of Punishment", as reprinted in his *Doing and Deserving: Essays in the Theory of Responsibility* (Princeton, NJ.: Princeton University Press, 1970), pp. 95–118, for similar remarks about the different practice of punishment in

The reactive account thus reveals that holding people responsible need not be wedded to attitudes of cruelty and vengeance. But it continues to tie this stance to emotions that are negative and disapproving, and this raises different questions. For instance, it seems that we hold people morally responsible not only for actions that violate moral obligations we accept, but also for the morally worthy actions they perform. There is a difference between doing something that inadvertently helps another person and deliberately aiming to help another person, and part of the difference seems to be that in the latter case, but not the former, we credit the agent for the good deed in a way that implies responsibility for it. Can this positive conception of moral responsibility be captured within the framework of the "reactive account"?

To answer this question, it will be useful to articulate a hitherto implicit equivocation in the notion of holding a person to a moral obligation (which one accepts). That stance, as presented so far, would seem to admit of a dispositional and an occurrent interpretation. On the occurrent interpretation, to hold a person to a moral obligation is either to be subject to an episode of reactive emotion, because the person has breached some moral obligation that we accept, or to believe that the violation would make it appropriate for one to be subject to such a reactive emotion. Obviously we cannot hope to understand responsibility for morally worthy acts in terms of this occurrent notion alone, because the person held responsible for a worthy action has not violated any moral obligation we accept, and is not believed to have done so. The occurrent reading yields an interpretation of holding a person responsible for some particular moral wrong; it tells us what it is to regard a person as having done something *blameworthy*.[28] But to regard someone as blameworthy for an action is miles away from the idea of responsibility for a morally worthy or admirable performance.

Consider, then, the dispositional reading of holding someone to an obligation. According to this construal, to hold a person to a moral obligation is to be *susceptible* to reactive emotions in the case that the person breaches the obligation, or to believe the person to be the sort of person whose violation of moral obligations would make it appropriate to be subject to a reactive emotion. This reading of the notion yields an interpretation not of regarding someone as blameworthy for a particular act, but of regarding someone as a morally *accountable* agent. To hold a person to moral obligations one accepts, in this dispositional sense, is to view the person as the sort of agent whose violation of moral obligations one accepts would render reactive

---

the law. Of course, legal punishment incurs a higher justificatory burden than the stance of holding people morally responsible, since the harms to which it exposes people are far graver and more systematic—there is a great difference between imprisonment and reproach. Expressive considerations help us to understand the nature of punishment, and perhaps to rebut the suggestion that the institution of punishment is essentially cruel, but they do not by themselves suffice to *justify* hard treatment of criminal offenders.

28 It is important to bear in mind that what is at issue is *moral* responsibility for a wrong. Of course I might hold someone *legally* responsible for an act without either being subject to resentment and indignation or thinking such emotions would be appropriate (by bringing charges against the person in court, for instance). This shows that we can hold people responsible without holding them morally responsible.

emotions appropriate.[29] But clearly one can view people as morally accountable in this way—adopting toward them the dispositional stance of holding them to obligations one accepts—even on occasions when they have done things that satisfy or exceed our moral obligations. This suggests the following account of responsibility for morally worthy actions; to hold a person morally responsible for such an action is (1) to hold the person to moral obligations one accepts, in the dispositional sense, and so to view the person as a morally accountable agent; and (2) to believe the person has done something that meets or exceeds the moral obligations one accepts.

Proceeding in this way, one in effect treats asymmetrically the cases of responsibility for morally worthy and unworthy actions. When we hold a person responsible for an unworthy act, we are subject to a negative reactive emotion because we believe the person to have violated a moral obligation we accept, or we believe that such an emotion would be rendered appropriate by the violation. By contrast, in the case of responsibility for worthy acts, we do not suppose there to be any particular positive sentiment that we are or ought to be subject to. We suppose only that the agent held responsible has done something that meets or exceeds the moral obligations we accept, and that at the time of action she was the sort of person we hold to such obligations, in the way that is dispositionally connected with the negative reactive emotions. This asymmetry in the accounts of the negative and positive cases seems to me to mirror our practice of holding people morally responsible, with its special connection to the negative responses of blame and moral sanction. Holding a person responsible for an unworthy action, or regarding the person as blameworthy because of the action, goes beyond believing the person to have done something morally unworthy in that it is linked with a range of disapproving emotions that hang together as a class (as I argued in the previous chapter). To hold a person responsible for a worthy action, on the other hand, does not seem presumptively connected to any positive emotions in particular. Of course when people exceed our moral demands in ways that benefit us (for instance, by suffering great inconvenience to do us a good turn), we are often subject to feelings of gratitude.[30] But gratitude is not called for in all cases where actions exceed the moral obligations we accept: consider the category of supererogatory acts that do not benefit us in any way. More generally, we hold people responsible for morally worthy acts that do not *exceed* the moral obligations we accept, but that merely comply with those obligations—acts such as keeping promises, telling the truth, not

---

29 Note that holding someone accountable, on this interpretation, is always relative to some set of moral obligations. A given agent is not held accountable *simpliciter*, but with respect to a specified set of moral expectations one accepts. It is accordingly possible to hold a person only *selectively* accountable—accountable with respect to some obligations one accepts, but not others ….

30 It has been pointed out to me that gratitude is sometimes also appropriate in cases where no action that is morally exceptional has been performed—one might feel grateful toward a secretary who has served one dutifully for many years. What one feels grateful for, in a case of this sort, is loyalty or dependability or service over time (which might itself be exceptional).

harming others, and so forth. In these cases it is especially clear that responsibility for worthy acts need not be connected with any distinctive sentiments.[31]

Even if this point about the morally worthy cases is granted, however, it might still be thought that the reactive account associates responsibility too closely with negative and potentially punitive emotions. Isn't it possible to hold people morally responsible without being subject to any malicious sentiments toward them when they violate the moral obligations we accept? Gandhi and King have been suggested as interesting cases in this connection, as persons who demanded conformity with important moral principles but forswore malicious or punitive responses toward those who had flouted such principles in the past.[32] Their example seems to tell against the claim that the stance of holding people responsible should be understood in terms of the susceptibility to such emotions as guilt, resentment, and indignation. As I defined them, these emotions are negative attitudes, in that they are forms of disapproval and include a disposition to sanctioning behavior that serves (I have suggested) to express the emotions when they are felt. But Gandhi and King apparently avoided disapproval and the sanctioning behavior that expresses it, while continuing to hold their opponents accountable for the moral wrongs they committed. Can this be understood as a refinement of the stance of holding people morally responsible, consistent with the reactive account of it that I have proposed?

I think it can, if we see the attitude of Gandhi and King toward moral transgressors as one of forgiveness and love. To forgive someone, in the spirit of love, is a complicated stance. It presupposes that one views the person to be forgiven as having done something that would make resentment or indignation a fitting response—one cannot rightly forgive a person for having done something that would not have rendered one of these reactive emotions appropriate in the first place (as with the actions of an infant). Rather, in forgiving people we express our acknowledgment that they have done something that would warrant resentment and blame, but we *renounce* the responses that we thus acknowledge to be appropriate.[33]

---

31 I have tried to account for *moral* responsibility for dutiful actions. But there is another kind of "deep" responsibility that one may have for such actions, [which we might refer to as] as autonomy. Thus an agent might be responsible for dutiful actions not just in the sense of being a morally accountable agent who complies with moral obligations, but also in the sense that those actions disclose her own values and commitments (her acceptance of the obligations with which she complies, for instance). It may be that this notion of autonomy yields a more interesting conception of responsibility for positive performances than the notion of moral responsibility.

32 See Lawrence Stern, "Freedom, Blame, and Moral Community", *Journal of Philosophy* 71 (1974), pp. 72–84; also Gary Watson, "Responsibility and the Limits of Evil: Variations on a Strawsonian Theme", in Ferdinand Schoeman, (ed.), *Responsibility, Character, and the Emotions: New Essays in Moral Psychology* (Cambridge: Cambridge University Press, 1987), pp. 256–86, at pp. 285–6 (reprinted in this volume, pp. 115–41; see pp. 139–40).

33 Renunciation is a complicated intentional stance: in renouncing the reactive emotions, we *deliberately* undertake to rid ourselves of those emotions, or refuse to behave in the ways that ordinarily express them, while recognizing that the conditions that would make the emotions appropriate are nevertheless present. For more detailed discussions of this double aspect of forgiveness, see Aurel Kolnai, "Forgiveness", as reprinted in *Ethics, Value, and Reality: Selected Papers of Aurel Kolnai* (Indianapolis: Hackett Publishing Co., 1978),

If this is correct, however, then forgiveness turns out to be a way of holding people morally responsible, according to the reactive account of responsibility. For on that account, it is sufficient for holding a person morally responsible that one believes that the person's violation of moral obligations would make it appropriate for one to be subject to the reactive emotions.

Ordinarily, forgiveness is a reaction to an acknowledgment of fault on the part of the person who is to be forgiven.[34] Where Gandhi and King seem to go well beyond ordinary responses, in the spirit of love, is in their adopting the stance of forgiveness *presumptively* toward people who have violated moral obligations, independently of whether those at fault have acknowledged wrongdoing. For my purposes here, however, the important point is that this attitude is compatible with their continuing to hold people morally responsible insofar as it includes the belief that violations of moral obligations they accept would render the reactive emotions appropriate. Of course, it would be possible for a moral reformer to try to abandon even this belief— for all I have said, this may well have been the aspiration of the historical Gandhi and King, at least some of the time. On the reactive account, one would have to say about such reformers that they are no longer in the game of holding people morally responsible at all. But this does not seem an implausible line to take. On the contrary, without the belief that violations of moral obligations one accepts would at least render the reactive emotions appropriate, the reformer's stance toward other moral agents would no longer have any connection with the kinds of deep assessment that distinguish moral responsibility. This point will be explained and defended in the section that follows.

The Reactive Account and Moral Judgment

The reactive approach, as presented so far, is a recognizable development of the account of responsibility found in Strawson's "Freedom and Resentment". Strawson there writes: "Only by attending to this range of attitudes [the reactive attitudes] can we recover from the facts as we know them a sense of what we mean, i.e. of *all* we mean, when, speaking the language of morals, we speak of desert, responsibility, guilt, condemnation, and justice."[35] Picking up on this idea, Gary Watson has taken Strawson to be making the "radical claim" that the reactive attitudes "are *constitutive* of moral responsibility; to regard oneself or another as responsible just is the proneness to react to them in these kinds of ways under certain conditions."[36]

Construed along these lines, Strawson's own approach appears to have a markedly noncognitivist character. Holding people morally responsible is understood not in

---

pp. 211–24 and Jean Hampton, "Forgiveness, Resentment and Hatred," in Jeffrie G. Murphy and Jean Hampton, *Forgiveness and Mercy* (Cambridge: Cambridge University Press, 1988), pp. 35–87.

34 See FR, 22–3/63, where this is built into the notion of forgiveness. Compare Jeffrie G. Murphy, "Forgiveness and Resentment", in Murphy and Hampton, *Forgiveness and Mercy*, pp. 14–34, especially pp. 24–9.

35 FR, 34–5/78.

36 Watson, "Responsibility and the Limits of Evil", p. 257 (this volume, p. 116).

terms of beliefs about the people who are held morally responsible, but in terms of the emotions one feels toward them. This apparent noncognitivism of Strawson's approach can make it seem vulnerable to the defects of other forms of noncognitivism in ethics. For example, T. M. Scanlon has criticized the Strawsonian approach to responsibility for failing to get at what is essential to moral judgment.[37] Scanlon evidently detects an emotivist undercurrent in Strawson's discussion, a tendency to emphasize too exclusively the fact that our practices of responsibility, blame, and sanction serve to express our emotions. Scanlon agrees that expressing attitudes is one of the things we characteristically do in making moral judgments—as is attempting to influence other peoples' behavior, as part of an economy of threats. But he does not think that this expressive function is the *essential* feature of moral judgment (any more than the function of influencing others' behavior is), since it is quite possible to endorse a moral judgment without feeling or expressing any attitude in particular.

Now it may or may not be the case that Strawson's own account of moral responsibility goes along with a general emotivism about moral judgment; but this does not seem to be a fair complaint to bring against the version of the approach that I have sketched above. The reactive approach to responsibility I have offered is not committed to the emotivist view that all moral judgments are expressive of reactive emotions. It makes no claim whatsoever about the general meaning or force of moral judgments, but says, at most, that judgments of moral *blame* are to be understood as involving the expression of reactive attitudes. Furthermore, the claim that judgments of blame essentially involve the expression of emotions does not entail that such judgments are *exclusively* expressive; and so even with respect to this more narrow class of judgments, the reactive account should not be confused with emotivist or otherwise noncognitivist accounts. On the reactive account, holding people responsible involves a susceptibility to a range of reactive emotions, so that to blame a person is to be subject to one of these reactive emotions, because of what the person has done. The special force of *judgments* of moral blame can then be understood as consisting in the expression of these reactive attitudes.[38]

Far from being implausible, this more modest claim seems to me to capture an essential dimension of blame, which is neglected by other conventional interpretations of responsibility.... As I have explained, blame is a form of deep moral assessment that goes beyond mere evaluative description of what an agent has done. Furthermore, the way in which blame goes beyond mere description cannot be understood behavioristically; it includes an attitudinal aspect, where the attitudes in question have a distinctive content and focus. It is this attitudinal aspect of blame

---

37 T.M. Scanlon, "The Significance of Choice", in Sterling M. McMurrin, (ed.), *The Tanner Lectures on Human Values*, vol. 8 (Salt Lake City: University of Utah Press, 1988), pp. 149–216, at pp. 165–6, 169–70.

38 Thus the account I have offered does not attempt to explain the "special force" of all moral judgments, but only, at most, of those judgments by means of which we blame people. Compare Scanlon, "The Significance of Choice", p. 169, where it is apparently assumed that an expressivist account of the special force of praise and blame would be part of an expressivist account of the special force of moral judgment generally.

that is accounted for by the reactive emotions. Those emotions are essentially backward-looking, being responses to particular violations of moral obligation, and in this respect they capture exactly the attitude characteristic of blame. Thus, I think it would indeed be strange to suppose that one might blame another person without feeling an attitude of indignation or resentment toward the person, or that one might blame oneself without feeling guilt; attempts to communicate blame generally do function, at least in part, to give expression to such attitudes.

Even if it is granted, however, that judgments of blame are essentially (if not exclusively), expressive of reactive emotions, one might still be in doubt as to whether responsibility can be understood more generally in terms of the susceptibility to such emotions. It is possible, after all, to think that someone has failed to meet the moral obligations we endorse, and to hold the person responsible for the failure—in the terms proposed above, to regard the person as having done something *blameworthy*—without feeling any particular emotion toward the person. Doesn't this confirm Scanlon's more basic point that the susceptibility to emotions is not the essential feature in terms of which we are to understand responsibility? In considering this objection, it is important to recall what is involved in holding someone to an expectation. When I introduced this notion above, I explained it in terms of a disjunction: for an agent to hold someone to an expectation is for the agent to be susceptible to the reactive emotions in cases where that expectation is breached, or for the agent to believe that such emotions would be appropriate for him to feel in those cases, and for him to believe that they would then be appropriate because expectations have been breached. It is this second disjunct that now needs to be emphasized. According to the reactive approach, to hold someone morally responsible is to hold the person to moral obligations that one accepts. This notion of holding a person to a moral obligation is in turn understood by reference to a certain range of emotions; but it is not required that we actually feel the relevant emotion in all the cases in which it would be appropriate to do so. All that is required is that we believe that it would be appropriate for us to feel the emotion in those cases, and that what would make it appropriate is the fact that some moral obligation has been breached.[39]

For example, you may believe that an especially charming colleague who has cheated and lied to you has done something morally wrong, insofar as he has violated a moral obligation not to cheat or lie for personal advantage, and yet you may have trouble working up any resentment or indignation about his case. In a situation of this sort it would perhaps be strange to say that you blame the colleague for what he has done. But you might, all the same, continue to hold him morally responsible—to regard him as having done something blameworthy—and that is allowed by the reactive account as I have presented it.[40] On the reactive account, blame requires that

---

39 Note that holding a person responsible does not involve the belief that the reactive emotions are *required* by the person's violation of moral obligations, or that one *ought* to be subject to them, but only the weaker belief that it would be *appropriate* or *warranted* for one to feel such emotions in response to the violation of those obligations.

40 Compare Scanlon, "The Significance of Choice", pp. 165–6, on believing a friend's action blameworthy without feeling moral indignation or disapprobation.

you actually are subject to a reactive emotion, but an emotional response of this sort is not necessarily required for you to hold your colleague morally blameworthy. It suffices for you to believe that indignation or resentment would be fitting responses on your part, and that they would be fitting because the colleague has done something morally wrong. This seems to correspond to our ordinary judgments of moral responsibility quite exactly. Thus if you know that a moral obligation you accept has been breached, and there are no exonerating circumstances that you are aware of, and you *still* do not believe that the moral response of indignation or resentment would at least be appropriate on your part, then it seems doubtful that you really do hold the colleague morally responsible for his actions or regard him as having done something blameworthy in this case. Of course you might continue to treat the colleague *as if* he were morally responsible, and engage in sanctioning behavior (for educational or deterrent purposes, say); but…this is not the same as actually holding the colleague morally responsible for what he has done.

In developing the reactive approach in this way, I am in effect exploiting the close connection between reactive emotions and expectations that I was at pains to emphasize in Chapter 2, for this connection is among the things that distinguish the account from cruder noncognitivist theories. Blame is construed essentially in terms of emotions, but the emotions in question are not arbitrary feelings of disapprobation and dislike; rather, they have propositional contents that are fixed by their connection to moral obligations that we accept. Moreover the nature of this connection with moral obligations is such that the reactive emotions are made appropriate by certain kinds of beliefs, about the violation of the moral obligations we hold people to. This connection is what gives the reactive emotions the backward-looking content and focus that is characteristic of the attitude of blame. But it also explains how we can continue to regard a person as having done something blameworthy even when we do not feel the emotions that would be appropriate responses to the person's behavior: namely, by persisting in the belief that such emotions would be warranted on our part, despite the fact that we happen not to feel them, and that they would be warranted in virtue of the fact that a moral obligation we accept has been violated. Because of this connection between reactive emotions and moral obligations, it seems misleading to refer to the reactive approach to responsibility, as I have developed it, as a distinctively noncognitivist strategy. The approach explicates moral responsibility in terms of our susceptibility to a range of emotions, but these emotions, in their turn, have an essential cognitive aspect that is given by their connection with moral obligations.[41]

This raises a question: if it is not really necessary to be subject to reactive emotions for one's stance to count as holding someone morally responsible, why bring in such

---

41 My remarks in this paragraph make clear the degree to which my understanding of the reactive attitudes differs from Bennett's. He writes of "the non-propositional nature of blaming, praising etc. in Strawson's account: feelings are made central, and are not tied systematically to any propositions about their objects" ("Accountability", p. 24). On my account, by contrast, the connection between reactive attitudes and obligations can only be understood if we suppose that those attitudes are systematically tied to propositions about their objects.

emotions at all? Could we not understand moral responsibility just as well in terms (say) of the acceptance of moral obligations, and beliefs that such obligations have been violated? On such an account, we might say that to hold someone morally responsible is to be willing to blame the person for violating moral precepts that we ourselves accept for purposes of practical reasoning, deliberation, and public normative discussion, where blame, in turn, simply expresses the belief that those precepts have been breached. But I take it that an account along these lines would not capture what is distinctive about the stance of holding people morally responsible. Blame would be rendered superficial on this account, reduced to a way of describing what an agent has done, and perhaps registering a causal connection between the agent and the action so described. True moral blame, by contrast, is a form of deep assessment, reflecting an attitude toward the agent who has acted wrongly that finds its natural expression in sanctioning behavior (avoidance, denunciation, reproach, censure, and the like). The reactive emotions are needed to explain this attitudinal aspect of true moral blame and to account for its natural connection with sanctioning behavior. And if the reactive emotions are needed to understand the phenomenon of moral blame, they will be equally necessary to make sense of blame*worthiness*. Thus one can hold a person blameworthy without actually being subject to an episode of reactive emotion; but, as I have argued, blameworthiness does require the belief that some reactive emotion would be appropriate. Without at least this degree of connection with the reactive emotions, we lose the idea that judgments of blameworthiness are forms of deep assessment, and with it the idea that they are ways of holding a person morally responsible.[42]

It is worth dwelling on this point a while longer, for a proper understanding of it is crucial if one is to appreciate the advantages of the reactive approach. How else might one try to explain moral responsibility for particular actions, and the related judgments of blame and blameworthiness? Scanlon has defended an alternative account that makes no special reference to reactive emotions.[43] He agrees that judgments of moral responsibility have a force that goes beyond "mere description" of people's actions, but he contends that this special force cannot be accounted for in terms of what the moral judge is doing in making the judgment (such as expressing a reactive emotion). Instead Scanlon makes the intriguing suggestion that the origin of the special force of judgments of responsibility should be located in the content of those judgments—in "what is claimed about the person judged".[44]

Scanlon explains the content of such judgments in terms of a contractualist moral theory. According to this theory, the basic moral obligations are derived from those

---

42 It follows from this that creatures to whom the reactive emotions were completely unfamiliar would not be capable of holding people morally responsible. This seems in line with ordinary thinking about responsibility. Thus, insofar as Mr. Spock (of *Star Trek* fame) was not susceptible to human emotions, he was depicted as being not quite able to make sense of such human responses as blame, and as not subject to such responses himself. (The question of whether Mr. Spock was completely incapable of such responses is complicated by the fact that he was of partially human ancestry, so that reactive emotions were perhaps not as utterly alien to him as he himself often made out.)
43 Scanlon, "The Significance of Choice", lecture 1, sec. 6 (pp. 167–72).
44 Scanlon, "The Significance of Choice", p. 169.

principles that could not reasonably be rejected by people seeking unforced general agreement on a common set of principles. "What is essential", he argues: "is that a judgment of moral blame asserts that the way in which an agent decided what to do was not in accord with standards which that agent either accepts or should accept insofar as he or she is concerned to justify his or her actions to others on grounds that they could not reasonably reject. This is description, but given that most people care about the justifiability of their actions to others, it is not *mere* description."[45]

Taken literally, this passage suggests that judgments of blame differ from mere descriptions of an action in that they describe the action as lacking a property— namely, accord with principles that could not reasonably be rejected as a basis for contractualist agreement—that people generally want their actions to possess. But as I noted earlier, and as Scanlon himself agrees, this alone does not distinguish moral blame from many other kinds of description (for instance, descriptions of people as handsome or clever), and so it does not seem to capture what is special about moral responsibility. The further element, he suggests, is to be found in the connection of moral blame with reasons and justifications. To blame *s*, or to judge *s* morally responsible for what *s* has done, is at least potentially a way of requesting an explanation or justification from *s*.[46] Blame is thus set apart from other forms of unwelcome description by its suitability to serve in a system of public codeliberation; it "differs from mere unwelcome description because it calls for a particular kind of response, such as justification, explanation, and admission of fault".[47] This connection of blame with reasons and justifications points toward the distinctive conditions of responsibility: blame can only be an appropriate response when it is directed at features of a person—such as intentions, actions, or decisions (in contrast to, say, appearance or intelligence)—that are open to assessment in terms of reasons and justifications.

This complicated proposal can be broken down into a plausible claim about the conditions of responsibility and a more dubious suggestion about the special force of judgments of blame. The plausible claim is that blame is an appropriate response only when it is directed at features of a person that are open to assessment in terms of reasons. What is not plausible is the suggestion that the connection with this kind of assessment sets blame apart from other forms of unwelcome description, accounting for its special force. Note, for instance, that beliefs are like intentions in their being explicable by reference to reasons, and hence are appropriate targets of assessment in terms of reasons. Thus we criticize peoples' political and aesthetic and scientific opinions if they do not seem to us to be well justified. Being concerned with justification in terms of reasons, such criticism could in principle influence the reflections of the person whose opinions are being criticized; it is thus suited for interpersonal exchange in a way that sets it apart from unwelcome description of a person's appearance or native talents. But criticism of a person's opinions in

---

45 Scanlon, "The Significance of Choice", p. 170.

46 What follows is an interpretation of Scanlon's difficult remarks on pp. 170–72 of "The Significance of Choice".

47 Scanlon, "The Significance of Choice", p. 171; for the reference to code liberation, see p. 167.

terms of reasons is normally very different from moral blame for a person's actions and decisions. Indeed it is different precisely in that it lacks the distinctive force of judgments of moral blame and moral blameworthiness, the connection to attitudes that gives those judgments their special "depth".[48] It is one thing to criticize a philosopher's views about causation and quite another thing to blame the philosopher for supporting racist or sexist hiring practices; the difference seems to consist in the fact that moral blame has a quality of opprobrium that is lacking in criticism of beliefs or opinions. Hence we cannot hope to account for this special force solely in terms of the connection of moral blame and responsibility with justification.

There is, in any case, something peculiar in the very idea that we might account for the special force of moral blame in terms of its concern with justification. Doing so leads Scanlon to trace the special force to the *conditions* that make blame appropriate; in particular, he looks to the fact that moral blame is appropriately directed only at aspects of persons that are susceptible to being influenced by reasons. But if, as Scanlon seems to agree, judgments of moral blame and moral responsibility have a force that goes beyond "mere description", it is obscure how one could hope to explain this in terms of the conditions that make such judgments appropriate. To try to do so is to look in the wrong place for the *force* of judgments of blame and responsibility. The right place would seem to be not in the conditions that make moral blame appropriate, but in the condition of the judge who assigns blame and endorses judgments of responsibility.

Conclusion

P.F. Strawson's "Freedom and Resentment" famously situates responsibility in relation to the reactive sentiments and the forms of interpersonal relationship with which those sentiments are connected. In these excerpts from my book *Responsibility and the Moral Sentiments*, I have attempted to develop and to defend one important strand in Strawson's rich and multifaceted discussion. Specifically, I have argued that the distinctive stance we adopt when we hold people morally accountable for their actions can best be made sense of in terms of the reactive emotions of resentment, guilt, and indignation. The plausibility of this position depends, however, on an improved understanding of the reactive emotions to which the stance of holding people responsible is constitutively connected. I have proposed a more constrained interpretation of these emotions than that suggested in Strawson's article, emphasizing the structuring role that demands or expectations play in the reactions of resentment, indignation, and guilt.

Strawson himself seems to think that once the reactive emotions are brought into the picture, "pessimistic" or incompatibilist conceptions of responsibility can fairly quickly be seen to be mistaken. In a naturalistic vein, his article suggests that the reactive sentiments are given to us with the fabric of human social life, so that there is no real question of opting out of the practice of moral responsibility in response

---

48 This is not to deny that there are differences in, say, the content and nature of moral and nonmoral justifications. But such differences do not alone account for the special force or opprobrium that seems to attach to moral criticism and blame.

to the (hypothetical) discovery that determinism is true. A different, Wittgensteinian line of argument in "Freedom and Resentment" contends that intelligible questions about our practices can be posed only from within them, so that there is no position from which a global challenge to the whole practice of moral responsibility might be mounted. Finally, Strawson argues that even if we could raise an intelligible global question about our practice of holding people responsible, the only touchstone for answering that question would be the gains and losses that the practice brings for human life; by this pragmatic standard, the connection of responsibility with the valuable forms of relationship to which the reactive sentiments are connected makes it robustly immune to pessimistic challenge.

I am not convinced by these influential parts of Strawson's larger argument. We should follow Strawson in understanding the stance of holding people responsible in terms of the reactive sentiments. But this interpretation of moral responsibility leaves plenty of room for a coherent and serious pessimistic challenge to the credentials of the practice. The question is not whether the reactive sentiments are inevitable, or whether they contribute to the enrichment of human life. It is whether it would be fair to adopt this stance toward people in a world in which their actions are the deterministic result of prior conditions and events. A Strawsonian interpretation of the practice of holding people responsible sets the terms in which this challenge should be understood. But the ultimate resolution of the issue between optimists and pessimists requires a detailed engagement with normative issues about the fairness of reacting to the things people do with such sentiments as resentment, indignation, and guilt.[49]

---

49 See the rest of my *Responsibility and the Moral Sentiments* (Cambridge, MA.: Harvard University Press, 1994), for a defense and development of this interpretation of the traditional debate about moral responsibility and its conditions.

Chapter 9

Blaming, Understanding and Justification
A Defence of Strawson's Naturalism about Moral Responsibility[1]

Kevin Magill

In this paper I discuss and defend Peter Strawson's ("Freedom and Resentment"[2]) argument that our practice of holding agents responsible for their actions is not something that can be given a justification or stands in need of one, since it is not something we could choose to give up. In Part 1, I outline Strawson's arguments and reply to some recent criticisms. In Part 2, I argue that despite our inability entirely to relinquish blaming and holding responsible, there are considerations about the role of acquired perspectives in the initiation of wrongful actions that give us reason to question whether these are ever appropriate responses to wrongdoing. In Part 3, I attempt to identify and diffuse the impulse to seek a justification for holding agents responsible. Finally, in Part 4, I go on to argue that the real force of the problem of moral responsibility lies in a tension in our moral sentiments about whether to blame or to try to understand particular instances of wrongdoing, and that, while there is no general philosophical resolution of this tension, we need not be faced with an irresolvable dilemma about whether to blame or understand whenever we are confronted with wrongdoing.

1.

To hold an agent responsible for his or her actions, according to Peter Strawson, is an expression of a moral attitude. Our moral attitudes, he argues, are the impersonal

---

1 This chapter previously appeared in T. van den Beld (ed.), *Moral Responsibility and Ontology*, (Dordrecht, Kluwer Academic Publishers, 2000), 183–97, and is reprinted with kind permission of Springer Science and Business Media. It also contains parts of Chapter 2 of my *Freedom and Experience: Self-Determination Without Illusions* (K. Magill, Houndmills, Macmillan (UK) and St Martin's Press (US), 1997), which are reprinted here with kind permission of Palgrave Macmillan.

My thanks are due to the organizers and participants of the conference on "Moral responsibility and ontology", Utrecht 1998, at which the first draft of the paper was presented, and especially to Paul Russell and R. Jay Wallace for commenting on my criticisms of their positions and Michael McKenna for his comments on the paper.

2 P.F. Strawson, "Freedom and Resentment", reprinted in this volume, pp. 19–36, and in *Free Will*, Gary Watson (ed.) (Oxford: Oxford University Press, 1982), 59–80. Page references will be to pages 19–36 of this volume, followed by (after the slash) the corresponding pages of Gary Watson (ed.), *Free Will*. Thus, 'FR, 16/59' refers to this volume, p. 16 / and *Free Will*, p. 59.

or generalized analogues of more personal attitudes such as resentment and hurt feelings, and also of gratitude, love (of certain sorts) and forgiveness: the interpersonal reactive attitudes. Strawson contrasts the moral and interpersonal attitudes with the 'objective attitude', in which our interpersonal expectations are withdrawn. To take the objective attitude is to put aside—perhaps only temporarily or partially—reactive attitudes like resentment and the expectations of good will and regard in which they are grounded. To adopt the attitude towards someone is in some way to view or, better, *to respond* to her as something other than a person. The two sorts of attitudes are not mutually exclusive, but they are opposed. To whatever extent one takes the objective attitude, one must forswear or modify resentment, indignation, blame and praise. There are various reasons for adopting the objective attitude and several ways of doing so: all of which involve some suspension of reactive attitudes.

We have criteria about what conditions warrant the suspension of the moral and interpersonal reactive attitudes, according to Strawson, and acceptance of determinism would not entail that those conditions apply to all actions. It is no consequence of determinism that everything anybody does must be accidental or unintentional or produced by psychologically abnormal or morally underdeveloped character. But even if determinism were thought to have threatening consequences for the reactive attitudes, this should not lead us to drop them on grounds of their lack of rational justification. Taken as a whole, the reactive attitudes are part of 'the general framework of human life',[3] and are not the sort of thing that can be given an overall justification or stand in need of one. It is simply not open to us to convert wholesale to the objective attitude (or not, at any rate, because of a theoretical conviction). But even if it were open to us, since the reactive attitudes are so pervasive and valuable a feature of the range of human relationships, our first consideration in deciding whether to persevere with them would have to be the likely effects for our lives of relinquishing them.

To think of someone's behavior as caused or determined is to adopt one kind of objective attitude towards her, but to adopt the objective attitude towards someone is not necessarily to think of her as determined: a doctor can think objectively of a patient as a healthy or an unhealthy body, without entertaining any ideas about the determination of her mental states or actions; a quantum physicist with libertarian inclinations might take an objective view of a person's decisions and actions as products of a neural system that is indeterministic and unpredictable,[4] and necessarily won't think of them as determined. The loss of confidence in the reactive attitudes that we can feel in response to thoughts of determinism, therefore, comes about because thinking of people as determined is one way of adopting the objective attitude and not, as such, because determinism is incompatible with the reactive attitudes. We may also note that while it is possible to think of persons in this way, it does not follow that this is how we ought always to think of them, and not thinking of them in this way does not imply that we thereby regard them as having contra-causal metaphysical powers.

---

3 *Ibid.*, 70.
4 See, for example, Robert Kane, "Free Will: the Elusive Ideal", *Philosophical Studies*, 75 (1994), 25–60.

The shift in focus from beliefs to attitudes in Strawson's discussion of moral responsibility represents an important challenge to the way the traditional debate has been conducted. If blaming people and holding them responsible were straightforwardly based on beliefs or judgments, it would always be possible to ask what ontological or metaphysical conditions are required for such beliefs or judgments to be true or warranted and to press the inquiry to the point where determinism (or, for that matter, personal identity, or agency, or whatever) becomes an issue. Attitudes, by contrast, are neither true nor false, and are not warranted by anything over and above their standard conditions of applicability. The shift from beliefs to attitudes as the focus of discussion therefore undercuts the characteristic assumption of the traditional antagonists that the problem is about what *justifies* us in treating people as responsible for their actions.[5]

Strawson's claim that it is not open to us, as things stand, to make a wholesale conversion to objectivity of attitude has been criticized on a number of grounds. Many of Strawson's critics have pointed out that while it may not be possible for us to relinquish our natural dispositions or proneness to the reactive attitudes, whether or not we give expression to those attitudes is something we *do* have a choice about, especially when it comes to punishing offenders. Strawson agrees:

> It is far from wrong to emphasize the efficacy of all those practices which express or manifest our moral attitudes, in regulating behavior in ways considered desirable; or to add that when certain of our beliefs about the efficacy of some of these practices turns out to be false, then we may have good reason for dropping or modifying those practices.[6]

What we are not capable of (as things stand), he thinks, is a universal objectivity of attitude. This claim has recently been criticized by what might be called *revisionist Strawsonians*: philosophers who are in agreement with Strawson's general claim that holding agents responsible for their actions should be seen as an expression

---

5 It is an assumption that remains central to the strategy of the main compatibilist rival to Strawson's treatment of moral responsibility in contemporary philosophy: that of Harry Frankfurt and his supporters, who argue that the ability to do otherwise than one does—characterised as a *principle of alternative possibilities*—is not necessary for moral responsibility. Some proponents of Frankfurt's position have attempted (not very plausibly, in my view) to co-opt Strawson's situating of moral responsibility within the reactive attitudes as a kind of qualification or finesse to Frankfurt's approach; notably John Martin Fischer and Mark Ravizza in *Responsibility and Control: A Theory of Moral Responsibility* (Cambridge: Cambridge University Press, 1998). See my review in *Mind*, 109, 433 (April 2000) for extensive criticisms of Fischer's and Ravizza's Frankfurtian arguments and a reassertion of Strawson's naturalism against them.

6 FR, 36/80. I have argued elsewhere ("The Idea of a Justification for Punishment", *Critical Review of International Social and Political Philosophy*, 1, 1 (Spring 1998), 86–101) that we have no real idea of how we might go about abolishing punishment, if it were found to lack a moral justification, and therefore that we have no choice about continuing with it (unless we—humanity at large, that is—ceased to care about laws being obeyed or underwent some other universal transformation in nature or values that would make laws or legal penalties unnecessary). The reasons for our lacking such a choice, however, are unrelated (or not directly related) to our natural commitment or proneness to the reactive attitudes.

of attitude, but who, for various reasons, reject or are skeptical of the claim that universal suspension of the reactive attitudes is not possible for us and that no justification is required for them.

Paul Russell has argued that, in making the argument that the reactive attitudes are natural to us and therefore that it is not open to us entirely to relinquish them, Strawson fails to distinguish between the claim that it is not open to us to relinquish our natural *proneness* to the reactive attitudes and the claim that it is not open to us universally to *abandon* entertaining or engaging in the reactive attitudes.[7] Those who seek a justification for our practices of holding agents responsible for their actions, according to Russell, may accept that our proneness to the reactive attitudes is an inescapable feature of our nature and therefore that there is no possibility of giving it up (and no sense in seeking a justification of it), while still maintaining that it *is* open to us to withhold the reactive attitudes where circumstances are judged to be such that they are unwarranted (which is insisted on by Strawson himself). They may also consistently argue that such circumstances might, in principle, include *all* instances in which reactive attitudes can be expressed. In that case it *would* make sense to seek a justification for our holding or manifesting the attitudes: a justification that would show either that the circumstances do not apply or that they do not render the attitudes unwarranted.

One reason why Russell rejects Strawson's claim that there are no circumstances or considerations that could lead us universally to withhold the reactive attitudes is that we might, for all we know, discover that human beings are universally morally incapacitated. Strawson allows that some individuals, and even some classes of individual (e.g. children), are thus incapacitated or lacking full moral capacities and if this is so there is nothing obviously incoherent in imagining that moral incapacity might—as a result of a virus, say—become universal. In that case, Russell thinks, we might legitimately conclude that the reactive attitudes, or, at any rate, blaming and holding responsible, are unwarranted. According to libertarians, if determinism is true we *are* thus incapacitated and blaming etc. are unwarranted.

In fact Strawson does not claim that there are *no* circumstances that could lead us universally to abandon the reactive attitudes, but rather that:

> we cannot, as we are, seriously envisage ourselves adopting a thoroughgoing objectivity of attitude to others as a result of *theoretical conviction* of the truth of determinism; and ... when we do in fact adopt such an attitude in a particular case, our doing so is not the consequence of a *theoretical conviction* which might be expressed as 'Determinism in this case', but is a consequence of our abandoning, for different reasons in different cases, the ordinary inter-personal attitudes.[8] (my italics)

Strawson's position is that our natural propensities and commitments are such that no theoretical commitment (whether about determinism or anything else) could lead us to abandon them. But a universally incapacitating disease of the kind envisaged by Russell is quite a different kettle of fish from a theoretical conviction. In such

---

[7] Paul Russell, "Strawson's Way of Naturalizing Responsibility", *Ethics*, 102 (1992), 287–302; reprinted in this volume, pp. 143–56.

[8] FR, 27/69.

a situation, we would imagine, our natural commitment to the reactive attitudes would be persistently challenged and undermined (assuming that we do not imagine ourselves to have fallen prey to the disease) by the *behavior* and *manifest attitudes* of others, rather than by some theoretical conviction, belief or judgment. The dislodging of the attitudes would not, in that case, result from any choice arising from theoretical conviction, but would rather be pressed on us by our circumstances. Thus, while it is possible to imagine circumstances that *might* lead us, gradually, universally to abandon the reactive attitudes, or realistically to consider doing so, this has no bearing on the status of Strawson's claims that no general theoretical conviction could lead us to do so or that, as things stand, whether in general to engage in the attitudes is not something about which we have a *choice*.[9]

R. Jay Wallace has argued that it is a mistake to think that we cannot relinquish the reactive attitudes, because there may have been societies that have been lacking in at least some of them, in which case, he thinks, while interpersonal relationships might be an inevitable fact of human life, "it does not necessarily follow that the reactive attitudes are similarly inevitable".[10] Whether there have been cultures that were completely lacking in the reactive attitudes is moot. If there have been such cultures, however, it would not follow from this that is open to *us* to give them up: that *we* could choose to divest our interpersonal relations of the reactive attitudes. In making the claim that the reactive attitudes are a feature of human nature, Strawson seemingly intends this to apply to all cultures, but those who agree with him that it is not open to us to give up the reactive attitudes need not take that view. Instead we might very plausibly argue that whatever might have been the case in the ancient world or (more recently) in the Trobriand Islands, it is simply not in *our* nature to be able to deliberately reorder our interpersonal relationships in such a way as to exclude the reactive attitudes. There have been many changes in human civilization that did not result from choice or design, in respect of many of which, moreover, it is implausible to imagine that they *could have* resulted from choice or design. What is true of the individual in this respect is true of cultures more generally: if I say that "it is not in his nature to (be able to) do that", the claim is not invalidated by remarking that "others can".

That it is not open to us to adopt a universal objectivity of attitude is a (highly general) empirical claim. As such, no watertight proof is available for it and, correspondingly, there is no general refutation of all denials of it. I have considered and rejected what appear to me to be the most plausible denials.[11] Those who maintain that universal objectivity is, in principle, an option for us need to say much

---

9 Although I disagree with Russell about the possibility of universally withholding the reactive attitudes, as I go on to suggest, there are certain reasons for thinking that the objective attitude is appropriate in particular cases of wrongdoing, and these reasons appear to generalize to all cases.

10 R. Jay Wallace, *Responsibility and the Moral Sentiments* (Cambridge Mass: Harvard University Press, 1994), 31.

11 Although there is certainly more to both Russell's and Wallace's critiques of Strawson's position than I have had space to cover.

more, I would argue, about how it might be accomplished, if their counter-claim is to be taken seriously.

2.

While it may not be possible for us to seriously envisage abandoning the reactive attitudes on the grounds of a theoretical conviction about determinism, there are more specific considerations about wrongful actions, which Strawson does not consider, that provide reasons for thinking that the objective attitude is an appropriate response in particular cases. Moreover, these considerations can be applied to all wrongful actions, thereby raising questions of fairness and consistency.[12]

As I have noted, thinking about the causes of someone's behavior is one form of the objective attitude. On the Strawsonian view, the reason for the loss of confidence we may feel about feelings of vengefulness, indignation and so on (and also about blaming and holding people to account) when thinking about the

---

12 Like me (see below), R. Jay Wallace takes the issue of fairness to be central to incompatibilist concerns about moral responsibility and determinism (although not their only concern). Wallace argues that Strawson implicitly treats questions about what would justify our practices of holding agents responsible for their actions as demanding an "external" justification of a sort that would provide reasons for buying into the practice. Strawson's arguments are less persuasive, according to Wallace, if questions about justification are taken as raising issues about fairness from a position that is *internal* to our moral practices. From this internal perspective, Wallace thinks, we have "moral terms for deciding whether it would be appropriate to hold people responsible in particular cases" (Wallace, *op. cit.*, 101–2), which, according to incompatibilists, would generalize to all cases if determinism is true. (Cf. Paul Russell's (*op. cit.*) distinction between questions about the justifiability of our proneness to the reactive attitudes and ones about the justification for particular *tokens* of expressions of those attitudes).

It seems to me, however, that an 'internal' inquiry into the fairness of holding agents responsible for their actions, which might yield the conclusion that they are never justified, and therefore that we should "buy out of" the practice, is no different in substance or intent from one generated by a supposedly "external" question about whether one should 'buy into' the practice. Moreover, and although I think that the demand for fairness is motivated by real concerns, I take the view (for reasons that cannot be defended in this paper) that sceptical questions about the fairness of the entire practice of holding agents responsible for their actions are incoherent. If questions about fairness, as I think Wallace is right to say, can only be raised from a position that is internal to our moral practices, they cannot coherently be raised in relation to *guiding* sentiments about responsibility, blameworthiness and desert. That (some of) the guilty should suffer for what they do, for example, is a sentiment that informs our judgments about what is fair and what is unfair treatment. To put a question about fairness in respect of that sentiment would require that it first be subtracted from the group of sentiments that guide our judgments about fairness. But if this subtraction were made, what we would be left would no longer be, authentically and recognizably, *our* sense of fairness or, indeed, *our* moral outlook.

I make the case for the position that certain moral sentiments are foundational to our moral outlook and practices, which places them beyond the scope of questions about fairness, in "Punishment: moral sentiments as an alternative to justification" (work in progress).

causes of behavior, is attributable to the fact that taking the objective attitude to someone necessarily involves setting aside our reactive attitudes towards them. According to Jonathan Bennett, since people tend not to think of blameworthiness and accountability in terms of feelings, those who are at all skeptical about moral responsibility—Spinozists, for example—are apt to misperceive the loss of their *feelings* of indignation etc. as a loss of a judgment that the wrongdoer is to blame.[13] But the loss of reactive feelings, brought on by taking the objective attitude, does not show those feelings or the practices that express them to be inappropriate, and there is no general reason for preferring the objective attitude to the reactive attitude. A Spinozist who strives always to view human actions as strictly necessitated and predictable natural phenomena forgets her own natural needs and inclinations.

As it stands, however, this response is insufficient to meet the Spinozist's concerns. We may allow that it would not be practicable or desirable universally to abandon our practices of holding people responsible for what they do or always to adopt the objective attitude towards the endeavors, achievements and misdeeds of others, but this still leaves us with judgments to make in respect of particular actions. Some are less inclined to blame and to resent than others. Their disinclination might be a result of Spinozist reflection on the causes and circumstances of wrongdoing, and of a general desire to understand, or of innate temperament. Now suppose that a person accepts Strawson's claim that there is no reason for, and no possibility of, entirely relinquishing blaming people for their actions, but is sufficiently impressed by considerations about the causes of human behavior to doubt whether blame is an appropriate response in many situations. Would Strawson and Bennett want to say that such individuals are simply mistaken? or that the reactive attitudes are always appropriate, providing the criteria for their application are fulfilled? Nothing in Strawson's arguments would support such a strong claim. All they establish is that there is no reason always to adopt the objective attitude.

There are circumstances in which it is thought inappropriate to blame, which are detailed by Strawson, but even these are not always clear cut. Some individuals are more patient and tolerant than others, and more inclined to try to view wrongdoings objectively than to engage in blaming and punishing; in some cases because they have thought a lot about the causes of wrongdoing. Advising them, when they have chosen not to blame, that it is sometimes appropriate to do so simply misses the point that such individuals often see no value or sense in blaming and punishing.

We know that there are various considerations that can lead people to refuse to engage in blaming, or to qualification or amelioration of their reactive feelings. Someone who knows that the spiteful remarks of her partner were caused by pressure of work can sometimes set aside her feelings of resentment. It does not follow that it would always be right for her to look to the causes of her partner's behavior or that it would be appropriate for anyone else to do so. Her response will follow partly from her other feelings towards her partner and partly, perhaps, from reflection about how the hurtful remarks relate to his character, how he would subsequently feel about having made them and so on.

---

13 Jonathan Bennett, "Accountability", *Philosophical Subjects: Essay Presented to P. F. Strawson*, Zak van Straaten (ed.), (Oxford: Clarendon, 1980).

Strawsonians could allow that this is so, and that there are indeed a range of cases in which the internal criteria for the reactive attitudes and practices give no unambiguous guidance about how we should respond to bad behavior, while insisting that there remain many cases where it is clear and uncontroversial that resentment, indignation or blame are in order. Indeed the cases are suggested by what complicates those in which how we should respond is not so clear cut. A person who is characteristically spiteful, *rather than reacting badly to pressure*, for example, is a proper object of blame. One who steals *without needing to,* and knowing full well the harm and distress his actions cause to others, gives proper cause for indignation.

Commenting on the Spinozist argument that our proneness to the reactive attitudes is causally dependent on ignorance of the determining causes of our actions, Strawson suggests that it is informed by an absurd vision of human behavior being brought entirely within the scope of scientific understanding (i.e. as entirely law governed).[14] But there is a different way of understanding the Spinozist position: one which Strawson (and compatibilists in general) would find harder to resist. Rather than attempting to conceive of human behavior as entirely law governed, the Spinozist may see misdeed and malice as caused by misconceptions and limitations of vision. The person who is characteristically spiteful could be understood as having acquired that characteristic as a misconceived response to his need for attention from others; a response that may have been reinforced by the reactions of others. It is possible to imagine how a child, because of the way it is treated and the limitations on what it knows, comes to see spiteful behavior as the most appropriate means to satisfy its need for attention. To imagine this is to see how we ourselves would respond were our horizons as limited as the child's. Once the spiteful characteristics are acquired they would become significant features of the child's personality, shaping the way it perceives and understands the world and guiding the way it responds. It is possible to imagine all the steps in a life history leading from an innocent child to a spiteful adult as ones we ourselves would have taken had our vision been similarly limited. Spite and malice, therefore, can be understood as resulting from limitations of vision and inferences drawn because of those limitations; and this, indeed, is the way in which such cognitive and imaginative limitations have been understood in a long tradition of thinking about wrongdoing from Plato, through Spinoza, to Freud.

The argument about limitations of perspective is a difficult line of reasoning for Strawsonians, and compatibilists generally, to resist, given their acceptance that ignorance and illusion provide reasons for withdrawing or tempering the reactive attitudes and withholding blame. The mistaken perspective of someone who is characteristically malicious may be so deeply ingrained that it is very difficult to isolate or dislodge, and such that their whole personality may be structured by it; and there is no obvious reason why it should not be viewed as a reason for taking the objective attitude towards their actions.

None of this exactly undermines Strawson's arguments about the reactive attitudes. The fact that a person's limitations of perspective can count against blaming them for what they have done, and that all bad behavior might be attributable to limitations of perspective, does not entail that no one ever knowingly does wrong (even if Plato,

---

14 P.F. Strawson, "Reply to Ayer and Bennett", van Straaten, *ibid.*, 262–4.

Spinoza and Freud may have thought that it does). Someone's acquired limitations of perspective may incline him to think and feel in characteristically despicable ways, but he may yet be a knowing sinner. The link between acquired limitations of perspective and bad behavior is no reason for thinking that all bad behavior must be excused, but it does leave us with doubts in many cases about how much weight we should attach to it, and these doubts can give rise to feelings of insecurity about blaming in any particular case. If we accept that all bad actions result from limitations of perspective and if we consider limitations of perspective as excusing wrongdoing in some cases, then why not in others? and why not in all?

3.

We face an impasse. Holding people morally responsible and the family of reactive practices and attitudes of which it is a part are seemingly ineradicable features of our natures and of our dealings with one another. Taken as a whole they cannot be justified, but neither do they require justification. Nevertheless, in any particular case of wrongdoing we face a choice about what attitude to take. To take the objective attitude is to forswear, to some extent, blaming and praising as we ordinarily understand and practice them. And yet there are reasons for adopting the objective attitude that Strawson does not fully consider, and no compelling reason for refusing to adopt it. Our feelings are very much at issue in all of this, but our feelings are not decisive: we must decide.

One way of responding to the impasse would be to decide emphatically always to refuse the objective attitude unless it is unambiguously called for. To do so, however, would be retributive humbug: a contrived response, which would be guilty of ignoring human feelings in much the same way as those one-eyed utilitarians, criticized by Strawson, who ignore the feelings that are expressed by our habits of praising and blaming. The feelings that such a strategy would ignore overlap with those that inform the reactive attitudes; namely sympathy and a sense of fairness. It is our human feelings, therefore, that issue in the judgment that it is "hideously unfair"[15] to blame someone for malicious behavior arising from misconceptions and limitations of vision that would have led anyone to behave in the same way.

But if it is unfair, would we think it any less unfair if we thought that wrongdoers were possessed of libertarian free will? According to those who are skeptical about moral responsibility, even though they may consider libertarian free will to be inane, the answer is yes, or, at any rate, that the concept of desert, which can be explicated as "fair reward" (whether for good or bad behavior), presupposes that of libertarian free will.[16] Presumably what has led them to this conclusion is the thought that it is impossible to think of behavior we regard as law-governed as also being blameworthy. Setting aside, for the moment, the argument that it is not the notion that all human behavior is law-governed that is really behind skepticism about moral responsibility, is it true that the concept of desert presupposes that of libertarian free will? Consider the

---

15 Bernard Williams, quoted by J. Bennett, *ibid.*, p. 25.
16 A.J. Ayer, "Free Will and Rationality", van Straaten, *ibid.*, 12. (Ayer's article is reprinted in this volume, at pp. 37–46; see p. 45).

following propositions about Bob's act of deceit: "he acted of his own free will", "it was his doing, and he was wholly and solely responsible for it" and "he categorically could have done otherwise than he did". Suppose we stipulate, if there is any doubt about it, that these propositions are all to be construed in the sense that incompatibilists believe to be required for moral responsibility: does any of the three propositions, taken on its own, logically imply or in any way entail that Bob deserves to be punished or blamed for what he did? The answer is clearly that none of them do; and supposing that there is something unfair about blaming and punishing, the truth of the any of the propositions would not entail or imply that it is any less unfair.

What makes it seem as if the concept of desert requires libertarian free will is awareness that thinking about the causes of behavior undermines the tendency to blame and resent (especially, as I have suggested, awareness of the thought that bad behavior arises from limitations of perspective which themselves have formative and ongoing causes). To think of a person's actions as free in the libertarian sense is to think of those actions as lacking any causes or that there is some point prior to which they have no causes, or no sufficient causes. That may make it seem as if the thought that someone deserves to be punished, which was undermined by considerations about causes, can be justified if their behavior has no causes or has uncaused causes or insufficient causes. But the notion that someone deserves to be punished is no more justified if their behavior lacks a sufficient causal history than if it has one. The sentiments that punishment is fair reward for bad behavior—that the guilty should suffer—and that people should be blamed for their wrongdoings are, I would argue, foundational to our moral thought and practices. And since any *moral* justification must be internal to our moral thought, there is nothing that could provide a moral justification for that sentiment.

If punishing offenders and treating individuals as morally responsible for their actions cannot, as practices and attitudes, be given a justification, what is it about them that could be thought of as monstrously unfair? The unfairness, I have suggested, might be thought to attach to the idea of seeing malicious behavior as the product of limited horizons and misconceptions that would have led anyone to behave wickedly. Presumably it would not be thought of as quite *monstrously* unfair if instead of punishing bad behavior, good behavior were always rewarded. What is thought to be unfair is the infliction of suffering on the wrongdoer who has done what we ourselves would have done given the same psychological circumstances. That we consider there to be something monstrous or bad about the infliction of suffering reflects another part of our moral thinking and practices. It is the idea or attitude that suffering, pain, disease, and so on are bad and that pleasure, happiness, well being and so forth are good. This is the part of morality, in other words, that utilitarians wrongly take to be the whole of it. Let us call it *the principle* (or *the sentiment) of well-being*.

The impulse to find a justification for punishment, desert and moral responsibility, therefore, comes from judging one strain or principle in our moral thinking and practice by another. If we put the matter like that, we may now ask whether the principle that the guilty should suffer needs to be justified just because it conflicts with the principle of well-being. Both are foundational to morality[17] (as we know it) and there is no reason to accept that one should be ranked inferior to the other as a moral principle, still less that one should have to be justified because it is thought to conflict with the other. The thought that punishment, desert and moral responsibility require a justification is therefore a kind of category mistake. It involves the employment of the principle of well-being beyond its meaningful sphere of application. The principle of well-being does not extend to treatment of the guilty, or, rather, it is qualified in respect of them.

4.

Is the forgoing argument persuasive enough for us to continue confidently to blame and punish, just as long as the usual criteria for the applicability of our reactive attitudes are satisfied? There are two related reasons for thinking that it is not.

In the first place, as I suggested above, the argument that our moral practices and judgments are bound up with attitudes and feelings, rather than metaphysical or ontological judgments, cuts both ways. The principle of well-being is no more justified in the light of some prior judgment that pain and suffering are self-evidently bad, than the principle of desert would be justified by our possessing libertarian free will. Our judgments that the pain and suffering of others are bad, as Hume rightly observed, are grounded in our feelings of sympathy: the capacity to be moved by the fortunes and misfortunes of others. The woman's judgment that her partner's spiteful words were brought on by stress and overwork does not simply repress or qualify her reactive feelings towards him, but expresses her feelings of sympathy and concern with his well-being. The Spinozist's judgment that it is inappropriate to hold the wrongdoer to blame for behavior that was understandable and predictable, given his cognitive circumstances, is likewise, presumably, informed by his or her concerns about suffering humanity.

Second, the fact that it is feelings or moral sentiments that are expressed by the principle of well-being, just as much as the principle of desert, undermines the claim that the impulse to find a justification for punishment and desert involves a straightforward category mistake. To say that the scope of application of the principle of well-being is limited by other principles, such as desert, private property, obligation to one's own community and so forth, is to imply that there is some rule or understanding that stipulates this. But there is no such rule and no such understanding. There is, I agree, a mistake (that of making one foundational principle subordinate to another) in arguing that desert and punishment require a justification because of the suffering they inflict. But this is not to say that there are no grounds for being troubled by the suffering caused by punishment and blame. The truth, as illustrated in the example of the woman who tries to be understanding about her partner's spiteful remarks, is that in many cases it is possible for us, rightly, to

---

17 Those who question this should ask themselves whether they could ever bring themselves always to feel that it is right to forswear blame or resentment in response to bad or injurious behavior.

blame and punish but also to decide instead to set aside the impulse to do so and to try to understand and accommodate.

Therefore, the impasse I identified, about whether in any particular case to respond objectively or reactively to wrongdoing, reflects deeper tensions in our moral thinking between the principle of well-being and other foundational sentiments, especially that of desert. These tensions, moreover, are grounded in conflicting feelings or sentiments we all (or almost all) share. Whether to respond reactively or objectively to wrongdoing—whether to blame or to try to understand—is a question for which there is no general answer. Our own moral thought, and our own natures, pull us in opposing directions. There is no reason universally to abandon our practices of praising and blaming, even supposing that we could; but there is no absolutely compelling reason in any particular case for holding anyone responsible for what they do or blaming them for it.

The philosophical inclination to ask whether moral responsibility is compatible with determinism assumes that it is possible to justify the practice of holding individuals responsible for their actions, but no general justification is either possible or required. The problem is rather that we face a decision in respect of any particular instance of wrongdoing about whether to blame or to adopt what Strawson has described as the objective attitude.

It is conceivable that if the principle of well-being assumes greater importance in moral attitudes, or if a universally incapacitating disease of the kind envisaged by Paul Russell were to occur, then moral responsibility, desert and punishment will no longer occupy the same proportions they have hitherto (although, as Strawson has argued, an overnight shift away from reactive attitudes and practices is barely conceivable). At any rate, the tension we face about whether to blame or to understand is not, as such, philosophical in nature or open to philosophical resolution. The tension is an inescapable feature of moral life, and if it ever can be resolved, it would be as a result of social and moral evolution.

Despite the lack of a general solution or answer to the problem, however, I think that there are considerations that can guide the individual in deciding whether to blame or to understand. In the first case, of course, blaming and understanding are not always exclusive. This is particularly true in respect of the treatment of children.[18] Nevertheless, there are many situations in which we can properly feel that there is a decision to be made about whether to blame. It would be wrong, of course, to think that whether to blame or understand is always something we make decisions about, but we sometimes do: we are not always simply carried along by our feelings in these matters. It is our feelings, however, that do, on the whole, guide us in making such decisions, and the feelings in question have to do with our interests (what we care about) in the behavior of others. The reactive attitudes, according to Strawson, are motivated by our expectations of and desires for good will and consideration on the parts of others with whom we are involved in interpersonal relationships of various sorts, and for the same kinds of consideration to be shown to others. I have argued that the objective attitude is also often connected with our interests in or feelings

---

18 Cf. FR, 32/75.

about the fortunes and sufferings of others.[19] The woman who resists the impulse to respond with resentment and blame to her partner's spite has both kinds of interest in his behavior. She values his good will and consideration while also being concerned with his well-being. Clearly these interests are not opposed but interdependent and mutually sustaining. But when the person in whom she has these interests behaves badly towards her, they can prompt conflicting responses. Her attempt to understand her partner's bad behavior reflects not only an interest in his well-being, but also a judgment that her interests in his good will and regard are not seriously challenged by uncharacteristic outbursts.

One can be led in the direction of the objective attitude, or to modify one's reactive attitudes, by a range of considerations and interests. The interest one has in the regard and goodwill of others might itself lead one to judge that the objective attitude is appropriate where protest and remonstration have persistently failed to alter another's hurtful behavior. In that case we might come to view the other person as incapable of responding to our hurt feelings. We would judge, in such cases, that there is a cause of the persistent behavior, and in doing so we would be drawn into the objective attitude.

There are considerations that for some of us would provide reasons for responding objectively, while leaving others unmoved. Someone who is committed to the view that poverty and inequality are avoidable evils has an interest in the misfortunes and suffering of those who are disadvantaged that may predispose her towards the objective attitude in respect of their wrongdoings and the causes thereof. A free marketeer, we may expect, would not be thus predisposed. It is possible that there are individuals—Spinoza may have been one—who are so saintly and detached from interpersonal relationships that their desires for the goodwill and consideration of others are very attenuated and their interests in the general well-being of humanity are unusually strong. Given what they care about, such persons will naturally tend to view wrongdoing objectively and without reproach. For them there will always be an interest in perceiving the sufficient causes of wrongdoing, and the thought that all behavior has sufficient causes will be a constant background to their desires, pursuits and dealings with others. But if there is a general reason why one should want or seek to be like Spinoza, it is not that all human behavior has sufficient causes, and there is no general reason why one should always strive to remind oneself that all behavior has sufficient causes.

Conclusion

I conclude, therefore, that the traditional problem of whether moral responsibility is compatible with determinism is misconceived. The real problem is a practical one about whether, in particular cases, to praise and blame or to try to understand. There can be no general resolution of the tension between the principle of well-being and sentiments and attitudes about blame and desert, and therefore we as individuals are

---

19 Although the objective attitude can also be informed by sheer intellectual curiosity—an interest in knowing more—in which concern for the well-being of others plays no necessary part.

inescapably confronted with conflicts of intuition about whether to blame or to try to understand particular instances of wrongdoing. Nevertheless, if we keep in mind that it is what we care about, informed by our personal, moral and political feelings and sentiments, that generally informs whether we take the objective or the reactive attitudes, we will not be faced with a hopeless dilemma every time we confront decisions about whether to blame or to understand.

Chapter 10

The Limits of Evil and the Role of Moral Address
A Defense of Strawsonian Compatibilism[1]

Michael McKenna

P.F. Strawson defends compatibilism by appeal to our natural commitment to the interpersonal community and the reactive attitudes. While Strawson's compatibilist project has much to recommend it, his account of moral agency appears incomplete. Gary Watson has attempted to fortify Strawson's theory by appeal to the notion of moral address. However, Watson then proceeds to argue that Strawson's theory of moral responsibility (so fortified) would commit Strawson to treating extreme evil as its own excuse. Watson also argues that the reactive attitudes do not lend unequivocal support to Strawsonian compatibilism and that the reactive attitudes are sometimes sensitive to considerations which suggest an incompatibilist or skeptical diagnosis. Watson attempts to provide a Strawsonian defense against these difficulties, but he ultimately concludes that the skeptical threats raised against Strawsonian compatibilism cannot be sufficiently silenced.

I believe that Watson has done Strawsonian compatibilism a great service by drawing upon the notion of moral address. In this paper, I attempt to defend the Strawsonian compatibilist position, as Watson has cast it, against the problems raised by Watson. I argue against Watson that Strawson's theory of responsibility, as well as the notion of moral address, do not commit the Strawsonian to treating extreme evil as its own excuse. I also argue that Watson misinterprets the point of certain reactive attitudes and thereby wrongly assumes that these attitudes are evidence against Strawsonian compatibilism.

---

1 This paper was written with funding from a *Cornell University Society for the Humanities Fellowship* provided by Ithaca College for the summer of 1996. I presented earlier drafts of this paper at the 1996 Annual Meetings of *The New York State Philosophical Association Creighton Club*, the 1996 Central Division Meetings of the *American Philosophical Association*, the 1996 Annual Conference of *The Society for Philosophy in the Contemporary World*, and the University of Virginia Department of Philosophy Metaphysics and Epistemology Discussion Group. Steven Lee acted as commentator at the *Creighton Club* meeting, Alison McIntyre acted as commentator at the *APA* Central Division meeting. I have profited greatly from both Professor Lee's and McIntyre's insightful remarks. I would further like to thank the following people for all of their generous advice and criticism: Scott Boltwood, David Copp, Richard Creel, Russell Daw, Dan Devereux, John Martin Fischer, Peter French, Carl Ginet, Ishtiyaque Haji, Rick Kaufman, Bob Klee, Kenton Machina, John Phillips, Paul Russell, Jorge Secada, Stephen Schwartz, George Thomas, two anonymous referees for the journal *Ethics*, and two anonymous referees for *The Journal of Ethics*. I am especially indebted to Gary Watson for providing me with a detailed set of encouraging comments on an earlier draft of this paper.

1.

In "Freedom and Resentment" P. F. Strawson presents the following argument for a compatibility between moral responsibility and determinism: Two categories of pleas are used to show that an agent should not be held morally responsible. One category *excuses* an agent when some piece of behavior, normally indicative of a lack of due moral regard towards others, does not in the particular case at hand actually manifest disregard. Pleas like: "I didn't know", or "I was shoved", or "I was threatened", or "I didn't mean to", fall into this category. The other category *exempts* an agent from membership in the class of competent moral agents. Exemptions show that an agent is incapacitated for ordinary interpersonal relations and, thus, for participation within the moral community. Pleas like: "She's only a child", or "She's a hopeless schizophrenic", or "She is mentally handicapped", fall into this second category. Call these two types of pleas local and global excuses.[2] Strawson argues that if we were to discover determinism to be true, we would have no grounds to excuse all persons locally or globally. For, the argument goes, if determinism is true, it does not follow that any local excuse applies universally (i.e., that we were all pushed, or that no one ever meant to do what she did). Nor, if determinism is true, does it follow that any global excuse applies universally (i.e., that everyone is only a child, or that every one is a hopeless schizophrenic). Therefore, the truth of determinism would provide no universal grounds for undermining the general practice of holding morally responsible. Call this Strawson's *argument from excuses*.[3]

Strawson's argument from excuses arises out of his naturalist theory of moral responsibility. In order to fully appreciate his argument, it is important to see why this is so. According to Strawson, moral responsibility is constituted by a range of attitudes:

---

[2] Strictly speaking, excuses and justifications show in different kinds of ways how a particular action does not demonstrate a lack of proper regard for others. Exemptions are designed to show that an agent is exempt from the demands of the moral community. For a helpful explanation of these distinctions see Gary Watson's "Responsibility and the Limits of Evil: Variations on a Strawsonian Theme", in F.D. Schoeman (ed.), *Responsibility, Character and the Emotions: New Essays in Moral Psychology* (Cambridge: Cambridge University Press, 1987), pp. 256–86; and also in J.M. Fischer, and M. Ravizza (eds), *Perspectives on Moral Responsibility* (Ithaca, NY: Cornell University Press, 1993), pp. 122–4. All references are to the latter [Watson's paper is also reprinted in this volume, at pp. 117–43—the editors]. See also R.J. Wallace *Responsibility and the Moral Sentiments* (Cambridge, MA: Harvard University Press, 1994), pp. 119–21. For purposes of convenience I will speak instead in terms of local and global excuses.

[3] P.F. Strawson, "Freedom and Resentment", *Proceedings of the British Academy*, vol. xlviii (1962), pp. 187–211. Also in G. Watson (ed.), *Free Will* (Oxford: Oxford University Press, 1982), pp. 59–80. [As in other essays in this volume, page references for "Freedom and Resentment" will be abbreviated as FR and are to pages 19–36 of this volume, followed by (after the slash) the corresponding pages of Watson's *Free Will* (1982). Thus, 'FR, 16/59' refers to this volume, p. 16/and *Free Will*, p. 59—the editors.]

Only by attending to this range of *attitudes* can we recover from the facts as we know them a sense of what we mean, i.e. of *all* we mean, when, speaking the language of morals, we speak of desert, responsibility, guilt, condemnation, and justice.[4]

These attitudes are situated within the framework of ordinary interpersonal relations and expectations central to social life. Most importantly, human susceptibility to this range of attitudes is a fundamental natural aspect of adult interpersonal life and is therefore not optional.[5] Thus, on the Strawsonian view, the attitudes which constitute moral responsibility arise out of circumstances endemic to the human condition.

To *hold* another (or oneself) responsible on Strawson's account is for one to be prone to a class of morally *reactive* attitudes towards another (attitudes of resentment, guilt or perhaps indignation).[6] These reactive attitudes are understood as appropriate *responses* towards attitudes of ill will (or disregard) made manifest in another's (or in one's own) behavior. As Gary Watson puts it, to hold another responsible means something in practice; it is not merely a judgment that a certain fact about another person obtains.[7] It involves certain attitudes and feelings seen as appropriate responses toward an offending party.

Because, on Strawson's account, the practice of holding responsible is a natural fact of adult interpersonal life, it requires no theoretical truth as a basis for its justification. Traditional theoretical justifications for the practice of holding morally responsible have involved, for instance, the libertarian claim that a responsible moral agent's will must be metaphysically free, or the compatibilist/utilitarian claim that it is appropriate to hold an agent morally responsible when doing so would optimize the utility of a system of rewards and punishments. In contrast, on the Strawsonian account, what is relevant to any justification regarding an ascription of responsibility is not the obtaining of any theoretical truth, but a set of practical questions related to the two categories of pleas mentioned above: First, is the person genuinely a member of the interpersonal community (is she a competent moral agent)? Second, does her particular piece of behavior indicate an attitude of ill will or general disregard for others (has she violated a moral demand)?[8] When the answer to one of these questions is no, some local or global excuse applies.

Understood as such, the two categories of excuses can be taken to define the conditions of moral responsibility.[9] This shows how Strawson's argument from

---

4 FR, 34–5/78 (emphasis on '*attitudes*' is mine; emphasis on '*all*' is Strawson's).

5 FR, 34–5/78.

6 In focusing upon resentment, guilt and indignation, I am restricting the discussion to holding one morally responsible for *blameworthy* behavior. A full theory would be able to accommodate praiseworthy behavior, as well as morally neutral behavior performed by a competent moral agent. For ease of discussion only, I will focus throughout exclusively upon Strawson's theory of responsibility as it applies to morally blameworthy behavior.

7 Watson, pp. 119–20.

8 This account of Strawson's general theory is based on both Gary Watson's "Responsibility and the Limits of Evil", pp. 129–30, and John Martin Fischer's and Mark Ravizza's introduction to *Perspectives on Moral Responsibility*, pp. 12–15.

9 This way of capturing the force of Strawson's argument from excuses was kindly suggested to me by Gary Watson in comments on an earlier draft of this paper.

excuses gains its force from his naturalist view of responsibility. According to the argument, determinism would not imply that some excuse applies universally. Because the excuses themselves, given Strawson's naturalist interpretation, define the conditions of moral responsibility, it follows (trivially) that determinism would not universally undermine any condition requisite for holding another morally responsible.

2.

Here is a problem with Strawson's argument from excuses: Global excusing considerations are designed to show an incapacity for responsible moral agency by showing an incapacity for adult interpersonal relationships. Perhaps such persons do not have the relevant capacities precisely because, for whatever reasons, they are determined. Until we understand the relevant capacities, we cannot maintain that if determinism were true, these capacities would not be undermined.[10]

Sympathetic to Strawson's compatibilist strategy, in "Responsibility and the Limits of Evil: Variations on a Strawsonian Theme", Gary Watson explores the notion of moral address as a way of explaining global excuses and, consequently, as a way of capturing the capacities requisite for membership within the moral community.[11] Strawson tells us that global excuses function *by* inhibiting the basic demands of morality.[12] Watson's suggestion is to draw upon moral address to explain *how* global excuses inhibit moral demands. The proposal is certainly appealing: If an agent cannot be addressed, then we cannot present her with demands.

Watson proceeds to argue, however, that the Strawsonian theory of moral responsibility (supplemented by appeal to the notion of moral address) appears to lead to paradox, and that the reactive attitudes are, as he puts it, not as "philosophically innocent" as Strawson has taken them to be.[13] According to Watson, Strawson's theory suggests that extreme evil should count as its own excuse. Furthermore, certain general skeptical reflections *would* seem to affect our morally reactive attitudes and, thereby, our willingness to hold responsible. Watson ultimately concludes that there are features of our reactive attitudes that are resistant to a Strawsonian compatibilist diagnosis.

I believe that Watson is right to appeal to moral address in defending Strawsonian compatibilism, and I take his skeptical conjectures to offer several significant and innovative challenges to Strawson's position. In what follows I would like to consider the problems Watson raises, and try to offer a more hopeful Strawsonian response.

---

10 This objection is carefully set out in Paul Russell's "Strawson's Way of Naturalizing Responsibility", *Ethics*, 102 (1992), pp. 287–302 (reprinted in this volume, at pp. 145–58).
11 Watson, p. 126.
12 FR, 30–31/73.
13 Watson, p. 120.

3.

Watson's arguments turn on a fairly plausible assumption about Strawson's theory of responsibility. Following Lawrence Stern, Watson argues that membership in the interpersonal moral community requires the possibility of moral address, the capacity to be seen as a potential interlocutor in our interpersonal exchanges.[14] As Watson explains, we can only address someone within the moral community if she *understands* our reactions and demands. This seems right. But Watson carries this insight a step further. The pertinent understanding seems to require some shared moral framework of values as a basis for our interactions.[15]

The demands of moral address, according to Watson, cannot be satisfied at the limits of evil, and here is where the trouble begins for Strawson's theory of responsibility. For example, Watson examines the horrible 1982 case of Robert Harris who brutally murdered two youths in order to use their car in a bank robbery. By virtue of his behavior, Harris ought to serve as a clear candidate for blame. The initial problem seems to be this: If a condition of responsible moral agency is membership within the moral community, then those individuals who are so evil that their behavior eschews the values of moral community altogether should fail to count as moral agents, and hence, fall outside the scope of our ascriptions of responsibility. They, *by virtue of their evil manner*, do not share our framework of values, and therefore cannot be seen as potential interlocutors in the moral community.

If Strawson wants to say that moral responsibility is constituted by the relations from within the framework of the moral community then, Watson suggests, it seems as if (according to the Strawsonian view) extreme evil should be its own excusing condition. But, of course, this ought to be taken as a *reductio*. If a case of clear, calculated, malicious behavior, *by virtue of being malicious behavior*, cannot be a candidate for our negative reactive attitudes, then what can? Where Strawson's theory, by appeal to moral address, should commit us to excusing, our reactive attitudes, in practice, commit us to holding responsible.[16]

4.

Watson's challenge is motivated by the presuppositions that membership in the moral community requires the potential for moral address, that moral address requires understanding, and that understanding requires a shared framework of values. This creates two problems: Individuals like Harris do not seem to be members of the moral community at all; and Harris cannot be morally addressed (and thus held responsible) unless Harris understands our demands (but understanding here appears to imply a shared framework of values, and Harris lacks this). I shall consider each problem separately.

---

14 Lawrence Stern, "Freedom, Blame, and the Moral Community", *Journal of Philosophy* 71 (1974), pp. 72–84.
15 Watson, p. 130.
16 *Ibid*, p. 134.

As to the issue of membership, there are two ways to meet the present challenge. One option is to argue that individuals like Harris remain members of the moral community, while a second option is to conclude that membership in the moral community is not necessary for moral responsibility. Both alternatives present troubles for Strawsonian compatibilism. The former is problematic because there is a clear sense in which someone like Harris is *not* a member of the moral community. As Watson points out, Harris' actions manifest a "repudiation of the moral community; he thereby declares himself a moral outlaw".[17] The latter is problematic since it departs from Strawson's naturalist attempt to explain moral responsibility purely in terms of the attitudes from within the framework of the interpersonal moral community.

Preserving membership within the moral community would fit Strawson's intentions best:

> The concepts we are concerned with ... (regarding offenders of moral demands) ... are those of responsibility and guilt, qualified as "moral", on the one hand—[together with membership of a moral community] ... The partial withdrawal of goodwill which ... (the morally reactive) ... attitudes entail ... is ... the consequence of *continuing* to view ... (an offender of moral demands) ... [as a member of the moral community]; only as one who has offended against its demands.[18]

Is it possible to argue that, in some relevant sense, Harris is a member of the moral community? Perhaps one might argue that Harris *is* a member of the moral community merely by virtue of his *capacity* to participate within the community, despite his refusal to do so. But this is implausible. Membership in a *community* appears to involve some shared ends or goals. It would be a great stretch of linguistic intuition, for example, to argue that I am a member of the community of Taos, New Mexico, simply because I have the capacity to engage in the activities which define membership for individuals in that community. I may in fact never have been to Taos, yet I do (as far as I know) have the capacity to engage in the activities definitive of membership in the Taos community. These considerations suggest that in the case of *community* some manner of *actual* participation or cooperative activity is essential to the notion of membership itself. Some acts of extreme evil, like Harris's, are themselves denunciations of the cooperative demands of the moral community. Therefore it is best to conclude that Harris is not a member of the moral community, even if he has the *capacity* for membership within the community.[19]

5.

If perpetrators of extreme evil are morally responsible for their actions, responsibility does *not* require membership in the moral community. Does this compromise the Strawsonian compatibilist project? The basis for Strawson's naturalist account is to

---

17 *Ibid*, p. 134.

18 FR, 33–4/77 (my parentheses, [my emphasis], *Strawson's emphasis*).

19 These views are influenced by Gary Watson's remarks on an earlier draft of this paper.

explain responsibility in terms of the "complicated web" of feelings and attitudes central to moral life. As Strawson sees it, these attitudes and feelings themselves only gain significance from *within* the moral community. But if individuals who commit extreme evil are both responsible, and yet *not* members of the moral community, then it appears that moral responsibility is not constituted by moral community alone.

I advise a slight modification to Strawson's account of moral responsibility. Strawson's basic naturalist insight can be preserved by explaining responsible moral agency in terms of a *capacity* for membership within the moral community. On this account one could *be* morally responsible for a particular action, yet *not* be a member of the moral community, just so long as one had the *capacity* for membership. This account of agency is consistent with the distinct thesis that the practice of holding morally responsible and the actual demands of morality are constituted by the moral community.

This modification does no damage to Strawson's naturalist theory of responsibility. Granted, Strawson intended to capture the entire range of concepts about moral responsibility from within the "web" of attitudes in the interpersonal community. This account permits some non-members the status of morally responsible agents. But on the present account, *that* status is dependent upon one's *ability* to participate within the moral community. Thus the conceptual status of the notion of morally responsible agency is itself still articulated in terms of the expectations and demands from within the framework of the moral community. This conceptual dependence should be enough to preserve Strawson's basic naturalizing move: The social framework itself, along with the interpersonal attitudes expressed within it, provides the conceptual foundations for our understanding of responsibility. No further theoretical justification is called for.

In the case of moral agency, it very well may be that an agent like Robert Harris is not a member of the moral community, but the question of whether Harris is a morally responsible agent will be decided by his *capacity* for membership in the moral community. If skeptical suspicions about extreme evil remain at this point, then it can only be about an account of the *capacity* for membership in the moral community. Following Watson, I believe that the Strawsonian would do well to explain the capacity for membership in the moral community by appeal to the capacity for moral address. But this leads to the second challenge posed by cases of extreme evil: In what meaningful sense can individuals like Harris be morally addressed?

6.

As Watson rightly points out, moral address requires understanding, and understanding appears to require a shared framework of values.[20] In what manner does

---

20 It is unclear whether Watson thinks that understanding essentially requires a commitment to a shared framework of values. In citing Lawrence Stern, he seems to endorse the connection (p. 130). However, immediately following an account of the Harris case, he then states that the case is arresting because, unlike the small child or psychopath, Harris, "exhibits an inversion of moral concern, not a lack of understanding" (p. 134).

understanding the pertinent demands require a shared framework of values? I might understand a shared framework of values and yet refuse to commit to those values. That does not even require that I remain unaffected by them; my reaction to them might be quite visceral. In the case of our ordinary interpersonal reactive attitudes, it seems quite plausible to suggest that understanding moral demands requires an understanding of the shared framework of values from whence such demands arise. But it is unclear that understanding those demands thereby requires an *adoption* of that shared framework of values. Rather, what *is* required is that there *be* some shared framework of values as the object of understanding. One could not have an understanding which had as its object the demands of the *moral* community, if those demands were themselves not constitutive of a shared framework of values.

In the case of Robert Harris, Watson recounts the brutal murder, the humor Harris found in the act, the pleasure he would have taken in going to the parents of the youths dressed as a police officer to inform the parents of their sons' deaths, and his wish to go out and just kill some cops.[21] No doubt, this is a person who has contempt for the moral order and who is unwilling to be a member of the moral community. Unlike a monster such as Godzilla,[22] however, the details of this case do not indicate that Harris failed to understand the framework of values which he chose to confront; rather, it appears that his evil, murderous mind was precisely so *because* he understood quite well the depth of those values. This is shown by his callous wish to inform the parents of their losses, his willingness to kill police (those who enforce the moral order), and the pleasure he took in shooting two young boys on a sunny summer day.

It might be objected that I have mislocated the relevant sort of understanding. The understanding in question, one might argue, requires not only *knowledge that* moral demands are made, but also *knowledge of how* to guide one's conduct in light of those demands, and *knowledge of why* one should do so.[23] Harris, it will be argued, must know more than that such and such demands are made upon him. He must also know how to guide his conduct in accord with moral demands, and he must be able to know why one ought to comply with those demands. But I see no reason why Strawson cannot simply incorporate this requirement into his account of global excuses.[24] Granted, it is certainly tempting to suppose that Harris lacked this second kind of knowledge, but this would be premature. We cannot move from the *fact* that Harris did *not* guide his conduct by the moral community's demands, to the conclusion that Harris *lacked the knowledge of how and why* to do so.[25] Had he genuinely lacked this knowledge, the case should be unproblematic for Strawson.

---

21 Watson, pp. 131–4.

22 The contrast between Godzilla's ignorance of the moral community and Harris's understanding of it was suggested to me by Carl Ginet.

23 Both Steven Lee and Alison McIntyre have objected to my account of understanding on these grounds.

24 In fact, Strawson mentions "being morally underdeveloped" as a global excuse (FR, 24/66).

25 Presenting this in terms of lacking knowledge (how and why) might be a bit misleading. Perhaps it is better to express this in terms of lacking the *ability* to know. I'll set this subtlety aside here since the relevant points could be revised accordingly.

Harris would be incapacitated for ordinary adult interpersonal relations and thus exempted. If Harris did *not* lack the knowledge, then there is no reason to exempt.

Watson suggests that we can only morally address someone who shares some framework of values with us. There is certainly the case in which someone turns a deaf ear to our admonishments; but a person who fails to share our framework of values is not thereby *immune* to our moral address. To understand us and interact with us, a person does not need to agree with us. True, as Watson points out, not all communication is dialogue. And it certainly seems, as Watson presents the case, that Harris was unwilling to engage in further dialogue with us:

> "He just doesn't see the point of talking", said a sister, ... who has visited him three times since he has been on Death Row. "He told me that he had his chance, he took the road to hell and there's nothing more to say."[26]

But it is important to appreciate that Harris' actions *were* a form of moral dialogue—a terrible and contemptuous form of dialogue. When *we* then turn to confront Harris, addressing him with our moral outrage, it is not as if Harris is unable to appreciate our point of view. In fact, more than likely he anticipates it. It is not so much that there is no dialogue between Harris and us; it is just that, as Harris sees it, the conversation is over.

If moral address requires understanding a shared framework of values, it does not follow that one must actually adopt that framework of values. It is not therefore evidence against Harris's capacity for moral address that he failed to adopt the values of the moral community. Furthermore, if our response to a perpetrator of extreme evil is met with icy silence, it does not mean that we fail to morally address this person; it may simply be that our moral address counts as the terminus of our conversation.

I hope that the discussion in this and the previous section is sufficient to show that the Strawsonian compatibilist is not committed to treating extreme evil as its own excuse. An effective Strawsonian reply to the charge does demand a slight modification to Strawson's expressed intentions: A person is a responsible moral agent so long as she has the *capacity* for membership within the moral community; she need not actually be a member. If she does have this capacity, she can be morally addressed, so long as she understands and is able to comply with moral demands. But she may understand all of this without thereby adopting that framework of values.

7.

I turn to Watson's suggestion that the reactive attitudes are sensitive to considerations which suggest an incompatibilist or skeptical diagnosis. Watson's fundamental concern is this: Sometimes historical considerations— in appeals to extremely unfortunate formative circumstances in particular— affect our antipathetic responses towards perpetrators of extreme evil. Yet, often such appeals do not provide evidence

---

26 Miles Corwin, "Icy Killer's Life Steeped in Violence", *Los Angeles Times*, May 16, 1982; cited from Watson, p. 134.

for any *incapacity* making the agent *unable* to participate in the moral community. Watson calls such appeals *nonevidential*.[27]

Were appeals to an agent's unfortunate formative circumstances cited as the causal origins of an *incapacity* for moral address, there would be no threat to Strawsonian compatibilism: Such an agent would simply be seen as falling under the rubrics of a global excusing consideration.[28] But if sentiments of antipathy are modified by *nonevidential* appeals to unfortunate formative circumstances, then it would seem that the sentiments constitutive of holding morally responsible are affected by historical origins *despite* the prospect that an individual might be a Strawsonian *competent* moral agent. This invites skeptical worries that historical factors can undermine responsible agency even if the "compatibilist friendly" capacities for moral agency are in place.[29]

To examine nonevidential appeals to unfortunate formative circumstances, Watson draws upon Robert Harris's biography, an account which has the understandable effect of (at least temporarily) diffusing antipathy. Harris's life began with a mother's neglect and an abusive father. He was rejected and scorned by both parents throughout his childhood. He spent a good deal of his teenage years in prisons for juvenile offenders and later, as an adult, in prisons and penitentiaries. A particularly noteworthy detail is that from early childhood Harris's mother did not permit him so much as to touch her. He was denied the most rudimentary human affections during the most vulnerable period in his life.[30]

When Robert Harris's life is recounted to us, our original antipathetic responses are affected. But how so?[31] We do not simply suspend negative reactive attitudes (and thus excuse) when we learn of Harris's past. But appeals to unfortunate formative circumstances *do* have *some* effect upon our sentiments. Such appeals tend to engender feelings of sympathy, creating an overall ambivalence in our attitude towards the perpetrator of extreme evil. As Watson explains, it is difficult to

---

27 Watson, p. 137.

28 In fact, Strawson includes amongst a list of global excusing considerations, "being unfortunate in formative circumstances" (FR, 25/66).

29 Kane makes exactly this claim about appeals to unfortunate formative circumstances. See Robert Kane, *The Significance of Free Will* (New York: Oxford University Press, 1997), p. 84.

30 It is, perhaps, contestable that this history is nonevidential of an incapacity for moral address. But the crucial point, and the role played by Watson's use of this particular example, is to understand those accounts which *are* nonevidential of incapacities, but yet *do* affect our antipathy. Thus, for purposes of this discussion, presume that the present biography does *not* provide evidence of any incapacity. Though, as Watson makes clear, the biography does provide *evidence* for understanding Harris's evil behavior as a response to his past:

... our interpretation of who Harris is depends upon his biography, upon our interpretation of his life. Harris' cruelty is a response to the shattering abuse he suffered during the process of socialization (p. 140).

31 My discussion of Watson in what follows has been influenced greatly by Alison McIntyre's insightful remarks on an earlier draft of this paper.

unequivocally sustain sentiments of antipathy when we see Harris as a victim and experience sentiments of sympathy.[32]

Furthermore, appeals to unfortunate formative circumstances invite thoughts about moral equality and moral luck. When we learn of the historical roots of extremely evil behavior, we are sometimes impressed by how (relatively) fortunate we are to have had the histories we have had. We come to see how such evil is an understandable response to that history and how our own moral place in the world is conditioned by a more fortunate past. According to Watson, this has a kind of chilling effect upon our willingness to cast blame. Our reactive attitudes are stifled by the sense that, given a similar history, we too might have acted likewise, that we therefore might be no better than the perpetrator of evil, and hence are not in a position to cast blame.[33]

8.

I believe that one can locate in Watson's discussion four distinct skeptical challenges which arise from the above reflections. Two arise from the effect of ambivalence, and two from thoughts about moral luck.[34] Consider first the effect of ambivalence. Learning of Harris' unfortunate past casts him as a victim, and we come to see his terrible behavior as a response to that history. This engenders an ambivalence in one's attitudes towards Harris. But, Watson continues, whenever any individual commits acts of extreme evil, will there not be *some* explanation of "what went wrong" in this person which explains her actions? Whatever the particular facts of that explanation are, whether they are facts about a person's past, or her genetic constitution, they can be cast as the circumstances which victimized this perpetrator of evil. Watson asks: "Can evil be the object of unequivocal reactive attitudes only when it is inexplicable?"[35]

This invites two kinds of skeptical threats. One issues from the possibility that determinism is true, the other, from simple human ignorance. Consider first the thesis of determinism. If determinism is true, then, as Watson explains: "evil is a joint product of nature and nurture".[36] If so, there will always be some facts of an agent's environment or constitution which explain why she does wrong when she does wrong. Just as learning of Harris' past portrayed him as a victim of his life, so too can each wrong doer be cast as a victim of the circumstances which determined her actions. It seems that determinism would imply that no cases of extreme evil—or even moderate evil—could be met with "unequivocal reactive attitudes" of moral indignation. We would face a state of universal ambivalence towards all persons whom we held responsible for evil.[37]

---

32 Watson, pp.138–9.
33 *Ibid*, p. 139.
34 I am uncertain as to whether my discussion properly accords with Watson's views.
35 Watson, p. 140.
36 *Ibid*, p. 141.
37 This is a skeptical threat which Watson *rejects*. He denies the view that determinism could affect our reactive attitudes in the way that they are affected by learning of Harris'

Ambivalence also poses another kind of skeptical threat to moral responsibility. As Watson points out, we are normally ignorant of most individuals' personal histories:

> If, for whatever reasons, reactive attitudes are sensitive to historical considerations, as Strawson acknowledges, and we are largely ignorant of those matters, then it would seem that most of our reactive attitudes are hasty, perhaps even benighted, as skeptics have long maintained. In this respect, our ordinary practices are not as unproblematic as Strawson supposes.[38]

9.

Now consider the effect of moral luck and moral equality. These also generate two skeptical concerns, one arising from reflections about determinism, another from ignorance.[39] If determinism were true, then, when confronted with a case of extreme evil, I might think that it is simply a matter of luck that I did not have the same kind of history as the history of the person who did evil. Perhaps if I did have such a history, I too would have done evil. This invites the thought that one is in no position to cast blame, that one is—quite possibly—no better than this perpetrator of evil. Therefore, if determinism is true, we all stand in a similar relation to any agent who commits extreme evil.

Watson rejects this brand of skepticism. We cannot, Watson argues, assume universally that we might have done the same as any evil perpetrator had we had the exact same determining history. Conditions of personal identity show that this thought experiment is incompatible with our respective identities.[40] For instance, if genetic heritage were a determining factor in an act of extreme evil, and if genetic heritage counted among one's essential identity conditions, then it would not be metaphysically possible for one to have another's genetic history.[41]

---

history. But Watson's reasons for rejecting this skeptical threat are based on reflections having to do with moral luck and personal identity (p. 141). His rejection is *not* based upon the considerations which (according to him) give rise to the effect of ambivalence. Thus, Watson's remarks are *not* sufficient to address this skeptical threat.

I believe that it is because Watson asks the question of how determinism would affect us in light of *both* the phenomena of ambivalence, *and* of moral luck, that he does not see that his rejection of the skeptical threat posed by determinism is only applicable to thoughts of moral luck. His appeal to conditions of personal identity leaves the problem of ambivalence untouched.

38 Watson, p. 145.
39 These are interesting skeptical challenges. Where most sources of skepticism about responsibility arise out of suspicions regarding the agent to be held responsible, these forms of skepticism focuses upon the status of the individual who holds responsible. They allow that a person might be seen as an appropriate object of moral address, but yet they challenge the presumption that it is appropriate for anyone to address her.
40 For a similar line of argument see Wallace, pp. 200–201.
41 Watson, p. 143.

Watson's rejection of this brand of skepticism is unsatisfactory. True, considerations of personal identity might show that it is not metaphysically possible, in many cases, for one to share the determining causes of another's evil behavior. But that does not dispel the worry that for any individual, there might be *some* determining causes *consistent* with her identity which also would have led her to equally evil ways. Hence, Watson's worries about moral luck and determinism remain unanswered.[42]

Another source of skepticism can arise from thoughts about moral luck, combined with ignorance of whether we too could withstand similar histories. It may very well be, as Watson argues, that some histories or determining factors in the lives of perpetrators of evil are incompatible with another's personal identity. But some may very well *not* be. We are left with the prospect that our *willingness* to hold responsible might be presumptuous.[43]

10.

I turn now to a response to each of these four skeptical threats. Consider first the two problems raised by the effect of ambivalence. Nonevidential appeals to unfortunate formative circumstances do often elicit an ambivalent attitude towards the perpetrator of extreme evil. Can the Strawsonian explain the phenomenon of ambivalence in a way that does not invite skepticism arising from worries about determinism or ignorance?

One explanation is to deny that these histories influence our antipathetic response. Rather, the attendant sympathy is a *distinct* response to a tragic past.[44] This strategy individuates responses according to the different facts which elicit them. Such histories, on this account, "give pause" to our antipathy, not because they modify the antipathetic response, but because our attentions are focused upon facts which do rightly elicit a distinct sympathetic response.[45] This would insulate the antipathetic response—constitutive of holding responsible—from historical considerations.

Will this do? Perhaps for a good number of cases, but not for others. Often times, as in the Harris case, appeals to unfortunate formative circumstances are not simply

---

42 This point was made clear to me by an anonymous referee for *The Journal of Ethics*.

43 Watson, p. 145.

44 George Thomas has pointed out that Joseph Rainsbury has developed an alternative interpretation. According to Rainsbury, one explanation for the influence of these biographical considerations is that sympathetic responses elicited are responses to the innocent child as victim and not to the evil person now before us. In this case our reactive attitudes are directed at different types of moral characters, though they have as their objects, the same person. I am less sympathetic with this alternative because it makes the response turn on the moral quality of the child which later became the evil person. However, it seems to me that our reactive attitudes towards horrific biographies do not turn upon whether the child was a little angel or a little monster. What seems to me to elicit the response is that such harms were done to any child.

45 Alison McIntyre has objected to this reply because, she argues, it makes holding responsible a matter of responding to the datable facts of a person's life (her particular actions, etc.), and not to the person as a whole. But this is not so. I might have distinct responses to a *person* which are elicited by my learning about distinct aspects of that person's life, without my responses therefore being merely responses to the facts and not to the person.

historical accounts of tragedies in earlier life. The point of the Harris narrative is precisely to show how such evil could be of a piece with a particular history. The historical considerations are intended to and actually do affect the original antipathetic response itself.[46]

Suppose that nonevidential appeals to horrible pasts *do* affect our antipathetic responses to perpetrators of evil. The Strawsonian might argue that this does not undermine the judgment that it would be *appropriate* to sustain sentiments of antipathy.[47] On this approach, the distinct facts motivating the antipathy and sympathy would not individuate distinct sentimental responses. Instead, the different facts would serve to individuate distinct judgments about the appropriateness of responding to an agent with antipathy or sympathy.

In order to show that this maneuver is not *ad hoc*, the Strawsonian must offer a general account of how the *propriety* of a morally reactive attitude can come apart from the attitudes which are *in fact* elicited. But, indeed, this is a modification to Strawsonian compatibilism required to explain the vagaries of our moral sentiments. R.J. Wallace uses the example of a charming colleague who has deceived us.[48] In the grip of our colleague's charm we may be unable to muster the pertinent reactive sentiments; nevertheless, we might judge that she is morally responsible for her actions. For the Strawsonian to explain this ordinary phenomenon (and preserve her thesis that responsibility can be captured purely in terms of the moral sentiments) she must distinguish the sentiments which *are* elicited from those which would be *appropriate*.

In Harris's case, assuming that his terrible history did not incapacitate him as a moral agent, an appeal to his history may very well affect our antipathetic reaction (constitutive of holding him responsible), but this does not itself show that it is inappropriate to sustain unequivocal sentiments of antipathy towards him. The modification of our antipathy can be understood as a psychologically unavoidable effect of learning of Harris's past.[49]

I believe that the above discussion provides an adequate reply to the skeptical challenge posed by the phenomenon of ambivalence. Our responses to cases like the Harris case may well result in ambivalence when confronted with accounts of unfortunate formative circumstances. This effect upon our reactive attitudes cannot, however, be generalized to show that it is never *appropriate* to unequivocally respond to extreme evil with sentiments of antipathy, even if, psychologically, it is often difficult to do so.[50]

---

46 Both Alison McIntyre and Gary Watson have persuaded me of this point.

47 Gary Watson has encouraged this line of thought, and has been instrumental in helping me to get clear the differences between this approach and the approach previously considered.

48 Wallace, p. 76.

49 This is not to suggest that the Strawsonian must be cold hearted and simply dismiss as weak sentimentalism the import of a history like Harris's. It is equally consistent with the account sketched here to maintain that Harris's past makes appropriate a *sympathetic* response, even though, in light of his evil, psychologically, it might be difficult to sustain such an attitude.

50 Tim Robbins's film, *Dead Man Walking* (1995) does an excellent job of illustrating many of these ideas. I am thankful to Kenton Machina for bringing this to my attention.

There may be some residual worries about this treatment of the Harris case. Views of responsibility over matters as delicate as this are contestable and reasonable persons have different intuitions. Some might feel that learning of Harris's unfortunate past does *indeed* make *appropriate* a response to Harris's evil quite different from what is called for in cases without such histories, irrespective of any incapacities Harris might have for moral address. An adequate defense of Strawsonian compatibilism should be able to capture this indeterminate area of our thinking about responsibility. Is there any way to avoid the skeptical consequences Watson draws and yet acknowledge that appeals to unfortunate histories *do* make appropriate a modification in our antipathetic responses?

R.J. Wallace has argued that we can explain many appeals to unfortunate formative circumstances as indications that an agent might find it "extremely difficult" to comply with the demands of morality.[51] On Wallace's account, an appeal to unfortunate historical circumstances would not be intended to show that an individual like Harris is incapacitated for moral agency. Rather, the *evidential* appeal would be intended to show that it is overwhelmingly burdensome for Harris to *exercise* the capacity for membership in the moral community which he *does* have. This approach opens the scope of global excusing considerations to include *mitigating* factors which modify the intensity of our judgments.

On Wallace's account, then, the proper Strawsonian reply to Watson's skeptical challenge is to modify Strawson's account of global excuses to include not simply incapacities for membership within the moral community, but also severe handicaps which make it reasonable for us to be less demanding about an agent's performances from within the moral community. This reply should also be sufficient to address the skeptical challenges posed by the phenomenon of ambivalence, for unless it can be shown that all (or most) individuals' histories are such that it is difficult for them to comply with the demands of the moral community, then there is no reason to suppose that all responses to extreme evil should be met with ambivalent sentiments.

I am inclined to think that each response, the one posed by Wallace, and the one I have offered, has a role to play in explaining how appeals to unfortunate formative circumstances affect our morally reactive sentimental responses to those who commit extreme acts of evil. The accounts are directed at conflicting intuitions about the legitimate role of appeals to unfortunate formative circumstances in our thinking about responsibility. Nevertheless, on either account, Watson's skeptical conjectures regarding the effect of ambivalence, while compelling, can be adequately addressed by the Strawsonian compatibilist.

11.

What about the problem of moral luck? According to Watson these terrible biographies affect our willingness to cast blame. Here the difficulty is that, for all we know, we might have acted similarly had we had similar histories (or different

---

51 Wallace, Ch. 8, especially pp. 231–5.

horrible histories causing us to act in similar ways). This engenders the thought that we might be no better, and therefore, are in no position to judge.

Often times we do feel as if we are in no position to cast blame. If Katherine drinks more than she ought and squanders money better left to her family's nest egg, I may think her behavior shoddy and selfish. Knowing, though, that I too have spent more at the local pubs than prudence allows, I might feel that it is not my place to cast judgment. But there is a substantial discrepancy between my reticence in this case, and the kind of cases Watson has in mind. In this case my reticence is explained by the way that I now am. It is not that, had I had different historical influences, then I too might have a tendency to drink too much, it is that I *do* have a tendency to drink too much.

Thus, when Watson argues that our reactive attitudes are affected by these biographies with the thought that "I too am a potential sinner", there is a sense in which this is clearly true, or at least highly likely, and another in which it is false, or at least highly unlikely. Considering the Harris case, it is certainly true that, had I had a radically different history than the history which I do have, I might have become a very different kind of person. I then might have become the monstrous kind of sinner which Harris is. But given the fact that I have had the history that I have had, there are certain options which are plainly unavailable to me; these limits reflect features essential to who I now am. I, as I am now, am *not* (to the best of my knowledge) a potential sinner in the way Harris is.[52]

Thus, the ontological shudder which Watson alludes to has little force. No doubt he is correct; had many of us had quite different formative years we might be quite different people—possibly morally contemptuous ones. But this thought does not seem to me to have the effect upon our reactive attitudes which Watson suggests it does. The thought that we ought not blame does not seem compelling in these cases since it is hard to take seriously that we might have been like that—for *we are now not anything like that*. Furthermore, for many of us, perhaps most of us, it is *essential* to our present selves that we *could not* be like that. The intuition that we ourselves ought not cast blame seems only to gain a purchase upon our sentiments when the condition of our present selves shares the same kind of moral fault or (minimally) shares the *potential* for the same kind of fault.[53]

---

52 These remarks are influenced by Harry Frankfurt's work on volitional necessity. See "The Importance of What we Care About", *Synthese* 53 (November 1982), pp. 257–72; "Identification and Wholeheartedness" in F. Schoeman (ed.), and the preface to Frankfurt's *The Importance of What We Care About* (Cambridge: Cambridge University Press, 1988). "Identification and Wholeheartedness", and "The Importance of What We Care About" are reprinted in Frankfurt's own *The Importance of What We Care About*.

53 As Stephen Schwartz has pointed out in conversation, even here, it is unclear that our reaction is to think that we are in no position to cast blame. We might see how someone could come to do a terrible thing, and we might further believe that we ourselves might have done a similar thing had we been in those circumstances. Even so, we might feel that it is perfectly appropriate for us to respond with antipathy, and that it would be perfectly appropriate for others (and ourselves) to respond to *us* with antipathy had we acted similarly. Schwartz used the Mai Lai massacres as an illustrative example here.

There is another way to respond to the problem of moral luck. Moral reactive attitudes are responses we feel on behalf of others who have suffered some harm. There is, therefore, a moral claim upon us to hold accountable. It might be true that we see in ourselves moral faults like those exemplified in another's actions or, as Watson might put it, we see in ourselves how, given different histories, we too might have had similar kinds of moral faults. Seeing this might evince the thought that we ought not cast blame. Given that our response is a response to harm done to someone other than ourselves, our own personal discomforts and moral short-comings should not dominate how we respond. There are competing demands here upon our moral sensibilities. One is that "the moral order" must find a voice somehow. Sometimes there is no one but oneself available to give voice to or enforce the moral order. The thought is that someone has to do it. Another demand is simply the protection of the innocent and of the victims of harms done. These kinds of moral considerations surely do not nullify the uneasiness we experience when thoughts of moral luck present themselves. But it seems that they should override them. In this way we might think that these feelings of moral luck will humble us and give us a due sense of the caution and understanding which ought to be exercised when holding another accountable. That is, moral luck might make us more compassionate in how we go about holding others accountable. Thoughts of moral luck might affect our reactive attitudes. There is, despite this, no compelling reason to think that the likely effect will be a sense of our impotence to hold others accountable.

12.

As explained in section 2, a serious difficulty with Strawson's argument from excuses concerns an adequate account of global excusing considerations. According to Strawson, global excusing considerations are designed to show that an agent is incapacitated for membership within the moral community. Strawson's argument from excuses states that determinism would not show that some global excuse applies universally. But until it is clear what relevant capacities are required for membership within the moral community, Strawson cannot convincingly maintain that determinism would not undermine them. Some might insist that the relevant capacities require the metaphysical freedom to do otherwise, a freedom which is incompatible with determinism.

Gary Watson has advised the Strawsonian compatibilist to explain the capacities relevant to morally responsible agency, and hence, global excuses, in terms of moral address. Moral address does not appear to invite any untoward theoretical commitments. It thus permits the Strawsonian compatibilist to preserve her basic naturalist project by providing an account of moral responsibility in terms of the natural framework of the interpersonal community, a framework which demands no more basic theoretical facts as a foundation for its justification.

Watson's suggestion does Strawsonian compatibilism a great service. It is, therefore, important to address the compelling challenges Watson raises against it. Watson's challenges arise from two different sources, one having to do with acts of extreme evil, the other arising from effects upon our reactive attitudes brought on by appeals to severely unfortunate biographies.

Contrary to Watson, I have argued that individuals who perform extreme acts of evil do not pose a serious difficulty for Strawsonian compatibilism. Granted, in order to adequately accommodate cases of extreme evil, the Strawsonian must make a slight modification to her theory: An individual is a competent moral agent so long as she has the *capacity* to participate within the moral community; she need not *actually* be a member. If she does have that capacity, she stands within the scope of our moral address. She need not embrace the moral community's framework of values in order to understand it. Nor must she share that framework of values in order for those who stand within it to morally address her.

If, as Watson suggests, our reactive attitudes are sensitive in certain ways to historical considerations, then the conditions of moral address would be influenced by various skeptical concerns. I also have argued that the historical considerations which do affect our reactive attitudes do not do so in ways which could be universalized in light of skeptical conjectures. A cautious Strawsonian response to Watson's challenges shows that the reactive attitudes do not themselves provide the seeds of skepticism about responsibility.

Strawson's basic naturalist position is defensible against a range of difficulties raised by Watson. If the conditions requisite for membership within the moral community can be specified in terms of moral address, and if the framework of the moral community is itself constitutive of responsibility, then by showing that moral address is compatible with determinism, one shows that responsibility is compatible with determinism. This is the compatibilist project which Watson has advised the Strawsonian compatibilist to pursue. I believe that she would be well advised to do so.

Chapter 11

Revising the Reactive Attitudes

Derk Pereboom

Strawson argues first for a psychological thesis, that the reactive attitudes cannot be affected by a belief in universal determinism, and then for a normative thesis, that they should not be affected by this belief. Here I develop three points of disagreement; first, the reactive attitudes can be affected by the belief that determinism is true; second, supposing that a belief in determinism did issue in theoretical conflict with the reactive attitudes, rational appraisal of these attitudes would sometimes favor rejection or revision over retention; and third, a theoretical challenge to the reactive attitudes from universal determinism is legitimate despite the concerns Strawson raises.

A note on my position in the free will debate: I contend that we would not be morally responsible if determinism were true, but also that we would lack moral responsibility if indeterminism were true and the causes of our actions were exclusively states or events. If our actions were caused exclusively by states or events, indeterministic causal histories of actions would be as undermining of moral responsibility as deterministic histories are. But if we were undetermined agent-causes—if we as substances had the power to cause decisions without being causally determined to cause them—we might well then have the sort of free will required for moral responsibility. However, although agent causation is not ruled out as a coherent possibility, the proposal that we are agent-causes is not credible given our best physical theories. Consequently, we need to take seriously the prospect that we are not free in the sense required for moral responsibility. I call the resulting view hard compatibilism.

From Chapter 4 of Living Without Free Will

The first route to compatibilism: Determinism as irrelevant to responsibility

According to a first type of route to compatibilism, the justification for claims of blameworthiness and praiseworthiness ends in the system of human reactive attitudes, and because moral responsibility has this type of basis, the truth or falsity of determinism is irrelevant to whether we legitimately hold agents to be morally responsible. This route was first suggested by David Hume, and then developed with sophistication by P.F. Strawson. In §VIII of *the Enquiry Concerning Human Understanding*, Hume discusses the effect the thesis of divine determinism does and should have on the moral sentiments. He first argues for a psychological thesis: that the sentiments of approbation and blame *cannot* be affected by a belief in divine determinism or in any philosophical theory. He then argues for a normative thesis: that these sentiments *should not* be affected by a belief in divine determinism or in any philosophical theory. Regarding the psychological thesis Hume claims:

> The mind of man is so formed by nature that upon the appearance of certain characters, dispositions, and actions, it immediately feels the sentiment of approbation or blame; nor are there any emotions more essential to its frame and constitution ... What though philosophical meditations establish a different opinion or conjecture; that everything is right with regard to the whole, and that the qualities, which disturb society are, in the main, as beneficial, and are as suitable to the primary intention of nature, as those which more directly promote its happiness and welfare? Are such remote and uncertain speculations able to counterbalance the sentiments, which arise from the natural and immediate view of the objects? A man who is robbed of a considerable sum; does he find his vexation for the loss any wise diminished by these sublime reflections?

Then, for Hume the psychological thesis that these sentiments of approbation and blame are inevitable and unalterable leads to a normative conclusion. The passage continues:

> Why then *should* his moral resentment against the crime be supposed incompatible with them [these sublime reflections]? Or why *should not* the acknowledgment of a real distinction between vice and virtue be reconcilable to all speculative systems of philosophy, as well as that of a real distinction between personal beauty and deformity? Both these distinctions are founded in the natural sentiments of the human mind: And these sentiments are *not to be controlled or altered* by any philosophical theory or speculation whatsoever.[1]

Because in certain circumstances having the sentiments of approbation and blame is inevitable and unalterable by us, having these sentiments is compatible with and should not be controlled or altered by any philosophical theory.

Strawson's view is similar.[2] He begins his account by characterizing two opposing participants in the controversy about determinism and moral responsibility, the "optimist" and the "pessimist". The optimist is a compatibilist of the sort who justifies the practices of moral disapproval and punishment not on the ground that

---

1   David Hume, *An Enquiry Concerning Human Understanding*, ed. Tom L. Beauchamp (Oxford: Oxford University Press, 2000), 8.35/102–3. [*The editors*: The now standard edition of Hume's *First Enquiry* is that edited by Beauchamp. The previous standard edition was that edited by L.A. Selby-Bigge and P.H. Nidditch (Oxford: Oxford University Press, 1975). Following the convention adopted in the Beauchamp edition, citations to the *First Enquiry* are provided as follows: "Section, Paragraph; followed by (after the slash) page references to the Selby-Bigge/Nidditch edition". Thus, *First Enquiry*, 8.35/102–3 indicates that the above quotation comes from Hume's *Enquiry Concerning Human Understanding*, Beauchamp edition, Section 8, Paragraph 35, followed by (after the slash) the Selby-Bigge/Nidditch edition, pages 102–3.] Similar claims about the affinity between Hume's and Strawson's views are made by Paul Russell in his *Freedom and Moral Sentiment*, (New York: Oxford University Press, 1995), pp. 71–84.

2   P.F. Strawson, "Freedom and Resentment", in Gary Watson, (ed.), *Free Will*, (Oxford: Oxford University Press, 1982), pp. 59–80, originally published in *Proceedings of the British Academy* 48 (1962), pp. 187–211 (and reprinted in this volume at pp. 19–36). [Page references for "Freedom and Resentment" will be to pages 19–36 of this volume, followed by (after the slash) the corresponding pages of Watson's *Free Will*. Thus, for example, 'FR, 16/59' would refer to this volume, p. 16/and *Free Will*, p. 59—the editors.]

they express reactive attitudes, but on the basis of their social utility.[3] The pessimist is an incompatibilist who wants libertarianism to be true. Strawson rejects the incompatibilism and libertarianism of the pessimist, but he also maintains, together with the pessimist, that the optimist is missing something important in the account of moral responsibility.

Rather than justifying the practice of holding people morally responsible solely on social utilitarian grounds, it is the participant reactive attitudes—the reactive attitudes to which people are subject by virtue of participation in ordinary interpersonal relationships—that play the crucial role in Strawson's account. He suggests that these attitudes supply what is missing in the optimist's explanation. It is the reactive attitudes, and the reactive attitudes alone, that provide the foundation for our holding people morally responsible. To secure his case for compatibilism, Strawson, like Hume, argues first for a psychological thesis, that the reactive attitudes *cannot be* affected by a belief in universal determinism, and then for a normative thesis, that they *should not be* affected by this belief. Consequently, what fills the role of that something which the pessimist rightly sees is missing in the optimist's account of our moral life—our reactive attitudes—cannot and should not be undermined by a belief in universal determinism.

Participant reactive attitudes are "natural human reactions to the good or ill will or indifference of others towards us, as displayed in *their* attitudes and actions", for example, gratitude, moral resentment, forgiveness and love.[4] These attitudes are central features of ordinary human interpersonal relationships. Would and should they be undermined by a belief in the thesis of universal determinism?

> ... would, or should, the acceptance of the truth of the thesis lead to the decay or repudiation of all such attitudes? Would, or should, it mean the end of gratitude, resentment, and forgiveness; of all reciprocated adult loves; of all the essentially *personal* antagonisms?[5]

According to Strawson, sometimes we can and at times we appropriately do forgo or suspend reactive attitudes. For example: "Type 1" considerations are those that "invite us to view an *injury* as one in respect of which a particular one of these attitudes is inappropriate", but "do not invite us to view the *agent* as one in respect of whom these attitudes are inappropriate". If someone spills his drink on your shirt but you find out that he did it by accident and not as a result of negligence, then you are capable of suspending normal reactive attitudes. But you do not then view the agent as an inappropriate subject of the reactive attitudes.[6]

"Type 2" considerations have more radical but nevertheless legitimate consequences. They invite us to view the *agent* as one in respect of whom these

---

3 For optimism of the sort Strawson describes, see Moritz Schlick, "When is a Man Responsible?" in *Problems of Ethics*, tr. David Rynin (New York: Prentice-Hall, 1939), pp. 143–56; reprinted in *Free Will and Determinism*, ed. Bernard Berofsky (New York: Harper and Rowe, 1966), pp. 54–63; and J.J.C. Smart, "Free Will, Praise, and Blame", *Mind* 70 (1961), pp. 291–306.

4 FR, 25/67.

5 FR, 25/67.

6 FR, 23/64–5.

attitudes are inappropriate. This involves adopting *the objective attitude* towards him:

> To adopt the objective attitude to another human being is to see him, perhaps, as an object of social policy; as a subject for what, in a wide range of sense, might be called treatment; as something certainly to be taken account, perhaps precautionary account, of; to be managed or handled or cured or trained; perhaps simply to be avoided ... The objective attitude may be emotionally toned in many ways, but not in all ways: it may include repulsion or fear, it may include pity or love, though not all kinds of love. But it cannot include the range of reactive feelings and attitudes which belong to involvement or participation with others in interpersonal human relationships; it cannot include resentment, gratitude, forgiveness, anger, or the sort of love which two adults can sometimes be said to feel reciprocally, for each other.[7]

Objectivity of attitude is befitting, for example, with regard to people who suffer from certain sorts of mental illness.

But none of this shows that a belief in universal determinism would lead to a suspension of reactive attitudes:

> The human commitment to participation in ordinary inter-personal relationships is, I think, too thoroughgoing and deeply rooted for us to take seriously the thought that a general theoretical conviction might so change our world that, in it, there were no longer any such things as inter-personal relationships as we normally understand them; and being involved in inter-personal relationships as we normally understand them precisely is being exposed to the range of reactive attitudes and feelings that is in question.[8]

Interpersonal relationships lie at the very core of the human way of existing. Being subject to the reactive attitudes is of a piece with participation in such relationships. Since no merely theoretical conviction could keep us from relating to each other in the ordinary interpersonal way, no such conviction could undermine our having the reactive attitudes. Because these attitudes comprise the foundation of our holding each other morally responsible, a belief in determinism is also incapable of dislodging this practice.

Strawson's answer to the "should" question, or more precisely, to someone who thinks that his answer to the "would" question leaves the "should" question unanswered is this:

> [F]irst, ... such a question could seem real only to one who has utterly failed to grasp the purport of the preceding answer ... This commitment [to ordinary inter-personal relationships] is part of the general framework of human life, not something that can come up for review as particular cases can come up for review within this general framework .... [S]econd, ... if we could imagine what we cannot have, viz. a choice in this matter, then we could choose rationally only in the light of an assessment of the gains and losses of human life, its enrichment or impoverishment; and the truth or falsity of a general thesis of determinism would not bear on the rationality of *this* choice.[9]

---

7   FR, 25/66.
8   FR, 26/68.
9   FR, 28/70.

Thus, according to Strawson, both the optimist and the pessimist are wrong in thinking that the reactive attitudes must be justified from outside of the practice in which these attitudes are embedded. This is, in fact, where their deepest mistake lies. The framework of these attitudes "neither calls for, nor permits, an external 'rational' justification".[10] Against the optimist Strawson also says: "Our practices do not merely exploit our natures, they express them."[11] This last claim echoes the anti-rationalist views of Hume and Wittgenstein, according to which all justification comes or must come to an end somewhere, and this end is (often) to be found in (the characterization of) a human practice such as induction, or mathematics, or interpersonal relationships. Demands for justification are legitimate only within such practices, and demanding justification for an entire practice is philosophical error.

Furthermore, assuming that a belief in determinism did challenge the ordinary reactive attitudes, and that we could choose to rid ourselves of these attitudes and the associated practice of holding people morally responsible, the decision would have to be made on the basis of practical considerations alone. A theoretical conviction would have no role to play in this assessment. By implication, Strawson maintains that the practical considerations would weigh very heavily in favor of retaining the reactive attitudes, and thus also our practice of holding people morally responsible.

Criticisms of Strawson's View

How should we assess the first route to compatibilism? Drawing on the ample work others have done on this issue, I will develop three points of disagreement that have special importance for my position.[12] Two of these are pertinent to the claim that living as a hard incompatibilist is a genuine and attractive possibility. The first of these is that Strawson is mistaken to hold that the reactive attitudes cannot be affected by the belief that determinism is true. The second is that supposing a belief in determinism did issue in a theoretical or epistemic conflict with the ordinary reactive attitudes, it is not clear that rational appraisal of these attitudes would always favor retention over revision. The third point of disagreement is germane to my defence of an incompatibilist condition on the causal history of actions. Strawson, I believe, is

---

10 FR, 35/78.

11 FR, 36/80.

12 See, in particular, Jonathan Bennett, "Accountability", in Zak van Straaten (ed.), *Philosophical Subjects* (Oxford: Oxford University Press, 1980), pp. 74–91; Galen Strawson, *Freedom and Belief*, (Oxford: Oxford University Press, 1986), pp. 84–92; Gary Watson, "Responsibility and the Limits of Evil", in *Responsibility, Character and the Emotions*, Ferdinand Schoeman (ed.), (Cambridge: Cambridge University Press, 1987), pp. 256–86, at p. 282; Robert Kane, *The Significance of Free Will* (New York: Oxford University Press, 1996), pp. 83–5; and Saul Smilansky, "Can a Determinist Respect Herself", C.H. Manekin and M. Kellner (eds), *Freedom and Moral Responsibility: General and Jewish Perspectives* (College Park: University of Maryland Press, 1997), pp. 85–98. pp. 95–6. Despite the criticisms he raises, Watson defends a broadly Strawsonian perspective, as does Michael McKenna in "The Limits of Evil and the Role of Moral Address: A Defense of Strawsonian Compatibilism", *The Journal Of Ethics* 2 (1998), pp. 123–42.

wrong to maintain that a theoretical challenge to the reactive attitudes based on the thesis of universal determinism is external to the practice of holding people morally responsible and therefore illegitimate. Rather, in my view, exemptions from moral responsibility that are widely regarded as acceptable and are thus internal to the practice will generalize to an incompatibilist condition on moral responsibility.[13]

First, then, as a matter of psychological fact, it is plausible that the reactive attitudes are not immune from alteration by a belief in determinism. Gary Watson provides a compelling example that may tell against the view that Hume and Strawson defend. A man named Robert Harris brutally murdered two teenage boys in California in 1978. Watson points out that when we read an account of these murders "we respond to his heartlessness and viciousness with loathing".[14] But an account of the atrocious abuse he suffered as a child "gives pause to the reactive attitudes".[15] Upon absorbing such information, not everyone relinquishes his attitude of indignation completely, but this attitude is at least typically tempered. It is not only that we are persuaded to feel pity for the criminal. Not implausibly, our attitude of indignation is mitigated by our coming to believe that there were factors beyond his control that causally determined certain aspects of his character to be as they were.

One might argue that although belief in determinism about a particular situation can affect reactive attitudes, the more general belief in universal determinism never can. Two possible reasons for this claim might be gleaned from Hume's rhetorical question "Are such remote and uncertain speculations able to counterbalance the sentiments, which arise from a natural and immediate view of the objects?"[16] A first reason is that the thesis of universal determinism is uncertain—as is any other responsibility-threatening general proposition. But while such general propositions, for example, that all events are alien-deterministic, partially random, or truly random are indeed uncertain, some may also be fairly well-substantiated. Moreover, some might well be no less well-grounded than other general claims that clearly can affect our attitudes and our actions, such as the proposal that if the rate of unemployment goes below 5.3 percent, significant inflation fueled by a wage-price spiral will result. Another reason for maintaining that the belief in universal determinism cannot affect the reactive attitudes is that this thesis is remote in the sense that it is not vivid. But while particular cases of determinism can be made especially vivid, the thesis of universal determinism can quite easily be made as vivid as other general propositions that can affect our attitudes and our actions, such as this last claim about inflation.

It would be implausible to maintain that in every case the presence or the intensity of one's reactive attitudes can be affected by a belief in determinism. Sometimes a wrong committed might be too horrible for such a belief to have any effect on one's reactions. The Stoics maintained that we can always prevent or eradicate attitudes like grief and anger, regardless of their intensity, with the aid of a determinist conviction. But they surely overestimated the extent of the control we have over

---

13 This is R. Jay Wallace's formulation, cf. *Responsibility and the Moral Sentiments* (Cambridge: Harvard University Press, 1994), pp. 114–17.
14 Watson, pp. 268–71.
15 Watson, pp. 272–4.
16 Hume, *First Enquiry*, 8.35/102.

our emotional lives. If someone were brutally to murder your family, it might well be psychologically impossible for you ever to eradicate feelings of intense anger toward the killer. This fails to show, however, that a determinist conviction cannot affect reactive attitudes, even in typical cases.

The second criticism of Strawson is that assuming a belief in determinism would conflict with the ordinary reactive attitudes, it is not clear that a rational assessment of these attitudes would always favor retaining as opposed to revising them. Suppose, for the sake of argument, that the practice of holding people morally responsible does make an indeterministic presupposition about human agency, and that we have a justified belief that determinism is true. Imagine that one is indignant with a friend—a normal human being—because he has intentionally betrayed a confidence. Strawson assumes that in this situation it would typically be rational to maintain one's indignation in such circumstances, for if one did not, interpersonal human relationships would be undermined.

A determinist who acknowledged that a theoretical conviction could affect the reactive attitudes, but that adopting an objectivity of attitude would be practically irrational by virtue of being destructive of human relationships, might well override theoretical rationality by retaining her normal reactive attitudes.[17] If she acted in this way, however, she would be reduced to the uncomfortable position of maintaining attitudes that are theoretically irrational. But the determinist is not clearly forced into such a predicament. For first, some ordinary reactive attitudes that would be irrational are not obviously required for good interpersonal relationships. In addition, the reactive attitudes one would want to retain might not be undermined, or else they could have aspects or analogues that have no false presuppositions. These aspects and analogues might well not be akin to Strawson's objectivity of attitude, and they may be sufficient to sustain good interpersonal relationships. I shall develop these claims in detail in Chapter 7 (the relevant parts of Chapter 7 are included below). For now, let us consider the examples of moral resentment and indignation.

For an interpersonal relationship to work well, is it necessary that the participants typically be morally resentful upon being wronged? An important function of resentment in such circumstances is to convey the distress suffered because of the wrongdoing. Such distress could certainly be discussed without such attitudes. But this procedure would be much too clinical, one might object. Emotional attitudes must be expressed in such circumstances if the relationship is to have significant psychological depth. However, consider again how one's attitude towards Harris might change as a result of learning of his past. Indignation gradually gives way to a kind of moral sadness—a sadness not only about his past but also for his character and his horrible actions. This kind of moral sadness is a type of attitude that would not be undermined by a belief in determinism. Furthermore, I suspect that it can play much of the role that resentment and indignation more typically have in human relationships, and that moral sadness will be at least as effective in sustaining

---

17 One is irrational in the theoretical sense when, for example, one has a belief that has no justification, or a belief one knows to be false, or knows might well be false, and one is irrational in the practical sense if, for instance, one does something one knows will frustrate what one wants, all things considered.

emotional depth as its more prevalent blame-ascribing counterparts. Indeed, in the final chapter I shall argue that human relationships and emotional depth may be improved by putting aside attitudes such as resentment and indignation, which depend on viewing agents as blameworthy for wrongdoing.

How can we deal with our ordinary reactive attitudes—those that are threatened by a belief in determinism—if they are inevitable or extremely difficult to alter, yet theoretically irrational and unfair? Imagine that we came to endorse hard determinism, or hard incompatibilism—the view that the sort of free will required for moral responsibility is incompatible with determinism, but also with the sort of indeterminacy specified by the standard interpretation of quantum mechanics, and that we have no free will of this sort. Suppose in addition that the ordinary reactive attitudes were inevitable or largely so. It would then seem inappropriate to maintain the way we regarded those attitudes. As R. Jay Wallace points out:

> Being caught up in the practice of holding people morally responsible, and also committed to the moral norms of fairness, we might well be led to the conclusion that the practice is essentially unfair, and this conclusion would remain an important and troubling one, even if it would not lead us to cease holding people responsible.[18]

Moreover, even apart from considerations regarding freedom and determinism, most of us have had unfair or irrational attitudes towards others that were difficult or even impossible to eradicate. One then is sad and embarrassed that one has the attitudes in question, avoids indulging or reveling in them, does what one can to rid oneself of them, and one certainly does not justify practical decisions on their basis. This is how it would be best to deal with inescapable resentment and indignation if hard determinism is true, and this way of managing these attitudes does seem to be within our range of capability.

The third criticism is that a theoretical challenge to the reactive attitudes based on the thesis of universal determinism is not external to the practice of holding people morally responsible, and hence could not for this reason be illegitimate. First of all, analogies from other areas of ethical concern show that a system of attitudes can be subject to justificatory pressures from highly general theoretical beliefs. For example, some sexist and racist attitudes could be undermined by the following reflection: there is no difference across race and gender in capacities for theoretical and practical reasoning, for creative achievement, and for developing good human relationships. This reflection could and should radically alter human attitudes and practices, even if they are deeply rooted and longstanding. Despite its general and theoretical nature, the way in which such reflection effects these changes is legitimate and normative. Furthermore, as Galen Strawson emphasizes, the idea that the incompatibilist challenge to the reactive attitudes simply opposes abstract theory to deep human commitments is implausible. For "the fact that the incompatibilist intuition has so much power for us is as much a natural fact about cogitative beings like ourselves as is the fact of our quite unreflective commitment to the reactive

---

18 Wallace, *Responsibility and the Moral Sentiments*, p. 99.

attitudes".[19] He adds that: "the roots of the incompatibilist intuition lie deep in the very reactive attitudes that are invoked to undercut it".[20] Indeed, many of us have a strong and visceral feeling that it is unfair to regard causally determined agents as deserving of blame for their wrongdoings.

In my view, the best way to challenge P.F. Strawson on this issue is by way of what Wallace calls a *generalization strategy*. An approach of this sort argues from widely accepted excuses or exemptions to the claim that there is an incompatibilist requirement on moral responsibility.[21] Since the excuses and exemptions that form the basis of the argument are widely accepted, they are plausibly features internal to the practice of holding people morally responsible. Moreover, generalization is also an internal feature of this practice. If no relevant moral difference can be found between two agents in distinct situations, it is a feature of the practice of holding people morally responsible that if one agent is legitimately exempted from moral responsibility, so is the other.

Added Material

Perhaps the strongest challenge to compatibilism in general develops the claim that ordinary causal determination presents no less of a threat to moral responsibility than does the sort of covert manipulation that determines the agent to decide as she does.[22] The incompatibilist initially devises an imaginary example in which an agent makes a decision and in doing so fulfils all of the prominent compatibilist conditions for moral responsibility, while she is causally determined to meet those conditions by, for instance, sophisticated neuroscientists. The intuition to be elicited is that the agent is not morally responsible, which would indicate that the compatibilist conditions are not sufficient for moral responsibility. The incompatibilist then argues that there is no difference between the manipulation case and the case of ordinary causal determination that can justify exemption from responsibility in the first but not in the second.

In a first type of counterexample to the compatibilist conditions the manipulation is local—it proceeds from moment to moment. One might imagine that the sophisticated neuroscientists manipulate the agent from moment to moment by radiotechnology to act in such a way that these compatibilist conditions are met. The manipulation takes place at the neural level, so that at the mental level of description the agent does not differ from one who is not manipulated. The incompatibilist argues that the agent is quite obviously exempt from responsibility in such a situation. Perhaps the best reply on the part of the compatibilist involves developing the claim that a locally manipulated agent in some sense lacks the metaphysical integrity required to be a morally responsible agent, perhaps that a morally responsible agent must be one whose character develops in the ordinary way over a significant period of

---

19 Galen Strawson, *Freedom and Belief*, p. 88; cf. Kane, *The Significance of Free Will*, pp. 83–5.
20 Strawson, *Freedom and Belief*, p. 88.
21 Wallace, pp. 114–17.
22 See my *Living Without Free Will*, pp. 100–111.

time and whose actions proceed from this character and not from external local deterministic manipulation. But then we might imagine a case in which an agent is deterministically programmed from the beginning of her life so that her character develops as it does, to all appearances in an ordinary way, and so that she inevitably makes a decision that meets all of the prominent compatibilist criteria for moral responsibility. Suppose the decision is for a crime of some sort. The incompatibilist again argues that the agent is not morally responsible. It would seem unprincipled to claim that here, by contrast with the local manipulation example, the agent can now be morally responsible because the length of time between the programming and the action is great enough. Whether the programming takes place two seconds or thirty years before the action seems irrelevant to the question of moral responsibility. Moreover, the incompatibilist contends that this exemption for responsibility generalizes to the ordinary deterministic situation in which the agent fulfils all of the prominent compatibilist conditions.

Strawson's variety of compatibilism is vulnerable to this sort of strategy, and this criticism is internal rather than external. The kinds of exemptions to moral responsibility exploited in this strategy are due to manipulation. It is a feature of our practice of holding people morally responsible that if no relevant moral difference is to be found between agents in two situations, then if one agent is legitimately exempted from moral responsibility, so is the other. If the incompatibilist is right, no relevant moral difference can be found between agents in the manipulation cases and agents in ordinary deterministic situations. So it would be the practice itself, in particular central rules governing the practice that makes it the case that universal determinism is relevant to moral responsibility after all.

From Chapter 7 of Living Without Free Will

Reactive attitudes and interpersonal relationships

As we have seen, Strawson contends that the justification for claims of blameworthiness and praiseworthiness ends in the system of human reactive attitudes, and because moral responsibility has this kind of footing, the truth or falsity of determinism is irrelevant to whether we legitimately hold agents to be morally responsible. Moral responsibility is founded in the reactive attitudes required for the kinds of relationships that make our lives meaningful. On the other hand, if the thesis of universal determinism did imperil the reactive attitudes, we would then face the prospect of a certain "objectivity of attitude", a stance that undermines the possibility of good interpersonal relationships.[23] I think that Strawson is right to believe that objectivity of attitude would destroy interpersonal relationships, but that he is mistaken to hold that it would result or be appropriate if determinism did pose a genuine threat to the reactive attitudes.

In my view, first, some ordinary reactive attitudes, although they would be undermined by hard determinism, or more broadly by hard incompatibilism, are

---

23 FR, 25/66.

not obviously required for good interpersonal relationships. Indignation and moral resentment, for example, might be theoretically irrational given hard incompatibilism, but all things considered do more harm than good. Secondly, the reactive attitudes that we would want to retain either are not undermined by hard incompatibilism or else have analogues that would not have false presuppositions. The attitudes and analogues that would survive do not amount to Strawson's objectivity of attitude, and are sufficient to sustain good interpersonal relationships.

In Strawson's conception, some of the attitudes most important for interpersonal relationships are indignation, moral resentment, forgiveness, gratitude, and mature love. A certain measure of indignation and resentment is likely to be beyond our power to affect, and thus even supposing that one is committed to doing what is right and rational, one would still be unable to eradicate these attitudes. As hard incompatibilists, we might expect that indignation, for example, would occur in certain situations, and we might regard it as inevitable and exempt from blame when it does. But we sometimes have the ability to prevent, alter, or eliminate indignation, and given a belief in hard incompatibilism, we might well do so for the sake of morality and rationality. Modification of this attitude, aided by a hard incompatibilist conviction, could well be a good thing for relationships.

One might object that indignation plays an important communicative role in relationships with others, and if one were to strive to modify or eliminate this attitude, relationships might well be damaged. However, when one is wronged in a relationship there are other emotions typically present that are not threatened by hard incompatibilism, whose expression can also communicate the relevant information. These emotions include feeling hurt or shocked about what the other has done, and moral sadness or concern for the other. These attitudes are not aggressive in the way that indignation can be, and all by themselves they do not typically have indignation's intimidating effect. But if aggressiveness or intimidation is required, a strongly worded threat, for instance, might be appropriate. It is not clear, therefore, that indignation is required for communication in interpersonal relationships.

The attitude of forgiveness would appear to presuppose that the person being forgiven deserves blame, and thus forgiveness would indeed be imperiled by hard incompatibilism. But there are certain features of forgiveness that are not threatened by this view, and these features can adequately take the place this attitude usually has in relationships. Suppose a friend has wronged you in similar fashion a number of times, and you find yourself unhappy, angry, and resolved to loosen the ties of your relationship. Subsequently, however, he apologizes to you, which, consistent with hard incompatibilism, signifies his recognition of the wrongness of his behavior, his wish that he had not wronged you, and his genuine commitment to improvement. As a result, you change your mind and decide to continue the relationship. In this case, the feature of forgiveness that is consistent with hard incompatibilism is the willingness to cease to regard past wrongful behavior as a reason to weaken or dissolve one's relationship. In another type of case, you might, independently of the offender's repentance, simply choose to disregard the wrong as a reason to alter the character of your relationship. This attitude is in no sense undermined by hard incompatibilism. The sole aspect of forgiveness that is jeopardized by a hard incompatibilist conviction is the willingness to overlook deserved blame or punishment. But if one has given up belief in deserved blame and punishment, then the willingness to overlook them is no longer needed for good relationships.

Gratitude might well require the supposition that the person to whom one is grateful is morally responsible for an other-regarding act, and therefore hard incompatibilism might well undermine gratitude.[24] However, certain aspects of this attitude would be left untouched, aspects that can play the role gratitude commonly has in interpersonal relationships. First, gratitude includes an element of thankfulness towards those who have benefited us. Sometimes being thankful involves the belief that the object of one's attitude is praiseworthy for some action. But one can also be thankful to a pet or a small child for some favor, even if one does not believe that he is morally responsible. Perhaps one can even be thankful for the sun or the rain even if one does not believe that these elements are backed by morally responsible agency. In general, if one believed hard incompatibilism, one's thankfulness might lack features that it would have if one did not, but nevertheless, this aspect of gratitude can survive.

Gratitude involves an aspect of joy upon being benefited by another. But no feature of the hard incompatibilist position conflicts with one's being joyful and expressing joy when people are especially considerate, generous, or courageous in one's behalf. Such expression of joy can produce the sense of mutual well-being and respect frequently brought about by gratitude. Moreover, when one expresses joy for what another person has done, one can do so with the intention of developing a human relationship.

The thesis that love between mature persons would be subverted if hard incompatibilism were true requires more thorough argument than Strawson has provided. Let us first ask whether loving another requires that she be free in the sense required for moral responsibility. One might note, first of all, that parents love their children rarely, if ever, because these children possess this sort of freedom, or because they freely (in this sense) choose the good, or because they deserve to be loved. Moreover, when adults love each other, it is also seldom, if at all, for these kinds of reasons. Explaining love is a complex enterprise. Besides moral character and action, factors such as one's relation to the other, her appearance, manner, intelligence, and her affinities with persons or events in one's history all might have a part. But suppose we assume that moral character and action are of paramount importance in producing and maintaining love. Even if there is an important aspect of love that is essentially a deserved response to moral character and action, it is unlikely that one's love would be undermined if one were to believe that these moral qualities do not come about through free and responsible choice. For moral character and action are loveable whether or not they merit praise. Love of another involves, most fundamentally, wishing well for the other, taking on many of the aims and desires of the other as one's own, and a desire to be together with the other. Hard incompatibilism threatens none of this.

One might argue, however, that we nevertheless desire to be loved by others as a result of their free will. Against this, it is clear that parents' love for their children—a paradigmatic sort of love—is often produced independently of the parents' will. Kane endorses this last claim, and a similar view about romantic love, but he nevertheless

---

24 cf. Honderich's discussion of gratitude, *A Theory of Determinism*, pp. 518–19.

argues that a certain type of love we want would be endangered if we knew that there were factors beyond the lover's control that determined it.

> There is a *kind* of love we desire from others—parents, children (when they are old enough), spouses, lovers and friends—whose significance is diminished ... by the thought that they are determined to love us entirely by instinct or circumstances beyond their control or not entirely up to them ... To be loved by others in this desired sense requires that the ultimate source of others' love lies in their own wills.[25]

The plausibility of Kane's view might perhaps be enhanced by reflecting on how you would react were you to discover that someone you love was causally determined by a benevolent manipulator to have the love she has for you.

Leaving aside *free* will for a moment, in which sorts of cases does the will intuitively play a role in generating love for another at all? When the intensity of an intimate relationship is waning, people sometimes make a decision to try to make it work, and to attempt to regain the type of relationship they once had. When a student is placed in a dormitory suite and is not immediately disposed to friendship with one of the suitemates, she may make the decision to attempt nevertheless to form an emotional bond. Or when one's marriage is arranged by parents, one may decide to do whatever one can to love one's spouse.

But first, in such situations we might desire that another person make a decision to love, but it is not clear that we have reason to want the decision to be *freely* willed in the sense required for moral responsibility. A decision to love on the part of another might greatly enhance one's personal life, but it is not at all obvious what value the decision's being free and thus praiseworthy would add. Secondly, while in circumstances of these kinds we might desire that someone else make a decision to love, we would typically prefer the situation in which the love was not mediated by a decision. This is true not only for romantic attachments, but also for friendships and for relationships between parents and children.

Perhaps the will plays a significant role in *maintaining* love over an extended period. Søren Kierkegaard suggests that a marital relationship ideally involves a commitment that is continuously renewed.[26] Such a commitment involves a decision to devote oneself to another, and thus, in his view, a marital relationship ideally involves a continuously repeated decision. A decision of this kind may include a choice not to pursue intimate relationships with others. Indeed, many of us might very much desire a relationship with this sort of voluntary aspect. But again, it is difficult to see what is to be added by these continuously repeated decisions being freely willed in the sense required for moral responsibility. It might well be desirable for each participant that the other make these decisions. But that the participants should in addition be praiseworthy for these choices seems hardly relevant.

Finally, suppose Kane's view could be defended, and we do have a desire for love that is freely willed, or free in the sense required for moral responsibility. If we indeed desire freely willed love, then we desire a kind of love whose possibility

---

25 Kane, *The Significance of Free Will*, p. 88.
26 Søren Kierkegaard, Either/Or, vol. 2, tr. Walter Lowrie (Princeton: Princeton University Press, 1971).

hard incompatibilism denies. Still, the possibilities for love that remain are surely sufficient for good interpersonal relationships. If we can aspire to the sort of love parents typically have towards children, or the kind romantic lovers ideally have towards one another, or the type shared by friends who are immediately attracted to one another, and whose relationship is deepened by their interactions, then the possibility of fulfillment in interpersonal relationships is far from undermined. Finally, of all the attitudes that Strawson thinks might be imperiled by a belief in universal determinism, love is surely the most crucial for our relationships. If the types of love important for mature human relationships can survive, as I have argued, then universal determinism's threat to such relationships has been largely defused.

Guilt and Repentance

It might be argued that the self-directed attitudes of guilt and repentance are also threatened by hard incompatibilism. There is much at stake here, one might claim, for these attitudes are not only essential to good interpersonal relationships for agents prone to wrongdoing, but are also required for the moral development and integrity of an agent of this sort. Depending of the attitudes of guilt and repentance, such an agent would not only be incapable of reestablishing relationships damaged because he has done wrong, but he would also be barred from a restoration of his own moral integrity in these situations. For in the absence of the attitudes of guilt and repentance there are no human psychological mechanisms that can generate a restoration of this sort. Hard incompatibilism would appear to undermine guilt because this attitude essentially involves a sense that one is blameworthy for what one has done. Plausibly, if one did not feel blameworthy for an offense, one would also not feel guilty for it. Moreover, one might argue that because feeling guilty is undermined by hard incompatibilism, feeling repentant is also no longer an option. For as a matter of psychological fact, feeling guilty is required for motivating an attitude of repentance.

However, suppose that you do wrong, but because you believe that hard incompatibilism is true, you reject the claim that you are blameworthy. Instead, you accept that you have done wrong, you feel deeply sad that you were the agent of wrongdoing, or as Bruce Waller advocates, you thoroughly regret what you have done:

> It is reasonable for one who denies moral responsibility to feel profound sorrow and regret for an act. If in a fit of anger I strike a friend, I shall be appalled at my behavior, and profoundly distressed that I have in me the capacity for such behavior. If the act occurs under minimum provocation, and with an opportunity for some brief reflection before the assault, then I shall be even more disturbed and disappointed by my behavior: I find in myself the capacity for a vicious and despicable act, and the act emerges more from my own character than from the immediate stimuli (thus it may be more likely to recur in many different settings), and my capacity to control such vicious behavior is demonstrably inadequate. Certainly, I shall have good reason to regret my character—its capacity for vicious acts and its lack of capacity to control anger.[27]

---

27 Bruce Waller, *Freedom Without Responsibility* (Philadelphia: Temple University Press, 1990), pp. 165–6, cf. 164–9.

Also, because you have a commitment to doing what is right, and to personal moral progress, you might resolve not to perform an immoral action of this kind again, and seek out therapeutic procedures to help treat one's character problems. None of this is undermined by hard incompatibilism.

Since such sadness and regret for one's actions and character do not involve considering oneself blameworthy, one might not then have the attitude of guilt. But even this supposition can be challenged. Given what is ordinarily meant by "feeling guilty", it may be that feeling intensely sad and regretful that you are the agent of wrongdoing is sufficient for having this attitude. Hilary Bok eloquently advocates a position of this sort:

> The relation between the recognition that one has done something wrong and the guilt one suffers as a result ... is like the relation between the recognition that one's relationship with someone one truly loves has collapsed and the pain of heartbreak. Heartbreak is not a pain one inflicts on oneself as a punishment for loss of love; it is not something we undergo because we deserve it ... Similarly, the recognition that one has done something wrong causes pain. But this pain is not a form of suffering that we inflict on ourselves as a punishment but an entirely appropriate response to the recognition of what we have done, for two reasons. First, our standards define the kind of life we think we should lead and what we regard as valuable in the world, in our lives, and in the lives of others. They articulate what matters to us, and living by them is therefore by definition of concern to us. If we have indeed violated them, we have slighted what we take to be of value, disregarded principles we sincerely think we should live by, and failed to be the sorts of people we think we should be. The knowledge that we have done these things must be painful to us.[28]

But even if, in the final analysis, merely feeling sad or regretful or pained does not constitute feeling guilty, it can nevertheless generate a repentant attitude, a resolution not to perform the immoral action again. One might object that a feeling of moral sadness and regret is an insufficiently strong motivation to an attitude of repentance, but this claim is not obviously true.

Hard incompatibilism, therefore, endangers neither relationships with others nor personal integrity. It might well undermine certain attitudes that typically have a role in these domains: indignation, gratitude, and guilt would likely be theoretically irrational for a hard incompatibilist. But these attitudes are either not essential to good relationships, or they have analogues that could play the same role they typically have. Moreover, some of the most crucial reactive attitudes, such as forgiveness, love, and repentance, are not clearly threatened by hard incompatibilism at all.

We can now see that hard incompatibilist need not adopt the objectivity of attitude so destructive to interpersonal relationships. The specter of this outlook arises from the sense that she is forced to regard other human beings as mere mechanical devices, to be used and not respected. She is not, however, constrained to view others in this way. The hard incompatibilist need not deny that human beings are rational and responsive to reasons, and no feature of her view threatens

---

28 Hilary Bok, *Freedom and Responsibility* (Princeton: Princeton University Press, 1998), pp. 168–9. I find the view she develops in the section "Excursus on Guilt" (pp. 167–79) very attractive.

the respect she has for them because of their rational capacities. Moreover, thinking and acting in harmony with her hard incompatibilist convictions would not endanger her relationships. She would resist anger, blame, and resentment, but she would not be exempt from pain, sadness, or regret. When hurt by another, she might admonish, and upon acknowledgment of wrongdoing on the part of the other, cease to regard it as a hindrance to the relationship. She could be thankful and express joy towards others for the good things they provide for her. Her convictions pose no obstacle to love. Only if she also had an unappealing tendency to control another would she see him "as an object of social policy; as a subject for what, in a wide range of sense, might be called treatment; as something certainly to be taken account, perhaps precautionary account, of; to be managed or handled or cured or trained; perhaps simply to be avoided ..."[29] But she would not be compelled to take on this objectivity of attitude by her hard incompatibilist beliefs.

---

29 FR, 25/66.

Chapter 12

Free Will: From Nature to Illusion

Saul Smilansky

Sir Peter Strawson's "Freedom and Resentment" was a landmark in the philosophical understanding of the free will problem. Building upon it, I attempt to defend a novel position, which purports to provide, in outline, the next step forward. The position presented is based on the descriptively central and normatively crucial role of illusion in the issue of free will. Illusion, I claim, is the vital but neglected key to the free will problem. The proposed position, which may be called "Illusionism", is shown to follow both from the strengths and from the weaknesses of Strawson's position.

We have to believe in free will to get along

– C.P. Snow

Sir Peter Strawson's "Freedom and Resentment" (2003, first published in 1962) was a landmark in the philosophical understanding of the free will problem. It has been widely influential and subjected to penetrating criticism (e.g. Galen Strawson 1986 Ch. 5, Watson 1987, Klein 1990 Ch. 6, Russell 1995 Ch. 5). Most commentators have seen it as a large step forward over previous positions, but as ultimately unsuccessful. This is where the discussion within this philosophical direction has apparently stopped, which is obviously unsatisfactory. I shall attempt to defend a novel position, which purports to provide, in outline, the next step forward. The position presented is based on the descriptively central and normatively crucial role of illusion in the issue of free will. Illusion, I claim, is the vital but neglected *key* to the free will problem. It is not claimed that we need to induce illusory beliefs concerning free will, or can live with beliefs we fully realize are illusory—both of these positions would be highly implausible. Rather, my claim is that illusory beliefs are in place, and that the role they play is largely positive. The proposed position, which may be called "Illusionism", can be defended independently from its derivation from Strawson's "reactive naturalism", but it is helpful to present the progression in this way. Since the role of illusion emerges only at a late stage of the train of arguments pertaining to free will, we will get to the final destination by "free-riding" most of the way on Strawson's train, and then continue a bit further by ourselves, into the uncharted and dangerous Land of Illusion.

This paper consists of six parts. Part 1 sets out reactive naturalism. Part 2 explains why it has been thought to improve on previous positions on free will. Part 3 shows why reactive naturalism is inadequate. Part 4 elaborates on the problems whose solution requires illusion. Part 5 presents Illusionism and motivates it philosophically. Part 6 reviews the road from reactive naturalism to Illusionism.

I. Strawson's "Humean Naturalism"

Naturalism, in the sense I am concerned with here, is a sort of "Humean" response to scepticism about our common free will related practices and reactions. It will be called here "reactive-naturalism" and "naturalism" inter-changeably. This sort of naturalism considers scepticism as idle in view of the natural inclinations of humanity, given which there is no need for countering the sceptic or, indeed, for offering any justification at all of our basic beliefs and attitudes (Strawson 1987, 38–41). Like the compatibilist, the naturalist claims that morality and human life are not dramatically affected by the absence of libertarian free will. However, he rests his case not on an analysis of the philosophical implications of this absence but on its insignificance in "real life".

Considering the predominance of human reactive attitudes and their centrality in human life, indeed, in being human, any intellectual considerations, such as the truth of determinism, cannot seriously be posed as a threat. And, even if we can imagine having a choice whether to engage in inter-personal relations, founded as they are on reactive attitudes, rational choice would be based on the expected gains and losses to human life, and the outcome would be clear (Strawson 2003, p. 83 [this volume, p. 28]). Strawson claims that the nature of morality is largely analogical, in that our demands for other persons' good will towards third parties (or demands from ourselves) resemble those we make for good will towards ourselves. This analogy is sustained by the various excusing conditions, in the particular irrelevance of considerations of the truth of determinism to them, and in the ridiculous nature of suggestions that the truth of determinism might abolish this part of life, the moral sphere being intimately connected with the sphere of inter-personal relations (p. 87 [this volume, p. 31]).

II. The Attractions of Reactive-Naturalism

II.1. Preliminaries

Reactive naturalism is a strange position to hold on the free will problem, since it is not really about whether we do or do not *have* free will or moral responsibility in an independent sense, in the way that traditional positions (libertarianism, compatibilism and hard determinism) clearly are. Rather, reactive naturalism focuses on our emotional lives and asks whether, in the light of our emotional make-up, common views are liable to be affected. That such a position can be a contender at all must be due then to a serious state of affairs; this is indeed the case. This state is, broadly:

(a) There is no libertarian free will.
(b) Compatibilism is insufficient as a basis for moral responsibility and related matters.

(c) We need to maintain common free will related attitudes and practices, so that compatibilist distinctions in terms of control and its absence should largely continue to be followed.

(d) Other alternatives, such as utilitarianism, are inadequate.

In considering the free will problem, the first[1] question is whether libertarian free will really exists, i.e. the libertarian Coherence/Existence Question. The second question is whether—if it does not—we are in trouble. It can be called the Compatibility Question, namely: are moral responsibility and related notions compatible with determinism (or with the absence of libertarian free will irrespective of determinism)? Compatibilism and hard determinism are the opponents on the Compatibility Question. Reactive naturalism, like the Illusionism I am offering, is best understood as an answer to the third-level question of the consequences of pessimistic answers to the first two questions—namely, that there is no libertarian free will, and that compatibilism is insufficient and hence we are in trouble. It can be called the Consequences Question.

It is the despair from the possibility of grounding our ethical and personal free will-related beliefs, practices and reactions on libertarianism, compatibilism or any other traditional alternative, which brought naturalism to the scene.

II.2. Why not libertarian free will?

First a few words on (a), i.e. the claim that there is no libertarian free will. I shall assume, with Strawson, that libertarian free will is incoherent (Strawson 1980, 265). In a nutshell, the conditions required by an ethically satisfying sense of libertarian free will, which would give us anything beyond sophisticated formulations of compatibilism, are self-contradictory, and hence cannot be met. This is so irrespective of determinism or causality. Attributing moral worth to a person for her decision or action requires that it follow from what she is, morally. The decision or action cannot be produced by a random occurrence and count morally. We might think that two different decisions or actions can follow from a person, but which one does, say, a decision to steal or not to steal, again cannot be random but needs to follow from what she is, morally. But what a person is, morally, cannot ultimately be under her control. We might think that such control is possible if she creates herself, but then it is the early self that creates a later self, leading to vicious infinite regress. The libertarian project was worthwhile attempting: it was supposed to allow a deep moral connection between a given act and the person, and yet not fall into being merely an unfolding of the arbitrarily given, whether determined or random. But it is not possible to find any way in which this can be done.

---

1 The free will problem can be structured in various ways, but the way presented here seems most useful: if there were libertarian free will, much of the point in asking the Compatibility Question would disappear, and so on. Nevertheless, one may begin by asking if compatibilism is insufficient and then move on to see whether libertarian free will could help. In any case, reactive-naturalism emerges at the end of such traditional explorations and, I claim, Illusionism follows from the weaknesses of reactive-naturalism.

Libertarians may well not be satisfied with my cursory treatment, but this should be accepted for the sake of the current discussion, for we need to journey far. We may then say that my argument, like that of Strawson, is primarily addressed to those who are not assured of the belief in the existence of libertarian free will.

II.3. Why not compatibilism?

I will now say something on (b), i.e. on why I think that compatibilism, its partial validity notwithstanding, is grimly insufficient. Not only is compatibilism a widely prevalent view in philosophy, and hence I need to combat the complacency it encourages if I am to motivate the need for illusion, but this need will emerge from the situation that makes compatibilism inadequate. (The case made here is my own, and it is not claimed that Strawson would view matters in exactly the same way.)

We can make sense of the notion of autonomy or self-determination on the compatibilist level but, if there is no libertarian free will, no one can be ultimately in control, ultimately responsible, for this self and its determinations. *Everything* that takes place on the compatibilist level, irrespective of the local distinctions in respect of control, becomes on the ultimate hard determinist level "what was merely *there*", ultimately deriving from causes beyond the control of the participants. If people lack libertarian free will, their identity and actions flow from circumstances beyond their control. To a certain extent, people can change their character, but that which changes or does not change remains itself a result of something, and there is always a situation in which the self-creating person could not have created herself, but was just what she was, as it were, "given". Being the sort of person one is, and having the desires and beliefs one has, are ultimately something which one cannot control, which cannot be one's fault; it is one's luck. And one's life, and everything one does, is an unfolding of this. Let us call this the "ultimate perspective" and contrast it with the "compatibilist perspective", which takes the person as a "given" and enquires about her various desires, choices and actions.

Consider the following quotation from a compatibilist:

> The incoherence of the libertarian conception of moral responsibility arises from the fact that it requires not only authorship of the action, but also, in a sense, authorship of one's self, or of one's character. As was shown, this requirement is unintelligible because it leads to an infinite regress. The way out of this regress is *simply to drop* the second-order authorship requirement, which is what has been done here (Vuoso 1987, 1681; my emphasis).

The difficulty is that there is an *ethical basis* for the libertarian requirement and, even if it cannot be fulfilled, the idea of "simply dropping it" masks how *problematic* the result may be in terms of fairness and justice. The fact remains that if there is no libertarian free will a person being punished *may suffer justly* in compatibilist terms for what is ultimately her luck, for what follows from being what she is—ultimately beyond her control, a state which she had no real opportunity to alter, hence neither her responsibility nor her fault. With all the importance of compatibilist distinctions, a morally serious compatibilist cannot escape the conclusion that if this person suffers—however justly in compatibilist terms—she is, from an important perspective, a victim. For it was *given* that being who she was she would (compatibilistically freely) choose as she did, and suffer the consequences.

A similar criticism applies to other moral and non-moral ways of perceiving and treating people. The compatibilist cannot maintain the libertarian-based view of moral worth or of the grounds for respect, and what she has to offer is a much shallower sort of meaning and justification. Desert, be it of praise or punishment, can make sense only on a shallow compatibilist level, where the underlying causes of the good or bad motives are not queried. Ultimately people are not deserving, they are simply the way they have been made, and hence equal in value, i.e. equally lacking in desert-based value. Compatibilism, in sum, is morally, even humanly, shallow, for it depends on our remaining on the level of people as more or less "givens", i.e. on blindness as to what we learn when we push our inquiries further, into the causes of this "given", beyond the limited internal compatibilist perspective. The picture of moral reality and of personal aspects of worth that we can aspire to as compatibilists is often tragic and inherently shallow. It is those two charges, of shallowness, and of a complacent compliance with the injustice of not acknowledging lack of fairness and desert, and in particular ultimate-level victimization, which form the backbone of my case against compatibilism.

II.4. *Why not hard determinism?*

If there is no libertarian free will and if compatibilism is insufficient, should we not then opt for hard determinism, which denies the reality of free will and moral responsibility in any sense? I will now briefly defend (c) above, namely the need to retain some of the "form of life" based on the value put on distinctions made in terms of compatibilist free will. I share with most free will philosophers the belief in the at least partial validity of compatibilism. In broad outline, the basis for this position combines the reality of distinctions in terms of local free choice even in a world without libertarian free will, such as a deterministic world, and the possibility to motivate ethically the making use of these distinctions. (Again, Strawson would not share this view in its particulars, but since this is not a work of historical interpretation this need not concern us. He *would* certainly share the thought that hard determinism should not guide our practice.)

The kleptomaniac and the alcoholic differ from the common thief and common drinker in the deficiency of their capacity for local reflective control over their actions (see e.g. Glover 1970, 136; cf. Fischer 1994 for a recent sophisticated compatibilist formulation). Here everyone should agree. But the point is that such differences are *morally significant*: in some ways the compatibilistically free may also be victims as viewing things from the ultimate perspective has helped us to see, and yet the importance of the commonplace compatibilist level distinctions will often be great. Consider, for instance, the notion of a valid Will and Testament made by a person wishing to arrange the distribution of her property after her death. The idea of a valid will requires that it be made of one's "free will". There are likely to be borderline difficulties but, in general, we are able to identify what it is about the agent and the situation when signing a document which makes the signatory's action free in a sense we care about (even without libertarian free will), and what limitations of free will (such as coercion and insanity) invalidate the will. And it is fairly obvious *why* we want to make use of these factors in our ethical judgements, reactions and social practices. We want our last wishes to be respected, as well as defended, if our will is tampered with, and an ethically decent social order will follow the compatibilist distinctions.

More generally, we want to be members of a Community of Responsibility where our choices will determine the moral attitude we receive, with the accompanying possibility of being morally excused when our actions are not within our reflective control, e.g. when they result from a brain tumor. The exceptions and excuses commonly presented by compatibilism should, in general, continue to carry weight. For if people are to be respected, their nature as purposive agents capable and desirous of choice needs to be catered to. We have to enable people to live as responsible beings in the Community of Responsibility, with their lives based largely on their choices, to note and give them *credit* for their good actions, and to take account of situations in which they *lacked* the abilities, capacities and opportunities to choose freely, and are therefore not responsible in the compatibilist sense. Even without libertarian free will, it is reasonable to desire that compatibilist distinctions concerning control affect the way one is treated, and to see this as a condition for civilized existence.

Such a community is possible on the basis of compatibilist-level distinctions. Except in extreme situations, we have no reason to accept at face value the words and deeds of a woman who admits that she continuously takes advantage of people and treats them shabbily, but claims as an excuse that "this is in her nature". Admittedly, it may be more difficult for her to control herself or to change than it is for others, but this can be only a mitigating element, and would not lead us to accept her presentation of things as simply an acceptable excuse. We shall see her self-justification as, at best, bad faith, but more probably as an attempt at self-serving manipulation. One is not normally in a *passive* relationship with such features of one's behavior, and is an agent who deliberates, decides and acts out one's decisions, not a spectator of forces carrying one along. This element of "up to us-ness" is why the compatibilist perspective is available, why we are allowed to hold this woman accountable and why we are permitted to attempt to influence her within a responsibility-based moral structure. Such a Community of Responsibility allows people to live lives of integrity based upon their choices, and is also a basis for a fair division of burdens. As Will Kymlicka points out: "It is unjust if people are disadvantaged by inequalities in their circumstances, but it is equally unjust for me to demand that someone else pay for the costs of my choices" (Kymlicka, quoted in Cohen 1989, 933). Hence, with all the moral importance of the absence of libertarian free will, we need not and must not escape from living according to the basic ethical paradigm of control and responsibility.[2]

We see, then, that we are in serious trouble, for (a) libertarian free will does not exist, (b) compatibilism is greatly insufficient, but (c) the basic free will related practices and reactions should be maintained.[3] Naturalism attempts to offer, as we have seen, a defence of our common attitudes and practices in this predicament.

---

2   We need to combine the insights of compatibilism and hard determinism into a joint position, for neither on its own is adequate; see Smilansky (1993) and Smilansky (2000, Part I).

3   Further views, such as utilitarianism, can be thought to be relevant. I cannot consider the general merits of utilitarianism here, but it seems to me to be fundamentally alien to the

III. Why Not Reactive-Naturalism?

Reactive-naturalism offers a highly significant contribution to the debate. When examined closely, however, it is much weaker than it seems at first, and if the basic attitude it favours is to be sustained it is necessary to interpret it along the lines of Illusionism.

III.1. Revisionist naturalism

Naturalism can be seen to split into two versions: a tough-minded, revisionist naturalism, and a softer, passive account. Revisionist naturalism seeks to change the perception that there is a theoretical need to justify common attitudes and practices, holding that there is no need for general grounding and that the reactions themselves provide all the (self-) grounding required. Strawson sometimes expresses views akin to revisionist naturalism (e.g. 1987, 32–3). In greater detail, Jonathan Bennett might be interpreted as working towards such a position in his attempt to apply Strawson's work to the issue of punishment (1980; cf. Wallace 1994). Bennett suggests that we see the reactive attitudes as the limiting addition (constituting "justice") to the regular consequentialist considerations regarding punishment, and this explains why we should not "punish" the innocent, for example—we cannot resent them, and to "punish" the innocent would be harmful to our reactive lives (pp. 48–9).

There is likely to be much affinity between the structure of our reactive lives and the basic ethical intuitions requiring the existence of free will. This depends, however, on the reality of distinctions in control, which influence our knowledge when a reaction is *appropriate*. Our reactive attitudes are not independent and self-validating. The concerns of the basic ethical intuition and reactive attitudes may differ and, in any case, the needs of our reactive lives cannot be the main consideration. Justice, for instance, involves matters other than safeguarding the reactive attitudes. If we doubt whether free action exists in a significant sense, this must be crucial to the view we take of the justification of blame and punishment, for example. Even with Strawson's paradigmatic attitude, resentment, a belief *transcending and underlying* the attitude itself seems necessary. As Joel Feinberg says: "It is clear, I think, that resentment without an ostensible desert basis is not resentment" (Feinberg 1970, 71).

Similarly, the wish to preserve the reactive attitudes could hardly be widely accepted as a basis for morality. Revisionist naturalism can be confronted with the same type of criticism that naturalism itself leveled at consequentialism in the

---

deep concerns of the free will issue. It is radically at odds with moral phenomenology: the seriousness of moral appraisal depends on our not viewing judgements merely as manipulative ways of influencing people, which can in principle be applied to the blameless if it is socially useful to do so. People would not be willing to be blamed, would not accept blame as appropriate, were it not assumed that they deserve blame on account of their freely taken actions. Utilitarianism is also opposed to our deepest moral intuitions (the inherent concern with control in general and the abhorrence for the "punishment" of the innocent example in practice). Even if one accepts utilitarianism the role of illusion with respect to free will can be demonstrated, but this paper can be taken to address those whose basic ethical views are not (only) utilitarian. I cannot consider other positions here.

free will context—that, like the consequentialist "effects of blame", safeguarding the reactive attitudes is just not the *kind* of reason bound up with free will-related moral life, and will not be recognized by most people as appropriate. Dependency on grounds is inherent in the notions under consideration, such as resentment, blame and punishment. The reactive attitudes follow the existence of such grounds (e.g. gratitude has to be deserved), and cannot in themselves replace it.

III.2. Non-revisionist naturalism

Perhaps a non-revisionist, passive naturalism is sufficient? Perhaps all the naturalist requires is that *in practice* common attitudes and behavior remain constant, whatever the theoretical case may be. However, even on its own naturalistic terms, naturalism is inadequate. Even someone such as Paul Russell, who follows Hume and Strawson in discounting the need for general justification of our moral attitudes as such, thinks that Strawson is too optimistic as to the stability of specific attitudes and practices (Russell 1992). But why are reactive attitudes insufficient?

III.3. Justice

One problem that has real practical substance concerns justice. It is not required that people think of some alternative moral position, unrelated to the reactive attitudes. It is enough that some segments of the population should become *cynical* or *doubtful*, about the moral difference between the guilty and innocent (in traditional terms) in the light of the causal role of crimogenic environments, in order for any confidence as to the assurance provided by reactive attitudes to be shaken. In such a case we might face a threat to the basis of moral life in the requirement for considering free will as a condition for punishment. Societies with very different conceptions of justice existed, and even if they cannot be reinstated, significant doubts as to the justness of our own institutions, resulting in an uncaring cynicism, cannot be ruled out.

A sense of "justice" has often been closely connected with feelings of revenge, concern with the existence of free will being non-existent or meager: it has often been thought that "just" revenge could be taken on the tribesmen or countrymen of the guilty person, without undue concern for their lack of responsibility. Today such attitudes are still expressed in societies organized largely on the basis of kinship, resulting in blood-feuds. Many terrorist actions, such as blowing up civilian airlines or buses in the name of "just" revenge, show the same disregard for the value of considering free will. Such beliefs, emotions and practices were long considered natural, and the danger has not been eradicated. Consider also the prevalence for hundreds of years in Christian Europe of the sentiment that Jews, as such, should suffer, because of the alleged role of some Jews in the Roman crucifixion of Jesus. Other religious beliefs, such as the common conception of Original Sin under certain interpretations, might also betray the lack of concern with "up-to-usness". Here we are faced with situations where even the *minimal* content of free will—agency—is not considered necessary in order for punishment to be just.[4]

Let us call the ethical demand for considering the existence of free will in justifying e.g. blame and punishment the "Core Conception" of justice. I believe that current acceptance of the Core Conception, in some societies, has a good claim to represent moral progress, perhaps the best claim there is: think about enlightened attitudes towards the "punishment" of the innocent or collective "punishment", for example. This progress is more fragile than we are wont to think. Moreover, such threats need not even arise from within the free will issue. There are various intellectual and social currents which might harm the value put upon free will. The call for "efficiency" in the fight against crime might suffice here. The point is that even a mild weakening of free will beliefs might reduce their power to make us *resist* such external influences.

III.4. Respect

We can highlight many of these points by considering the issue of (self-)respect. Just as with the issue of justice, I think consideration of this topic shows Strawson's position to be too optimistic. This becomes apparent if we substitute "respect" for "resentment" and consider the matter of "Freedom and Respect", respect being an attitude much more dependent on complex cognitive beliefs than resentment. Resentment may linger when we cease to see the issue of (dis)respect as pertaining to a person, in light of the issue of free will. We can hardly continue to respect ourselves in the same way if we really internalize the belief that all action and achievement is ultimately down to luck and not ultimately attributable to us. And there is every reason to believe that many educated people can internalize this thought to a degree that will *suffice* to cause serious harm to their self-respect. Similarly with the appreciation of and respect for others.

Moreover, the non-revisionist naturalist position, to the extent that it is deemed convincing, is itself harmful to our self-respect. If attitudes of respect are thought unjustifiable on the deepest level because of the lack of an ultimate basis for them in free will, then to say that it is "unavoidable" that we hold such attitudes means that we are caught in a humiliating state. To continue with the same attitudes and practices involving libertarian desert and worth when we know that there is no libertarian free will is hardly conducive to self-respect, even if no real choice is involved.

In sum, the issue of (self-)respect illuminates the danger of the ultimate hard determinist insight, and shows the weakness of a position such as Strawson's. Firstly, we realize that what we seek is a deep basis for being worthy of respect, and this Strawson cannot give us. The quest for respect is a quest for true appreciation and value, and cannot be satisfied in the way that the need for some of the more "emotional" reactive attitudes perhaps can. Secondly, we see that Strawson relies too

---

4 Natural human inclinations have not always been sufficient to safeguard our core conception. For more historical examples, from the ancient Geeks, medieval societies, and anthropology, see Sayre (1932, 977 and 981); Adkins (1960, 57, 68, 167); Hibbert (1963, 201f.); Von Furer-Haimendorf (1967, 216); Pollock and Maitland (1968, vol.2, 470f.).

heavily on our natural proneness to the reactive attitudes as a means of upholding these values, since many people may come to doubt the basis for their self-respect. Finally, even where they are effective, Strawson's pragmatic assurances are only comforting at the price of a further reduction in our self-respect, due to their very nature, and because of our very need for what might be taken to be mere palliatives.[5]

III.5. Why not reactive-naturalism? Conclusion

Reactive-naturalism originally appeared as a strong position for, unlike other compatibilist stances, it in a way encompassed the common libertarian assumptions, while neutralising them, so that they seemed to result, in practice, in compatibilist conclusions. But as we saw, this crucially depends on assuming that the reactive attitudes guarantee the status quo, with the cognitive status of the assumptions and resulting actions following the reactive attitudes. And this is unconvincing.

Free will and moral responsibility are the stuff of our beliefs and convictions and not mere secretions of our natural reactions. Instinctive nature is not in complete mastery in matters of free will, and our personal and ethical convictions can be led up grim paths if the absence of libertarian free will is internalized, as it may be, in part. Our ethical common-sense is not "built-in", and even those reactive attitudes that are more or less unavoidable cannot guarantee it. Reactive naturalism is a useful antidote to extreme cognitivism concerning free will, but in it the pendulum has swung too far the other way. Despite the role of the reactive attitudes, the free will problem can be important in practice, perhaps mainly in less subjective and moral areas, because we can have limited threats to the central values involved, threats that are perhaps largely unavoidable in the modern world, and should not be avoided by abandoning the Core Conception values, even if they could be.

IV. Elaborating "The Problem"

In order to see how illusion is crucial we must deepen our understanding of the difficulties which (would) prevail without it. There are fatal weaknesses in naturalism as a solution; but why is there an urgent problem in the first place? We have already seen some difficulties. In what follows I will give a number of further illustrations.

IV.1. The question of innocence

The danger concerning respect for moral innocence was mentioned above. Even in a world without libertarian free will, the idea that only those who deserve to be punished in light of their free actions may be punished is a condition for any civilized moral order (cf. Hart 1970). "Punishment" of those who did not perform the act for which they are "punished", or did so act but lacked control over their action in any sense, is the paradigm of injustice. Yet while the justification for

---

[5] I consider the issue of free will and self-respect in greater detail in Smilansky (1997) and Smilansky (2000, section 6.4).

these values does not require libertarian free will, in practice they might be at risk were the lack of libertarian free will internalized. Consider Anscombe's passionate remark that "If someone really thinks, *in advance*, that it is open to question whether such an action as procuring the judicial execution of the innocent should be quite excluded from consideration—I do not want to argue with him; he shows a corrupt mind" (Anscombe 1981, 40). Surely, if a moral system that seeks to preserve and guard vigilantly the common conception of innocence is to function well, such a sentiment should be prevalent, almost instinctive. But if this is to be so, the worst thing one could do would be to point out that, ultimately, none of this makes sense because the "guilty" are, ultimately, no more guilty than others. In a world imbued with a deterministic outlook the ethical-emotional weight of the Dreyfus affair, for example, is scarcely comprehensible.

IV.2. The ultimate conclusion as a practical threat to the taking of responsibility

We cannot tell people that they must behave in a certain way, that it is morally crucial that they do so, but then, if they do not, turn and say that this is (in every case) excusable, given whatever hereditary and environmental influences have operated in their formation. Psychologically, the attribution of responsibility to people so that they may be said to justly deserve gain or loss for their actions requires (even *after* the act) the absence of the notion that the act is an unavoidable outcome of the way things were, is ultimately beyond anyone's control. Morality has a crucial interest in confronting what can be called the *Present Danger of the Future Retrospective Excuse*, and in restricting the influence of the ultimate hard determinist level. To put it bluntly: people as a rule ought not to be fully aware of the ultimate inevitability of what they have done, for this will affect the way in which they hold themselves responsible. The knowledge that such an escape from responsibility, based on retrospective ultimate judgement, will be available in the *future* is likely to affect the present view, and hence cannot be fully admitted even in its *retrospective* form. We often want a person to blame himself, feel guilty, and even see that he deserves to be punished. Such a person is not likely to do all this if he internalizes the ultimate perspective, according to which in the actual world nothing else could in fact have occurred, he could not strictly have done anything else except what he did do.

IV.3. Failure

It might also be interesting to reflect upon *failure*. The threat of failure is central to the widespread motivation to study, work, and in general make an effort, i.e. in motivating achievement. The sense of achievement and the self-respect it generates are in everybody's interest; unfortunately these ideas make no sense without the notion of failure. Hence we need the idea of failure in order to be given the opportunity to succeed. By now, however, it will be obvious that the ultimate perspective poses a great threat here. If the boy at fifteen is to make something of himself, it cannot be the case that, were he to fail, at sixty he would have an easy way of dismissing his plight as all along beyond his control, for hard determinist reasons. Moreover, such an easy erasure of failure cannot but affect the fate of the sense of achievement:

it cannot be that failure is thought not to be in the end up to one, while attainment miraculously remains so. A cultural climate of guaranteed excuse is not conducive to effort and for encouraging success, nor is it a firm foundation for (self-)respect.

IV.4. A sense of value

From the ultimate hard determinist perspective, all people—whatever their efforts and sacrifices—are morally equal: i.e. there cannot be any means of generating "real" moral value. As we have seen, there is a sense in which our notion of moral self-respect, which is intimately connected with our view of our choices, actions and achievements, withers when we accept the ultimate perspective. From the latter any sense of moral achievement disappears, as even the actions of the "moral hero" are simply an unfolding of what he happens to be *no matter how devoted he has been, how much effort he has put in, how many tears he has shed, how many sacrifices he has willingly suffered*. True *appreciation*, deeply *attributing* matters to someone in a sense that will make him worthy, is impossible if we regard him and his efforts as merely determined products. All that the compatibilist can offer us in terms of value, although important in itself, is meager protection from the cold wind that attacks us when we come close to reaching the luck-imbued ultimate level. There is an obvious practical danger here to our moral motivation, which can be named the *Danger of Worthlessness*. But the concern is not only to get people to function adequately as moral agents, but with the very meaning we can find in our lives.

IV.5. Remorse and integrity

If a person takes the ultimate hard determinist perspective, it is not only others who seem to disappear as moral agents; in some way the person herself is reduced. In retrospect her life, her decisions, that which is most truly her own, appear to be accidental phenomena of which she is the mere *vehicle*, and to feel moral remorse for any of it, by way of truly *owning up* to it, seems in some deep sense to be misguided. Feelings of remorse are inherently tied to the person's self-perception as a morally responsible agent (see Taylor 1985, 107).

It sharpens our focus not to dwell upon those happy to escape accountability, but rather upon those who have good will. Here we confront what can be termed the *Danger of Retrospective Dissociation*, the difficulty of feeling truly responsible after action. One can surrender the right to make use of the "ultimate level excuse" for normative reasons, and yet perhaps not be able to hold oneself truly responsible (e.g. to engage in remorse), if one has no grain of belief in something like libertarian free will. One can, after all, accept responsibility for matters that were not up to one in any sense, such as for the actions of others, for normative reasons. But here we are dealing with a different matter: not with the acceptance of responsibility in the sense of "willingness to pay", but rather with feeling *compunction*. Compunction seems conceptually problematic and psychologically dubious when it concerns actions that, it is understood, ultimately one could not in fact help doing. But such genuine feelings of responsibility (and not mere acceptance of it) are crucial for being responsible selves! We see here the *intimacy* of the connection between moral and personal integrity and beliefs about free will; hence the danger of realising the truth also looms large.

Here the common person's incompatibilist intuitions, for all of their vagueness and crudeness, have captured something that has escaped philosophical compatibilists. Once this larger view of the need to have workable beliefs and sustaining self-images is taken we can no longer contemplate with equanimity the decline of libertarian-based beliefs. When we appreciate that it is not merely "external" or "theoretical" conclusions which may emerge, but that internalized beliefs regarding the free will problem could enter into our retrospective beliefs about *ourselves*, we see that the difficulties caused by the absence of ultimate-level grounding are likely to be great, generating acute psychological discomfort for many people and threatening morality—if, that is, we do not have illusion at our disposal.

IV.6. The "Problem": Some concluding reflections

The difficulties we have seen can be divided into two types. Firstly, reactions and practices which are at least partially valid (have compatibilist grounding) will not be sufficiently adhered to if the absence of libertarian free will is realized. The compatibilist categories are not erased by the absence of libertarian free will, but *over-reaction* to this absence may in practice occur. Secondly, the absence of libertarian free will is *in itself* grimly significant, hence its realization is potentially problematic irrespective of the danger to the compatibilistically-valid reactions and practices. Even if people continue to respect the compatibilist categories, they may come to see that the lack of libertarian free will is, say, corrosive of their self-respect. As we shall see shortly, illusion assists us with these two problems.

Belief can be fairly stable concerning libertarian free will but, if this current stability-point is broken, it is not the partially valid compatibilist categories that will be upheld. Rather, the risk is that belief will collapse to its next "natural" stability-point, to the denial of meaning to free will and moral responsibility, as it were, *If all is determined, everything is permitted*. And even when this is not the case, the poverty of the best that the compatibilist has to offer in terms of worth and desert is disheartening, and this grim situation can be realized to some extent.

In theory, alternatives to the concern with free will also present themselves: for example, a purely aesthetic view of life that does not treat achievements as reflecting on a person's value, except for a merely quasi-aesthetic ranking. Such abandonment of value and of self is at best a marginal possibility, at least within the framework of anything resembling Western forms of thought. Note that this extends beyond those with deep moral concerns. A true understanding of what is at stake concerning non-moral self-respect, for example, would lead one to the same conclusion. *There is no real substitute for the network of achievement, desert and value based on free action.* And within that framework, a deep view not diverted by illusion will find itself face-to-face with darkness.

V. Illusion as a "Solution"

V.1. What is Illusionism?

Illusionism is the position that illusion often has a large and positive role to play in the issue of free will. In arguing for the importance of illusion I claim that we can see why it is useful, that it is a reality, and that by and large it ought to continue. As I noted above, it is not claimed that we need to induce illusory beliefs concerning free will, or can live with beliefs we fully realize are illusory. Rather, my claim is that illusory beliefs are in place, and that the role they play is largely positive. Humanity is fortunately deceived on the free will issue, and this seems to be a condition of civilized morality and personal value.

The importance of illusion flows from the basic structure of the free will problem that we have seen. It flows in two ways: first, indirectly, from the fundamental dualism on the Compatibility Question—the partial and varying validity of *both* compatibilism and hard determinism. The partial validity of compatibilism does not reduce the need for illusion so much as it complicates it and adds to it, because of the need to guard the compatibilist concerns and distinctions, and the contrast and dissonance with the ultimate hard determinist perspective. Secondly, illusion flows directly and more deeply—from the meaning of the very absence of the sort of grounding that libertarian free will was thought to provide. We cannot live adequately with the dissonance of the two valid sides of the fundamental dualism, nor with a complete awareness of the deep significance of the absence of libertarian free will. We have to face the fact that there are basic beliefs that morally ought not to be abandoned, although they might destroy each other, or are even partly based on incoherent conceptions. At least for most people, these beliefs are potentially in need of motivated mediation and defence by illusion, ranging from wishful thinking to self-deception.

The sense of "illusion" that I am using combines the falsity of the belief with some motivated role in forming and maintaining that belief, as in standard cases of wishful thinking or self-deception. However, it suffices that the beliefs are false and that this conclusion would be resisted were a challenge to arise; it is not necessary for us to determine the current level of illusion concerning free will.

V.2. Why is there a need for illusion?

Our previous results supply the resources for an answer. Let us concentrate, for the sake of simplicity, on the concerns of a strictly "practical" point of view: if the basic ethical concern for free will, the Core Conception, is taken seriously, while the absence of libertarian free will is to some extent realized, and illusion does not prevail, then the ultimate level conclusion might tend to dominate in practice. It might very well pose a danger—especially because of the human tendency to over-simplify—to the "common form of life" and to the strict observance of the corresponding moral order. Many people would find it hard to think that the partial compatibilist truth *matters*, as in fact it ethically does, if they realized the sense in which both the compatibilistically free and the unfree were merely performing according to their mould. And this might lead them to succumb to "pragmatic" consequentialist temptations, or an unprincipled nihilism. The ultimate hard determinist perspective does not leave sufficient moral and psychological "space" for compatibilistically-defensible reactive attitudes and moral order. The fragile compatibilist-level plants need to be defended from the chill of the ultimate perspective in the hothouse of illusion. *Only if we do not see people from the ultimate perspective can we live in a way which compatibilism affirms*—blaming, selectively excusing, respecting, being grateful, and the like.

Within these parameters, there is a prima facie case for a large measure of motivated obscurity regarding the objections to libertarian free will: if libertarian assumptions carry on their back the compatibilist distinctions, which would not be adhered to sufficiently without them, an illusion which defends these libertarian assumptions seems to be just what we need.[6] The partial validity of the compatibilist distinctions is unlikely to overcome the practical salience of the ultimate perspective in such a situation, unless illusion intervenes. Determinists are not likely to cherish and maintain adequately the respect due to people in the light of their free actions, nor a free will-based moral order in general. The ethical importance of the paradigm of free will and responsibility as a basis for desert should be taken very seriously, but the ultimate perspective threatens to present it as a farce, a mere game without foundation. Likewise with the crucial idea of a personal sense of value and appreciation that can be gained through our free actions: this is unlikely to be adequately maintained by individuals in their self-estimates, nor warmly and consistently projected by society. A broad loss of moral and personal confidence can be expected. The idea of action-based desert, true internal acceptance of responsibility, respect for effort and achievement, deep ethical appreciation, excusing the innocent—all these and more are threatened by the "leveling" or homogenising view arising from the ultimate perspective. Illusion is crucial in pragmatically safeguarding the compatibilistically-defensible elements of the "common form of life". *Illusion is, by and large, a condition for the actual creation and maintenance of adequate moral and personal reality.*

V.3. How does illusion function?

When illusion plays a role, things can, in practice, work out. Two schematic answers can be made. Significant realization of the absence of libertarian free will and concern about ultimate level injustice, for example, can remain more or less limited to part of the population, say, those more concerned with policy making (an "elitist solution"). This maintains the widespread "intuition" that, for instance, "punishing" the innocent is an abomination whereas criminals deserve "to pay", while permitting the amelioration of treatment, resulting from the recognition, by some, that ultimately things are not morally that simple. Complex patterns of self-and-other deception emerge here. But, in addition to all the general practical and moral difficulties with

---

6   There are many complex ways in which illusion may be functional concerning free will, which we cannot consider here (see Smilansky 2000, section 8.4). We have focused on the main way, helping maintain false libertarian beliefs.

elitist solutions, which we cannot consider here, elitism can in any case be only a partial solution concerning free will. For, in the light of the reasons that we have already seen, people without illusions would have great difficulty in functioning.

The major solution will be one where, since two beliefs are vaguely but simultaneously held, yet commonly not set side by side (often, I claim, due to the presence of a motivated element), their contrary nature is not fully noticed. When acting in the light of compatibilist insights we suspend the insights of the ultimate hard determinist perspective (which we in any case are likely to be only dimly aware of). We *keep ourselves* on the level of compatibilist distinctions about local control and do not ask ourselves about the deeper question of the "givenness" of our choosing self; resisting threats to our vague, tacit libertarian assumptions. As Bernard Williams put it: "To the extent that the institution of blame works coherently, it does so because it attempts less than morality would like it to do … [it] takes the agent together with his character, and does not raise questions about his freedom to have chosen some other character" (1985, 194). The result is not philosophically neat, but that, after all, is its merit: the original reality was that we face practical dangers if we try to make our (incoherent or contradictory) conceptions *too clear*, but that we ought not to give any of them up entirely. Illusion, in short, allows us to have "workable beliefs".

We can *expect* people to be able to function adequately when they are compatibilistically free. There is ample basis in compatibilist local control for doing so, and enlisting such functioning is a condition of civilization. When we remain on the compatibilist level distinctions and excuses emerge which allow for normal human interaction, for our reactive lives, for the accumulation of moral credit and discredit and for moral discernment. However, awareness of the ultimate inevitability of any level of functioning endangers *good* functioning, and *darkens* our fundamental ways of appreciating ourselves as well as others; hence illusion is required. Illusion not only functions in motivated resistance to threats to our beliefs; but it also offers a positive view *underlying* our attitudes and practices. The affirmation of the responsible self is furthered by the vague tacit belief that one was and is able to do otherwise in the libertarian sense, and can have no general escape from the burden of responsibility. It is not that we find out the truth and then say "Let's keep quiet about this", but that illusion is intimately *entangled* with our free-will-related beliefs, reactions and practices. However, some awareness of deterministic elements can be useful, mitigating resentment of others or self-recriminations. Illusion allows us the advantages of the libertarian picture together with the mitigating element, without full awareness either of the incoherence of the libertarian picture or of the contrariness of the compatibilist and ultimate perspectives.

The interaction between illusion and reality is subtle: illusion is often the handmaiden of reality and, indeed, its constant support. Matters such as the acceptance of personal responsibility, adherence to the values and practices of a Community of Responsibility, and the sense of pride at having done "all that one could", are of immense value and find some grounding on the compatibilist level. They can be a non-illusory reality. However, they often depend upon lack of awareness of the ultimate perspective: illusion does not turn everything into falsehood but, on the contrary, is often the condition for the *emergence* of a valid and morally necessary reality.

Moreover, even those elements of our self-understanding that are solely illusory (and not compatibilistically-grounded reality merely assisted by illusion) may nevertheless be very important in themselves. Illusion not only helps to sustain independent reality, but is also *in itself* a sort of "reality", simply by virtue of its existence. The falseness of beliefs does not negate the fact that they exist for the believer. This is the way in which the libertarian beliefs exist. In addition to supporting the compatibilist non-illusory basis, illusion also *creates* a mental reality, such as a particular sense of worth, appreciation and moral depth associated with belief in libertarian free will, which would not exist without it. The effects of this illusory "reality" are sometimes positive. In a number of ways, then, illusion serves a crucial *creative* function, which is a basis for social morality and personal self-appreciation, in support of the compatibilist forms and beyond them.

The idea of illusion as morally necessary is repugnant and demeaning. As David Wiggins aptly put it:

> If a dilemma exists here it should first be acknowledged and felt as such. Only barbarism and reaction can benefit by concealment. If the unreformed notion of responsibility, the notion which is our notion, is a sort of metaphysical joke must we not at the very least create some safe time or place in everyday life to laugh at it? (Wiggins 1973, 55).

Nevertheless, I do not see any resources left to combat the ethical necessity of illusion in the free will case.

VI. From Naturalism To Illusionism

Revisionist naturalism sought to neutralize problems such as we saw by saying that we need not care, that there is no need to justify our attitudes and practices. Non-revisionist naturalism was more modest, merely insisting that in practice not much can change, and that for this reason there is little room for concern. Both stances were found to be unconvincing. We can understand the "conservative" instinct of naturalism but see that illusion is required. The insights of naturalism can be better defended in combination with an illusionistic element. We end up with the broad conclusion that our priority should be to live with the assumption of libertarian free will although there is no basis for this other than our very need to live with this assumption; but as we cannot accept this way of seeing things, and confront dangers to our beliefs, illusion must play a central role in our lives.

Reactive naturalism is important for Illusionism. Firstly, the failure of naturalism's "don't-worry" attitude leads to Illusionism. Naturalism has been seen by many as the last hope of compatibilism, and its weaknesses lead to recognition of the *role* and the *need* for illusion. Those who came to naturalism out of despair of previous alternatives now need to take a further step towards Illusionism. It can be said that naturalism and Illusionism are the last competitors. It is not by chance that they are located at the stage of the third question, the Consequences Question, unlike the more traditional positions. The progression to the third question reflects our acknowledgement that the answer to the Compatibility Question (are moral responsibility and the associated notions compatible with the absence of libertarian free will?), for all its importance, is not conclusive, and, moreover, that the deep meaning and practical significance of the free will issue is not fully encapsulated in the absence of libertarian free will and the answer to the Compatibility Question. The move to the third question (which asks about the consequences following from our previous results), and the insufficiency of naturalism on that question, serve to firmly identify illusion as the deep factor in the free will issue.

Finally, even more crucially, naturalism indicates the basis for illusion's practical *actualization*. Naturalism's partial successes, and not only its limitations, are instructive here. We are "naturally" tacit libertarians, and "naturally" resist threats to free will related beliefs, attitudes and practices: even when the defence of not seeing threats to libertarian free will in the first place is breached, the damage can be contained. The naturalistic foundation not only paves the way for illusion, but sets it at the heart of the human condition. Illusion is not some external, pragmatic, temporary way of coping with philosophical conclusions, but the very way humanity lives.[7]

References

Adkins, Arthur W.H., 1960, *Merit and Responsibility* (Oxford: Clarendon Press).
Anscombe, G.E.M., 1981, "Modern Moral Philosophy", *Collected Philosophical Papers*, vol. 3 (Oxford: Blackwell).
Bennett. Jonathan, 1980, "Towards a Theory of Punishment", *Philosophic Exchange*, vol. 3, pp. 43–54.
Feinberg, Joel, 1970, "Justice and Personal Desert", *Doing and Deserving* (Princeton: Princeton University Press).
Fischer, John Martin, 1994, *The Metaphysics of Free Will* (Oxford: Blackwell).
Furer-Haimendorf, Christoph Von, 1967, *Morals and Merit: A Study of Values and Social Controls in South Asian Societies* (London: Weidenfeld and Nicolson).
Glover, Jonathan, 1970, *Responsibility* (London: Routledge and Kegan Paul).
Hart H.L.A, 1970, *Punishment and Responsibility* (Oxford: Clarendon Press).
Hibbert, Christopher, 1963, *The Roots of Evil* (London: Weidenfeld and Nicolson).
Klein, Martha, 1990, *Determinism, Blameworthiness and Deprivation* (Oxford: Oxford University Press).
Kymlicka, Will, quoted in G.A. Cohen, 1989, "On the Currency of Egalitarian Justice", *Ethics*, vol. 99, pp. 906–44.
Pollock, Frederick and Frederic William Maitland, 1968, *The History of English*

---

[7] I am very grateful to Giora Hon, Hugh LaFollette, Iddo Landau, Jimmy Lenman, Andrew Moore, Paul Russell, Peter Strawson, Ralph Walker, and Jo Wolff, for helpful comments on drafts of this paper. Earlier versions were presented to the philosophy departments at Cardiff, Glasgow, the University of Kent at Canterbury, and Reading, and I have benefited from comments made by the participants. I am also very grateful to Michael McKenna and Paul Russell for including my paper in this collection.

Law, 2nd edn, vol. 2 (Cambridge: Cambridge University Press).

Russell, Paul, 1992, "Strawson's Way of Naturalizing Responsibility", *Ethics*, vol. 102, pp. 287–302.

Russell, Paul, 1995, *Freedom and Moral Sentiment* (New York: Oxford University Press).

Sayre, Francis Bowes, 1932, "Mens Rea", *Harvard Law Review*, vol. 45, pp. 974–1026.

Smilansky, Saul, 1993, "Does the Free Will Debate Rest on a Mistake", *Philosophical Papers*, vol. 22, pp. 173–88.

Smilansky, Saul, 1997, "Can a Determinist Respect Herself?", in C.H. Manekin and M. Kellner (eds), *Freedom and Moral Responsibility: General and Jewish Perspectives* (College Park: University of Maryland Press), pp. 85–98.

Smilansky, Saul, 2000, *Free Will and Illusion* (Oxford: Oxford University Press).

Snow, C.P., 1983, in John Halperin, *C.P. Snow: An Oral Biography* (Brighton: Harvester).

Strawson, Galen, 1986, *Freedom and Belief* (Oxford: Oxford University Press).

Strawson, P.F., 1980, "P. F. Strawson Replies" in Zak Van Straaten (ed.), *Philosophical Subjects* (Oxford: Clarendon Press).

Strawson, P.F., 1987, *Skepticism and Naturalism* (London: Methuen).

Strawson, P.F., 2003, "Freedom and Resentment" in Gary Watson (ed.), *Free Will* (Oxford: Oxford University Press).

Taylor, Gabriele, 1985, *Pride, Shame, and Guilt* (Oxford: Clarendon Press).

Vuoso, George, 1987, "Background, Responsibility and Excuse", *Yale Law Journal*, vol. 96, pp. 1661–86.

Wallace, R. Jay, 1994, *Responsibility and the Moral Sentiments* (Cambridge, MA: Harvard University Press).

Watson, Gary, 1987, "Responsibility and the Limits of Evil: Variations On a Strawsonian Theme" in Ferdinand Schoeman (ed.), *Responsibility, Character and the Emotions* (Cambridge: Cambridge University Press).

Wiggins, David, 1973, "Towards a Reasonable Libertarianism", in Ted Honderich (ed.), *Essays On Actions and Events* (London: Routledge and Kegan Paul).

Williams, Bernard, 1985, *Ethics and the Limits of Philosophy* (London: Fontana).

Chapter 13

Thinking with your Hypothalamus
Reflections on a Cognitive Role for the Reactive Emotions

David Zimmerman

In "Freedom and Resentment", P.F. Strawson argues that the "profound opposition" between the objective and reactive stances is quite compatible with our rationally retaining the latter as important elements in a recognizably human life. Unless he can establish this, he has no hope of establishing his version of compatibilism in the free will debate. But, because objectivity is associated so intimately with the rationally conducted explanation of action, it is not clear how the opposition of these stances is compatible with the rationality of the reactive attitudes. More to the point, it is not clear how an intellectual activity like shifting from the reactive to the objective stance can dispel reactive attitudes without thereby also rationally disqualifying them. I solve this puzzle by drawing on the idea that one cognitive component of emotions is the rationally optional "shift of attention", a feature which in turn helps to explain a lot about the role reactive emotions can play in the fixation of belief.

1. The Strawson Detente

P.F. Strawson's "Freedom and Resentment"[1] has had a pivotal influence on contemporary discussions of free will and responsibility. However, it has not been quite the influence Strawson had hoped for. Whereas he wished to effect a détente in the debate over the compatibility of determinism with free will and human responsibility, he succeeded merely in changing forever the terms in which this debate is posed. It will never again be posed simply as the question of whether a person whose actions are explainable in causal terms *is really* responsible for what he does, but always hereafter also as a question of whether he is an *appropriate object of the reactive attitudes*. This reposing has resolved little in the dialectic itself, but it has rendered it impossible for anyone to ignore the crucial importance of the reactive attitudes as an animating force in our practice of holding each other truly responsible.

---

1   P.F. Strawson, "Freedom and Resentment", reprinted in G. Watson (ed.), *Free Will* (Oxford: Oxford University Press, 1982), 59–80 (also reprinted in this volume, 19–36). [As previously mentioned, page references for "Freedom and Resentment" are to pages 19–36 of this volume, followed by (after the slash) the corresponding pages of Watson's *Free Will*. Thus, 'FR, 16/59' refers to this volume, p. 16/and *Free Will*, p. 59—the editors.]

Though it would be gratifying to make a dispositive contribution to Strawson's strategy of détente, I doubt that there is much new to be said about his ambitious project and the extent of its success.[2] But even if minimal progress is possible in that regard, Strawson's introduction of reactive attitudes into the general picture enables us to explore some little-noticed cognitive aspects of the emotions and the affective aspects of cognition, which remain little-noticed even in a time when "cognitivism" is still a dominant approach in the theory of the emotions. Naturally, I hope that they will turn out to illuminate some aspects of the free will debate as Strawson has reposed it, but I grant from the outset that incompatibilists are unlikely to be convinced.

As everyone knows, Strawson hoped to achieve a détente between incompatibilists and compatibilists (he called them "pessimists" and "optimists") about human freedom and causal determinism, by exacting "a formal withdrawal on one side in return for a substantial concession on the other". (Strawson, reprinted in Watson, 1982, 60. All page references are to this edition.) He hoped that the pessimists could be induced to retreat from "the panicky metaphysics of libertarianism" (80) if the optimists would only acknowledge that the twentieth-century compatibilism dominant then (circa 1960), of the sort generally associated with Schlick, Hobart and Foot,[3] offers an unrecognizably drab picture of the human practices which ground the concept of full-blooded responsibility. Strawson was confident that the lacuna in this exclusively consequentialist picture could be filled without resort to postulating agent-causes, noumenal selves and the like. Détente could be achieved at a relatively low price, he thought, if all sides would only recognize how "reactive attitudes", like resentment and gratitude, moral indignation and approbation, animate, indeed constitute, the human practice of responsibility.

His main line of argument has found few enthusiastic takers, especially not in the pessimists' camp. (This is what one would expect: Schlickian optimists have a lot less to lose.)[4] Few have been willing to grant that a full "objectivity" of attitude towards persons would result from or be appropriate *if* a general acceptance of

---

2 Some notable entries in a massive literature include, J. Bennett, "Accountability", in van Straaten (ed.), *Philosophical Subjects: Essays Presented to P. F. Strawson* (Oxford: Oxford University Press, 1980), 14–47; A.J. Ayer, "Free Will and Rationality", in van Straaten, 1980, 187–214; G. Strawson, *Freedom and Belief* (Oxford: Oxford University Press, 1986), Ch. 5; S. Wolf, "The Importance of Free Will", reprinted in Fischer and Ravizza (eds), *Perspectives on Moral Responsibility* (Ithaca: Cornell University Press, 1993), 101–18; R.J. Wallace, *Responsibility and the Moral Sentiments* (Cambridge: Harvard University Press, 1994), Ch. 2; P. Russell, "Strawson's Way of Naturalizing Responsibility", *Ethics* 102 (January, 1992), 287–302; and G. Watson, "Responsibility and the Limits of Evil: Variations on a Strawsonian Theme", in F. Schoeman (ed.), *Responsibility, Character and the Emotions* (Cambridge: Cambridge University Press, 1987), 256–86.

3 M. Schlick, *The Problems of Ethics* (New York, 1939), Ch. 7. R.E. Hobart, reprinted in "Free Will as Involving Indeterminism and Inconceivable without It", in B. Berofsky (ed.), *Free Will and Determinism* (New York: Harper and Row, 1966), 63–94; and P. Foot, "Free Will as Involving Determinism", reprinted in Berofsky, 95–108.

4 J. Bennett has been Strawson's most forceful champion on the optimists' side. Bennett, 1980.

determinism were completely to suppress our proneness to the reactive attitudes.[5] Fewer still have been convinced that the reactive attitudes are genuinely beyond the constraints of theoretical rationality.[6] But, still, Strawson has forever changed the way philosophers pose the central question ... no mean feat.[7]

2. The "Profound Opposition" of the Objective and the Reactive Stances

The centerpiece of Strawson's argument, and the point of departure for my investigation of the cognitive dimension of the emotions, is his contrast between two stances we take up toward people, the "objective" and the "reactive", and his claim that they stand in "profound opposition" to each other. In an oft-quoted passage he puts it this way:

> What I want to contrast is the attitude (or range of attitudes) of involvement or participation in a human relationship, on the one hand, and what might be called the objective attitude (or range of attitudes) to another human being, on the other. Even in the same situation ... they are not altogether *exclusive* of each other; but they are profoundly *opposed* to each other. To adopt the objective attitude to another human being is to see him, perhaps, as an object of social policy; as a subject for what ... might be called treatment; as something certainly to be taken account, perhaps precautionary account, of; to be managed, handled or cured or trained; perhaps simply to be avoided .... The objective attitude may be emotionally toned in many ways but not in all ways: it may include repulsion or fear, it may include pity, even love, though not all kinds of love. But it cannot include the range of reactive feelings and attitudes which belong to involvement or participation with others in inter-personal human relationships; it cannot include resentment and gratitude, forgiveness, anger, or the sort of love which two adults can sometimes be said to feel reciprocally for each other. If your attitude toward someone is wholly objective, then though you may fight him, you cannot quarrel with him, and though you may talk to him, even negotiate with him, you cannot reason with him. You can at most pretend to quarrel, or to reason, with him (66, Emphasis in the original).

Though many have questioned one detail or another in Strawson's catalogue of the objective and the reactive attitudes,[8] the broad distinction he draws has withstood the test of time: Strawson is obviously onto an important division in the kinds of inter-personal attitudes we take up toward each other. It is less clear precisely in what respect(s) these stances are "profoundly *opposed*" to each other. It takes us only so far to note that while the objective stance is animated principally by *epistemic or consequentialist* motives, the reactive stance never is. In Bennett's useful if negative

---

5 D. Pereboom, for example, suggests that rich enough surrogates for the reactive emotions would survive even a mass conversion to a belief in determinism. See his "Determinism *al Dente*", *Nous* 1995, 38–9.

6 G. Strawson, 1986, Ch. 5.

7 Whether this shift of perspective has advanced the causes of clarity and depth in our understanding of the conditions of human responsibility is another matter. The question is whether starting with the concept of "holding responsible" is the best way to pursue an investigation of the conditions of "being responsible".

8 See the Wallace, Bennett, and Pereboom references in note 2.

characterization, an attitude is reactive if and only if "it is a pro or con attitude which could *not* explain x's engaging in *teleological* inquiry into how y works" either as an end in itself, say to satisfy x's curiousity, or as a means to some further, perhaps policy-oriented or therapeutic, end of x's.[9] Illuminating though this is, it still leaves open *what kind of tension* exists between the stances, a matter crucial to Strawson's ultimate goal of détente. For, he clearly holds that taking up the objective stance even toward a normal person, that is to say, one who is subject to none of the standard excusing or exempting conditions, tends to drive out the reactive stance. The quoted passage clearly implies this. Moreover, Strawson goes on to say quite explicitly that "... we *can* sometimes look with something like this same eye on the behavior of the normal and the mature. We *have* this resource and can sometimes use it: as a refuge, say from the strains of involvement; or as an aid to policy; or simply out of intellectual curiousity." '(FR, 25/66–7; emphasis in the original). But until he can explain how this dispelling of one stance by the other is possible *without* thereby revealing the reactive emotions to be a rationally defective way to respond to the other, he has no chance of convincing incompatibilists that they are wrong to insist that a belief in determinism renders such attitudes incompatible with "the facts as we know them", and thus irrational. I pursue this question here, not because I think that Strawson still has a chance to make out his full case (I, along with many others, have long ago given up on that), but rather because no Strawsonian account of responsibility has yet made even the minimal case for the epistemic rationality of reactive attitudes in the face of a particularly puzzling feature of the relationship between cognition and affect.

3. Cognitive Dispelling without Rational Disqualifying

The puzzle is this: how is it possible that a specifically *cognitive* or *intellectual* operation *psychologically dispels* an attitude without in so doing also *rationally disqualifying* the attitude?[10] The psychological operation in question is, of course, the shift from the reactive to the objective stance. Its terminus is specifically cognitive or intellectual in that the constitutive feature of the objective stance is inquiry into how another person functions. And, on the face of it, any mental operation which increases a person's capacity to augment his or her justified belief or even knowledge ought also to count as a move toward greater rational control over her beliefs about the world. But that suggests that the shift from the reactive to the objective stance is by its very nature a move toward greater rational control over one's beliefs, which reflects badly upon the cognitive role and epistemic status of the reactive stance, and raises the question of how such a move away from it could possibly fail to reveal its cognitive or intellectual inferiority to the objective stance.

---

9 Bennett, 1980, 38.

10 This way of posing the question is (with the exception of a couple of adverbs) due to Bennett, 1980, 38.

3.1. Cognitive dispelling

Before we can solve the puzzle we must distinguish among kinds of psychological dispelling, for the question is not how one psychological state can *simply* dispel another, in the sense of crowding it out. This simpler phenomenon is a commonplace of what might be called "psychological ecology", for even the best of us can seldom consciously accommodate more than a few complicated psychological states or activities at a time. For example, the proverbial severe headache can dim any remnant of the lust one felt so recently and so insistently. In this case, the psychological item which does the crowding out is a non-intentional state, as is the state which is crowded out.[11] Sometimes, however, the state which merely ecologically dispels is distinctly intentional, as for example, when a long aesthetic or political argument produces the weary realization that your prospective sexual partner is an unregenerate devotee of *The Sound of Music* or of Marxist-Leninism, which in turn drives out your lingering lust. With mere ecological crowding, two crucial elements are missing (aside from the lust and a shared aesthetic or political outlook). One mental item, whether intentional or not, plays a purely causal role in dispelling the other, so that the crowding out cannot count as a cognitive operation. Moreover, there is no prospect for any distinctively *inferential* relationships between them. But where the possibility of inference is completely ruled out, so is the cognitive aspect of the relationship. The point is not that cognitive relationships among psychological items cannot be causal at all; it is rather that they cannot be *merely* causal. A rational inference can perfectly well supervene upon a causal chain; it just has to be the right kind.

And what kind is that?[12] Though the ultimate answer will probably come only from cognitive science, here is a provisional stab. A causal relationship between two mental states counts as "cognitive" or "intellectual" in the sense required only if the explanation of how MS1 drives out MS2 can plausibly be construed as engaging in "inferential activity" the person who instantiates the states. The key phrase is to be interpreted broadly in two respects, to include: 1) a full range of inferential processes from the most to the least conscious (in the sense of, "explicitly registered at the personal level"); and 2) a full range of inference patterns from the strictly deductive on down through the inductive, abductive, heuristic, and so on. (The vagueness is unavoidable.)

---

11 This partitioning of mental states into the intentional and the non-intentional is standard in the literature, but it has not gone unchallenged. M. Tye, for example, argues that allegedly non-intentional states like pains and itches do actually have intentional objects. (See *Ten Problems of Consciousness* [Cambridge, MIT Press, 1997)].) I cannot linger here to argue for the conventional view. Nor do I need to, for even if Tye is correct, the distinction suggested in the text between merely causal / ecological crowding out and genuinely cognitive dispelling still holds up. On a more specific level, one might also cavil at the idea that *lust* is always a non-intentional state. This is probably wise, because "lust" probably covers a range of mental states, some of which may well have intentional as well as merely carnal objects. I owe this insight to Andrea Scotland.

12 We encounter here a recurrent problem in spelling out causal theories or theories with an important causal component in any detail, namely, specifying the difference between "deviant" and the "right kind of" causal chains. Even if I could solve it, trying to do so here would take us too far afield.

Consider the paradigm case in which one psychological state or event cognitively or intellectually dispels another. Ivan is lying in his sick bed pondering the meaning of his life. Hitherto he has believed that he would live forever. But he reflects: "All men are mortal." "I am a man." "Therefore, I am mortal." "But if I too am mortal, then I cannot live forever." "And I am mortal!" "I no longer am able to believe that I will live forever." Thus the onset of Ivan's crisis: he entertains the familiar syllogism, applies it (with horror) to himself, and as a consequence one of his most cherished beliefs about himself is dispelled forever, and in the bargain it is disqualified from any further rational acceptance.[13]

Of course, Strawson would do well to resist this as his model of the sort of relationship of "profound opposition" between the reactive and objective stances, because embracing it would give the game away to the incompatibilist. She insists that what explains the evaporation of the reactive attitude is precisely the person's coming to form the belief that the other's action is to be explained causally, conjoined with his standing belief in the principle of macroscopic determinism. But if the underlying pattern which explains the psychological dispelling of resentment or moral indignation is strictly deductive in this fashion, then the fact of the dispelling *does* reveal that the reactive attitude is rationally disqualified.

But this leaves Strawson with a tough question to answer: how can the specifically cognitive operation of inquiring into the causes of another person's behavior, informed by the conviction that all (macroscopic) events are explainable in terms of causal laws and facts about the past, reveal in its course why the other person performed precisely the action one was nursing the resentment or indignation about, and can then drive out precisely that reactive feeling by the very fact of producing precisely that knowledge, *without* at the same time revealing the feeling to have been irrational, because based on precisely the ignorance of its origins that the shift to the objective stance rectified? This *is* a puzzle.

To solve it Strawson needs to identify a kind of psychological process which is (1) neither merely a matter of ecological crowding nor of doxastic-obligation-creating, but is at the same time, (2) a recognizably cognitive operation in the sense that it enters into and aids recognizably cognitive (i.e. inferential) processing, (3) in doing so tends to dispel or elicit or otherwise transform emotions, but (4) *nonetheless leaves the cognizing-emoting person with the theoretical option of reassuming the emotions without rational penalty.* This is a tall order. If he were able to fill it Strawson would have taken one modest leap forward in his campaign to convince the pessimists to give up their "panicky metaphysics" of the person. ... one leap, but not the whole

---

13 This is not to deny the important point that deductive logic is not, strictly speaking, a normative theory of inference per se, because even with such a "syllogism" in hand Ivan does have the rational option of either drawing the dreaded conclusion or rejecting one or more of the premises. See G. Harman, *Thought* (Princeton: Princeton University Press: 1973). Of course, when the deductive "inference" is so simple and its premises so empirically incontrovertible, such a recourse is bound to exact the price of irrationality elsewhere. For more on the "indeterminacy" of reasons at an especially crucial point in the argument of the present paper, see section 5.

way, for I don't think that is in the cards. For my purposes, however, it would be enough simply to come up with a likely *candidate* for such a process.

It is tempting to try to explain the phenomenon in question by simply weakening the "rules of inference" which drive the process of dispelling. In our paradigm case, they are strictly *deductive*. Bedridden Ivan employs *modus ponens* to arrive at his unhappy *apercu*. However, we can easily imagine cases in which a person's mental state is dispelled or elicited or otherwise transformed by virtue of the fact that he follows certain rules of *inductive* inference (if there are any), or even methodological guidelines for making inferences to the best explanation (if there are any rules of *abductive* inference). Consider a variation on the lust case: forming the belief that the other is a fan of Bolshevism or of the von Trapp family when conjoined with the "major premise" that (as the film critic Pauline Kael once wisely remarked) "sex is the great leveller, taste the great divider",[14] drives out a genuinely intentional state, namely the desire that one embark upon a long-term relationship with the other. This inference by no means yields a strictly deductive argument for the irrationality of pursuing the affair, but it provides a pretty good indication of it.

But loosening up the "rules of inference" in this fashion is not a very promising route to our ultimate goal, because even though there is considerably more slack between "premise" and "conclusion" when the rules of inference are *non*-deductive, the very fact that the cognitive operation employing them dispels the state *does* tend to reveal the irrationality of the latter. If this were not so, then induction and abduction could play no properly *normative* role in the regulation of belief and desire. But they do.

3.2. Rationally optional shifts of stance

Unfortunately, an even half-way satisfying explanation of the phenomenon of cognitive dispelling without rational disqualifying would require much better accounts than we have at present of both the kinematics of how emotions are summoned and dispelled, and the logical-cum-epistemological constraints on their rationality. But, as Amelie Rorty has observed, "behind debates about whether specific emotions are incorrigible stand yet further disagreements about the character of cognition and its relation to affect".[15] We seem to have painted Strawson (or perhaps ourselves) into a corner.

Happily, Rorty herself and Ronnie de Sousa[16] have done innovative work on the rationality of the emotions which presents us with a real candidate for solving the

---

14 In her review of the "Sound of Music", reprinted in Pauline Kael, *I Lost it at the Movies* (New York: Marion Boyars Publishers, 1965).

15 A. Rorty, "Introduction", in A. Rorty (ed), *Explaining Emotions* (Berkeley and Los Angeles: University of California Press, 1980), 3.

16 Rorty, "Explaining Emotions", in 1980, 103–26; R. de Sousa, "The Rationality of Emotions", in Rorty, 1980, 127–52, and *The Rationality of Emotions* (Cambridge: MIT Press, 1987).Though this was not always so. Along with Rorty and de Sousa, R.C. Solomon was also a key contributor to the "cognitivist revolution" in the philosophy of the emotions. See his "Emotions and Choice", in Rorty, 1980, 251–82, and *The Passions: The Myth and Nature of Human Emotions* (New York: Doubleday, 1976). There is a third alternative to regarding emotions as partly *constituted* by their cognitive components (whether fully or quasi-

puzzle about dispelling-without-disqualifying. For, it suggests that emotions have a kind of component with the following interesting properties: it is cognitive in that it plays an intellectual role in the fixation of a person's belief, but at the same time it is itself immune (mostly, anyway) from rational criticism in terms of the usual epistemic and logical standards of belief-formation. The emerging possibility which interests us (and should interest Strawson) is this: emotions partly constituted by such a component could be dispelled by intellectual operations driven by the component while at the same time remaining rational options for the person should he choose to encourage their reemergence or should they later simply befall him.

And what sort of component might that be? While it has become an orthodoxy in the philosophy of the emotions to stress their specifically *propositional* cognitive components, most notably the beliefs which partly constitute them, Rorty and de Sousa have been among the few to recognize their cognitive *sub*-propositional components. These might provide us with the cognitive dimension we need to explain the phenomenon of cognitive-dispelling-without-rational-disqualifying.[17]

Rorty implies that one serious over-simplification in the usual "cognitivist" conception of the emotions is its over-emphasis on their explicitly propositional components. She suggests, rather, that an adequate cognitivism recognizes a continuum ranging from (a) *explicitly propositional beliefs* with well-defined truth-conditions, all the way down to (e) *quasi-intentional states* which can, in principle, be specified in *(merely) extensional* terms (her e.g.: highly saturated colors are typically more salient for normal persons than less saturated ones). In between, she suggests, we find: (b) *vague beliefs* with truth conditions which can be only roughly specified; (c) *patterns of intentional salience which can be formulated as general beliefs* (her e.g.: a pattern of focussing on men's behavior as aggressive but competent, rather than hostile and insecure, which might be formulated as a set of predictions about behavior); (d) *patterns of intentional salience which cannot easily be formulated as beliefs* (her e.g.: focusing on the military defensibility of a landscape rather than on its aesthetic properties).[18]

We are especially interested in components of types (c) and (d), the *patterns of intentional salience* in an emoting person's *field of attention*. To be sure, reactive emotions can be and no doubt are frequently dispelled also by a change in a person's *beliefs*, both explicitly propositional and vague, as orthodox cognitivism would have it. But this familiar phenomenon is of no help in explaining the very possibility

---

propositional) and regarding the relationship as purely contingent. One could *individuate* instances of emotion-types in terms of their *essential* causal (cognitive) antecedents and/or consequents. J. Elster, defends such an alternative version in his *Alchemies of the Mind: Rationality and the Emotions* (Cambridge: Cambridge University Press, 1999).

17 For this suggestion to be defensible in the end, two hard questions must eventually be confronted: (1) given the rough characterization of cognitive states as those which are "inference-supporting", does the solution in the text presuppose that sub-propositional states can enter into inferential relationships? And, (2) If so, can they? These are hard questions which it would take us too far afield to try to answer here. I hope I have established a convincing enough explanation of the phenomenon of dispelling-that-is-not-also-disqualifying even without such answers.

18 Rorty, 1980, 112–13.

of cognitive-dispelling-without-rational-disqualifying, for the obvious reason that that is precisely the sort of intellectual operation the incompatibilist will seize on to make his case against Strawson. But is that the *only* available explanation of the phenomenon? With help from Rorty and de Sousa we can, I think, see that it is not.

It would be well at this point to remind ourselves of the present dialectic. I am not trying to provide a full vindication of Strawson's insistence that no merely theoretical commitment would, could, or should purge our lives of a tendency so deep as our proneness to reactive attitudes. I have already given up on that project by retreating to the more modest one of explaining how reactive attitudes are not irrational in one specific respect: that a distinctly cognitive operation can psychologically dispel them without by that very fact revealing them to have been irrational. This would not quite make Strawson's case, but it would advance the cause by (in his own phrase) "giving the optimist something more to say" (FR, 21/62) in response to the incompatibilist's likely charge that all psychological dispelling via recognizably cognitive processes must reveal irrationality. From full retreat to wary standoff is not a bad development for the compatibilist at this juncture in the debate.

4. A Case of Suspected Perfidy and Fading Trust

To fix ideas, let us bring the Rorty/de Sousa thesis to bear on a particular case in order to shed what light we can on the phenomenon of cognitive-dispelling-without-rational-disqualifying. Consider one in which the objective and reactive stances are in some tension with each other, as Strawson suggests, *but also in some respects mutually support each other* as the story unfolds. Suppose that you come to suspect that X, a long-time friend, has betrayed personal confidences you have shared with her over many an evening drink during an emotionally hard time. You thought she was a true *confidante* who could be trusted to keep counsel, but there is evidence that she has revealed to a perfect stranger Y aspects of your personal life which are nobody's business but trusted friends. Naturally, you start to feel hurt and angry and resentful. But because X has been such a good friend in the past you start to doubt the force of the evidence. Caught between lingering feelings of friendship and rising resentment, you become especially attuned to her behavior. You notice little things you would have missed before, like her tone of voice in recent encounters, and her too-persistent attempts to mention private aspects of your life in the presence of mere acquaintances, over your gentle requests that she change the subject.

But still, you are not really *sure* that X was the friend who betrayed your confidences. You *feel* (that does seem to be the word for it) that you need more evidence to justify your suspicion and thus your resentment. Again, you pick up on something you ordinarily would never have noticed, much less made anything of. A mutual friend Z lets it drop that he knows something about you which you have never told him and which no one could know unless a close friend of yours had disclosed it. Who? That sets you to thinking about which of your friends knows both Y *and* Z. There are several, but which one was the indiscreet chatterer? You go back over what Z said that the chatterer said. You come to realize that it involved things only X could have known. You start to become more certain that she was the one to have betrayed your confidences to Y.

As the evidence of her perfidy accumulates, it occurs to you (a bit late perhaps) that X might have had a good reason for saying what she said. You think back to all those occasions when she was a real friend to you. You start to become especially alert to the possibility that her motives this time were quite above reproach. Perhaps she truly thought that the troubles you had been having during that difficult time had left their mark and were so seriously affecting your spirits that other friends of yours should be alerted. To be sure, after you explicitly told X that you did not want your confidences to go any further, she did talk about them in public, but perhaps her loquaciousness was just a momentary lapse of judgment, not betrayal. Perhaps X thought that this was the best way to help you get solace and support from a wider circle of people. But you remember, again, that you explicitly asked her not to reveal the facts in question ... to anyone! Suddenly her reckless chatter does not seem like a (possibly misguided) attempt to help, but just that ... reckless chatter. But still, you remind yourself, X *has* been such a steady and understanding friend for all these years ....

These memories and the warm feelings they elicit set you to wondering whether *you* have done something to hurt *her* and to have provoke this kind of reaction ... or, whether something horrible is going on in her own life that she hasn't told you about which is clouding her judgment and sending her a bit out of control. But the more you go round and round, seeking some justifying or mitigating fact or other, the more frustrated you get: there simply aren't any. So, your anger and resentment keep mounting. To put it pedantically, you are becoming possessed by "negative reactive attitudes".

The story can take many different turns at this juncture. Scenario One: You still are not certain that X has betrayed your trust, so you keep an eye out for more evidence of her (un)trustworthiness. Scenario Two: Your resentment lingers without overwhelming you, so you are civil to X but remain wary of her. Scenario Three: You start to worry about the effect that all this resentment and anger is having on you, so you resolve to give X the benefit of the doubt and carry on your relationship as though no suspicions had ever arisen. Scenario Four: You have the same worry about being overwhelmed by anger and resentment, but this time you decide to become a motivational psychologist specializing in the dynamics of friendship, trust, and betrayal, in the hope that having a better understanding of both the general phenomenon and X's particular psychology will dispel your feelings once and for all. (And, perhaps into the bargain give you some insight into why you reacted so very angrily.) Scenario Five: You have the same worry, but this time you decide to steep yourself in the literature of incompatibilism. You ponder the arguments of hard determinists. You ponder the arguments of libertarians. As a result you become transformed from a complacent compatibilist into "a genuine incompatibilist determinist",[19] thoroughly convinced that because there is a causal explanation for why X did what she did, she was not free to do otherwise in any genuinely responsibility-grounding fashion. Your anger and resentment dissipate; you are amazed you ever could have felt them so strongly. And so on ....

---

19 G. Strawson, 1986, 281–6.

Whichever ending the story might have, one theme is pronounced during the narrative. Your reactive emotions—resentment, anger, the temptation to forgiveness, the warmth of friendly nostalgia, and so on—play a distinctively *cognitive* role throughout in regulating your inquiry into the question of whether X has in fact been perfidious. How? As Rorty and de Sousa would put it, by *shifting your attention* from one set of facts to another, and then back over the same set of facts, with more care the second time around; by inducing you to see *patterns of salience* in the facts which you would otherwise have missed; by sometimes slowing you down and sometimes speeding you up, as genuine opportunities for inquiry ebb and flow.[20]

This is where Rorty's components (c) and (d) and maybe even (e) might help us to understand the phenomenon in question. (Recall that they involve: (c) patterns of intentional salience which can be formulated as general beliefs; (d) patterns of intentional salience which cannot easily be so formulated; and (e) quasi-intentional states which can in principle be formulated only in extensional terms.) The incompatibilist might (just) be willing to concede that patterns of salience and shifts of attention are cognitive elements involved in the ebb and flow of your resentment and anger in the narrative proper and in culminating Scenarios One, Two, and Three. But this is an important concession (at least within our limited dialectical framework), for it involves the recognition that emotions have cognitive constituents other than explicitly propositional ones, which play important roles in the conduct of inquiry. In the narrative proper, you want to know whether X has in fact revealed aspects of your private life. If emotions are actually *constituted* (in part) by quasi-propositional components like patterns of salience in a person's field of attention, then your resentment and anger play an important role in your attempt to marshal evidence for and against your hypothesis about X's perfidy.

Moreover, if the items on the cognitive continuum Rorty identifies are not mutually exclusive in particular cases of taking on or shedding emotions, then compatibilists have an explanation of why your anger and resentment dissipate in Scenario Four which they can offer as a plausible competitor with the incompatibilist explanation. Incompatibilists insist that you no longer feel resentment and anger toward X because you have learned what there is to know about the psychological aetiology of her action. Compatibilists can now reply that there is an alternative explanation for why you have shed your reactive emotions toward X. In shifting to the objective, i.e. the explanatory-cum-therapeutic perspective, you shift also the patterns of salience in your field of attention. But since such patterns are part of what *constitute* an emotional state as the

---

[20] Rorty, 1980, 108–14; de Sousa, 1980, 134–42. Though I intend my title, "Thinking with Your Hypothalamus", to gesture figuratively and playfully toward the role of the emotions in directing cognition, there is good reason for a more literal construal. Antonio Damasio's investigation of patients with a certain kind of frontal lobe lesion indicates that "reduction in emotion may constitute an ... important source of irrational behavior". His hypothesis is that a specific area of the pre-frontal cortex is responsible for processing information it receives from the limbic system about past emotional responses to kinds of situations. When this area is destroyed patients are incapable of feeling certain emotions and thus very bad at practical reasoning in the real world (even though they perform at or above standard levels on reasoning tests). Evidently, the limbic system *is* importantly implicated in cognitive functioning. For the details, see Damasio, *Descartes' Error* (New York, Putnam, 1994). (The quotation is from 53.)

kind of emotion it is, this shift in patterns of salience *entails* that you no longer feel anger and resentment, just as surely as coming to believe (say) that your lover has not sexually betrayed you with another entails that the disagreeable feeling which lingers is not jealousy, or that coming to believe that P has no real connection to you entails that the warm feeling you have about her accomplishments is not pride. Just as explicitly propositional beliefs are among the cognitive *constituents* of emotions, so also are quasi-propositional aspects of attention. It is not simply that your shift of attention from X's behavior in the meeting room to (say) her childhood history contingently *causes* your resentment to dissipate; your shift of attention, more specifically your registration of certain patterns of salience in her behavior, is part of *what it is* for you no longer to feel resentment toward her. But with such an explanation in hand, Strawson can move a crucial step closer to an explanation of how a cognitive shift from the reactive to the objective stance can psychologically dispel an emotion like resentment without thereby revealing it to be irrational.

5. (One Reason) Why We Have Emotions

There is still a gap in the explanation, however, because we still have to make out a case for the rational *optionality* of such shifts of attention when they play their appointed role in the conduct of inquiry. If, instead, they were always rationally required, then the very fact that your resentment was dispelled (constitutively) by a *non-optional, rationally required* shift in the patterns of salience in your field of attention *would* reveal that you had indeed been irrational to have harbored such a reactive feeling towards X in the first place. So, we must ask whether such shifts of attention are really rationally optional in the sense the argument needs? To pursue an answer, let us consider the idea behind de Sousa's characterization of emotions as "determinate patterns of perceptual salience among objects of attention, lines of inquiry and inferential strategies", an intriguing formula he offers in the course of some tantalizing speculations about *what emotions are for*.[21]

First, try to imagine what a rational being completely devoid of emotions would be like. This turns out to be surprisingly difficult. The mere fact of a Mr. Spock's surface impassivity and constant invocation of the virtues of "logic" will hardly do the trick. (My banal example.) De Sousa speculates that such a being would be either "a Cartesian animal-machine" that functions as efficiently as (say) an ant or some kind of Kantian pure rational will. His hunch is that one reason we have emotions is precisely that we are neither insects nor angels, that is to say, neither beings completely equipped *ab initio* with a set of valences set to be triggered upon appropriate and relatively simple environmental prompting, nor beings blessed (or cursed?) with pure practical reasoning capacities which operate with perfect efficiency, always guiding us to the truth.

It is the way de Sousa develops this hunch that interests me. What the "reasoning" of actual insects and mythical angels have in common is "complete determinacy" at both the epistemic level and the practical level which rests upon it. In making their way through their worlds, neither insects nor angels need ever to consider the

---

21 Rorty, 1980, 108–14; de Sousa, 1980, 134–42.

possibility that they might go wrong. Therefore they have no need of techniques for dealing with the *indeterminacies* that the world might throw in their paths. But we human reasoners do, because for us "there is no such thing as fully determinate rationality" (Sousa, 135). This is not a concession to philosophical scepticism, but rather the acknowledgement of what actually happens when the various aspects of reason inform human theoretical inquiry about the empirical world and when they guide us on our practical path through it. One kind of *indeterminacy of application* infects all of the "rules and principles" which inform theory and practice, even in the context of justification, certainly inductive guidelines, abductive heuristics and theorems of decision theory, but even the rules of deductive inference, which are formally well-regimented.

This suggests a hypothesis: "the function of emotion is to fill gaps left by (mere wanting plus) 'pure reason' in the determination of action and belief" (Sousa, 136). And this in turn leads to a reformulation (in the manner quoted earlier) of the hypothesis about what the emotions are for, in a way that brings out nicely their guiding role in the conduct of inquiry both as end in itself and at the service of practice: "Emotions are determinate patterns of salience among objects of attention, lines of inquiry, and inferential strategies" (Sousa, 137). Emotions are valuable *qua* modes of attention for creatures like us, who live in highly variable worlds and whose behavior towards each other is not rigidly stereotyped, because logical considerations alone, even when supplemented by any of the well-recognized epistemic and methodological principles, "do not determine salience, what to attend to, what to inquire about" (136) in contexts in which this kind of focal efficiency is crucial to the advancement and protection of basic interests.

In the present dialectical context, we might take this as an observation about how rational constraints operate either in the context of justification or in the context of discovery. Let us consider each in turn. In the context of *justification* we apply whatever standards are available to the assessment of attitudes. But, as noted a moment ago, no standard determines its own application. Thus, even in the realm of justification, there is a horizon of indeterminacy, at least locally. But this suggests that patterns of attention might be well suited to fill whatever gaps there are in the application of these standards of belief-selection. Even if the members of the set are well-supported roughly equally, it is often important that one endorse one of these beliefs, if only to get on with inquiring, not to mention with living. Shifts of attention are well (though not uniquely) suited to do the job.

De Sousa's hypothesis is even more plausible as an explanation of what goes on in the context of *discovery,* because that is where the *rational optionality* of our attitudes is most unfettered. In our tale of suspected perfidy, for example, your resentment directs and redirects your attention to the facts before you, revealing some patterns to be salient in one way (perfidy) or the other (good faith) and others to be neutral. To be sure, there are more and less effective ways of deploying an emotion like resentment in guiding an "inquiry" about suspected perfidy, but none of them is rationally mandatory, for despite the high hopes of an earlier phase in the philosophy of science there is, after all, no "logic of discovery". An inquirer has a lot of rational slack in deciding what methodological heuristics to employ, including how to direct her attention.[22] Thus, the first four scenarios (and probably still others) are *rationally open* to you as you attempt to figure out whether your friend has indeed betrayed your confidence. That is, to say, in each you are free to move from the reactive to the objective stance and *then back again to the reactive*, without thereby revealing yourself to have made an irrational turn.[23] (Scenario Five is a special case. See below.)

Of course, this does not entail that the shift from the reactive to the objective and back again will in fact turn out to have been an equally reliable way in all four scenarios of discovering what the facts of the case are and what attitude you should take up toward your colleague, for there is always the possibility "that in pursuing a rationally optional course, someone may come to realize that one of her prior beliefs/attitudes is rationally disqualified".[24] This is certainly true, but epistemic rationality in the context of *discovery* is a preeminently prospective notion, in that a person might be equally rational at a time t in employing any member of a set of methods or heuristics, only a proper-subset of which end up actually yielding true and/or rational beliefs (full stop) at t+1.

To be sure, it might well turn out in the context of *justification* that "once one has taken the rationally optional step of considering the implications of determinism, it may not be rationally open for [one] to discount [one's] conclusions".[25] This too is no doubt true. In Scenario Five, for example, you become a genuine determinist incompatibilist,

---

22 This is not to deny for one moment that there are better and worse ways of conducting inquiry in the context of discovery. Philosophers often invoke hackneyed examples of how intuition, mystical belief, sheer prejudice and the like sometimes operate in the discovery of important scientific truths. But, even though Kekule did discover the structure of the benzene ring after an evening of staring into the fire which prompted a vision of a snake eating its tale, and even though Watson did co-discover the structure of DNA while treating Rosalind Franklin somewhat shabbily, these incidents provide no good reason to recommend to young chemists that they spend inordinate amounts of time hanging around fireplaces, or to young biologists that they take up a sexist stance toward their co-workers. Even absent a *logic* of discovery, there is better advice to give them. My point in this paper might be put this way: *taking up the reactive stance* might well be among the kinds of methodological techniques we might advise some inquirers to employ. Not all inquirers, to be sure. This advice is probably apt only in small-scale inter-personal contexts involving "inquiring" friends and acquaintances. Even there, moreover, the technique will no doubt have to be used with skillful *indirection*, given the essentially non-consequentialist structure of reactive emotions. On a related point, see Section 6.3: "Genuinely Reactive or Merely Epistemically Useful?".

23 Of course, it would over-intellectualize everything to suggest that these reactive emotions play a *solely* cognitive role. You *are* damned angry! You *do* resent X intensely! *Only* to have warm memories of genuine friendship overcome you! *Only* to have them swept away in turn by that same resurging anger and resentment. And so on. In fact, from a philosophical point of view, one of the most interesting things about the narrative is precisely how your reactive attitudes both have an emotional life of their own and at the same time play a distinctively cognitive role in your "inquiry". (Though at such an emotionally fraught time of your life, that is the last word you would use for it.)

24 This objection was raised by an anonymous referee for *Philosophy and Phenomenological Research*.

25 As was this one.

which does commit you to the belief that the truth of determinism is indeed incompatible with the rationality of resuming your reactive attitudes toward other people, which in turn commits you to the belief that all your reactive attitudes are irrational. But my argument is not designed to rule this out as a possibility, nor need it do so. The real threat to my argument would come, more specifically, from an *incompatibilist* resolution of the *original* dispute between the optimists and the pessimists over the question of whether free will, and the reactive attitudes which presuppose it, also presuppose the truth of indeterminism or agent-determinism. But in the current dialectical context that is not in the cards. The most I am trying to establish here is that there is a good explanation for how the shift from the reactive to the objective stance can cognitively dispel resentment without thereby revealing it to have been irrational.

Of course, under the very particular circumstances of Scenario Five, the shift in question does commit *you* to the belief that your reactive attitudes *there and then* are irrational. For, a genuine incompatibilist determinist is bound by consistency to purge himself of such attitudes. That's definitive of the position. But that in itself does not reveal that reactive attitudes themselves, yours or anyone else's, are *always* irrational. Thus there is no reason to suppose that this shift generally, say as it plays out in Scenarios One through Four, involves a consideration of "the implications of the thesis of determinism" which convinces you, must less actually reveals, that these attitudes are irrational.

I therefore conclude (with considerable help from Rorty and deSousa) that we have what we were looking for: a specifically cognitive or intellectual component of the reactive emotions, the deployment of which in the conduct of inquiry (whether as end in itself or in the service of practice) is rationally optional. Thus, we can place at Strawson's disposal the sort of explanation he needs for how the objective stance can cognitively dispel the reactive stance without in so far forth revealing it to be irrational. Thus, he does indeed "have something more to say" to the doubting pessimist. To be sure, it is not quite enough to convince everyone that we humans *must* retain the reactive emotions in our lives without pain of specifically theoretical irrationality, but it should be enough to convince many that we *may* do so.

6. Three Nagging Worries

I would love to leave matters right there, but for a few nagging worries about how this story might be received in some quarters. In ascending order of vexatiousness, there are (1) doubts about the very idea that emotions are partly *constituted* by patterns of attention; (2) doubts about the intelligibility of the distinction between an emotion e of type E which is *irrational* by virtue of some *defect* in its cognitive component, and an emotion e* which is simply *not an instance* of E at all because of some *difference* in its cognitive component; and (3) doubts about the story's seemingly *deflationary* stress on the epistemically *instrumental* role of reactive emotions in human life.

6.1. Constitution or causation?

You start to suspect X of betraying your trust. A feeling of resentment wells up in you. You suddenly (or gradually) see her in a new light; you notice inflections you missed before; your attention is directed to facts you never would have noticed, and so on. I can easily imagine that someone hearing this tale might wonder whether these shifts in patterns of salience in your field of attention are part of what *constitute* the emotion you feel as resentment or are, rather, *causal antecedents and/or consequences* of your emotional attitude toward X. The second way of regarding them does seem natural.

But then so was the parallel way of regarding the explicitly propositional belief-components of emotions before cognitivists came along to stress their constitutive role. Othello is happily in love with Desdemona. Upon Iago's prompting, he comes to believe that she has been unfaithful with Michael Cassio. A wave of jealousy wells up in him. Is the emotion (partly) constituted as jealousy by Othello's explicit belief in Desdemona's infidelity or is the jealousy merely a casual consequence of his change in belief? Before the "cognitivist revolution" in the philosophy of the emotions, we would unthinkingly have opted for the latter interpretation, but now it seems crudely regressive. But if Rorty and de Sousa are correct in arguing that we must also reckon quasi-propositional elements among the cognitive constituents of the emotions, then a parallel interpretation of their role as merely causal would be similarly regressive. If we can accept the idea that an emotion e is of type E partly by virtue of a person's having certain explicit beliefs, then we should have little more difficulty in accepting that it is of type E also partly by virtue of the person's being in certain quasi- or sub-propositional cognitive states.

6.2. *Irrationality or type-distinctness?*

The second nagging worry is not just about quasi- or sub-propositional cognitivism about emotions but about the whole cognitivist program, which is, after all, so much the keystone of the dispute between Strawson and the pessimists.

Suppose that my surname were Zimmerman, and that one day long ago I learned that Bob Dylan's real name is Robert Allen Zimmerman. Just suppose that my mischievous cousin Morris then told me that the Detroit, Michigan Zimmermans (suppose that's our home town) are closely related to the Hibbing, Minnesota Zimmermans (that is Bob Dylan's home town). "Bob Dylan is our cousin", he exclaims. Of course, I would never be so gullible as to believe him. But just suppose I were and I did. Suddenly, I feel a surge of pride about the Zimmerman family's amazing contribution to American music. "Wow! Bob Dylan is really Robert Allen Zimmerman!", I exclaim. (Morris also tells me that Ethel Merman's real surname was Zimmerman—this impresses me less.) Suppose that the mischievous Morris then bursts my balloon by admitting that it is all a hoax. "Schmuck. There are lots of Zimmermans. We aren't related to Bob Dylan, at all." I believe him this time too. However, perversely, I continue to feel pride. "Wow! Bob Dylan is really Robert Allen Zimmerman!", I continue to exclaim. (I become quite boring on the subject.)

But on the cognitivist account, certain belief-states are constituents of emotions. Therefore, this scenario verges on the unintelligible. If one of the constituents of my pride in the fact that Bob Dylan is a great singer/songwriter is the belief that I myself stand in a familial relationship to him, then the death of the belief entails the death of the pride. Whatever that warm feeling might be that I continue to have after my cousin Morris's antic revelation, it cannot be pride. It is not even pride if I continue to announce to all who will listen how *proud* I am of Bob Dylan ("whose *real* name is Zimmerman!").

But, then, what sense can the cognitivist make of the phenomenon of an irrational emotion that is irrational because based upon a false belief? Othello is jealous of Desdemona's sexual relationship with Michael Cassio. But since she has not really been unfaithful to Othello with his lieutenant and the evidence is not exactly conclusive despite Iago's worst efforts, Othello's jealousy is irrational. But it is jealousy nonetheless. On a cognitivist account of the emotions, wherein lies the difference between my *ersatz* pride in the accomplishments of Bob Dylan, and Othello's *genuine* but irrational jealousy of Desdemona?

The cognitivist does have some room for manoeuvre here. For one thing, I have explicitly disavowed the belief that I and Robert Allen are members of the same Zimmerman clan. (Moreover, I even acknowledge that the bare fact that he and I have the same last name is not enough of a relationship to sustain real pride.) Othello, on the other hand, continues to believe that Desdemona has sexually betrayed him. The belief-component which (on the cognitivist story) partly constituted my pride is gone; therefore so is my pride, properly so-called. On the other hand, the belief-component which partly constitutes Othello's jealousy endures (however irrationally); therefore so does his jealousy (however irrationally).

This explanation may seem glib, for we do after all talk about emotions in a way that seems to conflate the cases. Imagine a different (and much more boring play, say after a Bowdler got his hands on it) in which well-meaning friends, observing Othello's rising jealousy and rage, take him in hand and calm him down by managing to refute piece-by-piece all of Iago's "evidence" of the infidelity. ("The handkerchief? We can explain that!") They thereby achieve their purpose of wringing out of the tremblingly furious husband a (perhaps) grudging acknowledgement: "Alright. I see now that Desdemona could not possibly have had sex with Michael Cassio." Nonetheless, Othello might well go on to insist: "But I am still overwhelmed by this awful and oppressive feeling of jealousy! I still want to kill both of them!" And it might well be true: he does still want to kill both of them. (Therefore, it is a jolly good thing for both faithful wife and devoted lieutenant, if not for the tragedy, that these same well-meaning friends have spirited them well out of harm's way before disabusing Othello of his false suspicions.)

What does the cognitivist make of this? One course is for him simply to dig in his heels and insist that whatever the disagreeable (and potentially deadly) emotion is which Othello feels after his explicit disavowal of the constitutive belief, it is not jealousy. Another, slightly less stubborn, course for the cognitivist is to complicate the account by temporally indexing the attribution of emotion in a way that accommodates the vastly different speeds at which the neuronal belief-processing system and the endocrinal "visceral surge" system operate. This yields a slightly less counterintuitive interpretation of what Othello says after he is disabused of Iago's false testimony. Now, the cognitivist can comfortably acknowledge that at time t+1 Othello does still feel the lingering hormonal aftermath of the genuine (and partly belief-constituted) jealousy he felt at time t. This is more complicated, but it is accurate enough, and less evasive than the heel-digging response.

6.3. Genuinely reactive or merely epistemically useful?

The third nagging worry will not be restricted to those with questions about how the cognitivist theory of emotions plays out in the details, but will weigh upon all those who take seriously what Strawson says about the vital animating role reactive emotions play in human life as we know it. Recall Bennett's negative characterization of the reactive emotions as "pro or con attitudes which could *not* explain x's engaging in teleological inquiry into how y works". But, one might protest, doesn't the evolutionary story about the kind of help that the emotions give creatures like us in making our way sensibly through the world reduce the reactive emotions precisely to a merely *instrumental* role in the conduct of inquiry? Perhaps Strawson can have his convincing explanation of how the objective stance psychologically dispels the reactive stance without thereby rationally disqualifying it. But, does it not come at the rather high price of obliterating the very phenomenon up for explanation, by rendering the reactive stance so very ... objective?

This sort of deflationary concern plagues many evolutionary stories about the emergence of some humanly significant trait, activity or institution. There is a time-honored recipe for replying to it, which stresses the importance of the distinction between "phenotypic" and "genotypic" levels of explanation. Followed here, the recipe goes like this. The mistake of traditional Schlickian compatibilists was to suppose that *individual* human beings (and groups of human beings) take up reactive attitudes and engage in retributive practices in order to achieve exclusively utilitarian goals. But that is manifestly false. As both Strawson and Bennett insist, these attitudes and practices have a life of their own, a fact that is perfectly intelligible at the *phenotypic* level of description and explanation. But the evolutionary perspective speaks only of the natural selection of individuals qua members of species and of the "reasons" this process merely simulates. Nowhere need it even hint that phenotypes, individual human beings, like you in the narrative of sad perfidy, ever take up the reactive stance in order to achieve an end like making their way through the human environment more efficiently. An explicitly consequentialist "motive" for our having reactive emotions emerges only at the *genotypic* level. Therefore, despite appearances, the evolutionary perspective does not make cold-blooded consequentialist calculators of us all. On the contrary, it leaves intact all the "constitutive" richness of the reactive stance. Thus the recipe. Some will find it unconvincing, but, then, they probably have doubts about any explanation which appeals, however modestly, to natural selection.[26]

---

26 Acknowledgements: I owe the greatest debt to the published work of P.F. Strawson and Jonathan Bennett, Amelie Rorty and Ronnie de Sousa. Earlier versions of the paper improved as a result of the comments of three audiences, at The Hastings Center, at The Canadian Philosophical Association Meetings and at the Department of Philosophy of the State University of New York at Albany. I thank the following individuals for stimulating conversations on the topics herein: Steven Davis, Bruce Jennings, Andrea Scotland and two anonymous referees for *Philosophy and Phenomenological Research*. I also owe a debt of gratitude to my home institution, Simon Fraser University, for providing support for the research leave during which I wrote the current version of the paper.

Chapter 14

Doing without Desert

Erin Kelly

The idea of "moral responsibility" is typically linked with praise and blame, and with the notion of "the voluntary". It is often thought that if we are free, in the relevant sense, we may "deserve" praise or blame; otherwise, we do not. But when we look at whether and why we need the notions of praise and blame, we find that they are not as intimately connected with desert as many philosophers have thought. In particular, this paper challenges the idea that forms of evaluation and behavior tied to our "reactive attitudes" (especially resentment) best further morality's aims, properly understood.

Justice—who knows what it is? Do I know? Does your honor know? Can your honor tell me what I deserve? Do you think you can cure the hatreds and maladjustments of the world by hanging them? If you hang these boys, you turn back to the past. I'm pleading for the future.

– Orson Welles, *Compulsion*[1]

The idea of "moral responsibility" is typically linked with the notions of praise and blame, that is, with certain forms of moral evaluation. It is also usually associated with the notion of freedom, or "the voluntary". These ideas are drawn together by the following question: In what sense must we be free, or have acted voluntarily, in order to be appropriately subject to moral praise and blame? It is thought that if we are free (or our actions voluntary), in the relevant sense, we may "deserve" praise or blame; otherwise, we do not. While some philosophers find strict voluntariness to be too stringent a requirement, most concede that if an agent is to be thought deserving of praise and blame, it is important that he or she had or could have had some measure of control over his or her actions. Otherwise put, it is important that the agent had an opportunity to have acted otherwise. Moreover, it is thought that the extent of the agent's blame or praiseworthiness is related to her degree of control.

This brief depiction of the logic and metaphysical underpinnings of the concept of desert seems to me accurate. I will argue, however, that it is a mistake to attempt to rest the justification of praise and blame on that concept. Instead we should look to the normative role we think praise and blame should play in moral life. When we look at whether and why we need the notions of praise and blame, we will find that the forms of evaluation most important to morality are not as intimately connected with the notions of freedom and voluntariness as many philosophers have thought.

---

[1] *Compulsion*, dir. Richard Fleisher, with Orson Welles, Diane Varsi, Dean Stockwell, 20th Century Fox, 1959.

In asking whether and why we need the notions of praise and blame, I mean to be asking about the utility of these notions and whether their employment furthers the practical aims of morality.[2] The many powerful criticisms of utilitarianism notwithstanding, we should not lose sight of the important sense in which morality aims fundamentally to bring about a good result. J.J.C. Smart once proposed that instead of asking: "Who is responsible?" we should be asking: "Whom would it be useful to blame?"[3] This proposal comes off as outrageous, but I submit that we should not dismiss it altogether. We should investigate the value of engaging in blaming behavior, and where doing so generally is not morally beneficial, we should refrain from it. Our recoil at Smart's proposal may largely be the result of our rejection of the utilitarian goals of Smart's conception of morality, rather than its practical concern with consequences. The idea that morality's aim is to maximize happiness overall (or to maximize anything else, for that matter) may not be tenable, but although utilitarianism appears to get the practical aims of morality wrong, its teleological orientation with respect to the reasons we have for dealing out blame and various forms of punishment is a virtue.

In what follows, I will explore a certain conception of the nature and practical aims of morality. On this conception, the content of morality is determined by persons who have some concern for one another's basic needs and would be motivated to reason together as equals to reach an agreement on moral principles to regulate their social interactions.[4] In other words, I will assume that the content of morality is (metaphysically speaking) up to us, when we think of ourselves as engaged in a certain sort of common enterprise, and that its normative force is conferred by our common will, or what would be our common will, were we to reason together as equals to further that common enterprise. The moral motivation and basic interests of participants to moral reasoning act as normative constraints on the content of a reasonable agreement. They can be used to assess the relevance of considerations persons introduce; they are, in that sense, procedural constraints. Beyond this, however, there are no prior or independent moral facts that could be used to determine the agreement moral agents should make. Thus there is no room on this view for the position that reasonable persons must agree to treat each other in a certain way because that is what they deserve. What persons deserve, on this view, can be determined only by how we agree to distribute praise and

---

2   Because my account justifies praise and blame directly by appeal to the aims and principles of morality, rather than via an analysis of the conditions under which agents act freely, it can be thought of as a version of what Stephen White calls "direct compatibalism". See his *Unity of the Self* (Cambridge, MA: MIT Press, 1991), 236.

3   J.J.C. Smart, "An Outline of a System of Utilitarian Ethics", in J.J.C. Smart and Bernard Williams (eds), *Utilitarianism: For and Against* (Cambridge: Cambridge University Press, 1973), 54.

4   For a similar philosophical conception of morality, see T.M. Scanlon, *What We Owe To Each Other* (Cambridge, MA: Harvard University Press, 1998), Ch. 5; and Jürgen Habermas, "Discourse Ethics: Notes on a Program of Philosophical Justification", in *Moral Consciousness and Communicative Action*, tr. Christian Lenhardt and Shierry Weber Nicholsen (Cambridge, MA: The MIT Press, 1990).

blame; it does not provide a normative basis for determining what the content of the agreement should be.[5]

An advantage of this philosophical conception of morality is that it avoids relying on the vague and metaphysically contested moral concept of desert. It seems that persons do not share an understanding of what persons deserve, at least not one detailed enough to serve as a guide to blaming behavior. Morality need not assume otherwise; it can serve as a framework of thought within which persons could work out a standard for distributing praise and blame that serves shared interests. This conception of morality is more feasible for a pluralistic and secular society than a morality that relies on the notion of desert. Because it is focused on the practical task of identifying and securing shared aims, I will refer to this conception of morality as a practical conception. Within the framework of a practical conception of morality, we can develop an account of the grounds of moral judgment and the reasons we have for engaging in moral criticism and other blaming behavior.

Praise and blame enter into a practical conception of morality in the following ways. First of all, morality will articulate a set of obligations and prohibitions to guide our behavior. These standards constitute the standards of *moral judgment*; our behavior can be evaluated relative to our moral obligations and prohibitions. But on what I am calling a practical conception of morality, we do not judge persons simply for the sake of judging. Moral judgment does not have a life of its own. It has an important role, but one that must serve morality's practical aims. The second section of this paper explores this role.

In addition to standards for moral judgment, morality also needs mutually acceptable criteria for determining how we are to treat people in view of moral evaluations, especially negative ones. Call these the standards of *blaming behavior*. The third section of this paper argues that the question that should guide our formulation of these standards is the following: what sort of expressions of our moral evaluations do we have reasons to endorse, when we reason together as equals and respect the basic interests of all? Appropriate notions of praise and blame should bring about a good result and not be unfair. I maintain that the best principles to utilize as guides to blaming behavior will protect people's rights but will not be much concerned with free will. They will make claims about the moral relevance of an agent's reasons for acting and her causal responsibility for harms. This information, however, falls short of what is needed to determine whether an agent deserves blame and punishment.

Some will say that it is not enough that our notions of praise and blame promote good results and do so in ways that do not violate people's rights. In addition, it will be claimed, our notions must allow for the (public) expression and validation of certain moral sentiments; what counts as a mutually acceptable and reasonable way

---

5 Cf. Rawls's contrast between the idea of legitimate expectations within an institutional framework and a pre-institutional concept of desert. Erin Kelly (ed.), *Justice as Fairness: A Restatement* (Cambridge, MA: Harvard University Press, 2001), 73–9. For criticism of political liberalism's avoidance of the notion of desert, see Samuel Scheffler, "Responsibility, Reactive Attitudes, and Liberalism in Philosophy and Politics", *Philosophy and Public Affairs*, vol. 21, no. 4 (Fall 1992), 299–323.

to promote good results cannot neglect our moral sentiments and must be involved with their expression. I agree that there are moral sentiments to which a practical conception of morality should be responsive, but I mean to raise serious questions about whether the forms of evaluation that track our "reactive attitudes" best further morality's practical aims, as they are properly understood. Reactive attitudes, and in particular, resentment, are commonly associated with a desire for retribution—with the thought that it is a good thing in itself that the offender pay a price. The social costs of collectively expressing such attitudes can be very high.

Many of these costs are incurred in the criminal justice system. The United States, for instance, now incarcerates two million persons, two-thirds of whom are non-violent offenders. It has been estimated by some that this is the highest incarceration rate in the world, having recently surpassed that of Russia.[6] The cost is about $40 billion a year. The death penalty, which enjoys widespread popular support, imposes additional costs.[7] In the state of Texas, a single death penalty case costs taxpayers an average of $2.3 million—three times the cost of life imprisonment of one inmate for forty years. In Florida, it costs six times more to execute than to imprison for life without parole. It is estimated that the state of California could save $90 million a year by abolishing capital punishment and that New York could save $118 million. The extra costs of capital punishment would appear to rely for their justification on the value of expressing retributive sentiments, since its deterrent value is in serious doubt.

Of course, the expression of our reactive attitudes, such as resentment and indignation, need not take the form of a legal sanction. We may, more simply, withdraw our goodwill toward a wrongdoer, break off a relationship, or engage in public criticism and censure. But while we may sometimes have good reasons for these responses, it is not clear that they need always, or normally, be regarded as morally desirable.[8] On a practical conception of morality, whether we have reasons to express ourselves in these ways depends on an assessment of the associated benefits.

Part of the practical task of morality is to limit the expression of our reactive attitudes, to call attention to the social and moral costs the expression of such attitudes may impose, and to construct social structures that may better serve our shared needs. Insofar as it is natural for us to seek channels for the public expression of our reactive attitudes, morality may need to serve a corrective function. The public expression of our reactive attitudes, I will argue, should itself be a practical aim of morality in only a limited way. I turn now to a fuller account of such attitudes.

---

6 Anthony Lewis, "Abroad at Home; Punishing the Country", *The New York Times* 21 Dec. 1999, (late edition), A31.

7 The following statistics are from Richard C. Dieter, "Millions Misspent: What Politicians Don't Say About the Hight Costs of the Death Penalty", in Hugo Adam Bedau (ed.), *The Death Penalty in America* (New York: Oxford University Press, 1997), 402–3.

8 John Stuart Mill pointed to the power of the sanction of public opinion, regardless of legal enforcement. He was especially sensitive to the morally detrimental effects of expressions of majority opinion. See *On Liberty* (1859).

I. The Reactive Notion of Responsibility

In his article "Freedom and Resentment", P.F. Strawson illuminates what seems to be an important connection between the idea of moral responsibility and the reactive attitudes, in particular, resentment, love, gratitude, forgiveness, hurt feelings, and the like.[9] I will refer to this notion of responsibility as the reactive notion. Strawson analyzes the moral psychology of praise and blame in terms of the conditions that make possible our experience of the reactive attitudes he identifies. Our reactive attitudes indicate, he claims, that a personal interaction has fallen short of or exceeded our normal and ordinary expectations with regard to the attitudes of other persons toward us, and they represent our personal reactions to this shortcoming or special merit. In particular, our reactive attitudes indicate the importance within personal life of the attitudes of good or ill will (or indifference) that others display towards us in our interactions with them.[10] Resentment is a reaction to injury or indifference, a reaction we have when excusing conditions that would undermine the connection between the harm and ill will do not apply.[11] Strawson thus thinks our reactive attitudes make sense against the background of people's engagement in personal interaction in which ordinary standards of due regard for one another are normally satisfied. His view is that the expectation of this sort of personal regard is simply part of what it is to be involved or to participate in a normal human relationship.

Now our moral notions of condemnation and disapproval, Strawson thinks, can plausibly be thought of as the vicarious or impersonal analogues of these personal reactions: they are reactions to the quality of others' wills, not only towards ourselves, but also towards others.[12] (We may also feel guilt at the vicarious appreciation of others' reactions to our ill will.) These moral attitudes are at the core of our concept of moral responsibility, according to Strawson. In fact, he claims the making of moral demands *just is* the proneness to such attitudes.[13] The demands of our collective sense of morality carry with them the threat of sanction by our negative moral reactions for noncompliance.

Strawson describes our moral attitudes generally as having two notable features, both of which link them with what I will call blaming behavior. First of all, the experiences of moral indignation, disapprobation and condemnation, he claims,

---

9 Peter Strawson, "Freedom and Resentment", reprinted in Gary Watson (ed.), *Free Will*, (Oxford: Oxford University Press, 1982) (and in this volume, pp. 19–36), FR 21–2/62.' [As previously noted, page references for "Freedom and Resentment" are to pages 19–36 of this volume, followed by (after the slash) the corresponding pages of Watson (ed.), *Free Will*. Thus, 'FR, 21–2/62 refers to this volume, pp. 21–2/and *Free Will*, p. 62—the editors.]

10 FR, 28–9/71.

11 FR 28/70. Strawson groups excusing conditions into two categories. The first consists in conditions that undermine the connection between the injury and the agent's ill will (e.g., the agent was pushed). The second category concerns the existence of abnormal conditions that reveal that the ill will demonstrated is uncharacteristic of the agent (e.g., the agent was under great strain, or affected by posthypnotic suggestion, et cetera), or that the agent herself is psychologically abnormal or undeveloped. See FR 23/64ff.

12 FR, 28/70.

13 FR, 34/77.

"tend to promote an at least partial and temporary withdrawal of goodwill; they do so in proportion as they are strong; and their strength is in general proportioned to what is felt to be the magnitude of the injury and to the degree to which the agent's will is identified with, or indifferent to, it."[14] Thus the first step in our moral reaction is to withdraw, to an extent we deem proportional to the degree of intentional harm, our goodwill. The second is that our attitudes give rise in us to a further interest in punishing the offender. Strawson says, "[T]he preparedness to acquiesce in that infliction of suffering on the offender which is an essential part of punishment is all of a piece with this whole range of attitudes of which I have been speaking."[15] In these two ways, Strawson asserts an essential connection between our moral attitudes and blaming behavior. If we think of moral judgments as expressing our moral attitudes, then his view seems to be that making a (negative) moral judgment conveys our preparedness to engage in blaming behavior. I will argue that this identification of moral judgment with (potentially) blaming behavior is a mistake.

Strawson thinks we can, however, avoid launching into the varieties of blaming behavior, by deliberately suspending our moral attitudes. We may shift to a more "objective" point of view. This is a point of view from which we regard other persons as suitable subjects for therapeutic treatment or social policy, as persons "to be managed or handled or cured or trained; perhaps simply to be avoided ...."[16] From this point of view, we are no longer full participants in human relationships with them. We may observe our interactions with interest and strategize accordingly for the sake of constructive results, but the fact that we are not vulnerable to the full (normal) range of moral reactions means that we are not personally or morally engaged. We have suspended our moral attitudes at the cost of no longer viewing those we interact with as fully capable moral agents, and thus we have lost a moral dynamic that is normally central to interpersonal relations and interactions, or so Strawson claims. As we shall see, however, there is an important sense in which a practical conception of morality narrows the gap between the objective and participant points of view.[17]

Strawson's reactive account has generated considerable attention, for it presents itself as able to avoid metaphysical questions about whether we have free will by showing that the most illuminating account of moral judgment will be given by an analysis of when it is that our reactive attitudes tend to occur and how deeply those attitudes are implicated in our relationships with other people. As we have seen, Strawson's view is that to hold someone responsible is *just* to be vulnerable to these

---

14 FR, 34/77.

15 FR, 34/77.

16 FR, 25/66.

17 Psychiatric treatment itself may challenge the distinction between the objective and participatory stances by requiring the therapist to walk the line between the two. See, for instance, Dennett's interesting discussion of how successful therapeutic treatment of "multiple personality disorders" may require that the therapist demonstrate an attitude of respect for the alters, without actually endorsing or, one might say, fully embracing the participatory stance with regard to them. Daniel Dennett, *Brainchildren* (London: Penguin Books, 1998), 57–8. The understanding of morality and agency I develop in this paper is intended to press us to think about how the objective and participatory stances intersect in our ordinary social and moral relations, and possibly also in the deliberative stance we assume with respect to our own action.

reactive emotions in one's dealings with that person (or vicariously). Moreover, he maintains that the conditions that give rise to the reactive emotions would not be undermined by our acceptance of the truth of causal determinism, because the excusing conditions that tend to diffuse our reactive attitudes, or assessments of incompetence that trigger our shift to the objective point of view, are not examples of how we would be forced to view all human behavior if we were to come to acknowledge the truth of causal determinism. But it is not clear that the reactive account can succeed in substituting moral psychology for a metaphysics of the will, and I believe there is an alternative approach that clarifies the significance of our moral practices while more successfully avoiding the sticky metaphysical issues.

One of the distinctive features of Strawson's account is that he does not attempt directly to justify our reactive attitudes. Rather, he is interested in describing their importance to us in a way that illuminates the essential role they play in our social lives. In that sense, his approach is not strongly normative. Yet it is interesting that discussions of the moral psychology of resentment often lead in a more avowedly normative direction. R. Jay Wallace asks, when *is it fair* to subject someone to our negative moral attitudes? The answer, he claims, refers us to the general rational powers of an agent, what he calls "the powers of reflective self-control". These powers include the general ability of persons "to grasp and apply moral reasons and to regulate their behavior by the light of such reasons".[18] Wallace argues that it is reflective self-control, rather than deep metaphysical freedom, that is presupposed by the psychology of blame and resentment. (When people lack reflective self-control, Strawson confirms, we tend to suspend our reactive attitudes.)

The Strawsonian approach, even as its emphasis is shifted by Wallace and others, retains a deflationary character: it aims to deflate the importance and urgency of sorting out the metaphysical underpinnings of our concept of moral responsibility by stressing that however those philosophical investigations might turn out, we cannot and would not want to give up the reactive attitudes that express our concept of moral responsibility. In other words, the fact that the experience and expression of the reactive attitudes is so highly valued and practically unavoidable within our normal interpersonal relations makes the truth of causal determinism irrelevant to moral philosophy, or so it is claimed. But despite the deflationary ambitions of the reactive account, it remains vulnerable to worries about whether the reflective self-control we possess is thoroughgoing enough to "justify" resentment. This appears to point to an important feature of the moral psychology of resentment: the concept of responsibility it presupposes is the concept of *justified* liability to sanctions (i.e., the sanction of our reactive attitudes and behavior). We seek a justification for resentment and find it (on Wallace's analysis) in the idea that a blameworthy (or praiseworthy) agent possesses a sufficient measure of reflective self-control. Resentment is justified by a defect in the agent's moral reasoning: it is directed at a person who understands moral reasons, and is able to guide her behavior accordingly, but fails to do so. We think such an agent *deserves* the sanction of our reactive attitudes and behavior and, generally, we think that it is a good thing if people get what they deserve.

---

18 R. Jay Wallace, *Responsibility and the Moral Sentiments* (Cambridge, MA: Harvard University Press, 1994), 155.

But why shouldn't we worry, then, about what caused the agent's defect (or success), and what would make it sufficiently willful? The concern to justify our reactive attitudes may lead us to look at the psychological history and social context of the agent's defective choice, and then to be skeptical about whether we can pin down a notion of reflective self-control that is suitably robust to support judgments of desert. Agents lack control over many factors that influence the formation of their characters, dispositions, and ends. How much control do we really have? We might, for that matter, be skeptical about whether we can articulate a suitably circumscribed notion of the agent. Does Ulysses deserve praise for overcoming his weakness by having himself tied to the mast? He does succeed in overcoming, but not without the assistance of others. Think also about the importance to us that conferring with our friends about important decisions may have. The help this may provide us in coming out all right should lead us to check our reactive attitudes to persons who fail to get help and support under difficult circumstances. Yet we may not really be able to question their capacity for reflective self-control without questioning our own. We might thus come to worry about whether Strawson's catalogue of excusing conditions is thorough enough, or whether his distinction between the objective and participant points of view really holds up.

The reason the reactive account of responsibility is pressed to isolate a person's sphere of reflective self-control is that the account ties moral assessment and blaming behavior closely together. When negative moral assessment is understood to carry with it the withdrawal of goodwill and an interest in inflicting some further form of punishment, and since these are meant to be proportional to the amount of reflective self-control possessed by the agent, the justification of moral assessment depends on a fairly precise measure of the agent's freedom. This is difficult, perhaps even impossible to achieve. But I will argue that we need not accept this close association of moral assessment with blaming behavior and, therefore, we need not worry about the metaphysics of free will. The moral basis for assessing other people's conduct can be separated from our reactions to such assessments, including the reactive interest we may have in engaging in blaming behavior. We can then raise the question of whether something other than our reactive attitudes should guide blaming behavior as well.[19] In fact, we can raise the possibility of developing an account of moral assessment and behavior that bears no essential connection to the reactive attitudes; their role is a crutch we can do without. Rejecting it may have some real advantages.

II. Moral Judgment

I propose that the conditions under which moral qualities can be attributed to an agent's character or behavior can be examined and justified apart from our reactions to such attributions. The question whether and when we ought to engage in blaming

---

19 My criticism here is similar to one made by T.M. Scanlon, although, as discussed below, the view I defend breaks the connection between moral judgment and the reactive attitudes more radically than his does. See "The Significance of Choice", *The Tanner Lectures on Human Values 1988* (Salt Lake City: University of Utah Press, 1988), 160–66.

(or praising) behavior can be treated separately. My proposal is similar in certain respects to one made by Gary Watson.[20] Watson argues that judgments of an agent's faults need not imply that she deserves adverse treatment or "negative attitudes" in response to her faulty conduct, but may instead concern whether the agent's activities and ways of life are choiceworthy.[21] He claims we are interested in what is choiceworthy in order to develop "models and ideals of human possibility".[22] These consist in examples of virtue and vice that we aspire to emulate and avoid, respectively. Watson considers someone who betrays her ideals by choosing a dull but secure occupation instead of a riskier but potentially more enriching one, or endangers something of deep importance to her life for trivial ends (by sleeping too little and drinking too much before important performances, for example), and he concludes that we might judge that she has acted badly—cowardly, self indulgently, or unwisely.[23] But from this it does not follow that we withdraw our goodwill toward her or are inclined to attempt in some other way to punish her. When it comes to that, we might think that her behavior is none of our business.[24] Rather, our interest in appraising her may be to further our understanding or underscore our conviction about which considerations ought to guide future choices, our own and other people's.

What Watson says seems right thus far, and it emphasizes what I take to be the most fundamental reason why judgment of present and past behavior is important to morality: we rely on such judgments to guide present and future action. I also agree that when we appraise someone's choices or dispositions, we see her as someone who adopts ends for reasons, that is, as someone with evaluative capacities. We think her choices or dispositions can meaningfully be appraised morally insofar as they express evaluative commitments. Watson's point is that the basis of this appraisal does not deliver the justification sought by and for our reactive attitudes.

Recall that the reactive notion of responsibility seems to depend on whether we can isolate and defend the sphere of an agent's reflective self-control. This is important because our reactive attitudes reach beyond what an agent has done; they are directed toward the agent herself. They are involved with a judgment of what she is like, and they presuppose, importantly, that the agent is responsible for what she is like.[25] Our appraisals of an agent's evaluative commitments, however, need not depend on the truth of this presupposition, and thus they may fall short of justifying our reactive attitudes.

Now Watson appears to limit his analysis of "responsibility as attributibility" to assessments of virtue and vice that do not directly entail judgments about whether an

---

20 See also Scanlon, Ch. 6 (see note 4, above); J.J.C. Smart, "Free Will, Praise and Blame", *Mind*, vol. 70 (1961), 291–306; Joel Feinberg, "Collective Responsibility", in Larry May and Stacey Hoffman (eds), *Collective Responsibility*, (Savage, MD: Rowman and Littlefield, 1991), 74–5; and Wallace, 52ff.

21 Gary Watson, "Two Faces of Responsibility", *Philosophical Topics*, vol. 24 (1996), 231.

22 Watson, 243.

23 Watson, 231.

24 Watson, 231.

25 This concerns what Susan Wolf refers to as "deep responsibility", *Freedom within Reason* (New York: Oxford University Press, 1990), 41.

agent has violated a moral duty. The latter sort of judgment, he thinks, is tied to the question of when moral sanctions are appropriate. But I do not see why this need be so. While Watson does not commit himself to any particular view of the source of morality's claims upon us, I have proposed that our moral reasons are determined with reference to principles that could be the object of agreement among persons who care for one another's basic needs and acknowledge one another as equals. These principles can be relied upon to guide our judgments about where our duties and obligations lie and whether or not an agent has satisfied her obligations. But the suitability of these moral principles to serve as a guide to judgment may not entail that our reactive attitudes and blaming behavior are an appropriate response to an agent's failures. This is because an agent may not be sufficiently accountable for her failures.

The basis for our evaluations of what an agent is like would seem potentially to fall short of what is required to justify our reactive attitudes toward that agent even if we attempt to separate the reactive attitudes from blaming behavior, as T.M. Scanlon proposes. Scanlon denies that the justification of our reactive attitudes takes us into the territory of desert. Instead of separating the basis of moral judgment from the reactive attitudes, as Watson does in appraising a person's virtues and vices, Scanlon denies that the notion of responsibility that underlies our reactive attitudes need be understood as a desert-entailing notion.[26] He holds that we may justifiably experience resentment without experiencing a further propensity to engage in punitive behavior or to think that it would be a good thing if the offending party were to suffer. Thus we may speak about what justifies resentment without implying that blaming behavior is thereby warranted. A person is justified in feeling resentment when that person has been wronged.[27] The justification of blaming behavior should be based on further considerations.

Surely it is possible to separate the experience of certain sentiments from the conditions under which one ought to express those sentiments. In that sense, we may agree with Scanlon that our reactive attitudes need not be understood as guided by a desert-entailing notion of responsibility. Even so, it is not clear that the basis for our moral judgment of an agent's choice, action, or character suffices to justify our reactive attitudes toward that agent. I have argued that assessing whether an agent has violated a moral principle that represents a mutual agreement between persons who are morally motivated need not depend on an overall assessment of the agent's rational capabilities, and in particular, it need not lead us deeply into an assessment of the metaphysics of her self-control.[28] Suppose that someone who disregards an accident victim in order to be on time for a business meeting has acted wrongly. We can make this appraisal without knowing what has made her care so much about

---

26 Scanlon, 274, 276–7.

27 Scanlon, 271.

28 Scanlon would agree with this because he believes that the justification of our reactive attitudes is provided by the reasons we have for thinking that an agent has acted wrongly. I question his claim that the reactive attitudes do not presuppose that an agent is responsible for her actions and character. But perhaps our attitude of resentment, for instance, can take different forms. See footnote 54 below.

business meetings or so little about accident victims or whether we can rightly say how fully her values are under her control.[29]

In other words, moral assessment of an action or attitude need not require us to determine the extent to which various causal influences on an agent's adoption of (good or bad) reasons threaten her reflective self-control.[30] We judge what she is now like only to the extent needed in order to isolate the reasons for her behavior. An agent's evaluative commitment may remain strong even when reflective self-control is uncertain, as in the case of a willing addict. The agent's causal history and the extent of her reflective self-control seem important when we wish to hold her responsible for what she is like. But when our aim is to understand what behavior to model ourselves after or avoid, the agent's attitude, character traits, deliberation and choice stand as model-types to emulate or avoid, and the particularities of her history and abilities become much less important.[31] This means that our moral evaluations may fall short of justifying our reactive attitudes.[32] Certain reactions toward an agent, such as resentment or indignation, may well be understandable, given what she has done or what she is like. But this is not to say that we are giving them a deeper sense of justification in terms of the agent's accountability for her actions and character.

Thus moral appraisal of an agent's action or attitude is less metaphysically complicated than moral appraisal of an agent's responsibility for her choice, character and dispositions. I have maintained that our reactive attitudes are directed toward the latter and that they are bound up with an assessment of the agent's self-control. Of course, some measure of control is involved in adopting and acting on reasons, and Watson concurs with this. He says: "absence of control indicates that the action was not attributable to the agent".[33] His point is that the basis for attributing an action to an agent points to an aspect of our concept of responsibility that is separate from, and no less important than, what is analyzed by the reactive account. On the core notion of "responsibility as attributability", Watson claims, an agent is responsible for her ends in the sense that she has adopted those ends for reasons that express her practical identity as an agent. But here we should be wary. It is misleading to

---

29 Cf. Michael Slote, "Ethics Without Free Will", *Social Theory and Practice*, vol. 16, no. 3 (Fall 1990), 369–83. Slote describes a non-utilitarian and non-egoistic virtue ethics that avoids the notions of moral praise, blame and responsibility altogether. The account I offer does not eliminate reference to praise and blame in this way, but it nevertheless bears some resemblance to Slote's approach.

30 Scanlon denies that moral assessment requires us to determine whether a wrongdoer is responsible for having become the kind of person she now is (284). In that respect, his view is close to mine. Nevertheless, Scanlon is more concerned than I am with whether the agent has a coherent psychology that is stable over time (278–9). I believe that this is because he is interested not simply in articulating the grounds for moral judgment, but also in the further task of justifying our reactive attitudes.

31 This is so even though character traits cannot be understood apart from knowing the person. We may know a person well without being familiar with her developmental history.

32 Scanlon holds that the justification of our reactive attitudes need not presuppose that the wrongdoer is responsible for what she is like (284–5). I believe this significantly revises our familiar concept of resentment. See footnote 54.

33 Watson, 234.

employ the language of responsibility to describe the conditions of attributability because doing so seems to lead naturally to questions about the causal history of and possibilities for the formation of the agent's practical identity—what was the agent's role in shaping his or her own identity? How much control do we have over our characters? Are we responsible for our flaws? More to the point is the idea that an analysis of how actions (or reasons) are morally attributable to agents can bypass the notion of responsibility altogether. Establishing that the conditions of attributability are in place is a matter quite different from investigating the agent's mind and history as required by the moral psychology of blame and desert. The conditions of attributability should thus not be identified with the concept of responsibility.

Moral judgment, as I shall understand it, appraises an agent's reasons for action relative to the practical aims of morality; it assesses the extent to which those reasons help to realize a mutually agreeable form of social life and are consistent with its principles. We situate actions in order to understand their significance as models of behavior relative to this ideal. Should we emulate them? Should we encourage others to adopt them? Simply attending to consequences, which could be radically contingent, will not enable us to answer these questions. We want to know what the agent intended to do and why. That is, we want to know what justification the agent thought (or could have thought) she had for what she aimed to do. Thus the paradigm case of the object of moral assessment is an agent's action situated in the context of her reasons for acting.[34] (According to Kant, this is captured in an agent's maxim.) But, in particular, we want to know what reasons the agent had for thinking that certain kinds of claims on other persons are warranted—claims that bear upon the rights, liberties, and basic needs that would be acknowledged by moral principles we can share.[35] Moral appraisal remains, in this way, quite focused.[36]

We can think of people's reasons as organized, normatively, in a hierarchy or in chains. Suppose I quickly take my change from the countertop and put it in my pocket so that the clerk will not notice the $5 bill she has mistaken for a $1 bill. There are several reasons here that might figure into an explanation of what I have done. I took myself to have reason (1) to pick up the change quickly and (2) to put it in my pocket. The reasons are instrumental to the end of (3) hiding the clerk's mistake. But so far we have not made much progress in understanding the justification I take myself to have for my action. Suppose that my behavior can further be described as self-interested. We have now ascended into the normative hierarchy of my reasons. A potentially morally neutral action (the quick pocketing of change) serves a morally relevant end (promoting my self-interest at certain costs to others). My opportunistic pursuit of self-interest represents a point in my cluster of reasons that is relevant to moral appraisal and, presumably, the appraisal would be negative.

---

34 For a discussion of the complexities of moral interpretation, see Michele M. Moody-Adams, *Fieldwork in Familiar Places: Morality, Culture, and Philosophy* (Cambridge, MA: Harvard University Press, 1997), especially Chs 4 and 5.

35 We also appraise people's failure to assess the bearing of their actions on other persons' rights, liberties, and basic needs.

36 Watson's criteria of choiceworthiness would seem to extend beyond what I am identifying as the province of moral appraisal.

Situating actions relevantly in their rational context, however, does not necessitate an evaluation of the causal history of an agent's adoption of her reasons for action, or of how an agent became someone who fails, within deliberation and self-regulation, to take certain moral reasons seriously. We need not, for instance, understand how I came to be someone who would act in such an instinctively self-serving manner, or whether I could come to alter my character. In that sense, we need not take up the issue of the extent or purity of an agent's reflective self-control. In fact, we need not even be particularly concerned with the agent's practical identity. We are interested in the agent's rationality in a more limited sense. It is enough that the agent has reasons that figure informatively into a certain kind of explanation of what she does. The explanation we seek is one that examines the reasons for an agent's actions in view of how those reasons and the actions that serve them bear on the moral interests of other persons. Once we have identified a piece (or lack) of reasoning we can appraise morally, we can carry out our appraisal without exploring the causal conditions under which the agent acquired a disposition to reason as she has.

I have said that we are interested in assessing an agent's reasons because we are interested in what kind of behavior to model and emulate. Thus our interest in explaining an agent's actions in accordance with her reasons is connected with an investment we have in taking up a deliberative point of view in order to decide how to act or how to advise others. Nevertheless, the explanatory and deliberative points of view have different presuppositions.[37] When we deliberate about what to do, we aim to decide what to do based upon our assessment of the merits of the alternatives. Making a decision for what we regard as good reasons is fundamentally different from making a predictive claim based upon a survey of the causal factors impinging upon us.[38] The former excludes at the same time doing the latter. As Stuart Hampshire puts it,

> It is essential to human action ... that it should be impossible that while I am deciding what to do, and while I am therefore working towards the state of being certain what I shall do, I should at the same time ask myself the question—"Knowing myself as I do, what am I in fact likely to do?"[39]

---

[37] For a discussion of these two "standpoints", see Hillary Bok, *Freedom and Responsibility* (Princeton: Princeton University Press, 1998), Ch. 2.

[38] On the distinction between a prediction and a decision, see Stuart Hampshire, *Thought and Action* (New York: The Viking Press, 1967), 107–12. See also my "Clarke's Unlikely Success Against Hume", forthcoming in *Archiv für Geschichte der Philosophie*, vol. 84 (2007), 297–318; Christine M. Korsgaard, "Morality as Freedom", in Yirmiahu Yovel (ed.), *Kant's Practical Philosophy Reconsidered: Papers Presented at the Seventh Jerusalem Philosophical Encounter* (Dordrecht: Kluwer, 1989), 26–7; Christine M. Korsgaard, *The Sources of Normativity*, ed. Onora O'Neill (Cambridge: Cambridge University Press, 1996), especially 94–7 of Ch. 3 entitled, "The Authority of Reflection"; Thomas E. Hill, "Kant's Argument for the Rationality of Moral Conduct", in *Dignity and Practical Reason in Kant's Moral Theory* (Ithaca: Cornell University Press, 1992), 116–22; and Hill, "Kant's Theory of Practical Reason", in *Dignity and Practical Reason in Kant's Moral Theory*, 131–8.

[39] Hampshire, 109.

Deliberation proceeds under the presupposition that we are free to act on what we take to be the best reasons, otherwise it would be pointless. This does not mean that we are in fact free or even that we must believe that we are.[40] It only means that when we deliberate we think not about what is likely to happen, but about what we ought to do, in view of our survey of possible reasons for action. We imagine what we would do, if it were the case that nothing but the best reasons to act determine our judgment and will. By contrast, when we explain someone's actions by reference to reasons they have endorsed, we need not assume or imagine that they were free to have deliberated more soundly or to have acted on better reasons. In fact, there is some tension between a presupposition of the agent's freedom and our explanatory ambitions. In explaining human behavior we attempt to show that actions are the necessary result of antecedent conditions. We need not project onto the agent the libertarian presuppositions of the deliberative point of view.

I have argued that in moral appraisal, we aim to identify how a person's actions or dispositions bear on the morally relevant interests of other persons. We then attempt to determine why the action or disposition in question seems reasonable from the agent's point of view, and whether or not we can endorse that judgment. If the agent's action or disposition lacks normative structure because the agent appears to have no evaluative commitments that bear on what she has done—for instance, what happened was an accident—then moral appraisal comes to a dead-end. It comes to a dead-end, that is, unless the agent was accident-prone for morally interesting reasons. It is useful here to draw an analogy with the "principle of quiescence" in chess. The principle states: always look a few moves beyond any flurry of exchanges to see what the board looks like when it quiets down.[41] In ethical assessment, we examine the network of reasons that explain what an agent does or is disposed to do, searching for "hot spots" where the agent's reasons (or lack thereof) have a bearing on the moral interests of other persons. These hot spots become the focus of moral appraisal, and what lies beyond them in the agent's normative network of reasons is of diminishing import unless examining them calls attention to other hot spots.

The point is that we can do this without taking up the question of whether or not the agent has the capacity to adopt and live up to better reasons (or, for that matter, whether the agent took herself to have the reasons it makes sense to ascribe to her). We need not determine whether the agent freely or autonomously adopted her reasons or, if she acted badly, whether she could have known better or cared more about acting well. Thus the question of whether the agent "deserves" the moral assessment we confer upon her, i.e., how responsible the agent is for having turned out as she did, is drained of its urgency. The moral judgment of agency (i.e., the production of actions in accordance with reasons) should be less concerned with the causal history of an agent's adoption of reasons for action than many who have worried about moral responsibility have thought.

---

40 See Korsgaard, "Morality as Freedom", 26.
41 Daniel Dennett, *Darwin's Dangerous Idea* (London: Penguin Books, 1995), 499.

III. Blaming Behavior

My account separates our interest in and grounds for moral judgment from the reactive attitudes. I now take up the question when or whether we should engage in blaming behavior. By "blaming behavior" I intend to refer to the expression of moral judgment and criticism, as well as to more intrusive forms of interference and physical restraint. In addressing the matter of blaming behavior, do our reactive attitudes surface again as essential guides to what is appropriate? On Watson's view they do, but I disagree. He is right that responsibility as attributability is not enough to tell us how to act toward an offender, but wrong to think that the reactive account of responsibility is what must further direct us. In other words, I believe that the reactive account of responsibility can be separated as well from the question of how morality should counsel us to act toward one another. What counts as fair and appropriate treatment, especially with regard to those persons who have acted badly, is not determined by consulting our reactive attitudes. If this is true there are, of course, (further) deflationary implications for the reactive notion of responsibility—it would be left with a highly restricted domain.

I have argued that moral evaluation is concerned with the questions: Can we endorse the agent's aim in acting, or did the agent act for the wrong reasons? I will now defend the idea that if the agent's reasons are bad, we have grounds for expressing our negative moral judgments, because and insofar as doing so furthers aims that mutually concerned parties could endorse. I give only a bare sketch of how this might go, but enough to suggest a variety of reasons that need not rely on the notion of desert. Below are four ways in which the activity of moral criticism and censure can promote moral interests that we share:

(1) Moral criticism and censure can have deterrent force. They have this force for those who assign importance to their membership in the moral community, since for them moral failure is uncomfortable and to be avoided.[42] Criticism may lead to a person's loss of self-esteem as well as to a loss of her esteem in the eyes of others, by calling attention to her failure to live up to moral principles she accepts and takes herself to share with others. Deterrence is a familiar reason for moral censure and I won't say more about it.[43] The principle worry about forward-looking accounts of blaming behavior that invoke the value of deterrence is that such accounts are implausible when they rest entirely on that value.[44] So I turn to the further reasons.

---

42 See Scanlon, *What We Owe To Each Other*, 276.

43 For discussion of the justification of punishment on grounds of deterrence, see Daniel M. Farrell, "The Justification of General Deterrence", *The Philosophical Review* 94 (July 1985), 367–94. Farrell stresses the difficulties of justifying punishment for the sake of general deterrence, that is, punishing an offender for the sake of deterring others from committing similar crimes. I agree that general deterrence lacks justification when we cannot establish a causal connection between the offender's behavior and the harms we aim to avert.

44 See Wallace, 54–9. See also Jonathan Bennett, "Accountability", in Zak van Straaten (ed.), *Philosophical Subjects: Essays Presented to P. F. Strawson*, (Oxford: Oxford University Press, 1980), especially 19–21.

(2) Moral criticism and censure can be instructive. They serve as an occasion to clarify on publicly accessible grounds the principles we expect others to accept if they are reasonable.[45] They do so in a context in which we address those reasons either directly or indirectly to someone who has acted for morally unacceptable reasons. This can provide the opportunity for further reflection on and argument about the nature of our moral principles. The grounds of moral justification are thus examined publicly and, if all goes well, they are strengthened.

(3) Moral criticism and censure serve the end of reconciliation. Understanding and acknowledging harms suffered is an important step in the process of recovery from them, and it is often especially important for this acknowledgment to come from people the harmed person respects and has confidence in, i.e., members of what she identifies as her moral community. These will be persons who share the moral principles on which the criticism is based.

(4) Finally, the activities of moral criticism and censure can facilitate a sense of solidarity in the moral community.[46] This point must be treated carefully. Solidarity in the relevant sense is created not through a sense of righteousness, but by underscoring a collective commitment to bringing about a better society. As I construe it, this is a commitment we make to helping one another to regulate our conduct by appropriate (shared) moral principles, and to the idea that this commitment has a high priority in our overall scheme of values.[47]

None of the points I have gone over so far need involve significant interference with "blameworthy" persons, so clearly the account given thus far is incomplete. What about the justification of penalties and restraints? On this question, we should take seriously the large role played by (simple) causal responsibility, as opposed to moral desert, in justifying the regulation and restraint of persons who cause or imminently threaten harms to others.[48] The role within morality of what most would regard as a shallow notion of causal responsibility is under-appreciated by moral philosophers;

---

45 This reasoning is similar to that found in moral education theories of punishment. See, for example, Jean Hampton, "The Moral Education Theory of Punishment", *Philosophy and Public Affairs* 13 (1984), 208–38; and Herbert Morris, "A Paternalistic Theory of Punishment", in Antony Duff and David Garland (eds), *A Reader on Punishment*, (Oxford: Oxford University Press, 1994). Moral education theories of punishment tend to focus on the aim of morally educating the offender. Morris writes, for example, "a principle justification for punishment is the potential and actual wrongdoer's good" (97). I am stressing, however, the benefit to the wider community.

46 Durkheim argues that this is the primary function of punishment. See Emile Durkheim, *The Division of Labor in Society* (New York: The MacMillan Co., 1933), 108–10.

47 Cf. Joel Feinberg on the expressive function of punishment in *Doing and Deserving* (Princeton: Princeton University Press, 1970), 95–118. Feinberg stresses that the function of punishment is to express our reactive attitudes, in particular, to express a kind of vindictive resentment.(100) I agree with Feinberg that punishment has an expressive and symbolic significance, but I am suggesting a different understanding of what it can and should convey.

48 I am indebted to Lionel McPherson for this point.

judgments of causal responsibility contribute substantially to our judgment about proper treatment. If true, this means that the moral justification of our appropriate responses to and interference with the behavior of persons who cause harms should be less preoccupied with our assessment of the agent's will, much less its freedom, than many have thought.

The guiding principle is simple: we are usually justified in preventing harms by interfering with their causes.[49] An agent's causing harm to others provides us with grounds for restraining her. This idea receives considerable support from common sense and social policy. For example, we often restrain persons who have assaulted others and continue to pose a threat. We seem to feel justified in doing this pretty much regardless of the origins of the aggressor's anti-social behavior, provided that we do not violate his rights. On the approach I have endorsed, a person's rights are determined by reference to principles that equal and mutually concerned moral agents could agree upon. They protect our moral status and our freedom to lead a life compatible with a similar freedom for others. The limits of freedom should be negotiated with due attention to the equal moral status and basic interests of all persons. Restrictions would be unlikely to secure agreement unless they are necessary for the protection of shared and fundamental interests. When harms constitute a violation of such interests they provide grounds for restricting the harmdoer. If our understanding of the relevance of causal responsibility to the justification of penalties and restraints is constrained by this notion of people's rights, we can mostly avoid evaluations of the origins of harmful behavior. The origins of an aggressor's anti-social behavior may, however, enter into determining which restraint is appropriate. If the aggressor is not capable of being deterred by a prison sentence (much less by moral criticism), we may opt for some form of treatment instead. The deterrent value of punishment is not undermined by exempting some persons.[50] On the principle I am examining, the rationale for restraint is preventing harms, and more severe restraint than would be necessary to achieve this aim is not warranted.

The moral significance of the role of causal responsibility is highlighted by what we would concede to the interests of others from the first-person perspective. We tend to believe it is not unreasonable for other persons to prevent us from harming them, even if we do not think that the threat we pose to them is our fault. For example, if I fall off a roof and am about to land on someone, I would not think it unreasonable of that person to move out of the way, even if that would mean more serious injuries for me. Or if a hypnotist causes me to aim a loaded gun at someone and instructs me to shoot, I would not think it would be unreasonable for the intended victim to preempt me, if that is the only way she could protect herself. Similarly, if I become infected with a serious and highly contagious disease, quarantine may be justified

---

49 This is a principle of blaming behavior that lacks moral content and perhaps should not even be classified as a principle of blaming behavior.

50 Daniel Dennett stresses that punishing those incapable of being deterred would undermine the rationale for punishment as deterrence. See his *Elbow Room* (Cambridge, MA: The MIT Press, 1984), Ch. 7. This point depends, of course, on the idea that it is the agent who is punished that we aim to deter. It does not count against the prospects of deterring others. But general deterrence is, for other reasons, difficult to justify. See footnote 43.

even supposing that I have done nothing wrong. According to the practical principle we are considering, however, the use of restraints must head off harms that would otherwise (imminently) occur, or it is not justified. Restraint is not here understood as a form of retaliation.

Consider another sort of case. We sometimes think it is justifiable to fight against and attempt to contain a society or group of persons who have unjustly aggressed or who threaten to aggress against another society or group (e.g., Serbian aggression in Kosovo), and that we may do this without investigating the source of the aggression in culture or history or political agendas of social control to see whether those who perpetuate it "deserve" the harms we may inflict upon them in response. Here it is important that the threat be imminent, if a transgression has not already occurred. If it has occurred, we must reasonably believe the threat continues to be a live one. In choosing our targets, we attempt (or ought to attempt) to incapacitate those who are causally responsible for the perpetuation of the unjust aggression, and to use minimum necessary force.

Also, we commonly think (or, I submit, we ought to think) that it is justified for a group to rebel against another group that oppresses it (e.g., the struggle against apartheid) without first investigating whether the individual members of the dominant group are "responsible" for their causal role in the oppression.[51] These acts of self-defense, as we might call them, are not about dealing out desert. They are motivated by concern to stop harms from occurring and to prevent them from reoccurring. This motivation is at the heart of a practical conception of morality.

These examples have focused on the moral importance of identifying and restraining individuals who have not only caused harms, but also continue to pose threats. Restraints are justified to stop harms from occurring and to deter further harms threatened by the agent who is subject to our blaming behavior, and only to the extent necessary to accomplish this. But I acknowledge as well that those who have caused harms yet do not pose further threats may rightly be penalized for the sake of the three additional reason-types outlined above (instruction, reconciliation, and solidarity). In these cases, of course, we reach beyond the principle that allows us to prevent harms by interfering with their causes and return to the various reasons that justify moral criticism. In order to be justified, the penalties inflicted must advance these aims and not exceed what is required for doing so. This means restraints and other penalties can be justified only when it is reasonable to think that the agent (1) was causally responsible for harms or imminent threats, and (2) had morally faulty reasons for acting.[52]

---

51 Cf. Cheshire Calhoun, "Responsibility and Reproach", in Cass R. Sunstein (ed.), *Feminism and Political Theory* (Chicago: University of Chicago Press, 1982). Calhoun argues that in certain abnormal contexts, we may be justified in using moral reproach as a tool for social improvement even when the individual being reproached is not blameworthy. The point I am making here, however, does not involve making use of moral reproach.

52 Farrell argues plausibly for the relevance of the following principle of distributive justice: "a person's (informed) choices make her liable to suffering certain harms if, in the light of those choices, it is inevitable that someone be harmed and she is one of the individuals who can be harmed in order that someone else be saved" (Farrell, 373).

IV. The Moral Sentiments

I may seem to be coming dangerously close to the sort of flat, reductive view found in utilitarian accounts, one that does not appear to do justice to the role and complexity of our moral sentiments. Let me briefly turn to the question of how moral emotions bear upon or appear within a practical conception of morality.

I have been criticizing accounts of moral responsibility (and, in particular, accounts of moral blame) that are centered around the reactive attitudes: resentment, indignation, and guilt. It is important that in rejecting the centrality of the reactive attitudes to the practical aims and orientation of morality, I am not rejecting altogether the role and importance of moral sentiments within morality. My positive account can and does maintain a sensitivity to moral emotions, although it presents a somewhat alternative take on which emotions are central to morality. Very briefly, I will make this case.

The view of morality I have been advocating focuses on our collective attempt to approximate an ideal, namely, a mutually acceptable form of social life that is suitably responsive to people's basic needs. The class of emotions most relevant to consider thus concerns our relationship to ideals: what it means to us to pursue an ideal, to fall short of it, or to embody it, however imperfectly. Pursuing an ideal may involve, for instance, the attitudes of respect and hope. The gains we make can give rise to pride and joy. Failing to attain an ideal may bring disappointment, sadness, anger, regret, and even shame.[53] Emotions such as these will be moral when the ideal to which they are responsive has moral content. I have proposed an abstract characterization of such an ideal. We may feel moral emotions, however, not simply with regard to abstract moral principles and the ideal they serve (although we may feel them in this way). We may also feel them toward other persons with whom we share a commitment (more or less) to realizing this ideal in human relationships. The ideal, after all, makes sense only because human beings and how they relate to one another matters. Our moral judgments are sensitive to what persons are like: how helpful and even adventurous they are in realizing our common sense of morality, and such assessments give rise, importantly, to emotions such as the ones I have indicated. From the point of view of a practical conception of morality, we tend to feel respect and appreciation for someone's virtues. When persons fail, we feel disappointment in their shortcomings. Our disappointment is measured by our sense of the possibilities and opportunities lost, and is not, like resentment, fixed by a notion of what a person deserves.[54] Even our anger need not depend on our sense of how responsible persons are for having turned out as they did: what part exactly

---

53 It is interesting that people often feel shame about things that are not in their control, such as their heritage or height. A similar point can be made about regret: we may regret actions and consequences of actions that are beyond our control. Moreover, we tend to regret harms that we have caused, regardless of their relationship to our will. See Bernard Williams, "Moral Luck", in his *Moral Luck* (Cambridge: Cambridge University Press, 1981). See also his *Shame and Necessity* (Berkeley: University of California Press, 1993), Chs 3 and 4.

54 As discussed above, Scanlon proposes an understanding of resentment that separates it from the notion of desert. See Scanlon, Ch. 6. I believe his understanding of resentment moves resentment closer to disappointment.

they played in their own failure. We may be sad, regretful, or angry that a person, for whatever reasons, did not turn out to be the person we hoped she would be, or thought she might have been. When human relationships work out well, on the other hand, we may celebrate the moral possibilities realized in and through them, and this can give rise to mutual love and admiration. The role each person has played in a relationship or community may not be sharply differentiated; and that is partly why the love and admiration that may emerge is not centered around feelings of gratitude. We may also feel gratitude toward persons who have done more than is expected, but this gratitude need not be thought of as the counterpart of resentment. It may not be important to distinguish the agent's "responsibility" for her accomplishment from the conditions that enabled it: we may simply be grateful for its possibility.

V. Beyond the Psychology of Blame

I have argued that the prominence of the reactive attitudes in moral thought is not defensible on moral grounds. What, then, accounts for their persistence? Since a normative account is lacking, we must turn to psychology, history and sociology for an answer.

The best-known psychological account comes from Nietzsche.[55] Nietzsche thought that the notion of the will itself is an artifact of the psychology of *ressentiment*: when we become conscious of our powerlessness, and especially when others hurt us, we come to hate the power associated with their agency. In an attempt to give meaning to our suffering and to gain control over it when we are unable to act on it, we moralize this hatred and express it in the form of resentment and moral blame. In its purest form, blame attempts to isolate the power of agency in "the will". It positions the agent clearly behind and separate from the deed as its proper focus. It is thereby possible to posit that the harm need not have occurred—the agent could have prevented it by an act of will.[56] This frees us from an inevitable consignment to the status of victim.[57] Nietzsche maintained that, in this way, the psychology of blame reflects and serves a position of weakness: the perspective of the powerless. It serves this position by reactively elevating the moral status of the victim above the "evil" of the agent who is supposed to have caused harm intentionally and voluntarily.[58] But

---

55 Friedrich Nietzsche, (1887) *The Genealogy of Morals*.

56 Bernard Williams, "Nietzsche's Minimalist Moral Psychology", in his *Making Sense of Humanity* (Cambridge: Cambridge University Press, 1995), 73. Williams adds that blame actually involves trying to make its subject into such an agent (i.e., into someone who would have prevented the harm through an act of will). He writes that it involves the thought that: "I, now, might change the agent from one who did not acknowledge me to one who did" (73). In other words, the psychology of blame involves the fantasy that the expression of blame itself might retrospectively have prevented the injury. See also Bernard Williams, "Internal Reasons and the Obscurity of Blame", in his *Making Sense of Humanity* (Cambridge: Cambridge University Press, 1995).

57 See Nietzsche, *Genealogy of Morals*, Essay 1, section 13.

58 Durkheim argues that the moralization of our reactive sentiments leads to a sense of alienation, for in avenging them we project them outside of ourselves, and attribute them to the

this moral perspective is not liberating, he argued, for it is ultimately involved with the ascetic denial of desires and impulses, most notably our anger and aggression, that are implicated in the causal order of nature—a denial that is especially destructive and costly when it becomes internalized and thought to be good in itself.

Nietzsche's story seems to me plausible, but its details need not concern us here.[59] The point is that if the argument of this paper is valid, normative ethics will not be able to explain our attachment to the reactive attitudes. This means some other account must be found. If Nietzsche's story is not entirely correct, then something like it must be true.

The alternative to a psychology of blame I have proposed is to free our investment in the power of rational thought and control from the reactive attitudes and to connect it instead to the possibility of realizing the cooperative ideal of a just society. Justice, as I understand it, is not the meting out of resentment, but represents an alternative to and an overcoming of it.[60] While the Strawsonian picture rightly points to the fact of our investment in rationality, and to its importance to social relations, our investment in rationality need not be so tightly linked to the reactive attitudes. The reactive account of responsibility Strawson presents as an alternative to a metaphysics of desert does not succeed because the quest for a metaphysics of desert is driven by our reactive attitudes. It is because we seek a justification for our reactive attitudes and the blaming behavior that so often accompanies them that we attempt to stake out the conditions of desert. A practical conception of morality, on the other hand, can abandon the reactive account of responsibility and its metaphysics of free will and desert; it represents a collective response to our needs and conflicts that can replace the relief (perhaps misguidedly) sought in our experience of the reactive attitudes. The forward-looking, constructive quality of moral thought means that morality involves, in a sense, taking what Strawson refers to as an "objective" attitude in the collective construction and realization of moral ideals: it requires us to engage in practical reasoning about how to define and satisfy our aims as moral agents.

Recall the features of a practical conception of morality. Moral motivation involves each party taking some interest in the morally urgent needs of other people. The norms of morality are not the outcome of self-interested bargaining between persons. They presuppose that moral persons will take an interest in realizing a form of association that affirms the value of each person's basic interests, provided that others do so as well. This is expressed in persons' willingness to reason together with others as equals to arrive at a set of moral norms all who are similarly motivated could share. We might think of the "objective" point of view, then, as prescribing that we take one another's morally basic interests and equal status into account in our social interactions. Morality would have us acknowledge the intersubjective validity of a certain set of needs and interests and the rights and liberties we ascribe to persons in view of these needs and interests.

---

idea of morality or a divinity, which we regard as superior to ourselves. See Durkheim, 100–101.

59 For further analysis and discussion, see Max Scheler, *Ressentiment*, ed. Lewis A. Coser (New York: The Free Press, 1961).

60 Nietzsche, *Genealogy of Morals*, Essay 1, section 11.

A form of social life that is responsive to the morally urgent needs of each person must cultivate incentives for promoting shared aims.[61] Ideally, this involves enabling each person to realize his or her capacity and desire for moral agency. I have suggested that our moral attitudes are largely directed toward the relevant potentials and capacities in persons, and that our respect for persons as moral beings is expressed in our acknowledgment of these potentials and capacities.[62] When persons fail to realize their potential as moral agents, however, practical deliberation involves negotiating how acceptably to distribute this burden in the interest of most effectively promoting shared practical aims. This can lead us to important forward-looking rationales for identifying and responding to past wrongs. Expressing our disapproval of people's wrongdoing and penalizing them for it can play a crucial role in the process of halting abuses, compensating victims, returning stolen property, redistributing wealth, overcoming ethnic and racial conflict and, generally speaking, working toward greater justice. But this is a matter quite different from dealing out blame on the basis of desert. Our interest in the "stains" on people's records remains firmly linked to our interest in bettering the prospects for a tolerant and just society.

Thus we can see that on this view, morality is not the impersonal analogue of resentment, but an alternative to it. Morality need not attempt to isolate the self-generating power (or self-control) of the rational will. It depends not on a presumption of the autonomous forms of self-control that seem to underwrite the reactive attitudes but, rather, on the possibility of cultivating reasonable and just interrelations that generally offer sufficient incentives for compliance and safeguards for dealing with the failure of some persons to be motivated by morality.

I have argued that we should understand the moral value of the activities of praise and blame to be relative to the practical aims and ambitions of a morality. We should not confuse the psychology of blame and resentment with the moral interest we have in cultivating people's rationality (i.e., our capacity to recognize and act for reasons) for collectively acceptable aims and purposes. Our interest in fairness, furthermore, can be detached from our preoccupation with justifying resentment and extends more appropriately to the matter of how we are justified in treating others as we pursue our collective moral aims. I do not deny that people experience resentment and may sometimes have reason to seek acceptable channels for its expression. The psychology of resentment, the appeal of blame as punishment to inflict suffering because we think it is deserved, may well be a primitive psychology we may not be able fully to divorce ourselves from.[63] The importance to people of expressing such attitudes is something that may need to be taken into account in our social policy on punishment. But we should attempt to minimize the importance of these expressions, for their social costs are high, they rest on dubious metaphysics, and they are not essentially linked to the practical aims of morality.

---

61 A practical conception of morality must also solve coordination problems.

62 Moral education as an aim of punishment is relevant here, as are the aims I have connected with the activity of moral criticism. See footnote 45 and Section II.

63 See, for example, J.L. Mackie, "Morality and the Retributive Emotions", in Joan Mackie and Penelope Mackie (eds), *Persons and Values: Selected Papers, Volume II*, (Oxford: Oxford University Press, 1985).

Acknowledgments

I would like to thank members of the philosophy departments at the University of California, Santa Cruz and the Universitá Degli Studi Roma Tre for fruitful discussion of this paper. This paper was also presented at a seminar for the Program on Ethics and Public Life at Cornell University and at the Central Division APA, 2000. I thank the participants for their challenging questions as well as my commentators Michele Moody-Adams and Joan McGregor. I am grateful to Arnold Davidson, Daniel Dennett, Sean Greenberg and Gary Watson for their very helpful critical responses to an earlier draft. And finally, I acknowledge a special debt to Lionel McPherson—conversations with him have shaped much of this paper.

Chapter 15

Responsibility and the Aims of Theory
Strawson and Revisionism

Manuel Vargas

Strawsonian approaches to responsibility, including more recent accounts such as Dennett's and Wallace's, face a number of important objections. However, Strawsonian theories can be recast along revisionist lines so as to avoid many of these problems. In this paper, I explain the revisionist approach to moral responsibility, discuss the concessions it makes to incompatibilism (including the point that compatibilists may not fully capture our commonsense understanding of responsibility), why it provides a fruitful recasting of Strawsonian approaches, and how it offers an alternative to the pattern of dialectical stalemates exhibited by standard approaches to free will and determinism.

In recent years, reflection on the relationship between individual moral responsibility and determinism has undergone a remarkable renaissance. Incompatibilists, those who believe moral responsibility is incompatible with determinism, have offered powerful new arguments in support of their views. Compatibilists, those who think moral responsibility is compatible with determinism, have responded with ingenious counterexamples and alternative accounts of responsibility.

Despite the admirable elevation of complexity and subtlety within both camps, the trajectory of the literature is somewhat discouraging. Every dialectical stalemate between incompatibilists and compatibilists seems to be superseded by a similar though often more subtle stalemate.[1] The stalemates have two sources. On the one hand, incompatibilists again and again find powerful intuitive support from our folk concept. On the other hand, compatibilists seem right to insist that even if determinism were true, this would not mitigate our need for a concept of responsibility.

In this paper, I attempt to show how principled and systematic pursuit of an approach I call *revisionism* might push us through this stalemate. The central idea of revisionism is that an adequate theory of responsibility will depart significantly from our commonsense understanding of responsibility. My point of departure is P.F. Strawson's justly influential "Freedom and Resentment" and some of the work that

---

1 The term "dialectical stalemate" is John Martin Fischer's. On a Fischer-related note, I should mention that my characterization of (in)compatibilism is meant to be neutral with regard to whether or not free will is required for responsibility. Thus, any references to free will will be treated as references to a kind of agency, condition, or power required for morally responsible agency or moral responsibility. This device is not meant to reflect implicit acceptance of a substantive position on this issue (i.e., the relationship of responsibility and any or all notions of free will).

article has inspired.[2] I start with Strawsonianism because careful attention to *how* it fails suggests a way to rehabilitate it along systematically revisionist lines. This recasting requires that we make some important concessions to incompatibilists, including the idea that no compatibilist theory may be able to respect the constraints of the ordinary concept of moral responsibility.[3] However, if we adopt my approach we have good reason to think we can make real progress against the pattern of dialectical stalemates.

This paper is divided into three parts. In part one, I describe Strawson's original account and the main lines of criticism it provoked. In part two, I argue that no standardly compatibilist Strawsonian account has the resources to answer traditional incompatibilist worries. In part three, I say what the revisionist alternative is, how it can be pursued, and why it constitutes a promising alternative to standard forms of compatibilism and incompatibilism.

1.

a. Strawson on responsibility

In "Freedom and Resentment", Strawson sought to put compatibilism on a new and more persuasive footing. Strawson aimed to give the compatibilist an account of our moral practices showing that they were justified and did not depend on, as he memorably put it, the "panicky metaphysics" of libertarianism. He argued that responsibility is to be understood in terms of a set of distinctive attitudes and associated practices. According to Strawson, if we carefully reflect on the way these attitudes and practices function, we would find nothing internal to our practices to suggest that the truth of determinism should prevent us from engaging in those practices.

---

2 P.F. Strawson, "Freedom and Resentment", originally in *Proceedings of the British Academy*, xlviii (1962), p. 187–211; reprinted in Gary Watson (ed.), *Free Will* (New York: Oxford, 1982), pp. 59–80. [Also reprinted in this volume, pp. 19–36. Page references for "Freedom and Resentment" will be to pages 19–36 of this volume, followed by (after the slash) the corresponding pages of Gary Watson (ed.), *Free Will*. Thus, for example, 'FR, 34–5/78 in note 14 below, refers to this volume, pp. 34–5/and *Free Will*, p. 78)—the editors.] For important developments and critiques, see Jonathan Bennett, "Accountability" in Zak van Straaten (ed.), *Philosophical Subjects* (New York: Clarendon, 1980), Daniel Dennett *Elbow Room* (Cambridge: MIT, 1984), Watson, Gary in Ferdinand Schoeman (ed.), *Responsibility, Character and the Emotions* (Ithica: Cornell 1987), T.M. Scanlon "The Significance of Choice" in Sterling M. McMurrin (ed.), *The Tanner Lectures on Human Values* VII, (Cambridge: Cambridge, 1988) and his *What We Owe to Each Other* (Cambridge: Belknap Harvard, 1998), R. Jay Wallace, *Responsibility and the Moral Sentiments* (Cambridge, Harvard, 1996), Michael Bratman "Responsibility and Planning" *The Journal of Ethics* 1 (1997), pp. 27–43, John Fischer and Mark Ravizza *Responsibility and Control* (Cambridge: Cambridge, 1998), and Michael McKenna "The Limits of Evil and the Role of Moral Address" *The Journal of Ethics* 2 (1998), pp.123–42.

3 Further uses of the term "responsibility" should be understood to stand for the more cumbersome term "individual moral responsibility".

Strawson described two kinds of cases in which we do not hold people responsible: (1) when agents act in a way that does not reflect a poor "quality of will" and (2) in cases where the target of assessment is not the right sort of agent to be a target of our practices and attitudes. I will follow Watson in identifying the suspension of the attitudes characteristic of holding people responsible in the former case as *excuses*, and in the latter case as *exemptions*.[4] Excuses do not depend on truths about determinism. When we excuse someone, we typically do so because the targeted agent fails to have a criticizable quality of will. For example, if I accidentally step on your foot, I will be excused from responsibility not because determinism entailed that I stepped on your foot, but rather because I did not step on your foot out of ill will. According to Strawson, my ill will is what matters for our attitudes and practices, not whether my will had been determined. The case of exemptions is similar: when we exempt agents from responsibility, it is not because they are determined, but because they are simply agents of the wrong kind.[5] These agents typically lack the right sensitivity to moral practices because they have not yet developed the relevant capacities (children), they have lost them (the injured, diseased, or aged) or the agents never had them. It is a departure from ordinary adult capacities that exempts agents from responsibility, not the threat of determinism. In short, neither excuses nor exemptions are sensitive to abstract truths about determinism.

Since the truth of determinism does not affect our practices through either excuses or exemptions, nothing internal to the practices of holding people responsible suggests that we need to be worried about determinism. But, Strawson recognized that one might challenge the entire framework of practices and the attitudes they express. The critic might argue that the framework presupposes something false or that it stands in need of some further justification. Strawson responded that the practices (and the attitudes they express) are part of an inescapable framework of interpersonal relationships and thus do not require further justification.[6] There is a strand in Strawson's discussions that suggests that questions about this framework are unintelligible, for the framework in question is somehow foundational or necessary for our thinking about responsibility. The main thrust of his argument, though, is that because we cannot help having attitudes that give rise to our practices of holding people responsible, demand for further justification is inappropriate. The demand for justification of our practices comes to an end when the root of those practices, the responsibility-characteristic attitudes, turns out to be inescapable features of human

---

4   *Op. cit.*, p. 260.

5   Recall that consequentialist compatibilists were criticized for failing to take seriously the distinction between kinds of agents. Strawson's move seems to give the consequentialist a response: the distinction between responsibility practices and other kinds of practices *does* reflect a difference in moral agency precisely because the mark of moral agency is susceptibility to certain distinctive mechanisms of social and psychological influence. Only moral agents can be effectively influenced by considerations rooted in the characteristic attitudes and practices and this susceptibility is what marks them out as distinctive. Whether we should attribute this move to Strawson is perhaps disputable, but it is available to consequentialists of Strawsonian inspiration.

6   Strawson later cites Carnap and Wittgenstein as the inspiration for this move see Strawson's *Skepticism and Naturalism* (New York: Columbia, 1985), Chs 1–2.

psychology. Finally, Strawson suggests a possible pragmatic defense. Even if we could give up the framework of attitudes, this would be to give up many of the rich social-psychological features that make our lives worth living. Consequently, determinism does not and could not pose a real threat to responsibility.

b. Reactions to Strawson

Strawson's theory provoked criticism from a number of directions. Several philosophers have offered rigorous criticisms of various aspects of Strawson's substantive account of our practices and what they require. For our purposes, we need not consider them in any detail, though they point to something widely recognized about Strawson's account: his analysis of our practices, while insightful and suggestive, is seriously underdeveloped.[7] In particular, Strawson says too little about who is exempt from responsibility and why. One way of understanding the threat of determinism is to think that it might show that we are all exempt from responsibility because we are not the kinds of agents whom it would be appropriate to treat as responsible in the sense presupposed by our practices.

A second line of criticism concerns the claim that our responsibility practices and attitudes are an inescapable part of the basic framework of human social life.[8] Several philosophers question whether the attitudes characteristic of responsibility—what Strawson calls the *reactive attitudes* in cases in which one is reacting to some personally directed responsibility-bearing act, and the *vicarious analogs* in cases in which one is responding to an action directed at others—are truly inescapable human reactions.[9] If these critics are right, then the responsibility-characteristic attitudes *can* be called into question precisely because they are malleable in a way that does not presuppose abandonment of our entire network of interpersonal attitudes. Consequently, the justification of our responsibility-characteristic attitudes, and the practices that depend on them, is still in order.

Although it is far from clear that our attitudes are as plastic as these critics of Strawson suggest, others have convincingly argued that we can intelligibly raise questions about the framework of attitudes even if the attitudes are ultimately inescapable. This third sort of criticism can (though it need not) concede the inflexibility of our psychology, but resists Strawson's claim that these attitudes cannot be subject to further justificatory demands because of their place in the framework of our lives. It could turn out, Susan Wolf argues, that we are not truly responsible even though we cannot help treating people as though they are responsible agents.[10] Believing

---

7 See Bennett, *op. cit.*, Paul Russell "Strawson's Way of Naturalizing Responsibility" *Ethics* 102 (1992), pp. 287–302, and Watson, op. cit.

8 Strawson admits that we can temporarily suspend the personal "reactive" framework that is partially constituitive of our inescapable social framework to "relieve the strains of commitment" that come from reactive engagement with others. However, he emphasizes that such suspensions are only temporary.

9 Lawrence Stern "Freedom, Blame, and the Moral Community" *Journal of Philosophy* (1974), pp. 72–84, Galen Strawson *Freedom and Belief* (Oxford: Oxford, 1986), and Derk Pereboom "Determinism *al Dente*" *Nous* 29 (1995), pp. 21–45.

10 "The Importance of Free Will" *Mind* 90 (1981), pp. 386–405.

people are responsible and treating agents as responsible would be species-wide instances of what Dennett calls "the familiar class of life-enabling or life-enhancing illusions: the illusion that one is still loved by one's loved ones; the illusion that one has several more years to live when one hasn't; the illusion that in spite of one's physical ugliness, one's inner beauty is readily manifest to others".[11] Even if our responsibility-characteristic attitudes are inescapable, there are other parts of our doxastic and value framework from which questions about our practices might be raised. To paraphrase Wolf, our interest in living in accord with the truth can ground challenges to even highly implastic attitudes. On this line of criticism, the framework of responsibility turns out to be only a sub-set of our more complete conceptual, axiological, and connative framework. It is from the perspective of other aspects of that framework that the responsibility framework can be called into doubt.

One way to get at this family of criticisms is to focus on the apparently cognitivist character of responsibility. This is the idea that claims of responsibility admit of truth and falsity, and our "grounding beliefs"—the beliefs that provide the foundations for our judgments that someone is responsible—might well be false. Call this worry the *cognitivist criticism*. To see why we might worry about the apparently cognitivist dimension of responsibility (i.e., the grounding beliefs), we need only recall the hackneyed example of judgments about the location of the sun in pre-Copernican times. Before the Copernican revolution changed much of our thinking about cosmology, people believed that during midday the sun was objectively above them. This judgment was made against a background of other beliefs, including fixed and absolute spatial relations. The problem was, of course, that some of these background beliefs were false. The worry that motivates the question of responsibility is similar: Do our practices and attitudes characteristic of responsibility depend on a judgment that presupposes false or incoherent things? Strawson downplayed this worry, instead directing our attention to the inescapability of the reactive framework. But Wolf and others are right to insist that we cannot rule out this question and the metaphysics that its answer might bring, simply by declaring that the attitudes triggered by our judgments are an inescapable part of our social psychology. Assuming that we do care about whether or not we are truly responsible in the ordinary sense of the phrase, Strawson needs to show that the expression of our attitudes does not depend on a judgment or judgments (however inevitable) that is or are false. Strawson never does this.

Bernard Berofsky recently noted "Strawson's celebrated proposal to construe freedom and responsibility as constituitive of human society failed to convince enough of us that metaphysical issues cannot have a bearing on the attitudes and perhaps even the practices associated with these notions.[12] Berofsky's comment points to an important similarity between two of the three lines of criticism I have mentioned. The point of the first criticism was that Strawson lacks a sufficiently detailed account of when someone is or is not exempt from responsibility. The upshot of the third criticism, the cognitivist criticism, is that Strawson lacks a sufficiently

---

11 *Op. cit.*, p. 168.
12 "Ultimate Responsibility in a Deterministic World" *Philosophy and Phenomenological Research* XL (2000), p. 135.

detailed account of our grounding beliefs for responsibility ascriptions. In both cases, the main worry turns out to be the possibility that a more complete account of the conditions for responsibility will invoke a troublesome metaphysics, which might undermine the normative integrity of the existing practices. In short, Strawson needs to be given something more to say.

2.

a. Strawsonians

Several contemporary compatibilists have attempted to rehabilitate Strawson's theory in a way that answers the cognitivist criticism and the more general implication that a full accounting of our beliefs might or must yield an unacceptable metaphysics. Among the most sophisticated and thorough attempts to do so are R. Jay Wallace's *Responsibility and the Moral Sentiments* and Daniel Dennett's *Elbow Room*.[13] Both works attempt to show that the beliefs presupposed by judgments of responsibility are neither metaphysically robust nor especially troublesome. Here, I will show that even sophisticated Strawsonian theories such as these cannot give an adequate accounting of the beliefs that matter for our judgments of responsibility. These theories answer the cognitivist criticism because they can accommodate the cognitive structure of responsibility claims and beliefs. Given the kinds of things these theories postulate in accounting for those cognitivist features, however, incompatibilists will remain unsatisfied.

For both Wallace and Dennett's accounts, there is a delicate issue concerning interpretation. Are these accounts supposed to capture and cohere with our ordinary beliefs and intuitions? Or, are we to understand these accounts as attempting to tell us about the property of responsibility, whatever its relationship to our commonsense concept? Here, I cannot do the full exegetical work required to defend one or the other interpretation. So, I will begin by assuming that whatever else the accounts are committed to, at the very least they are intended to capture and cohere with our ordinary beliefs and intuitions about responsibility. I take it that this assumption is in keeping with P. F. Strawson's original project of trying to account for "what we mean, i.e., of *all* we mean" by responsibility.[14] However, in accepting the assumption that these accounts are supposed to capture the contents of our ordinary beliefs about responsibility, this does not mean that the accounts cannot or are not also

---

13 Both *op. cit.*

14 FR, 34–5/78. Though Bennett is inclined to read Strawson more along the revisionist lines I propose to make a systematic part of Strawsonianism in part 3, I think it is pretty clear that Strawson and many subsequent Strawsonians have been reluctant to see their project as conceptually revisionist. For example, consider that Strawson viewed libertarian metaphysics not as something given by conceptual analysis, but rather something postulated in an attempt to fill "a lacuna" in our understanding of responsibility. The account Strawson proposed was therefore not intended as an attempt to overturn ordinary thinking, but rather, to show that our beliefs, practices, and attitudes were not committed to a very robust metaphysics, libertarian or otherwise. Of course, all of this is of a piece with Strawson's descriptive metaphysics.

intended to be accounts of the truth conditions of responsibility. This only means that the accounts cannot be committed to providing truth conditions for responsibility irrespective of our folk beliefs. I will return to the significance of this assumption in part three.

b. Wallace

Wallace's main innovation is something he calls the *normative interpretation* of responsibility. On the normative interpretation, and *pace* Strawson, judgments of responsibility do depend on facts about whether an agent is truly responsible. These background facts (upon which our responsibility judgments rely) are facts about the fairness of adopting the distinctive stance of holding someone morally responsible. That stance is understood in terms of a characteristic psychology and its associated practices. The complex metaphysics of agency defended by many incompatibilists turns out to be unnecessary, because the background facts are primarily facts about the fairness of a certain way of treating other agents. And, these facts do not require an incompatibilist metaphysics of agency.

Wallace characterizes the normative interpretation of responsibility in the following way:

(*N*): *S* is morally responsible (for action *x*) if and only if it would be appropriate to hold *s* morally responsible (for action *x*).[15]

The first thing to note is that N gives an answer to the cognitivist criticism that plagued Strawson's theory. N is consistent with there being facts about whether we are truly responsible, and those facts can be important for our judgments of responsibility. This gives the language of responsibility a cognitivist construal, but the view retains the Strawsonian spirit of analyzing the concept of responsibility because the stance of holding responsible is understood in terms of a characteristic psychology and its associated practices.

Also worth noting is that N includes no specification of appropriateness. As it turns out, the details of Wallace's theory depend on understanding the appropriateness of N in terms of fairness. This yields a slightly different specification of the normative interpretation that we can call F:

(*F*): *S* is morally responsible (for action *x*) if and only if it would be *fair* to hold *s* morally responsible (for action *x*).

Though the move from N to F does not receive much discussion in *Responsibility and the Moral Sentiments*, F is a natural, though certainly contentious, refinement of N.

Wallace's acceptance of F turns on his view that the fairness (or not) of our responsibility-characteristic practices is, in some important way, prior to our being responsible. This assumption is not made clear by the schema itself, but it makes explicit what is innovative about Strawsonians. The difficulty, though, is

---

15 *Op. cit.*, 91.

that the innovation invites the charge that Strawsonians are failing to respect our commonsense understanding of responsibility.

Consider what is likely the standard view about the relationship between our being responsible and the appropriateness of our practices. Most incompatibilists and non-Strawsonian compatibilists believe that our being responsible is, roughly, a matter of an agent standing in a particular relation to an action. On this view, facts about responsibility are practice-independent facts about agency and action. If there is a relationship between responsibility and the appropriateness of our practices, facts about fairness depend on facts about being responsible. Call this the *agent-based account* of responsibility facts.

In contrast, Wallace maintains that our being responsible is *not* fixed by some facts antecedent to the appropriateness of our practices.[16] Rather, an agent's being responsible depends on the fairness of treating that agent as responsible. Wallace's particular account might be described as a *normative practice-based account*. On this account, the "truth maker" for claims about responsibility is some normative feature of responsibility-characteristic practices (e.g., the fairness of the practices in general and/or in that specific instance). What makes it characteristically Strawsonian is that it is a member of the more general class of practice-based accounts, accounts where the truth maker is based on some feature of our practices.

As incompatibilists and other non-Strawsonians see it, Strawsonian accounts either misconstrue or fail to capture some core features of commonsense thinking about responsibility. The starting point for agent-based accounts is the idea that it is natural to think that responsibility facts are fixed by features of the agent and the agent's actions. This does not mean that responsibility-ascriptions cannot play other roles. Responsibility ascriptions may frequently play a dual role in our moral lives, both marking out facts about responsibility and indicating an assessment about the appropriateness of certain practices. But, what facts there are about responsibility are facts that supervene on agents and their actions, not on the practices directed at the agents.

As agent-based theorists see it, there are only two things we need to know to learn the facts about responsibility in any particular case: what kind of agent is involved, and the agent's connection to the considered action (or state of affairs). Wallace-style Strawsonians, however, maintain that we need to know a further thing: whether deployment of responsibility-characteristic practices is appropriate (or fair, etc.) in general and in the particular case. But, what evidence could they offer for thinking that we need to know these things as well? Everything we need to know seems to be settled by knowledge about the agent and his or her connection to the evaluated action or state of affairs. Indeed, the further normative facts of interest to

---

16 Wallace opens his book by writing that, "if we wish to make sense of the idea that there are facts about what it is to be a responsible agent, it is best not to picture such facts as conceptually prior to and independent of our practice of holding people responsible." Later he reiterates the claim, emphasizing "on the normative approach, the facts about whether people are morally responsible are not yet available to be appealed to at this stage in the inquiry. Those facts are fixed by the answer to the question of when it is appropriate to hold people responsible, and so they cannot be invoked to decide that very question" (*Ibid.*, pp. 92–3).

normative practice-based theorists are, by their own admission, largely determined by facts about agents and their connection to actions or states of affairs. It seems gratuitous to insist that the normative property of being responsible is parasitic on a further, more basic normative property (e.g., the fairness of the practices), which is itself dependent on properties of agency and action on which the status of being responsible was initially thought to depend. Moreover, it seems possible to think that someone can be responsible, regardless of whether or not it is fair to hold them responsible in this or that particular case. Suppose we have a policy of never holding people responsible for their first moral infraction, even if we would normally be inclined to think of them as a fully responsible agent. Now suppose that we arbitrarily suspend this policy for a randomly selected person. It seems plausible to think of this as a case where it would be unfair to hold someone responsible all the while thinking that they are responsible. If so, this shows that in our commonsense moral ontology, the property of responsibility is not dependent on some further and more basic normative property of our responsibility practices.[17]

Given the power of agent-based accounts to capture our commonsense thinking about responsibility, Strawsonians have to muster some compelling arguments to get incompatibilists and others to abandon the agent-based picture of our concept of responsibility. Wallace's main argument for a normative practice-based interpretation of our commonsense convictions is the fruitfulness of his account, which relies on this assumption.[18] But this kind of argument, especially given apparent counterexamples of the sort I mention above, is not likely to convince the majority of incompatibilists and non-Strawsonian compatibilists who find a practice-independent account of the folk concept more plausible. Thus, if Strawsonians want to sustain the claim that they can adequately capture folk thinking about responsibility, we need to look elsewhere for a defense of their compatibility with ordinary moral thinking.

c. *Dennett*

Dennett's work is a promising place to look for a defense of practice-based accounts. Like Wallace, Dennett endorses a roughly Strawsonian interpretation of being and holding responsible. (Though unlike Wallace, he does not emphasize the importance of fairness in how we hold people responsible.) More importantly, Dennett offers direct arguments against interpreting the concept of responsibility as having practice-independent purport.

Dennett rejects the agent-based picture of responsibility for three reasons. First, he thinks that taking the status of being responsible as prior commits you to a metaphysical interpretation where the invoked metaphysics cannot provide the requisite normative justification. Second, he argues that treating the status of being responsible as prior to holding responsible engenders intractable epistemological

---

17 Randolph Clarke, who credits Scanlon as the source of his idea, suggested this case to me.

18 In conversation, Wallace has confirmed that he does not take himself to have given a "direct" argument for the practice-based interpretation.

problems associated with responsibility. Finally, he thinks that there is no way to make the agent-based approach's presumed metaphysical story coherent.[19]

All of these reasons are inadequate for abandoning what Dennett admits is the common-sense assumption that we take *being* responsible as fundamental in our thinking about responsibility. For our purposes, the discovery that our folk metaphysics does not provide normative justification does not count as a reason for thinking that our concept has no such metaphysical commitments. It could well turn out that our ordinary concept of responsibility has metaphysical commitments that are not normatively justified. But, that would be a discovery about our concept, not something we should rule out as a matter of principle. The same is true of Dennett's third argument, about the coherence of the metaphysical story. Our folk metaphysical commitments might indeed be incoherent, but again, that would be a discovery worth making, not a possibility we should close off at the start of inquiry.

As for Dennett's other charge, that a metaphysical grounding of responsibility would make assessments of guilt or innocence tricky things (inasmuch as facts of metaphysical independence would likely be epistemically inaccessible), it is difficult to see why this should count as a reason for thinking that our concept lacks metaphysical commitments.[20] Even if we can never demonstrably prove that someone has satisfied all the metaphysical conditions for true responsibility, Dennett's charge—at best—points to a need for practical ways of dealing with assessments of responsibility. But, this is hardly unique to the moral realm. We are always in need of practical solutions for problems about which we know we can never be certain of the best answer, even when we are confident that there is such a thing. Dennett himself makes this point in his 1988 Tanner lecture.[21]

In sum, neither Dennett nor Wallace offer arguments that would change the mind of an antecedently convinced incompatibilist or agent-based compatibilist. Thus, if Strawsonianism is to make good on its promise to end the pattern of dialectical stalemates, it will have to do so in a fundamentally different way from what it has attempted so far. In the rest of this paper, I attempt to show how this might be done.

---

19 *Op. cit.*, p. 166.

20 Note that if Dennett's argument did work, it would seem to work just as well against Wallace's account, for facts about fairness seem no more or less metaphysically spooky than facts about responsibility.

21 See Dennett "The Moral First Aid Manual" in McMurrin (ed.), *The Tanner Lectures on Human Values* VII (Cambridge: Cambridge, 1988). I take it there is more that can be said about this issue, though I do not think that it will change anyone's mind about these issues. For instance, Dennett could point out that our ordinary attributions seem to presume some confidence in assessments that ought to have at least some evidence. But the incompatibilist will just reply that we ordinarily assume people are metaphysically free unless we have *countervailing* evidence. What makes the issue of free will and moral responsibility an issue at all just is that it seems to threaten our unreflectively assumed belief that we have the kinds of metaphysically demanding powers we ordinarily assume. It is worth noting, though, that we should not simply assume that our current stock of philosophically interesting concepts is optimal, accurate, metaphysically innocuous, or worth keeping. More on this in section 3.

3.

a. A concession and two reactions

The key to adequately rehabilitating the Strawson project and moving closer to a resolution of the deadlock between compatibilists and incompatibilists is for Strawsonians to concede something to incompatibilists. The concession is this: *the folk concept of responsibility may be incompatibilist.*

We can expect two different (and opposed!) reactions to this suggestion. The first reaction will go something like this: "You are groundlessly claiming that compatibilists should simply capitulate on the crux of the compatibility debate. Why in the world would any compatibilist agree to this?"

In response, it is important to consider what we (Strawsonian revisionists), are not giving up. We are not necessarily giving up on the idea that the *property* of responsibility is compatible with determinism, nor are we necessarily giving up on the idea that we can be responsible agents in a deterministic world. What we are giving up is the idea that an adequate theory of responsibility is one that fully captures folk beliefs about responsibility. In short, revisionist Strawsonians will admit that the best theory of responsibility might well be *revisionist* in the sense that it will depart (to some extent) from our commonsense understanding of responsibility, and ultimately, require some revision of commonsense. But, nothing in such a concession requires that revisionist Strawsonians give up a commitment to the property of responsibility being compatible with the truth of determinism.

The kind of revisionism I propose is not altogether unheard of among Strawsonians. We find clear suggestions of it in Dennett's slogan of "the varieties of free will worth wanting" and in Wallace's conditional acceptance of "modest revisionism" about our retributivist folk beliefs, in light of the fairness demands imposed by F.[22] Moreover, there are some who have maintained that the only charitable way to interpret Strawson or compatibilists of any stripe is as revisionists.[23] If one already thought that revisionism was a central feature of compatibilism, the alternative reaction we can expect is something like this: "How is revisionist Strawsonianism any different than Strawsonianism? This is what Strawsonians have been trying to do all along. If what they have been doing isn't working, we should hardly expect that calling it revisionism will move us any closer to ending the dialectic of stalemates."

This reaction gives too much credit to extant Strawsonians. Despite sporadic awareness of it, the revisionist insight is almost never fully appreciated, even by those who admit it into their theories. Revisionism, when recognized at all, is usually admitted only cautiously and with some ambivalence.[24] For instance, suppose we read the texts of the afore-mentioned Strawsonians as arguments about the truth

---

22 Wallace, pp. 228–9.

23 Bennett (1980) and Frank Jackson *From Metaphysics to Ethics* (New York: Oxford, 1998).

24 Bennett, *op. cit.*, is an important exception. In that paper he (implausibly, I think) claims that Strawson's original theory was "excisionary". Despite important differences with Strawson he seems to endorse something like the revisionist strategy I have proposed here. However, his recent statement of a particular methodological approach in *The Act Itself*

conditions for responsibility, where these accounts succeed or fail independently of the theory's conformity to the folk concept of responsibility. Such a reading does considerable violence to the structure of their texts. For example, there is a pervasive ambiguity in Dennett's account regarding whether the varieties of free will (or morally responsible agency) worth wanting are the one(s) we ordinarily do want. Sometimes, as in his analysis of control, he is concerned to give an account of *our ordinary concept*.[25] At other times, when he considers intuitions in support of agent causation, for example, he does not argue that we do not have these intuitions or that we just need to understand their content properly. Rather, his aim is to give a naturalistically acceptable account of agency that does not rely on such intuitions, dismissing them as "a sort of cognitive illusion".[26] Similarly for Wallace; his admission of potential revisionism rests uneasily against a background of substantial argument directed at showing that we need not adopt metaphysical interpretations of our folk concept. If revising our folk concept of responsibility is acceptable in light of pursuing a normatively adequate account of responsibility, it is difficult to see why he should be concerned to undermine the intuitions that drive metaphysical accounts of responsible agency. It would seem better just to admit that we have a metaphysically demanding picture and then to argue that this picture should be abandoned in favor of the account he proposes.

A more thorough examination of the work of Strawsonians and other compatibilists would doubtlessly find more passages that are suggestive of one or another form of revisionism.[27] To the extent that various Strawsonians intended to propose a revisionist project, what follows will already seem appealing. My goal, though, is to sketch how intentional, systematic, and rigorous pursuit of Strawsonian revisionism might constitute a genuine advance in our theorizing about responsibility.

I will begin by discussing the outlines of a general revisionist approach to responsibility. Then, I will argue for the advantages of a revisionism informed by Strawsonian insights.

b. Outlines of a revisionist project

Let us start by clarifying what the revisionist gives up to the incompatibilist. Suppose the revisionist concedes to the incompatibilist that our folk concept of responsibility really does suppose metaphysically demanding alternative possibilities, but that

---

(New York: Oxford, 1995) and the way he links that approach to his earlier work make a straightforward interpretation of Bennett's project too complicated to pursue here.

25 *Op. cit.*, n.52, italics in original.

26 *Ibid.*, p. 77.

27 For example, Fischer and Ravizza pursue a theory of responsibility that might be thought of as "revisionist" in the sense that it holds that serious reflection about our concept of control makes us realize that it need not be as metaphysically demanding as we initially suppose it to be. As I understand it, they think that our concept of responsibility-relevant control really is metaphysically innocuous, though they admit that there are intuitions that initially suggest otherwise. This relatively mild form of revisionism contrasts with, for example, Wallace's and T.M. Scanlon's revisionism about retribution. They cautiously claim that their accounts may altogether depart from the commitments of folk thinking.

(for a variety of reasons), it is implausible to think that we have them. In principle, revisionists do not need to hinge their revisionism on alternative possibilities being a part of the folk concept. Revisionism could be adopted if our folk concept does not require alternative possibilities, but rather, some kind of agency that amounted to "unmoved mover-hood" or agent causation. As long as there is *some* incompatibilist condition required by the folk concept that is not likely to be met, there is room for a revisionist theory. Call the account of the (likely) unsatisfied incompatibilist condition the *folk conceptual error theory*.

Often there is an inclination to move from the conviction that the folk concept of responsibility is implausible to the conclusion that we are not responsible. It is important to note that such a move supposes a particular semantics of moral language. It supposes that reference to responsibility properties is largely or completely fixed by our concept of responsibility. But, we could hold a causal or some other externalist account of the reference of the relevant moral terms. If so, an error in our folk concept does not mean that we systematically fail to refer to some property of responsibility. It might only mean that we believe false things about responsibility. This insight, then, allows us to push past the stalemate between incompatibilists and compatibilists. We can concede that certain aspects of our thinking about responsibility are incompatibilist, without being committed to incompatibilism about the property of responsibility. It might well turn out that incompatibilism about the property of responsibility is true, too. But if an externalist semantics for responsibility is correct, then we will not learn this fact solely from reflection on our concept. The upshot is that we need not be held hostage to what we might call the *connotational content* of the concept.

Of course, there are surely many who would defend an internalist account of the reference of moral terms. For our purposes, though, we do not need settle the issue one way or another. We can proceed with a fairly timid position: agnosticism about whether conceptual analysis tells us about the property of responsibility. Call this *semantic agnosticism*.[28]

---

28 Just how the proposed revision is understood will be something for revisionist metaphysics and semanticists to decide. However, one might worry that their answers have important consequences for the revisionist project. On the one hand, if our folk concept does fix reference, one might criticize revisionist theories as failing to be theories of *responsibility*. I'm inclined to think this is not a large worry. First, to the extent that the proposed revision is conservative, preserving the bulk of responsibility-characteristic beliefs, practices, and attitudes should be enough to earn the right to claim to be a revisionist theory *of responsibility*. Moreover, if we really do lack responsibility, it is hard to see how the fact that a proposed package of concept, attitudes, and practices does not pick out the exact same property (and note, in this case, a non-existent property) counts as a reason to think the theory is inadequate. In this case we might think of the theory as a charitable "paraphrasing" of our metaphysics of responsibility. On the other hand, if our concept does not fix reference and something else does, then one might think that any revision should be guided by whatever it is that fixes references. With respect to this latter criticism, the semantic agnostic revisionist need not disagree. However, I think that even if we could specify the truth conditions for responsibility in a folk-conceptually independent way, there might still be other reasons for taking up the revisionist's questions. For example, it could well turn out that the property we were tracking and calling

Given acceptance of both semantic agnosticism and a folk conceptual error theory, how can the revisionist proceed? I propose to adopt two standards, perhaps hinted at in Strawson's own work, for the revision of the folk concept of responsibility. The first is a standard of *normative adequacy* and the second is a standard of *naturalistic plausibility*.

The standard of normative adequacy holds that however the revision goes, the result must include a concept that is justified and well integrated with our network of mutually supporting norms and practices. A revised concept of responsibility that made responsibility-characteristic practices immune to considerations of (for example) fairness, proportional praise or punishment, and differences of moral agency (from moral patients to fully moral agents) would hardly count as being well integrated. A revised concept of responsibility that played no justified normative role in our moral thinking, that systematically conflicted with other pieces of justified moral thinking, or that lacked normative force altogether would also fail to meet the standard of normative adequacy. Thus, the normative standard forces some degree of conservatism about the revision in order to preserve the normatively significant parts of our practices.

In order to satisfy the normative standard, a revisionist account will need to be justified independently of the non-revised concept of responsibility and concepts that depend on it. For instance, a revised concept would fail to count as justified if the attitudes and practices it is intended to preserve were justified solely in virtue of some normative notion that is itself conceptually dependent on the non-revised concept of responsibility. For example, if desert relies upon the non-revised concept of responsibility, then desert is an inappropriate basis for revising the concept of responsibility when we accept a folk conceptual error theory.

One might worry that the normative standard is problematic because it rules out justification involving concepts dependent on the current folk concept of responsibility. This might seem to deplete the stockpile of available normative concepts too much. However, it is not clear whether the integrity of many, or any, normative concepts depends at all on the adequacy of the *concept* of responsibility. It is more sensible to think that the dependency would be on the property of responsibility. And, as we have seen, a folk conceptual error theory does not by itself entail an error theory about the property of responsibility. Even if we admit that there are some normative notions whose justification or integrity depends on the folk concept of responsibility, there is no reason to think that their loss would significantly deplete the availability of normative concepts that might serve as a basis for revision. Fairness, virtuousness, rationality, and other important normative concepts seem to be underived from the

---

"responsibility" is not normatively binding in the way we ordinarily suppose (and of course, this possibility must be allowed for once we separate the specification of the property from our conception of it). In that case, we could still be interested in trying to ground the cluster of practices, attitudes, and beliefs characteristic of our old understanding of responsibility even if none of these things were justifiable in turns of the features of actually responsible things. See Manuel Vargas, "The Revisionist's Guide to Responsibility", *Philosophical Studies*, 125 (2005), pp. 399–429.

folk concept of responsibility. Thus, the justification of the bulk of our responsibility-characteristic practices and attitudes might come in terms of these notions.

This result is important when we consider the range of theories available to the revisionist. Recall schemas N and F:

(*N*): *S* is morally responsible (for action *x*) if and only if it would be appropriate to hold *s* morally responsible (for action *x*).

(*F*): *S* is morally responsible (for action *x*) if and only if it would be *fair* to hold *s* morally responsible (for action *x*).

Suppose we decided to construe these schemas as claims about the kinds of commitments our folk concept *should* have. In that case, the variation between N and F points to a variation between the kinds of normative claims that we are allowed to appeal to in a revisionist theory. In the case of N, as long as there is something that makes it appropriate to hold someone responsible (where we understand this as the distinctive stance of adopting the responsibility-characteristic attitudes and practices), we can justify those characteristic practices and attitudes. Appropriateness could, in principle, be decided in diverse ways, ranging from considerations of rationality, self-interest, and other values only contingently connected to morality. However, this is one place where it matters that the standard of normative adequacy restricts our revisionism in a particular way. If it turns out that the norms that justify the continuation of the bulk of responsibility-characteristic attitudes and practices are not, at some significant level, *moral* norms, it is difficult to see how what would be left could possibly count as moral practices and attitudes. If a revision of the concept of moral responsibility entails that the revised concept does not play the same sort of role (as a moral concept) in our network of norms, the revision will fail to meet the standard of normative adequacy. Hence, acceptance of the normative standard means our revisionist theory must be of a more specific sort than some allowed for by N.

The unsuitability of N suggests F as a candidate for understanding the constraints of a revisionist theory under the normative standard. On F, the revised concept of responsibility is restricted to justification solely in terms of fairness. However, the normative standard does not restrict theory as much as F proposes. To the extent that we accept that other moral notions survive acceptance of the folk conceptual error theory of responsibility, revisionisms based on these other justified moral concepts will meet the standard of adequacy. We might put things this way: a theory will count as satisfying the normative standard if it adheres to the following schema

(*M*): *S* is morally responsible (for action *x*) if and only if it would be *morally appropriate* to hold *s* morally responsible (for action *x*).[29]

Under this schema (and following Wallace's suggestion of what it is to hold someone responsible), the revisionist is committed to changing our folk concept of responsibility so that by "S is responsible" we understand *that there is some justified*

---

29 In keeping with the argument thus far, I am assuming that the revisionist will give priority to the idea that being responsible is to be understood in an intersubjectivist way.

moral consideration or collection of considerations that entitles us to adopt towards S the stance characterized by those responsibility-characteristic beliefs, practices, and attitudes that are morally justified in a way not dependent on our current folk concept of responsibility. Once the revision is firmly in place, when we say that "S is responsible" what we will have in mind is that our then-current responsibility-characteristic beliefs, practices, and attitudes concerning *S* are morally justifiable in light of whatever conditions the particular revisionist theory specifies.

The normative standard moves us closer to a plausible picture of revisionism, though a satisfactory revisionism will need to specify the particular conditions in light of which the bulk of responsibility-characteristic attitudes and practices are justified.

Let us turn to consider the standard of naturalistic plausibility. According to this standard, a revision must not require things that are implausible under some broad-minded conception of substantive naturalism. As I use it here, "naturalism" need not be understood in an especially contentious way (e.g., as committed to strict reductionism).[30] Rather, we should think of it as helping to adjudicate a proposal's plausibility, based on what we know about science and the kinds of demands the considered theory makes on future science.[31]

We can see how the standard of naturalistic plausibility works in the following example. Suppose we learned that agent causation is scientifically implausible, if not impossible. In this case, commitment to the standard of naturalistic plausibility would prevent an agent causalist revision of our picture of responsible agency. Or, suppose we thought that the viability of a particular picture of agency depended on a very particular neurological structure, which we had no independent reason to believe in. Again, the naturalistic standard would treat this kind of theory as less plausible (ceteris paribus) than one that required no such structure.

What gives the naturalist standard some bite is that it effectively blocks a large class of theories from counting as viable revisionist accounts. Without some tool to reduce the total number of viable theories, admitting revisionism into our spectrum of theories might, by itself, seem to only double the number of accounts of the folk concept of responsibility. For any existing theory, we might suppose that it could be rendered in both revisionist and a non-revisionist ways. Thus, rather than ending the pattern of stalemates, revisionism might seem to make things worse. As is the case with the normative standard, adoption of the standard of naturalistic plausibility reduces the number of viable revisionist theories. In my judgment, though I will not attempt to adequately defend it here, it does this by ruling out virtually all revisionist theories that presuppose libertarian agency. Given that we accept the need

---

30 See Strawson's own discussion of responsibility in light of naturalism in Strawson, *Skepticism and Naturalism*, especially Chs 1–2.

31 In adopting this standard I am assuming that realism about moral properties is compatible with naturalism. Even if one rejects this assumption there are still two options. First, one might accept the standard of naturalistic plausibility, but take a different view about how to talk about the issue of a revisionist picture of moral responsibility. Second, one might pursue a kind of revisionism compatible with only the standard of normative adequacy. Either way, these would count as revisionist theories, though not of the sort that I pursue.

or possibility of conceptual revision, it would be prima facie undesirable to adopt a revision that makes significant demands on how the world must turn out (e.g., that indeterminism shows up in just the right place in the deliberative process and not in some other place, or that emergent causal powers appear at just the right level of ontological organization).[32] Even though libertarians have made great strides in showing how their theories might be consistent with various forms of naturalism, it is an altogether different thing to convince us that the theories are naturalistically plausible. Moreover, it is a further challenge to show these are burdens we would want to impose on our revised concept. If we have a warrant for revising our folk concept in a number of different ways, why would we want to do it in a way that shoulders the burdens of libertarianism? Other than the already excluded motive of conserving our folk concept of responsibility, what motive could there be for putting our newly revised concept and its commitments at the mercy of speculative accounts of indeterminism?

c. *Revisionist Strawsonianism*

Acceptance of a folk conceptual error theory and the standards of naturalistic plausibility and normative adequacy give considerable shape to a plausible revisionism. What we need, though, is some idea of how revisionists might go about filling in the indeterminate condition of moral appropriateness specified in M. In what follows, I sketch some of the ways in which reasonable revisionist theories can give some content to the schema provided in the previous section. My goal is not to argue for a particular account—this would be too much to attempt here. Rather, I hope to point out the ways in which development of a particularly Strawsonian revisionism will be well suited for giving an account of the moral appropriateness of some suitably large collection of our responsibility-characteristic beliefs, attitudes, and practices.

There are at least three reasons why specifically *Strawsonian* revisionism is promising. First, the revisionism sidesteps many of the complaints directed against Strawsonians. For example, Strawsonian revisionists need not deny those intuitions that suggest that our ordinary concept of responsibility is committed to alternate possibilities (or some other incompatibilist condition). All the favorite arguments of the incompatibilist can be accepted, as long as they are construed as arguments about our folk concept. This moves us closer to overcoming one stalemate with incompatibilists and it also gives new life to practice-based accounts of responsibility. For instance, even if practice-based accounts fail to fully capture the purport of the folk concept of responsibility, practice-based accounts may be appealing when recast as revisionist theories about the conditions for application of a revised concept of responsibility. That means that any benefits of practice-based approaches to

---

32 For a sophisticated account of the former, see Robert Kane, *The Significance of Free Will* (New York: Oxford, 1996). For sophisticated version of the latter, see Timothy O'Connor, *Persons and Causes* (New York: Oxford, 2001). Again, I do not mean to suggest that my remarks constitute adequate criticism for either theory. Rather, the point is merely to illustrate the greater burden of ontological commitment typically carried by libertarian theories.

responsibility can be co-opted by revisionists. So, in the spirit of Strawsonianism, we might maintain that a practice-based account is the preferable way of avoiding the "panicky" metaphysical commitments created by our agent-based folk concept.

A second advantage of Strawsonian revisionism is that it can provide principled adjudication of debates in the theory of agency. Unlike standard compatibilists, revisionists need not worry whether their pictures of moral agency satisfy all of our pre-theoretical intuitions. We can expect that given the revisionist's focus on normative adequacy and naturalistic plausibility, revisionists will offer refinements of existing theories of moral agency that more closely track naturalist and normative standards than theories developed under concerns of intuitiveness. For instance, Fischer and Ravizza maintain that a theory of moral agency has to include a historical condition on the ownership of the agent's reasons-responsive mechanism.[33] Given the concern of preserving ordinary intuitions, this may be true. However, a rigorously revisionist approach might find little normative justification for retaining the historical condition. If so, this illustrates one way in which the very best parts of compatibilist theories might be re-deployed in the service of Strawsonian revisionism.

Finally, Strawsonian revisionists can benefit from traditional Strawsonianism's robust account of the moral psychology of holding agents responsible. For instance, if it turns out that Strawson was right that certain reactive attitudes and the practices they give rise to are genuinely inescapable, then the Strawsonian revisionists have an answer as to why at least those attitudes are justified or not in need of justification. Of course, there are likely to be complicated issues concerning the way belief revision affects other attitudes, and vice-versa.[34] But the point is that Strawsonian revisionism can help itself to all the available moral psychology. By incorporating these insights, revisionists can avoid accusations of psychological implausibility of the sort that have dogged some hard determinist theories.

Though this sketchy discussion of some advantages of revisionist Strawsonians is still some distance from a well-developed theory, we know enough to see some of the ways in which the Strawsonian revisionist can provide the foundations of a justification for the bulk of our responsibility-characteristic beliefs, attitudes, and practices. In particular, we can expect that the justification will be practice-based and tied to a revisionist-refined account of moral agency (whether hierarchical, reasons-responsive, or other). We can also expect the account to be informed by a robust account of the moral psychology of the attitudes and practices characteristic of responsibility.

---

33 *Op.cit.*

34 A complicated issue concerns the role of the cognitivist criticism in light of this possibility. In particular, one might worry that this argument suggests an abandonment of the cognitivist criticism. It need not, though. The revisionist will point out that even if our attitudes are inescapable, and even if those attitudes presuppose false or implausible beliefs, those false beliefs are not the basis of justification in a revisionist theory. So even if we cannot, as a matter of everyday human psychology, fully replace folk beliefs with suitably cleaned up "revisionist beliefs", the revisionist will insist that our theorizing about responsibility reflect the beliefs we *ought* to have. In this way, a revisionist theory of responsibility might be a bit like some theories of physics which might be implausible candidates for replacing folk thinking, but true and theoretically necessary all the same.

Although the above-mentioned considerations are fairly abstract, it is enough to give us a method for developing concrete theories of responsibility. Here is the method:

1. Take your favored compatibilist theory of responsibility and invoke standard revisionist tropes (e.g., a folk conceptual error theory, the naturalist and normative standards, etc.) to justify the theory's partial departure from common sense.
2. Revise the theory's account of morally responsible agency so that it reflects our best picture of moral psychology.
3. Strip the account of morally responsible agency of any features that do not meet the naturalist and normative standards.
4. Show how the resultant specification of conditions for holding people responsible meets schema M.

There we have it—a method to build revisionist theories.

Of course, Strawsonian revisionism will not end every debate about free will and moral responsibility. Among revisionists there will be serious disputes about whether one package of revisions is more desirable than another. But, this just means that there is likely to be rich and fertile discussion between competing incarnations of revisionism. The chief advantage, though, is that these theories will be much better focused on what matters for responsibility and why.

d. Reactions to revisionism

Here I want to consider two different reactions, the first being the relationship of revisionism to normative ethics, the second being revisionism and incompatibilism.

Despite everything that has been said so far, one might reasonably wonder whether *any* kind of revisionism will be possible in the absence of a substantive moral theory. What a substantive theory of ethics gives us, among other things, is some account of the relations between various moral concepts and norms. Though the mentioned accounts of moral agency and psychology bring us closer to the specification of moral appropriateness that a revisionist needs to invoke, it might seem that at the end of the day we will still need a substantive theory of ethics to tell us what things are morally justified independent of our folk concept of responsibility. If so, then Strawsonian revisionism can only tell one part of the responsibility story.

I think this reaction is basically right. It seems implausible to think even a Strawsonian revision of moral responsibility can be done in a way that is *completely* independent of more general theories of morality. We should, however, be cautious about moving too quickly from the idea that there will necessarily be interaction between a theory of responsibility and a broader moral theory to the idea that a revisionist theory of responsibility should simply be the output of utilitarianism or virtue theory, for example.[35] Without additional arguments for the priority of one

---

35 For a brief exploration of revisionism in light of virtue theory, see Michael Slote "Ethics Without Free Will" *Social Theory and Practice* 16 (1990) pp. 369–83. For a classic,

kind of theorizing over another, we might even think the opposite: considerations grounded in a revisionist theory of moral responsibility will change the way we view broader theories of ethics.

For anyone agnostic about the truth of more general theories of ethics, or unsure about the appropriate direction of influence between theories of responsibility and broader theories of ethics, the best path will be to develop a theory of responsibility that is compatible with a wide array of plausible moral theories without being dependent on one in particular. We even have a model of how this might be done. Consider Wallace's own account of responsibility. It is guided by the idea of interpreting our practices and attitudes in terms of fairness. Now suppose a systematically revisionist recasting of his theory succeeds in justifying some sizeable subset of our practices in terms of a fairly thin notion of fairness. This proposal represent one example of how a revision might be justified on specifically moral grounds (i.e., fairness), without explicitly invoking a particular substantive theory of ethics.[36] The key seems to be starting with a fairly primitive and uncontroversial moral notion. Nonetheless, we should acknowledge that selection of nearly any moral notion, regardless of its "primitiveness", is likely to rule out one or another moral theory. The best we can hope for is an initial revisionist theory that makes relatively thin demands on a substantive theory of ethics.[37]

I will conclude by commenting on the relationship of revisionism to standard incompatibilist accounts. As we have seen, the clearest thing that revisionism offers incompatibilists is a willingness to concede that incompatibilist arguments do show that our folk concept of responsibility has incompatibilist commitments. In return, though, revisionists ask a high price: that we accept that our folk concept of responsibility should be revised so that it better conforms to the revisionist's interpretation of M. By the incompatibilist's lights, this price may well be too steep to pay. I think, however, that revisionism should be of concern for incompatibilists for at least two reasons.

First, libertarians ought to have an interest in revisionism for purely pragmatic reasons. Because libertarians generally understand their own proposals to be defeasible, they should have an active interest in what alternatives exist if

---

but sometimes misunderstood statement of utilitarian revisionism, see J.J.C. Smart "Free Will, Praise, and Blame" *Mind* 70 (1961), pp. 157–63. On Smart's view, practices ought to be reorganized around procedures that promoted the good, which required a notion of praise and "dispraise", distinct from ordinary praise and blame. Smart's view is unusual in that he explicitly endorses a revisionist approach to moral blame.

36 The revisionist Strawsonianism I propose departs from Wallace in at least three important ways. First, it is explicitly revisionist. It may also be revisionist to a greater degree than Wallace would accept. Second, it is open to grounding the normative integrity of our practices in terms other than just fairness. Third, it is strongly concerned to satisfy a standard of naturalism.

37 I say "initial revisionism" to allow for two possibilities. The first is that as we learn more about what ethical systems are preferable, we will have reasons to advocate different kinds of revisions. This might motivate several rounds of "stages" of revisionism. Second, as the particular facts of our circumstances change what practices and attitudes are justifiable, we will have reason to call for more revisions in our folk concept of responsibility.

libertarianism is falsified by future science or other means. The revisionism proposed might be treated as a more adequate "second best" theory of responsibility than standard compatibilist accounts.

There is also a philosophically deeper motive that should drive libertarians to care about revisionist proposals. Once revisionism is a viable theory, libertarians come under special pressure to say why we should not just pursue revisionism, regardless of one's favored view about determinism and responsibility. To the extent that revisionists are able to give a folk conceptually independent normative basis for the bulk of the beliefs, attitudes, and practices that are characteristic of responsibility, we are forced to ask ourselves why we should want the libertarian network of concepts, practices, and attitudes over the revisionists'. Typically, libertarians do not feel a need to argue for their relative merits against compatibilist theories because compatibilists have been so quick to accept that an adequate theory of responsibility must fall within the constraints of the folk concept of responsibility.[38] As we saw in parts 1 and 2 of this paper, as long as this constraint is accepted by compatibilists (and inadequately met in the eyes of incompatibilists), incompatibilists will not feel compelled to answer challenges about why the beliefs, attitudes, and practices they account for are worth wanting. Libertarian freedom seems worthwhile at least because it is the only kind of theory that preserves our ordinary concept of responsibility. But, by calling into question the privilege of our folk concept, revisionists force libertarians to say why it matters so much that we preserve *all* the beliefs and attitudes characteristic of it.[39] Of course, libertarians and revisionists will disagree whether or not a folk conceptual error theory is likely to be true. The point, however, is that once we acknowledge that we can change some of our beliefs, practices, and attitudes in this domain, compatibility questions (including arguments about alternate possibilities) will be much less important than answers to why responsibility-characteristic practices, attitudes, and beliefs are important and worth keeping.[40]

---

38 One libertarian who has been a notable exception to this criticism is Kane, *op. cit.*

39 Once this issue is opened up, revisionists will already be standing on the high ground because their theories are necessarily out to capture everything that is genuinely normatively binding and justifiable about our responsibility characteristic practices. By contrast, libertarian theories will start at a disadvantage because they will have been constructed to capture all of our ordinary intuitions and practices of responsibility. And, unless they can show the prima facie implausible, there is no reason to suspect that our current folk concept and practices track *only* what is plausible and justifiable.

40 Part of the intractability of the incompatibility debate concerns an unarticulated difference in the range of ends that are considered primary for a theory of responsibility. For many, the appropriate end of a theory of responsibility is to provide a philosophical account consistent with our folk concept. For those engaged in "descriptive metaphysics" questions regarding the normative adequacy of these beliefs or categories are secondary, if they have any status at all. Opposed to the purely descriptive character of the metaphysical approach are theorists who also want to invoke concerns continuous with moral theorizing in general. These theorists include among the aims of a theory of responsibility a defense of the normative adequacy of the concept, attitudes, and/or practices constituitive of responsibility. Revisionism allows us to appreciate the truths of both projects.

Revisionism will also be of particular interest for more pessimistic forms of incompatibilism. Though the revisionism I present grows out of a compatibilist tradition, it is easy to see how, for example, hard determinist theories might be rewritten in revisionist terms. That is, we might take hard determinists to be arguing for a particularly stark version of revisionism. If such a reinterpretation is successful, that means that revisionism creates a bridge between the concerns of traditional compatibilists and the claims of pessimistic incompatibilists. Both kinds of revisionism would be joined in asking questions about what justifies the beliefs, practices, and attitudes that we have. If such convergence can be achieved, this would be no small accomplishment. Indeed, its mere possibility might be taken as a further reason to believe that revisionism provides a way to escape from some of our stalemates.[41]

---

41 I owe thanks to many people for useful comments and valuable criticisms on this paper since it was first written, including Randolph Clarke, John Martin Fischer, Nadeem Hussain, Miriam McCormick, Michael McKenna, Derk Pereboom, John Perry, Tamar Schapiro, Ken Taylor, R. Jay Wallace, participants at the 2001 Inland Northwest Philosophy Conference, and Al Mele for his excellent referee work on this paper. Special thanks to Michael Bratman, Agnieszka Jaworska, and Michael McKenna for their considerable help with this paper and these ideas over the past few years.

Suggested Further Readings

Other Related Writings by P.F. Strawson

Strawson, P.F., *Skepticism and Naturalism: Some Varieties* (London: Methuen, 1985). [Ch. 2: "Morality and Perception".]
—— *Analysis and Metaphysics: An Introduction to Philosophy* (Oxford and New York: Oxford University Press, 1992). [Ch. 10: "Freedom and Necessity".]
van Straaten, Zak. *Philosophical Subjects: Essays Presented to P. F. Strawson* (Oxford: Clarendon Press, 1980). [Contains Strawson's replies to papers on "Freedom and Resentment" by A.J. Ayer and Jonathan Bennett.]

Classical Sources and Background Readings

Berofsky, Bernard (ed.), *Free Will and Determinism* (New York: Harper & Row, 1966).
Butler, Joseph. "On Resentment", [*Fifteen Sermons* (1726), Sermon 8], in *The Works of Joseph Butler*, ed. Samuel Halifax (Oxford: Oxford University Press, 1849).
Campbell, C.A., "Is 'Freewill' a Pseudo-Problem?", *Mind*, 60 (1951), 446–65. Reprinted in Bernard Berofsky, (ed.), *Free Will and Determinism*.
Hume, David. *A Treatise of Human Nature* [1739–40], D.F. Norton and M.J. Norton (eds), (Oxford: Oxford University Press, 2000).
Nowell-Smith, Patrick, "Freewill and Moral Responsibility", *Mind*, 57 (1948), 45–61.
Schlick, Moritz. "When is a Man Responsible?" [1930], reprinted in Bernard Berofsky, (ed.), *Free Will and Determinism* .
Smith, Adam. *The Theory of Moral Sentiments* [1759], D.D. Raphael (eds), (Oxford: Oxford University Press, 1976).
Westermarck, Edward, *Ethical Relativity* (London: Routledge & Kegan Paul, 1932).

Selected Contemporary Commentary

Arneson, Richard J., "The Smart Theory of Moral Responsibility and Desert", in S. Olsaretti (ed.), *Desert and Justice* (Oxford: Oxford University Press, 2003).
Campbell, Joseph, "Strawson's Free Will Naturalism" [Manuscript].
Fischer, John M. and Ravizza, Mark, Introduction to *Perspectives on Moral Responsibility* (Ithaca: Cornell University Press, 1993).
Greenspan, Patricia, "Responsible Psychopaths", *Philosophical Psychology,* 16 (2003), 417–29.

Haji, Ishtiyaque, "Compatibilist Views of Freedom and Responsibility", in Robert Kane (ed.), *The Oxford Handbook of Free Will* (Oxford: Oxford University Press, 2002).

Kane, Robert, *A Contemporary Introduction to Free Will* (Oxford: Oxford University Press, 2005). [Ch. 10]

Knobe, Joshua and Doris, John M., "Strawsonian Variations: Folk Morality and the Search for a Unified Theory", in J. Doris et al. (eds), *The Handbook of Moral Psychology* (Oxford: Oxford University Press: forthcoming).

Mackie, John L., "Morality and the Retributive Emotions" [1988], reprinted in Mackie, *Persons and Values: Selected Papers Volume II* (Oxford: Oxford University Press, 1985), 206–19.

McKenna, Michael. "Compatibilism", *Stanford Encyclopedia of Philosophy*. Edward N. Zalta (ed.), URL = http://plato.stanford.edu/entries/compatibilism/

—— "Where Frankfurt and Strawson Meet", *Midwest Studies in Philosophy*, 29 (2005), 163–80.

Nagel, Thomas. *The View From Nowhere* (Oxford: Oxford University Press, 1986). [Ch. 7]

Pears, David, "Strawson on Freedom and Resentment", in Lewis Hahn (ed.), *The Philosophy of P. F. Strawson* (Chicago and LaSalle, IL: Open Court, 1998). [See also Strawson's reply to Pears in the same volume.]

Pritchard, Michael, *On Becoming Responsible* (Lawrence: University of Kansas Press, 1991). [esp. Ch. 4]

Russell, Paul, *Freedom and Moral Sentiment: Hume's Way of Naturalizing Responsibility* (Oxford and New York: Oxford University Press, 1995). [esp. Ch. 5]

—— "Responsibility and the Condition of Moral Sense", *Philosophical Topics*, 32 (2004), 287–305. [Special Issue on Agency, ed. by John M. Fischer]

—— "Hume on Free Will", *Stanford Encyclopedia of Philosophy*: (Winter 2007 Edition), Edward N. Zalta (ed.), URL = http://plato.stanford.edu/archives/win2007/entries/hume-freewill/

Scanlon, T.M. "The Significance of Choice", [1988] reprinted in Watson (ed.), *Free Will*.

Scheffler, Samuel, "Responsibility, Reactive Attitudes, and Liberalism in Philosophy and Politics", *Philosophy and Public Affairs*, 21 (1992), 299–323. Reprinted in L.P. Pojman (ed.), *What Do We Deserve?*, (Oxford and New York: Oxford University Press, 1999).

Shoemaker, David, "Moral Address, Moral Responsibility, and the Boundaries of the Moral Community", *Ethics*, 118 (2007), 70–108.

Sher, George, *In Praise of Blame* (Oxford and New York: Oxford University Press, 2006).

Sneddon, Andrew, "Moral Responsibility: The Difference of Strawson, and the Difference it Should Make", *Ethical Theory and Moral Practice*, 8 (2005), 239–64.

Sommers, Tamler, "The Objective Attitude", *Philosophical Quarterly*, 57 (2007), 321–42.

Stern, Lawrence, "Freedom, Blame and Moral Community", *Journal of Philosophy*, 71 (1974), 72–87.

Tabensky, Pedro A., " Moved Movers: Transfiguring Judgement Practices", in Pedro A. Tabensky, (ed.), *Judging and Understanding: Essays on Free Will, Narrative, Meaning and the Ethical limits of Condemnation* (Aldershot: Ashgate, 2006).

Thorton, J.C., "Determinism and Moral Reactive Attitudes", *Ethics*, 79 (1969), 283–97.

Watson, Gary (ed.), *Free Will*, 2nd edn (Oxford and New York: Oxford University Press, 2003).

Index

Abelard, Peter 135
accountability 4, 48–9
  conditions for 49
  and determinism 49, 49–50, 55–7
  Dostoyevsky on 57–8
  and moral pressure 52
  Schlick's explanation 51–2
  criticism 52–3
  Strawson on 53–4
actions, physical determination of 42–4
ambivalence
  Harris case 211, 212, 213–15, 224, 225
  towards moral responsibility 211, 212
Anscombe, G.E.M. 171, 172, 245
attitudes, objective, vs reactive 257–8, 260
  see also reactive attitudes
Ayer, A.J., on determinism 40–41

beliefs
  and reactive attitudes 158
  and reason 183
Bennett, Jonathan 193, 241, 272
Berofsky, Bernard 301
blame 120, 273, 274, 277–8
  and forgiveness 229–30
  Harris case 205
  justification, need for 183, 184
  and moral luck 215–17
  and moral responsibility 182
  psychology of
    alternative to 293
    Nietzsche on 292–3
  and reactive attitudes 179–81, 182, 194–5, 293
  refusal to 193, 197–8, 278
  in shame cultures 172
  and understanding 198–9, 200
  Williams on 250
  see also blaming behavior; moral responsibility; praise
blaming behavior 86, 287–90
  deterrent effect 287
  instructive effect 288
  justification for 289
  meaning 287
  prevention of harm 289–90
  reconciliation outcome 288
  sanctions 288–9
  solidarity effect 288
Bok, Hilary 233
Butler, Joseph 157

Campbell, C.A. 50
causality 1, 3, 237
  of reason 92, 101
chance 2, 3, 42, 45, 49, 251
children
  moral capacities 122
  as responsible agents 122
cognitive dispelling 259–61, 262, 263
cognitivism, Rorty on 261, 262, 265
compatibilism 2, 85, 202, 210, 217–18
  challenge to 227
  definition 119 n7
  insufficiency of 238–9
  natural 101–5
compatibilists
  definition 297
  vs incompatibilists 297
  Strawson on 4
  see also optimists
consequentialism 122
  and human agency 117
  as social regulation 116–17
Core Conception, justice 243, 248
cruelty, paradigm of 173–4

de Sousa, Ronnie 261
  on emotions 266–7
Dennett, Daniel
  Elbow Room 302
  on moral responsibility 305–6
desert concept 3, 38–9, 44–5, 196, 273, 275
  and resentment 241

determinism
    and accountability 49–50, 55–7
    Ayer on 40–41
    consequences of 72–3, 79–83, 86
    dilemma 1–2, 116–17
    divine, Hume on 219–20
    drug addict example 75–6, 78
    and fatalist mistake 97–8
    freedom, incompatibility 88
    hard 239–40
    Harris case 133–4, 211
    and human relationships 73
    and ignorance 133–4
    and moral responsibility 2, 70–71, 86, 143, 145, 198, 199, 202, 221, 297, 298, 299
    and pessimists 144–5, 154
    and rationality 88–92, 97
    and reactive attitudes 72, 81–2, 92, 92–3, 98, 146, 192, 221–2, 223, 224
    and responsible agents 307
    robot example 76–9
    and the self 79–82, 86, 94–9
    Strawson on 6, 39–40
    thought experiment 94–7
    see also "Freedom and Resentment"; indeterminism; Spinozism
Dewey, John, on moral responsibility 115
Dostoyevsky, Fyodor, on accountability 57–8
drug addict, determinism example 75–6, 78

Einstein, Albert
    on moral responsibility 138–9
    on need for solitude 139
emotions
    cognitive dimension 257, 262, 269, 272
    examples 263–6, 269–71
    de Sousa on 266–7
    definition 267
    and expectations 159–60
    function of 267
    and reactive attitudes 147–50, 159–60
    and reactive naturalism 236
    Stoic attitude to 224–5
evil
    Harris case 125–31, 140–41
    individual response to 135
    as product of free will 134–5
    roots 128–31, 133
expectations
    conflicts of 160
    and emotions 159–60
    expression of 160
    meaning 160
    moral 165
    and reactive attitudes 160–62, 163, 169, 181
    support of 160

failure, basis of motivation 245–6
fairness 192 n12, 195, 226, 238, 239, 294, 303, 304, 305, 307, 310, 311, 316
fatalist mistake, and determinism 97–8
fear, reactive attitudes 147–50
Feinberg, Joseph 241
Fischer, John Martin 12
forgiveness
    and blame 229–30
    and moral responsibility 177–8
free will
    causal necessitation 2
    evil as product of 134–5
    importance of 82–3
    libertarian 237–8, 247, 252
    and moral responsibility 2, 195–6, 244, 273
free will debate 1, 3, 14, 37, 69–70
    illusion, role of 235, 248
    solutions 9
freedom
    commitment theory of 85–6, 105–10
    determinism, incompatibility 88
    essence of 104
    and self-determination 97
    see also satkāyadṛṣṭi
"Freedom and Resentment" (Strawson) 1, 70
    achievement 59
    critical themes 9–14
    criticism 12–14, 85–113, 300–302
    determinism 19–20, 25–6, 27
        behavior 32
        and rationality 88–92
    dichotomies 11–12
    forgiveness 22
    freedom 21
    gratitude 22
    influence of 235, 255, 297–8
    libertarianism 5, 8, 36, 256, 298
    moral community 34
    moral responsibility 12, 20, 88, 116, 139–40, 143–4, 184–5, 206–7, 277, 298–300

objective 4
objective/participant dichotomy 11–12
optimists 19, 20, 21, 33, 35
pessimists 19, 20, 33, 35
punishment 20, 21
reactive attitudes 5, 6, 7, 12, 13–14, 23, 29–30, 47–8, 53, 60–64, 72, 116, 117, 144, 147, 164–5, 178, 188, 277, 279, 300
  and determinism 28, 31
  participant 25, 26
resentment 5–6, 22, 28
  modification 23–5
strategy 5
text of 19–36
Watson on 116

Gandhi, Mahatma 140, 177, 178
gratitude 100
  in interpersonal relationships 230
guilt 164–5, 232–3
  as reactive attitude 169

Harris, Robert
  ambivalence towards 211, 212, 213–15, 224, 225
  blame, candidate for 205
  and determinism 133–4, 211
  as example of evil 125–31, 140–41
  and moral community 125–31, 205–6, 208–9
  remorse, absence of 130, 141
  as victim 131–2, 210–11
Hobart, R.E. 50
human agency, and consequentialism 117
human relationships, and determinism 73
Hume, David 8, 224
  on divine determinism 219–20
  Enquiry Concerning Human Understanding 101, 219

illusion
  free will debate, role in 235, 248, 252
  functioning of 249–51
  need for 248–9, 251
  reality, interaction 250–51
  Wiggins on 251
incompatibilism 92, 112, 221, 298, 309, 315, 318
  hard 226, 228–30, 232–3
  natural 104, 105

incompatibilists 2, 3, 119, 227–8
  definition 297
  and revisionist moral responsibility 308–9, 316–18
  Strawson on 4
  vs compatibilists 297
  see also libertarians; pessimists
indeterminism 2, 56, 70, 89, 137, 269, 313
  see also determinism
indignation *see* moral indignation
innocence 65, 68, 244–5, 306
interpersonal relations
  gratitude in 230
  and reactive attitudes 228–32

justice 241
  Core Conception 243, 248
  and free will 242–3
  and revenge 242
justification 267, 268
  and blame 183, 184
  reactive attitudes 72–82, 195

King, Martin Luther 140, 177, 178
Kroll, Michael 140, 141

libertarianism 136–7, 221
libertarians 3, 42, 117, 134, 136, 316–17
loving
  freely willed 231–2
  and moral responsibility 230

meditation 112
metaphysics, descriptive, Strawson on 10
moral agency 204, 205, 207, 210, 215, 294, 299 n5, 310, 315
  theory 314
moral community
  blaming behavior, outcome 288
  capacity for membership 206, 207
  Harris case 125–31, 205–6, 208–9
  and moral responsibility 125, 205, 206, 240
moral equality 132, 213
moral indignation 28, 29, 30, 33, 38, 40, 159, 229
  expression of 52, 53
  as reactive attitude 63, 64, 117, 164, 169, 260, 276
  reasons for 194
moral judgment

aim 286
basis 284
example 284
morality 275, 280–86
Watson on 281–2
moral luck 132, 135, 137, 212–13, 291
and blame 215–17
moral obligations 170
and moral responsibility 171, 172
as theological concept 171
moral pressure, and accountability 52
moral responsibility 45, 168–9
ambivalence towards 211, 212
and blame 182
cognitivist criticism 301–2
Dennett on 305–6
and determinism 2, 70–71, 86, 143, 144–5, 198, 199, 202, 221, 297, 298, 299
Dewey on 115
Einstein on 138–9
excuses, argument from 202, 204, 208, 215, 217, 299
exemption from 202, 299
expressive theory of 119–20, 137–8
and children 122
and forgiveness 177–8
foundation of 228
and free will 2, 195–6, 244, 273
"Freedom and Resentment" (Strawson) 12, 20, 88, 116, 139–40, 143–4, 187–8, 206–7, 277, 298–300
impossibility of 3
incapacity for 210
limits of 125
and loving 230
and moral community 125, 205, 206, 240
and moral obligations 171, 172
naturalist theory 202–4, 207
normative interpretation 303–5
and pessimists 145
reactive account 173
and reactive attitudes 116, 118, 125, 144–5, 157, 169–78, 181–2, 221, 222, 255, 256, 277–80, 281
and retributive justice 13
revisionism 297–8, 307–18
and incompatibilists 308–9, 316–18
naturalistic plausibility 310, 312–13
normative adequacy 310–12
reactions to 315–18

Strawsonian 313–14
Scanlon on 179, 182–3, 184, 282
for the self 136–7
in shame cultures 172
theories, development of 315
Wallace on 303–5
see also blame
moral sadness 225–6, 229, 233
moral sentiments 10, 35, 100, 147
and morality 291–2
see also reactive attitudes
morality
aim 274
moral judgment 275
and moral sentiments 291–2
practical conception of 275–6, 291, 293
motivation, and failure 245–6

Nagel, Thomas 132
naturalism
non-revisionist 242, 251
revisionist 241–2, 251
token 150, 151, 152, 156
type 152, 156
see also reactive naturalism
naturalistic thoughts 58
naturalistic turn, Strawson 5, 9–10
sources 8–9
Nietzsche, Friedrich, on the psychology of blame 292–3
nirvana 112, 113

optimists 4, 70, 71–2, 73–4, 75, 83, 256
Strawson on 7, 19, 220–21
see also compatibilists; pessimists
over-intellectualizing, Strawson on 7–8, 11

pessimists 4, 19, 20, 33, 35, 70, 71, 72, 73–4, 75, 79, 82, 83, 144–7, 256
and determinism 144–5, 154
fear-type 149, 150
and moral responsibility 145
naturalistic strategy against 145, 151–2, 156
critique of 152–3
rationalistic strategy against 145–6, 146–50
critique of 153–4, 155
Strawson on 7, 19, 143–4, 144–7, 221
token 149, 150
see also incompatibilists; optimists

praise 273, 274
    see also blame
praising 86, 120
punishment 37, 38, 196–7, 198, 241, 244, 278
    and choice 189
    desert justification for 66, 196–7, 198
    in "Freedom and Resentment" (Strawson) 20
    as retribution 68, 196–7
    a theory of 66–8
    utilitarian approach 65–6

rationality
    and determinism 88–92, 97
    Strawson's 44, 88–92
Ravizza, Mark 12
Rawls, John 157
reactive account
    moral judgment 178–84
    moral responsibility 173
reactive attitudes
    absence of 191
    and beliefs 158
    and blame 179–81, 182, 194–5, 293
    characteristics 157–8
    classification 115 n5
    cognitive dimension 162–3
    commitment to 89–91, 94, 190–91
    and determinism 72, 81–2, 92, 92–3, 98, 146, 192, 221–2, 223, 224
    and emotions 159–60
    and expectations 160–62, 163, 169, 181
    fear 147–9
    as form of evaluation 158–9
    in "Freedom and Resentment" (Strawson) 5, 6, 7, 12, 13–14, 47–8, 53, 60–64, 72, 116, 117, 144, 147, 164–5, 178, 188, 222–3, 279, 300
    and guilt 169
    Harris case 125–8
    insufficiency of 242
    and interpersonal relations 228–32
    justification 72–82, 195
    moral 64, 165–6
        nonmoral, distinction 163–4
    moral indignation as 63, 64, 117, 164, 169, 260, 276
    and moral responsibility 116, 118, 125, 144–5, 157, 169–78, 181–2, 221, 222, 255, 256, 277–80, 281
    negative
        examples 120
        excusing 118, 121
        exempting 118–19, 121, 122, 123–4, 125
    non-principles 64
    objective view 119, 222
    personal 164
    propositional content 158, 163
    resentment as 122–3, 169, 276, 277
    as social constructs 10
    type 1 considerations 221
    type 2 considerations 221–2
    Wallace on 191, 214
    Watson on 178, 203
    see also blame; moral sentiments; resentment
reactive feelings 53–5, 58
    harmful 59–60
reactive naturalism 241–4
    and emotions 236
reality, illusion, interaction 250–51
reason
    and beliefs 183
    causality of 92, 101
    Strawson on 11
Reid, Thomas, Strawson on 8–9
remorse 38–9, 59, 60, 63, 64, 246
    Harris case 130, 141
resentment 100, 162, 225, 229
    and desert concept 241
    justification for 279
    as reactive attitude 122–3, 169, 276, 277
    reinterpretation 123–4
    setting aside of 193
responsibility *see* moral responsibility
responsible agents 2, 3, 42, 43, 87, 110, 115–16, 207, 300–301
    children as 122
    and determinism 307
retribution
    costs of, US 276
    punishment as 68
retributive justice, and moral responsibility 13
revenge 38, 48, 68
    and justice 242
robot, determinism example 76–9
Rorty, Amelie, on cognitivism 261, 262, 265
Russell, Paul 190, 242

satkāyadṛṣṭi concept 111–13
Scanlon, T.M., on moral responsibility 179, 182–3, 184, 282
Schlick, Moritz, accountability theory 51–2
   criticism 52–3
the self
   delusion of 111
   and determinism 79–82, 86, 94–9
   responsibility for 136–7
self-control, reflective 279–80
self-respect 243–4, 246
shame cultures 167–8, 171–2
   blame in 172
   moral responsibility in 172
Smart, J.J.C. 274
Smith, Adam 8, 67
social regulation, consequentialism as 116–17
solitude, need for, Einstein on 139
Spinozism 56, 58, 193, 194, 197
   see also determinism
spite 194, 199
Stern, Lawrence 125, 205
Stoicism, and emotions 224–5
Strawson, P.F.
   on accountability 53–4
   anti-pessimist strategies 145–7
   critique of 146–7
   on compatibilists 4
   on descriptive metaphysics 10
   on determinism 6, 39–40
   freedom, commitment theory of 85–6
   on incompatibilists 4
   on moral responsibility 139–40, 187–8
   naturalistic turn 5, 9–10
      sources 8–9
   on optimists 7, 19, 220–21
   on over-intellectualizing 7–8, 11
   on pessimists 7, 19, 143–4, 143–7, 221

rationality, concept 44
   on reactive attitudes 5, 6, 7, 12, 13–14, 47–8, 53, 60–64, 72, 116, 117, 144, 147, 164–5, 178, 188, 222–3, 279, 300
   critique of 223–7
   on reason 11
   on Reid 8–9
   works
      Individuals 10
      Skepticism and Naturalism 8, 152
      see also "Freedom and Resentment" (Strawson) main entry
Strawsonians 302–6
Strawson's Theory 116–17

Trobriand Islands 191

understanding, and blame 198, 198–9, 200
US, criminal justice system, costs 276

Wallace, R. Jay 215, 226, 279
   on moral responsibility 303–5
   on reactive attitudes 191, 214
   Responsibility and the Moral Sentiments 157, 184, 302
Waller, Bruce 232
Watson, Gary 217–18, 224
   on "Freedom and Resentment" 116, 178
   on moral judgment 281–2
   on reactive attitudes 178, 203
   "Responsibility and the Limits of Evil" 204
well-being, principle of 196–7
Welles, Orson 273
Wiggins, David, on illusion 251
will, exercise of, obstacles 51
Williams, Bernard 56, 168, 171, 172
   on blame 250